THE OPEN SOCIETY IN THEORY
AND PRACTICE

THE OPEN SOCIETY IN THEORY AND PRACTICE

edited by

DANTE GERMINO
University of Virginia

AND

KLAUS VON BEYME
Heidelberg University

MARTINUS NIJHOFF / THE HAGUE / 1974

ISBN 90 247 1630 6

PRINTED IN THE NETHERLANDS

TABLE OF CONTENTS

BIOGRAPHICAL DATA

Dante Germino, who organized the conference on which this volume is based, is Professor of Government and Foreign Affairs at the University of Virginia, Charlottesville, Virginia. He is the author of *Modern Western Political Thought, Beyond Ideology,* and other works.

Alexander Passerin d'Entrèves is Dean of the Faculty of Political Science, University of Turin, Italy. He is author of *The Notion of the State, Dante as a Political Thinker,* and numerous other works.

Anthony Parel is Professor of Political Science, University of Calgary, Alberta, Canada. He is editor of *The Political Calculus: Essays on Machiavelli.*

Ali Mazrui is Chairman of the Department of Political Science at Makerere University, Kampala, Uganda. He is author of *Towards a Pax Africana: A Study of Ideology and Ambition.*

Leon Bramson is Chairman of the Department of Sociology and Anthropology, Swarthmore College, Swarthmore, Pennsylvania. He is author of *The Political Context of Sociology.*

Melvin Richter is Professor of Political Science at the Graduate Center, City University of New York. He is author of *The Politics of Conscience: T. H. Green* and other works.

Klaus von Beyme is Professor of Political Science at Heidelberg University. He is author of numerous works in political theory and comparative government, including *Die parlamentarischen Regierungssysteme in Europa, Interessengruppen in der Demokratie.*

John H. Hallowell is Professor of Political Science, Duke University, Durham, North Carolina. He is author of *Main Currents of Modern Political Thought, The Moral Foundations of Democracy,* and other works.

C. L. Ten is Lecturer in Philosophy, Monash University, Clayton, Victoria, Australia. He is author of articles on John Stuart Mill and on liberalism.

George Kateb is Professor of Political Science, Amherst College, Amherst, Massachusetts. He is author of *Political Theory: Its Nature and Uses* and other works.

Ehud Sprinzak is a member of the Eliezer Kaplan School of Economics and Social Studies, The Hebrew University of Jerusalem, Israel. He is author of articles on the "new left" and on Max Weber.

Marek Sobolewski is Professor of Philosophy, University of Cracov, Poland. He is author of numerous articles on Marxist political thought.

Bernard Crick is Professor of Politics, Birkbeck College, University of London. He is author of *In Defence of Politics, The Reform of Parliament* and other works.

David Spitz is Professor of Political Science, Graduate Center, City University of New York. He is author of books on liberalism and on democratic theory.

Anthony Storr of Harley Street, London, is a psychiatrist and author of numerous books, the most recent of which is entitled *Creativity*.

Henry S. Kariel is Professor of Political Science, The University of Hawaii, Honolulu, Hawaii. He is author of *Open Systems, Saving Appearances,* and other works.

John Rodman is Professor of Political Science, Pitzer College, Claremont, California. He is editor of *The Political Theory of T. H. Green.*

INTRODUCTION

From June 28 until July 4, 1972, a group of scholars, all of them academicians committed to the critical study of man and society which may be called political theory, met at The Rockefeller Foundation's Villa Serbelloni in Bellagio, Italy, to present papers on and discuss the subject of "The Open Society." These papers, as revised, are published here, most of them for the first time. They reflect no consensus of view, nor were they intended to do so. That such a consensus did not emerge from the conference is not in our judgment a cause for regret; it may rather be regarded as a manifestation of a healthy and desirable plurality of approaches which itself indirectly tells us something important about the nature of the open society.

All the papers deal in different contexts and from a variety of philosophical and theoretical perspectives with the interrelated themes of openness and the open society. Some of the panelists are skeptical of the capacity of modern industrial, or "post-industrial," society, with its heavy emphasis upon technological rationality to foster authentic openness under currently prevailing assumptions about man and nature. Within this group, in turn, some would emphasize recovery of the modes of openness in myth, philosophy, revelation, and mysticism as essential preconditions of a new breakthrough to the open society, while others would stress the need for radically new departures on the basis of a changed ecological and world cultural perspective and a recognition of man's capacity for continuous imaginative reconstruction of his symbolic world. Another significant group of contributors argues, at least implicitly, that it is chiefly in the modern, secular world, and particularly in western liberalism, that values of authentic openness such as tolerance, diversity, freedom to dissent, and the legal protection of individual rights have flourished. At least one contributor contends that the perspective of Marxist thought is needed to extend and deepen the contributions of liberalism in relation to the open society. It is, of course, possible that both the critics and proponents of modern industrial society might come closer together on certain points had "we but world enough and time." But they do seem to be divided on the issue of whether contemporary society is in need of a decisively new consciousness (or pre-intellectual disposition) toward the world. The latter group tends in varying degrees to be committed to the prevailing symbols of "reason" and "science," while the former insists that vital dimensions of experience have been omitted, neglected, or even suppressed by the secular and scientific world-view which has come to predominate in the west, at least since the time of the Enlightenment.

We have entitled our volume *The Open Society in Theory and Practice* because the papers span a range of concerns from the philosophical and theoretical to the institutional and sociological. The more institutionally-oriented papers included here suggest such key questions as: How much openness can societies tolerate? What is the relationship between political form and cultural substance? May a variety of regimes contribute equivalently to openness? What are the characteristics of a "closed society" and is it a viable concept for the analysis of political institutions? What are the pressures – sociological, economic, cultural, ecological – which affect the realization of equal educational opportunity and the possibility of social mobility for the majority of the people? These questions are scarcely resolved within the pages of our book, but perhaps the fact that they are raised will in a modest way contribute to a revival of interest in them.

Professor d'Entrèves, at the conclusion of his paper, quotes Dante's lines about "the tower of the true city" which might be seen dimly in the distance. This image is particularly appropriate for the open society, for such a society, the editors suggest, should not be conceived either as an established fact or as a revolutionary blueprint but as an intimation of a fuller life for all mankind stretching before us at the outer limits of possibility. Every model of the open society which we make will be an imperfect attempt to fill in the outlines of that true city of which Dante spoke and of which at best we may see only the tower. At the same time, the inevitably defective models of the open city which have been offered by political theorists from Plato onwards are not to be dismissed as irrelevant to the world of practice. That world we all know to be one of boundaries and of limitations. But the vision of Dante's non-literal city beckons to us across the centuries and perennially inspires that mode of inquiry and of critical reflection on man and society known as political theory.

There remains the pleasant task of acknowledging the assistance of those individuals and institutions that made the conference and this volume possible. The Rockefeller Foundation provided a generous grant in support of the conference and publication of the papers. Various officers of the Foundation were helpful in this undertaking, but we should particularly like to express our appreciation to Dr. Kenneth W. Thompson, Jr., then Vice President of the RF and now Director for Higher Education for Development of the International Council for Educational Development, Dr. Joseph E. Black, Director of Social Sciences, and Dr. Jane Allen, Conference Coordinator for the Foundation's Villa Committee. The editors also wish to thank President Edgar F. Shannon, Jr. of the University of Virginia for agreeing that the University would administer the grant and serve as official sponsor of the conference. Professor David C. Jordan, Chairman of the University's Department of Government and Foreign Affairs, also assisted and encouraged the publication of this work through providing departmental support, for which the editors wish to express their appreciation. Miss Frances Lackey, Mr. Robert H. Webking, and Mr. James Piscatori rendered able service at crucial points in the editorial process and also deserve a vote of appreciation. Neither The Rockefeller Foundation nor the University of Virginia is responsible for any views expressed herein, however, and any errors of fact or judgment which may remain are the responsibility of the authors. We wish also to thank, Mr. Michael J. Taylor for expert assistance in arranging the air travel of the conference participants, Dr. and Mrs. William C. Olson for helping to insure that our stay at the Villa Serbelloni was both pleasant and profitable, and Martinus Nijhoff for its invaluable assistance in insuring that the papers will reach a wider audience.

DANTE GERMINO
KLAUS VON BEYME

June, 1974

PRELIMINARY REFLECTIONS ON THE OPEN SOCIETY: BERGSON, POPPER, VOEGELIN

DANTE GERMINO

Let me briefly explain why I chose to begin our conference with a consideration of Bergson, Popper, and Voegelin. So far as I am aware, it was Henri Bergson who first employed the term "the open society" in print, in a book published in French in 1932 and translated into English in 1935.[1] After Bergson, it is logical to move to Karl Popper's *The Open Society and Its Enemies* (1945), which did so much to give the phrase wide currency in the English-speaking world, but which differs from Bergson's treatment in significant respects. Finally, Eric Voegelin, consciously drawing inspiration from but also modifying Bergson, has made the "open society" a key concept in his important philosophy of history in his *magnum opus* now in progress, *Order and History,* and in other writings.

HENRI BERGSON

For Bergson, the open society stands forth as a paradigm of development for the community of man. "Our civilized communities," he declares, far from resembling the open society, are all outgrowths of the "morality of pressure" demanded by the initial promptings of nature. These communities, which are "closed societies," may be "very extensive compared to the small agglomerations to which we were initially drawn by instinct," but "their essential characteristic is nonetheless to include at any moment a certain number of individuals and to exclude others."[2]

According to Bergson, all politics which we have known up to the present has been conducted upon the premises of the closed society. However unpleasant it may be for us to contemplate, the politics of the past – *all* the

[1] Henri Bergson, *Les deux sources de la morale et de la religion* (Paris, Felix Alcan, 1932), translated as *Two Sources of Morality and Religion* by R. A. Andra and C. Brereton (New York, Holt, 1935).

[2] *Ibid.,* p. 22.

past, including *our* past – has ultimately been a politics geared for war. And in war, "murder and pillage and perfidy, cheating and lying become not only lawful, they actually become praiseworthy." Peace itself

> has always hitherto been a preparation for defence or even attack, at any rate for war. Our social duties aim at social cohesion: whether we will or no they compose for us an attitude, which is that of discipline in the face of the enemy. This means that, however much society may endow man, whom it has trained to discipline, with all it has acquired during centuries of civilization, society still has need of that primitive instinct which it coats with so thick a varnish. In a word, the social instinct which we have detected at the basis of social obligation always has in view . . . a closed society, however large. It is doubtless overlaid with another morality. . . . But it is not itself concerned with humanity. For between the nation, however big, and humanity there lies the whole distance from the finite to the indefinite, from the closed to the open.[3]

Bergson repeatedly emphasizes that the distinction between the closed and the open society is one of *kind* rather than *degree*. One does not attain to the concept of the open society by any mere "broadening out" from the family or the nation to humanity. What is required is a leap of insight, a qualitatively distinctive mode of experiencing human existence. "Our sympathies," the French philosopher tells us, "are supposed to broaden out in an unbroken progression, to expand while remaining identical, and to end by embracing all humanity. This is *a priori* reasoning, the result of a purely intellectualist conception of the soul." [4]

The family and civil society are indeed "closely connected"; "domestic virtues are indeed bound up with civic virtues." "But between the society in which we live and humanity in general there is . . . the same contrast as between the closed and the open; the difference between the two objects *is one of kind and not simply one of degree*." [5]

The route to the open society, grounded on the love of all mankind, is indirect and promptings toward it do not flow from our primitive natural instincts to self-protection and solidarity with the in-group. How then, do men come to be drawn to the open community at all? Through religion (but as we shall see, not simply any form of religion) and philosophy:

> . . . it is only through God, in God, that religion bids man love mankind; and likewise it is through reason alone, that Reason in whose communion we are all partakers, that philosophers make us look at humanity in order to show us the pre-eminent dignity of the human being, the right of all to command respect.

[3] *Ibid.*, pp. 23-24.
[4] *Ibid.*, p. 24.
[5] *Ibid.* Emphasis added.

Neither in the one case nor the other do we come to humanity by degrees, through the stages of the family and the nation. We must, in a single bound, be carried far beyond it, and, without having made it our goal, reach it by outstripping it.[6]

In this passage, so full of meaning, Bergson captures the drama of the opening of the soul. Philosophy and revelation are grasped by him as the twin sources of the open society and the open morality in history. Furthermore, the appearance of these two experiential forces constitutes a decisive break in the continuity of history. This is what Eric Voegelin (in *Order and History*) has called the "leap in being." Such a break with cosmological modes of symbolization could not have been foreseen or predicted. The occurrence of openness in history is at once a – or even the – supremely important "fact" and an impenetrable mystery.

"Exceptional men," the heroes and *virtuosi* of the spirit, are the carriers in time of the vision of the open society and the open morality. "Before the saints of Christianity, mankind had known the sages of Greece, the prophets of Israel, the Arahants of Buddhism, and others besides. It is to them that men have always turned for that complete morality which we had best call absolute morality." [7]

Henri Bergson finds that, in contrast to the "closed morality" of "the city," which is reducible to "impersonal formulae," the "open morality" of the great seekers and mystics of mankind "must be incarnate in a privileged person who becomes an example. The generality of the [closed morality] . . . consists in the universal acceptance of a law, that of the [open morality] . . . in a common imitation of a model." [8] The former is a morality of "pressure," while the latter is one of "aspiration."

Notice how vividly *personal* Bergson reveals the love of mankind, authentically construed, to be! Here we do not have a preoccupation with Humanity in the abstract, as in the anti-theistic "religions of Humanity" constructed by Saint-Simon and Comte, and which Max Scheler diagnosed as being based more on a revolt against God than upon an affirmative love for man. To reach humanity in our affections we must, "in a single bound, be carried far beyond it, and without having made it our goal, reach it by outstripping it." Thus it happens that "a generous nature, eager to sacrifice itself, experiences a sudden chill at the idea that it is working 'for mankind.' The object is too vast, the effect too diffuse." [9]

We come to the love of mankind through the example of a concrete

[6] *Ibid.*, p. 25.
[7] *Ibid.*, p. 26.
[8] *Ibid.*
[9] *Ibid.*, p. 28.

person whose psyche has opened itself in charity to embrace all nature. The "pioneers in morality" introduce us by their example to "unsuspected tones of feeling," rather like a great composer "draws us after him" into some new symphony. Only, for the *virtuosi* of the open morality, the result is not only contemplation and delight, but a new consciousness, a new mode of being in the world which has results in the sphere of action.[10]

Bergson characterizes openness as "the strength to love mankind." It is a "love which absorbs and kindles the whole soul." [11] In fact, he adds, to say that the open soul "embraces all humanity" is not going far enough, "since its love may extend to animals, to plants, to all nature. And yet no one of these things which would thus fill it would suffice to define the attitude taken by the soul, for it could, strictly speaking, do without all of them. Its form is not dependent on its content." [12]

A psychology which is "too purely intellectualist," the French philosopher tells us, "will doubtlessly define feelings by the things with which they are associated; love for one's family, love for one's country, love for mankind, it will see in these three inclinations one single feeling, growing ever larger, to embrace an increasing number of persons." But between the first two emotions and the third, a difference in kind exists. Love of family and love of country "imply a choice" between objects of affection; they focus on some men to the exclusion of others, and "may act as incentives to strife," for they "do not exclude hatred." Love in the open soul, however, "does not yield to the attraction of its object; it has not aimed at this object, it has shot beyond and reached humanity only by passing through humanity." [13]

In the open soul we see a new morality reflected, a morality which unlike that of the closed soul, is not derived from nature, but which is "acquired" by means of a new passion animating the soul. In allowing itself to be seized by this new passion, the open soul breaks with the nature which "enclosed it both within itself and within the city." [14]

The open souls experience "liberation" from the goals of everyday existence in the world of the closed society: "Well-being, pleasures, riches . . . leave them indifferent. In breaking away from them they feel relief, and then exhilaration." Not that these goals are in themselves wrong; it is rather that "the amenities which are real comforts at home would become

[10] *Ibid.*, p. 32.
[11] *Ibid.*, p. 30.
[12] *Ibid.*
[13] *Ibid.*, pp. 30-31.
[14] *Ibid.*, p. 44.

hindrances, burdensome impedimenta, if we had to take them on our travels." [15]

Again and again Bergson underscores his insight that the concept of the open soul and the open society involves a qualitative leap in man's experience. We cannot attain it by any incrementalist view of reform, or by any mere "broadening out" of concepts already familiar to us. Here, if you like, we have the "radicalism" of Bergson's philosophy of man:

> Never shall we pass from the closed society to the open society, from the city to humanity, by any mere broadening out. The two things are not of the same essence. The open society is the society which is deemed in principle to embrace all humanity. A dream dreamt, now and again, by chosen souls, it embodies on every occasion something of itself in creations, each of which, through a more or less far-reaching transformation of man, conquers difficulties hitherto unconquerable.[16]

There is, then, for Bergson no halfway house between the closed and the open society. What is involved is a leap from "action confined in a circle [i.e., the closed morality] to action developing in the freedom of space, from repetition to creation, from the infra-intellectual to the supra-intellectual." Anyone halting in between "practices that half-virtue, detachment." [17] Of course, it is true that to follow the path of ascent to the open society requires heroism of the mind and spirit. But the truth is that "heroism may be the only way to love." [18] Heroism itself "cannot be preached," but can only "show itself" and thereby "stir others to action." [19]

The above conclusions, of course, are not taken by Bergson to imply that unless the entirety of mankind is won over to the open morality all is lost; to argue in this fashion would be to lose sight of the character of the open society as a *paradigm*. It is of the very nature of the paradigm always to be beyond our grasp, always serving as a standard by which to measure our relatively imperfect response. Without the paradigm of the open society the very aspiration to break loose from the confines of the closed society would be absent. The open society is the end for which we hope – against hope:

> ... to obtain a complete effect, the privileged soul would have to carry the rest of humanity with it. But if a few follow, and if the others imagine they would do likewise on occasions, this already means a great deal; henceforth, with the

[15] *Ibid.*
[16] *Ibid.*, p. 256.
[17] *Ibid.*, p. 56.
[18] *Ibid.*, p. 45.
[19] *Ibid.*

beginning of accomplishment, there will be the hope that the circle may be broken in the end.[20]

Just as the distinction between the closed and open society is one of kind rather than of degree, so the transition from the former to the experience of openness that could be the basis for the latter occurred at a precise period in history, thanks to new spiritual and intellectual forces, rather than being the result of a steady gradual evolution over time. The "door" to the open society (which in Bergson's view "probably will for all time stand open,") "must have been opened" by some specific cultural development. The answer Bergson gives to the question of when the opening decisively occurred reminds one of the formulation of Clement of Alexandria: Christianity marks the point of decisive advance from the closed to the open mode of existence, with both the Judaic prophets and Greek (and neo-Platonic) philosophy serving as forces preparing the way for this decisive event.[21] Anticipations, preparations for the open society, can thus be found in the teaching of Socrates and in the Stoics, but "humanity had to wait until Christianity for the idea of universal brotherhood. . . ." [22]

It would be an error to think that Bergson is regarding Christianity in a sectarian way. (Like Simone Weil, Bergson was of Jewish descent, but came to have strong affinities for Catholicism. In fact, in his will he wrote that he "would have become a convert" had it not been for the "formidable wave of antisemitism which is to break upon the world." He "wanted to remain among those who tomorrow will be persecuted." Quoted in Jacques Maritain, *Bergsonian Philosophy and Thomism* [New York, Philosophical Library, 1955], p. 337.) It is not the victory of Christianity as an institutionalized religion that interests Bergson, but rather the influence and effect (whether direct or indirect) of Christ's teachings as reported in the Gospels on the lives and actions of succeeding generations of men. In other words, he was concerned with the effect of the Gospels on the quality of life led by those who are receptive to them. Jesus is the paradigm of the mystic who becomes a "great man of action." It is not philosophers but "mystic souls who draw and will continue to draw civilized societies in their wake." [23] "Our admiration for the speculative function of the mind may be great; but when philosophers maintain that it should be sufficient to silence selfishness

[20] *Ibid.*, p. 44.
[21] *Ibid.*, pp. 54, 68. Plotinus in particular is hailed as a representative of the open society. Bergson does not entirely ignore non-Western contributions (he cites Buddhism, for example), but his discussion is insufficient to indicate their quality and extent.
[22] *Ibid.*, p. 69.
[23] *Ibid.*, p. 75.

and passion, they prove to us . . . that they have never heard the voice of the one or the other very loud within themselves." [24]

Before we yield to the temptation to dismiss Bergson's call that we follow the great mystics as evidence of the "irrationalism" which some critics have attributed to him, let us explore more fully his concept of the mystic experience and society. What Bergson describes as "mystical" is the antithesis to the "static" world-view of the closed society. The open morality of the great mystics is not the antithesis to intelligence, for mysticism in itself is "supra-intellectual" rather than anti-intellectual. The opposite of the supra-intellectual vision of the mystic is not intelligence but the "infra-intellectual" consciousness of the inhabitant of the closed society. While "static morality" is infra-intellectual, "dynamic morality" is supra-intellectual. "Nature intended the one, and the other is a contribution of man's genius." The supra-intellectual consciousness of the mystic "contains any amount of intellectuality; it is more than intelligence." Between the two [i.e., the infra- and the supra-intellectual] lies intelligence itself.[25]

Socrates himself (whom Karl Popper is to call the champion of reason conceived of as intelligence in opposition to the taboos of closed society) is hailed by Bergson as one of the great "mystic souls." In following his *daemonion* to his death, Socrates conceived of his mission as "of a religious and mystic order . . .; his teaching, so perfectly rational, hinges on something that aims to transcend pure reason." [26] Socrates inspired "enthusiasm" in his disciples with his "lyrical sayings," and his presence decisively influenced a host of movements and thinkers from the Cynics to the Stoics.[27]

Although Bergson does not say so, what he charts in his account of the opening of the psyche to transcendent Being is a development from compactness to differentiation (to employ Eric Voegelin's terminology). The closed, or "archaic" society (Mircea Eliade), is bound by the confines of the sacred myth, and the individual is experienced as part of a collective politico-religious order. The morality of this order is one of "pressure," "discipline," and "pleasure," rather than of "liberation," "aspiration," and "joy." The man of the closed society "is part and parcel of society; he and it are absorbed together in the same task of individual and social preservation. Both are self-centered." [28] From the standpoint of the closed morality, the "cell lives for itself and also for the organism, imparting to it vitality and borrowing vitality from it; it will sacrifice itself to the whole if

[24] *Ibid.,* p. 78.
[25] *Ibid.,* p. 55.
[26] *Ibid.,* p. 53.
[27] *Ibid.*
[28] *Ibid.,* p. 29.

need be; and it would doubtless then say, if it were conscious, that it made this sacrifice in its own interest." In its unadulterated form (rarely if ever encountered in reality) the relationship of the individual to the closed society is comparable to that of an ant to an ant-hill.[29] The closed society, in summary, "is that whose members hold together, caring nothing for the rest of humanity, on the alert for attack or defence, bound, in fact, to a perpetual readiness for battle." [30]

Bergson's great service for political theory is to have formulated the "mystic" or "open" society as paradigm, in contradistinction to the reverse paradigm of the "closed" or "static" society. These two paradigmatic societies function as the "ideal limits" of man's field of action:

> Now, a mystic society, embracing all humanity and moving, animated by a common will, towards the continually renewed creation of a more complete humanity, is no more possible of realization in the future than was the existence in the past of human societies functioning automatically and similar to animal societies. Pure aspiration is an ideal limit, just like obligation unadorned.[31]

That the paradigm may not be realized in its fulness is not to imply its irrelevance to the actual course of history, however. Indeed, that very course has been decisively changed by the discovery of the cosmopolis of the spirit binding all men:

> ... the great moral figures ... join hands across the centuries, above our human cities; they invite [us] into a divine city which they bid us enter ... from the real society in which we live we betake ourselves in thought to this ideal society; to this ideal society we bow down when we reverence the dignity of man within us, when we declare that we act from self-respect.[32]

The marks of the open spirit are joy and enthusiasm; these qualities flow from the realization that the dominion of instinct and habit, of the self-centeredness of nature, has been breached. We follow the examples of the "founders and reformers of religions, mystics and saints, [and] obscure heroes of moral life ... as if we were joining an army of conquerors. They are indeed conquerors: they have broken down natural resistance and raised humanity to a new destiny." While the closed morality "becomes more perfect as it becomes more impersonal" and the closer it is to "those natural forces we call habit or ... instinct," the open morality becomes the more powerful as it is "aroused in us by definite persons, and the more it apparently triumphs over nature." [33] The very special "will to power" (or

[29] *Ibid.*
[30] *Ibid.*, p. 255.
[31] *Ibid.*, p. 75.
[32] *Ibid.*, p. 59.
[33] *Ibid.*, p. 42.

rather the experience of being empowered by something better than ourselves), which mysticism experiences has nothing in common with "imperialism"; it aims at "a sovereignty, not over men, but over things, precisely in order that man shall no longer have so much sovereignty over man." [34]

In a recent book, Gerhard Niemeyer has written of Bergson's juxtaposition of the open and closed moralities as essentially a "confrontation of rationality with higher rationality in a mode of gentle persuasion, resulting . . . in supersession of the lower by the higher authority and a 'leap' in the level of existence." [35] Niemeyer manages here to make Bergson sound more complacent than his analysis permits: to speak of the closed society as based on "rationality" ignores the Bergsonian view that such a society is based on "infra-intellectual" experience and that it is geared for war and the destruction of human life.[36] Instead of "gentle persuasion," one finds in Bergson an anguished exhortation to man to take his destiny into his own hands before it is too late. The voyage across the troubled seas of modernity to the open society is possible, because the way had been opened for modern man by Greek philosophy and the Judeo-Christian religious consciousness.

Contrary to many utterly false impressions that he deserves somehow to be linked with fascism, Bergson regarded democracy as the modern, secular political expression of man's striving for the open society. "Of all political systems," he wrote, democracy "is indeed the furthest removed from nature, the only one to transcend, at least in intention, the conditions of the 'closed society'." [37] For Bergson democracy is much more than a piece of electoral machinery, but rather rests, as John Hallowell later expressed it in the title of a book,[38] upon moral foundations – and precisely upon the foundations of the open morality. The French philosopher sensed the danger that in the process of being transposed into the idiom of contemporary secular thought, the rationale of democracy would be increasingly given in utilitarian terms, and thereby "risk turning into an incurvation in the direction of private interest." [39] For Bergson quite unabashedly held democracy to be "evangelical in essence" and in principle to have "love" for its "motive power." [40] This was not to say that its immediate intellectual antecedents were the great

[34] *Ibid.*, p. 300.
[35] Gerhard Niemeyer, *Between Nothingness and Paradise* (Baton Rouge, Louisiana, 1971), p. 187.
[36] Bergson, *Two Sources*, p. 268.
[37] *Ibid.*, p. 270.
[38] John H. Hallowell, *The Moral Foundations of Democracy* (University of Chicago Press, 1954).
[39] Bergson, *Two Sources*, p. 272.
[40] *Ibid.*, p. 271.

world religions or that modern philosophy played no role in its development. On the contrary, its great modern progenitors were Rousseau and Kant. But Rousseau and Kant were themselves explicable for Bergson only in the light of the earlier decisive opening of the soul in Athens and in Israel. As he summed up his views on the intellectual and spiritual roots of contemporary democracy:

Its sentimental origins could be found in the soul of Rousseau, its philosophic principles in the works of Kant, its religious basis in both Kant and Rousseau: we know how much Kant owed to his pretism, and Rousseau to an interplay of Protestantism and Catholicism.[41]

Bergson was well aware that the struggle for the open society would be an arduous one, for the "innate beliefs of our ancestors subsist in the depths of our inner selves; they reappear as soon as they are no longer inhibited by opposing forces." [42] Furthermore, he observed, in a comment about as far as one can get from the attitude that all is sweetness and light, "the difficulty of abolishing war is greater even than is generally recognized by most people who have no faith in the abolition of war." [43]

How is it possible to break out of the tunnel in which mankind has so long travelled, able to see the light from the open society at the end, but unable to clear the path of obstacles thrown up by the (often massive) vestiges of the closed society? Perhaps a new "privileged soul," or great religious reformer will come to lead us out of the tunnel (cave?), a mystic genius who will

yearn to make of it [humanity] a new species, or rather deliver it from the necessity of being a species, for every species means a collective halt, and complete existence is mobility in individuality.[44]

The advent of a new spiritual *dux* for a new age was not what Henri Bergson had in mind, however. It will be "just as well," he informs us, "not to count too much on the coming of a great privileged soul. Failing that, some other influences might divert our attention from the baubles that amuse us, and the vain shadows for which we fight." [45]

What "other influences" did Bergson have in mind? He does not say, presumably because for the theorist of the open society the future is alive with new possibilities:

[41] *Ibid.*
[42] *Ibid.*, p. 300.
[43] *Ibid.*, p. 276.
[44] *Ibid.*, p. 300.
[45] *Ibid.*, p. 301.

How is it possible to ask for a precise definition of liberty and equality when the future must lie open to all sorts of progress, and especially to the creation of new conditions under which it will be possible to have forms of liberty and equality which are impossible of realization, perhaps of conception, today? [46]

Bergson's theory of the *élan vital,* or vital impetus, inclined him to an optimism reminiscent of another evolutionist writer absorbed in both theology and natural science, Teilhard de Chardin. Both writers share a faith in the meaningfulness of natural processes, and yet both see the final result in terms of man's capacity to transcend these processes and what had been understood to be their limits. They are not determinists, however, any more than Marx was a determinist. It is only that they see the natural environment as congenial, rather than as hostile, to man if only he will use his capacity for thought to organize his resources in a way compatible with the development of the person.

Thus, for Bergson, there was in principle no opposition between spirit and matter, the "mystical" and the "mechanical," the person and technology. He would not have agreed with his compatriot Jacques Ellul that, barring a miracle, there is something implacably dehumanizing about technology which in the "technological society" develops its own imperative independently of human thinking and willing. On the contrary, Bergson held with characteristic faith in man and his future that

Man will rise above earthly things only if a powerful equipment supplies him with the requisite fulcrum. He must use matter as a support if he wants to get away from matter. In other words, the mystical summons up the mechanical. This has not been sufficiently realized, because machinery, through a mistake at the points, has been switched off on to a track at the end of which lies exaggerated comfort and luxury for the few, rather than liberation for all.[47]

The reversal of the domination of man by the machine and the employment of the latter in the service of the open society can come only at the hands of man himself, however:

Humanity must set about simplifying its existence with as much frenzy as it devoted to complicating it. The initiative can come from humanity alone, for it is humanity and not the alleged force of circumstances, still less a fatality inherent to the machine, which started the spirit of invention along a certain track.[48]

The great closing paragraph [made highly controversial by its concluding words, which must not be taken literally, of course] of *Two Sources* consti-

[46] *Ibid.,* p. 271.
[47] *Ibid.,* p. 298.
[48] *Ibid.,* p. 296.

tutes a ringing reaffirmation of Bergson's conviction that man is free – in the words of Hegel *all* are free – to shape his own destiny and to make of "this refractory planet" a place "worthy of the human spirit to inhabit.":

> Mankind lies groaning, half crushed beneath the weight of its own progress. Men do not sufficiently realize that their future is in their own hands. Theirs is the task of determining first of all whether they want to go on living or not. Theirs the responsibility, then, for deciding if they want merely to live, or intend to make just the extra effort required for fulfilling, even on their refractory planet, the essential function of the universe, which is a machine for the making of gods.[49]

Where does Henri Bergson end with respect to the present political condition of mankind? In the in-between, between the closed and the open society, but with the accent upon the possibilities for openness. Still, strait is the gate and narrow is the way which leads to the city of humanity, for the "tendencies of the closed society have . . . persisted . . . in the society on the way to becoming an open one. . . ." But Bergson chose to write, and apparently also to live, as someone who already was a member of the city of the future. This was his ultimate act of faith: that mankind can and will be moved by a new awareness and a new consciousness to achieve the open society within time. Many will have trouble with the biological support he claimed for this faith; others with the fact that it partakes of the nature of faith at all. But Bergson appears to have been convinced that there is more "evidence" for things unseen and "substance" of things "hoped for" (Hebrews 11) than is contained in faith itself. Perhaps this is only another way of stating that authentic faith can have no other anchorage than the possibilities of existence. Only, it can aid us in seeing those possibilities which the eye of natural reason inclines us to overlook.

KARL POPPER

Karl Popper wrote his *The Open Society and Its Enemies* in New Zealand during the terrible years of World War II, when it seemed that Nazism and Fascism might triumph. It was first published in 1946. The book's at times ferociously intense argument reflects the critical period during which most of the work was composed. Popper clearly felt that he was either writing for posterity (in the event of a German victory) or to prevent a repetition of the totalitarian threat in the event of a German defeat. In either case, his purpose was in part highly polemical. He emerges in these pages as in

[49] *Ibid.*, p. 306 (End).

intention a deeply humanitarian man, and his conception of the open society has more similarities with that of Bergson than one might at first think. Nonetheless, it is now generally recognized by historians of political thought that Popper wildly caricatured, in varying degrees, the three major figures whom he attacked as the chief "enemies" of the open society: i.e., Plato, Hegel, and Marx.

It is not my purpose to enter into his interpretations of any of these figures; there are other participants at the conference who will be considering his treatment of Plato, for example. In these remarks I wish only to indicate the broad contours of his conception of the open and closed societies respectively, particularly by way of comparison with Bergson's teaching.

According to Popper, the "attempt to build up an open society" originated with the Greeks, and specifically with the "Great Generation" of the sophists and Socrates. The open society "rejects the absolute authority of the merely established and the merely traditional while trying to preserve, to develop, and to establish traditions, old or new, that measure up to [the] standards of freedom, of humaneness, and of rational criticism." [50]

Popper was aware that Bergson had used the terms open and closed society, and he remarked in a note on the relationship between his analysis and that of the Frenchman:

> In spite of a considerable difference (due to a fundamentally different approach to nearly every problem of philosophy) between Bergson's way of using these terms and mine, there is a certain similarity also, which I wish to acknowledge. (Cp. Bergson's characterization of the closed society, *op. cit.* [a reference to the *Two Sources*], p. 229, as 'human society fresh from the hands of nature.') The main difference, however, is this. My term indicates a *rationalist* distinction; the closed society is characterized by the belief in magical taboos, while the open society is one in which men have learned to be to some extent critical of taboos, and to base decisions on the authority of their own intelligence (after discussion). Bergson, on the other hand, has a kind of *religious distinction* in mind.[51]

Actually, there are other important differences between the conceptions of Bergson and Popper of the open and closed society than the one indicated by Popper. Bergson is at one with Popper in linking *a certain kind* of religious attitude (which the French thinker calls "static" as opposed to "dynamic" religion) with the closed society, and Bergson is scarcely against "reason," objecting instead to its confinement to the sphere of "intelligence"

[50] Karl R. Popper, *The Open Society and Its Enemies* (London: Routledge and Kegan Paul, 1950), Preface, p. ix. (In two parts: all but the final quotation are from Part I.)

[51] *Ibid.*, I, Notes, p. 202.

to the exclusion of "intuition." It is by intuition that we get *inside* phenomena instead of imposing a conceptual scheme from the outside: in the philosophy of the French thinker, concepts should be conformed to reality rather than reality to concepts.

The differences between Popper and Bergson have to do with the question of openness toward what? For Popper the emphasis is upon *horizontal* openness, openness to the experimental method of trial and error, to critical thought as conceived by the natural scientist. (Popper's most outstanding work has been in the area of epistemology of scientific investigation as exemplified in his famous *Logik der Forschung*). Although his thought is not dogmatically closed to religious insight, Popper expresses his idea of the open society primarily within the framework of secular liberalism. He sees the sophists and Socrates as precursors of modern liberal democracy as represented by Locke, the Enlightenment, the French Revolution, and John Stuart Mill. Bergson, on the other hand, emphasizes *vertical* openness, the opening of the psyche toward the ground of Being. To employ a distinction I have made elsewhere, Bergson's thought revolves around the experience of *theocentric* humanism, while Popper is more inclined to anthropocentric humanism. It is no accident that Protagoras ("man is the measure") is a hero to Popper while Plato ("God is the measure") is a model for Bergson. The Greek philosophers – Plato and his precursors such as Parmenides and Heraclitus – and the Hebrew prophets and Christian mystics are the paradigmatic "heroes" of the open society for the Frenchman. Popper disagrees fundamentally with Bergson on Plato; for him, the Ireek philosopher is the arch-enemy of the open society and a proponent of obscurantist myth and a closed society based on taboos, while for the Frenchman he is one of the key discoverers of philosophic openness which challenges and shatters the authority of taboos. Popper draws a sharp distinction between Socrates and Plato, accusing the latter of cynically expropriating the former's prestige to make his infamous teaching appear more palatable to unsuspecting readers. For Bergson, Plato is a faithful colaborer with the "mystical" Socrates in the vineyards of the open society. With regard to Christianity, there is closer agreement, although not convergence, in the works of Popper and Bergson, although the former tends to confine his remarks entirely to the New Testament and to regard Christian mysticism, like all mysticism, as "irrational." Both writers see democracy, properly understood, as the authentic contemporary expression – indeed culmination – of the idea of the open society, but they have quite different views of the meaning of democracy. Popper is much more *individualistic,* whereas Bergson, like Rousseau, emphasizes *fraternity* as the mediating term between liberty and equality. Popper holds that there is such a thing as a good or liberal form of "imperialism" (as represented by the Athens of Pericles and presumably by the "Anglo-Saxon" powers in our own time), whereas Bergson rejects all imperialism and insists that the open society must advance through cultural permeation rather than through power. Perhaps most importantly of all, Bergson speaks of *the* open society "embracing all mankind," while Popper frequently refers to open soci*eties,* which are in competition, and perhaps at war, with other societies, themselves either closed or open. For Bergson the achievement of the open society entails the elimination of war and the creation of some type of world community. Popper does not insist upon this development, and risks thereby having his theory transformed into a weapon in the ideological struggle of what has since come to be called the "cold war."

To pursue Popper's theory of the open society in greater detail, let us turn to Chapter 10 of Volume I of *The Open Society and Its Enemies:*

> In what follows, the magical or tribal or collectivist society will also be called the *closed society*, and the society in which individuals are confronted with personal decisions, the *open society*.
>
> A closed society at its best can be justly compared to an organism. . . . A closed society resembles a herd or a tribe in being a semi-organic unit whose members are held together, sharing common efforts, common dangers, common joys, common distress. It is still a concrete group of concrete individuals, related to one another not merely by such abstract social relationships as the division of labour and the exchange of commodities, but by concrete physical relationships such as touch, smell, and sight.
>
> . . . in an open society, many members strive to rise socially, and to take the places of other members. This may lead . . . to . . . [the] class struggle . . . [The closed society rejects] competition for status among its members . . . [and] its institutions, including its castes, are sacrosanct – taboo . . .
>
> As a consequence of its loss of organic character, an open society may become by degrees, what I should like to term an 'abstract society.' [52]

Popper concedes that the "abstract," impersonal quality of social groups in "modern open societies" has left "many people" in a condition of "anonymity and isolation, and consequently of unhappiness." "For although society has become abstract, the biological make-up of man has not changed much; men have social needs which they cannot satisfy in an abstract society." [53]

Nonetheless, such a condition, Popper implies, is the necessary price of incalculable gains. "Personal relationships of a new kind can arise when

[52] *Ibid.,* I, pp. 174-175.
[53] *Ibid.,* p. 175.

they can be freely entered into, instead of being determined by the accidents of birth; and with this, a new individualism arises. Similarly, spiritual bonds can play a major role where the biological or physical bonds are weakened, etc." [54]

What Popper calls the "strain of civilization," occasioned by the breakdown of the closed society and by the "endeavor to be rational, to forgo at least some of our emotional needs, to look after ourselves, and to accept responsibilities," is asserted to be "the price to be paid for every increase in knowledge, in reasonableness, in cooperation and mutual help [in an 'abstract society'?] and consequently in our chances of survival, and in the size of the population [how strange that last phrase sounds to contemporary readers who hardly link the 'increase of population' to increasing our 'chances of survival'!] It is the price we have to pay for being human." [55]

Imperialism – of the "benevolent" variety – was reckoned by Popper, along with the renunciation of "at least some of our emotional needs," as part of the "necessary price" to be paid for advancing from the closed to the open society. He vigorously champions the cause of Athenian expansion, taking Thucydides and later historians who followed him, to task for their "anti-democratic" and pro-Spartan biases. Nonetheless, Popper adds,

> I am far from defending everything that Athens did in building up her empire, and I certainly do not wish to defend wanton attacks (if such have occurred), or acts of brutality; nor do I forget that Athenian democracy was still based on slavery. But it is necessary, I believe, to see that tribalist exclusiveness and self-sufficiency could be superseded only by some from of imperialism. And it must be said that certain of the imperialist measures introduced by Athens were rather liberal.[56]

Among the "liberal" measures "introduced" by Athens were, we are told, the offer to the Samosians to become Athenians and to merge their *polis* with that of Athens (of course retaining "freedom" to order their "internal affairs" as they chose), and the Athenian system of requiring money tributes from cities in her control, which was not all exploitative because their trade was in turn encouraged and protected by the Athenian fleet! [57] These cheerful remarks of Karl Popper will surely produce a chilling effect on a good

[54] *Ibid.* Popper does not elaborate on this last reference to "spiritual bonds." Did he foresee a new religiousness?
[55] *Ibid.,* p. 176.
[56] *Ibid.*
[57] *Ibid.*

many readers today. If such imperialism is truly the "necessary price" for the open society, how many will want to be thus "liberated"?

To dwell on Popper's conclusions on imperialism would be to neglect the forest for the trees, however, for there is a nobility of moral vision in his work that is incompatible with his endorsement of expansion and conquest, of a new "crusade," as it were, that could end, to the extent that it was successful, only in erecting another, more vast, and more dreary closed society. For like Bergson, Popper also sensed, in his best moments, that the idea of the open society was a revolutionary idea – or better, *the* truly revolutionary idea – against which all other conceptions must be judged deficient.

For Karl Popper, the "transition from the closed to the open society can be described as one of the deepest revolutions through which mankind has passed." The Greeks "started for us that great revolution which, it seems, is still in its beginning – the transition from the closed to the open society." [58] During the Fifth Century B.C. at Athens Socrates and the other great critical minds such as Protagoras, Democritus, and Gorgias, discovered "a new faith in reason, freedom, and the brotherhood of all men – the new faith, and, as I believe, the only possible faith, of the open society." [59] Here we have echoes of Bergsonian universalism, and when a little later Popper quotes Democritus with approval as observing that "Not out of fear but out of a feeling of what is right should we abstain from doing wrong" we are very near to Bergson's contrast between the closed morality of "pressure" based on fear and the open morality of "aspiration" grounded in love.[60]

Popper describes the "rise of philosophy" as coextensive with the "breakdown of the closed society." Philosophy involves the replacement of the "magical faith" with "rational faith." Philosophy "modified tradition" by "establishing a new tradition – the tradition of challenging theories and myths and of critically discussing them." [61]

In contrast to Bergson (and even more markedly, to Eric Voegelin) who counted the pre-Socratic philosophers among the (largely unsung) heroes of the open society, Popper regards Anaximander and Heraclitus as having given way to the 'strain of civilization" after making a promising beginning in critical thought. Anaximander, we are told, regarded "individual ex-

[58] *Ibid.*, p. 175. One page later, however, he makes the puzzling statement that the "revolution was not made consciously," but was the result of "population growth" and rapid social change. What is philosophy if it is not self-conscious thought?
[59] *Ibid.*, p. 185.
[60] *Ibid.*, p. 185.
[61] *Ibid.*, p. 188.

istence" as *hubris*, while Heraclitus "rationalized his feeling of drift by developing the first anti-democratic ideology and the first historicist philosophy of change and destiny . . . *Heraclitus* was the first conscious enemy of the open society." Xenophanes is the only pre-Socratic thinker to merit Popper's praise. However, the Professor does not think we can "blame them for their hostility towards the new developments in the way in which we may . . . blame their successors. The new faith in man, in equalitarian justice, and in human reason, was perhaps beginning to take shape, but it was not yet formulated." [62]

In Popper's interpretation, the greatest figures in the "Great Generation" of Fifth Century Athens in the advocacy of the open society were Protagoras, the theorist, Pericles, the statesman, and Socrates, the martyr. Pericles was the founder of Athenian democracy and Socrates its leading critic. However, Socrates was a "friendly" rather than a "hostile" critic of democracy. His type of criticism must be seen as "the very life of democracy" and must not be confused with the "totalitarian" threat of such men as Plato, and later Hegel and Marx.[63]

What appealed to Popper about Socrates was his "intellectualism, i.e. his equalitarian theory of human reason as a universal medium of communication; his stress on intellectual honesty and self-criticism; his equalitarian theory of justice, and his doctrine that it is better to be a victim of injustice than to inflict it on others." [64] Socrates, we are told, "had only *one* worthy successor, his old friend Antisthenes, the last of the Great Generation. Plato, his most gifted disciple, was soon to prove the least faithful. He betrayed Socrates, just as his uncles had done . . . Plato tried to implicate Socrates in his grandiose attempt to construct the theory of the arrested society; and he had no difficulty in succeeding, for Socrates was dead." [65] Antisthenes, the founder of Cynicism, radically juxtaposed nature (*physis*) and convention (*nomos*). And yet Popper takes Plato to task for allegedly doing the same thing: for Plato, we are told, the "end must be the complete return to nature, a complete cleaning of the canvas." [66] Plato made a tremendous "effort to close the door which had been opened." [67]

Popper's conception of the open society seems to center on a re-affir-

[62] *Ibid.*, p. 189.
[63] *Ibid.*
[64] *Ibid.*, p. 190.
[65] *Ibid.*, p. 194. Antisthenes, of course, was the founder of the Cynic School. It is rather surprising to see Popper hailing the founder of Cynicism, who delighted in iconoclasm and exhibitionism, as a champion of "rational criticism." See L. Edelstein, *The Meaning of Stoicism* (Cambridge, Mass., Harvard University Press, 1966), for a discussion of Antisthenes.
[66] *Ibid.*, p. 198.
[67] *Ibid.*, p. 199.

mation of liberal individualism with a strong dose of Stoic fortitude mixed in. There are only two alternatives facing man: a reactionary return to primitive tribalism and collectivism or a decisive advance to the open society. The former road leads eventually to the brutalization of man and his reduction to the level of a beast (a common charge, incidentally, against the Cynics). The latter way is the only path to a fully human life for all men:

> For those who have eaten of the tree of knowledge, paradise is lost. The more we try to return to the heroic age of tribalism, the more surely do we arrive at the Inquisition, at the Secret Police, and at a romanticized gangsterism. Beginning with the suppression of reason and truth, we must end with the most brutal and violent destruction of all that is human. *There is no return to a harmonious state of nature. If we turn back, then we must go the whole way – we must return to the beasts.*[68]
>
> It is an issue we must face squarely.... If we dream of a return to our childhood, if we are tempted to rely on others and so be happy, if we shrink from the task of carrying our cross, the cross of humaneness, of reason, of responsibility, if we lose courage and flinch from the strain, then we must try to fortify ourselves with a clear understanding of the simple decision before us. We can return to the beasts. But if we wish to remain human, then there is only one way, the way into the open society....[69]

Some of Popper's best writing about the open society comes in his concluding Chapter 25, entitled "Has History Any Meaning?" I shall not attempt to summarize his argument, but it should be pointed out that in this chapter one finds many judgments which go far toward redressing the balance of his earlier statements about "benevolent" imperialism. He roundly condemns the worship of power in historical writing, and eloquently affirms the capacity of man self-consciously to shape his own destiny in reason and freedom rather than to serve as the plaything of anonymous deterministic "forces" beyond his control.

Karl Popper's *The Open Society and Its Enemies,* for all its limitations and questionable interpretations of particular philosophies of the past, constitutes an eloquent restatement of the liberal ideal of a society based on "open questions," as John Stuart Mill observed in *On Liberty.* And yet to link Popper and Mill too closely may be to fail to do full justice to the latter. Mill championed spontaneity and variety, and self-expression, and through his own harrowing experiences was not oblivious of the emotional needs of man as indispensable for his true fulfillment. Mill's sympathy for Coleridge indicates that he could never have agreed with Popper's careless dismissal of "romantic" concern with self-expression as in the following sentence: "We can train ourselves to use our language as an instrument not

[68] *Ibid.,* pp. 200-201.
[69] *Ibid.,* p. 201.

of self-expression (as our romantic educationists would say) but of rational communication."

Nonetheless, for all its deficiencies and polemical excesses, how many of us would disagree with the concluding paragraph of *The Open Society and Its Enemies:*

Instead of posing as prophets we must become the makers of our fate. We must learn to do things as well as we can, and to look out for our mistakes. And when we have dropped the idea that the history of power will be our judge, when we have given up worrying whether or not history will justify us, then one day perhaps we may succeed in getting power under control. In this way we may even justify history, in our turn. It badly needs a justification.[70]

ERIC VOEGELIN

Voegelin's political teaching is particularly resistant to bald summarizing. He writes in a formidable style and with enormous compactness, so that to expound with reasonable sufficiency upon a single paragraph would require pages. No attempt will be made to deal with his political philosophy *in extenso* here; rather, I shall limit myself to a few observations on what I find to be his significance in the ongoing attempt to refine and clarify the concept of the open society.

Although Voegelin's references to Bergson are relatively rare, there is no doubt that the French philosopher, particularly through his *Two Sources,* exercised a major influence on Voegelin's philosophy of history. Voegelin, in fact, has gone so far as to argue that as a symbol, the open society stands for nothing less than the history of mankind:

The history of mankind, thus, is an open society – Bergson's, not Popper's – comprehending both truth and untruth in tension. It is true, the balance of the tension can shift . . . toward one or the other of the poles; and the shifts in balance can be characterized as periods of history. . . . But social predominance of one pole does not abolish the other pole and together with it the tension. . . .[71]

Elsewhere, Voegelin has characterized existence as having "the structure of the In-Between, of the Platonic *metaxy,* and if anything is constant in . . . history . . . it is the language of tension between life and death, immortality and mortality, perfection and imperfection, time and timelessness; between order and disorder, truth and untruth . . . between *amor Dei* and *amor sui, l'âme ouverte* and *l'âme close*; between the virtues of openness toward the

[70] *Ibid.,* II, end.
[71] Eric Voegelin, "Immortality: Experience and Symbol," 40 *Harvard Theological Review* (July, 1967), pp. 235-279, at 239.

ground of being such as faith, love, and hope, and the vices of unfolding closure such as hybris and revolt. . . ." [72]

Here, it seems to me, Voegelin has posed the fundamental, decisive philosophical issue which has implications for all of our discussions on the open society: to what extent is the open society exclusively a paradigm, "laid up in the heavens," as Plato has Socrates say toward the end of the *Republic,* and to what extent can it be realized here and now, within time and the world?

To say, as Voegelin does, that existence is a state of tension between different poles, is to affirm that the open society can never prevail within time and the world but must represent a goal or target forever beyond the reach of men. This is obviously at variance with the progressivist flavor of Bergson's original formulation. For although the French philosopher frequently expressed himself upon the extreme difficulty of the human species' advancing from the closed to the open society, the conclusion of the *Two Sources* left no doubt but that he foresaw such a breakthrough, while not inevitable, as being at least possible and perhaps even probable. What is absent in Voegelin's formulation is any concept of human development's being undergirded by an *élan vital.* Voegelin is reticent about explicitly attacking Bergson – perhaps out of appreciation for the latter's achievement in articulating the symbols of *la société ouverte* and *la société close* – but it is clear that he regards the tenor of the closing pages of the *Two Sources* as a regrettable capitulation to evangelical progressivist fervor.

A key distinction in Voegelin's philosophy is that between *metanoia* and *metastasis. Metanoia* (or inward conversion – literally a change of the *nous* or of consciousness) is presupposed by the open morality; *metastasis* (or fixation with a qualitative change of existence) represents for Voegelin an intellectual and spiritual disease of enormous proportions. Voegelin tends to use the terms "metastatic faith" and "gnosticism" interchangeably to represent a hankering after an impossible perfection or fulfillment within existence. The gnostic or metastatic ideologue commits the sin of *hybris* and revolts against the human condition, with its inevitable ambiguity and tension. The real world of human existence is declared to have been replaced by what is in truth an illusory "second reality" which by the gnostic ideologue is claimed to constitute a dramatic qualitative improvement over all the past of mankind.

[72] Voegelin, "Equivalences of Experience and Symbolization in History," unpublished ms., p. 7. (To be published in Volume IV of *Order and History* Louisiana State University Press. I am most appreciative of Professor Voegelin's willingness to share this essay with me.)

A key term which Voegelin employs in *Order and History* to designate the opening of the psyche to world-transcendent reality is "leap in being." Perhaps his most succinct explanation of the meaning he attaches to this term is to be found in the Introduction to Volume II:

> The leap in being, the epochal event that breaks the compactness of the early cosmological myth and establishes the order of man in his immediacy under God . . . occurs twice in the history of mankind, at roughly the same time, in the Near Eastern and the neighboring Aegean civilizations. The two occurrences, while they run parallel in time and have in common their opposition to the Myth, are independent of each other; and the two experiences differ so profoundly in content that they become articulate in the two different symbolisms of Revelation and Philosophy. Moreover, comparable breaks with the myth, again of widely different complexions, occur contemporaneously in the India of the Buddha and the China of Confucius and Laotse.[73]

Let us listen to Gregor Sebba, one of Voegelin's most gifted interpreters, describe the concept of the leap in being:

> The framework of *Order and History* is the transition from cosmological, compact civilization to differentiation. This occurs in five "leaps in being" of different degrees of radicalism and with different characteristics. Two of them, in India and China, have remained incomplete. The other three (Israel, Greece, the Incarnation) have been radical, merging in the end into Western civilization. The leaps in being are "transcendental irruptions" in which the ground of being (God) becomes manifest as world-transcendent. These leaps in being, where radical, open the era of human existence immediately under God. They constitute "history" as man enters existence in "historical form." [74]

The "leap in being" is accomplished in the psyche of the individual philosopher or spiritual (pneumatic) personality, and the experiences of such a man become representative for all mankind. The understanding of society as a *micro-cosmos* articulated in the cosmological myth of the closed society is replaced with the understanding of society as the soul of the representative human exemplar writ large (*macro-anthropos*). The measure of right action is discovered in the depths of the psyche rather than in the order and motion of the visible heavens. As the new insights into the human condition resulting from the leap in being are disseminated, mankind acquires a sense of liberation, an awareness of a new richness and depth to

[73] Voegelin, *Order and History, II: The World of the Polis* (3 volumes, Baton Rouge, Louisiana State University Press, 1957), p. 1. "The initial leap in being, the break with the order of the myth, occurs in a plurality of parallel instances, in Israel and Hellas, in China and India. . . ." *Ibid.*, p. 3.

[74] Gregor Sebba, "The 'Leap in Being'. Eric Voegelin's Construction of History," unpublished ms., pp. 1-2. (To be published in the *Proceedings* of the Symposium in honor of Voegelin, University of Notre Dame, April 28-29, 1971.)

inner experience, and a capacity – troublesome to the authorities – for criticizing existing institutions and policies in the light of a transcendent standard. The "whole duty of man" is conceived to go decisively beyond conformity to the external requirements of a given society's code of "law and order," to require a striving for "attunement" of the soul with the "order of being." With the discovery of participation in the divine ground of being as man's ultimate defining characteristic, the open society breaks upon the scene.

Gregor Sebba has perceptively noted that in Voegelin's more recent writings (dating from "Ewiges Sein in der Zeit" of 1964) the term "tension" begins to take the place of "attunement."

> From now on, [writes Sebba] *tension* becomes a fundamental symbol, together with another one: the *metaxy* or Inbetween, taken from Plato's *Symposium*: "the spiritual realm lies between God and man." Philosophical experience of the divine ground of being is then a movement of the soul *between* life and death, time and eternity, reality and deformed "reality," and so on.[75]

Sebba does not say so explicitly, but it would appear that with this shift in emphasis from attunement with, to tension toward the ground as the crucial experience of the open soul, we encounter a potentially significant blunting of the critical cutting edge which the open society concept possessed at the hands of Bergson. Bergson wrote of the experiences of openness and closure as if they were different in kind; Voegelin's metaphor of the "leap in being" also conveys this impression. However, the perception of existence as a state of tension *between* good and evil, life and death, perfection and imperfection, etc., implies that there are only differences of *degree* between different modes of experience, some relatively closed, others relatively open. While the above approach may represent a gain for "realism" in some respects, in others it tends to divest the open society concept of its radical importance.

Here it seems to me that we come upon a key *aporia* – or even "tension" if you like – in Voegelin's thought: i.e., if the "leap in being" results only in confirming that in historical reality we are bound to implacable limitations on what we may hope to achieve, and if the rents and tears in the community of man endure as men continue to inhabit their closed societies (in the Bergsonian sense), what is the importance of the discovery of the open society for temporal politics?

Already in the *New Science of Politics* and in *Order and History,* in other words long before "Ewiges Sein in der Zeit," with its replacement of

[75] *Ibid.*, p. 4.

"attunement" with "tension," Voegelin had formulated the concept of the leap in being in such a way as to play down or remove its transformational "sting." Thus, in *Order and History* we find him observing:

For human nature is constant in spite of its unfolding, in the history of mankind, from compact to differentiated order: the discernible stages of increasing truth of existence are not caused by 'changes in the nature of man' that would disrupt the unity of mankind and dissolve it into a series of different species. The very idea of a history of mankind presupposes that constancy of nature; and the reality of that constancy is attested beyond a doubt by the experiences of the leap in being, by the experience of a transition from untruth to truth of existence in which the same man is the 'old man' before, and the 'new man' after he has suffered the infusion of divine Being.[76]

Or, as he expressed the matter in Volume I of the same work, "the leap upward in being is not a leap out of existence." Man's "partnership with God," experienced through philosophy and revelation, "does not abolish [his] partnership in the community of being at large. . . . Man and society . . . must remain adjusted to the order of mundane existence." [77]

"Adjusted . . . to mundane existence"! Has the psalmist sung, the prophet excoriated, the mystic extolled, the suffering servant experienced martyrdom all for this, that man remain "adjusted to mundane existence"? Such a conclusion flies in the face of Voegelin's own eloquent and profound explication of the inner meaning of these experiences. It contrasts markedly with St. Paul's exhortation to "be not conformed to this world" but to be "transformed by the renewing of [our] mind."

What is the source of Voegelin's cautious conclusion to his bold analysis? Perhaps it is the same source which produced the same result in Camus' *L'homme révolté* or in J. L. Talmon's *Political Messianism*; i.e., Voegelin, Camus, and Talmon, sickened by the ideological and practical excesses, indeed bestiality, of so much of twentieth century politics, have understandably overreacted to *any* conceptions of a basically transformed political order. They have witnessed so many "crimes of logic," so many insane "wars of principle," that they are led to confine their energies to attempts to defuse the ideological climate of our time and to articulate the implacable confines and limits of collective human efforts.

One takes heed of the warning which men of the stature of Voegelin, Camus, Talmon, de Jouvenel, Strauss, and Oakeshott give to us about the dangers involved in attempting to bring an impossible perfection to the

[76] Voegelin, *Order and History,* II, p. 5.
[77] Voegelin, *Order and History,* I: *Israel and Revelation* (3 volumes, Baton Rouge, Louisiana State University Press, 1956), p. 11.

political world. We ignore their insights at our peril. But cannot more be done to show the possibility of leavening our existing political structures and practices with the experience of openness and of the open morality than appears evident in their philosophy? Perhaps Eric Voegelin will deal with the question of the conditions and possibilities for the greater social efficacy of the experience of openness toward transcendent Being in future writings. In any event, Voegelin has rendered a signal service in his magisterial efforts to recall for us today the meaning of philosophy and revelation as experienced during the Age of the Breakthrough, and we can learn from him that a crucial task of those who today seek to live in accord with the fullest possibilities of an open existence is "to recover what has been lost and found again and again" by men "whom one cannot hope to emulate." (T.S. Eliot, *Four Quartets,* East Coker.)

As Henri Bergson continues to remind us:

> The great moral figures that have made their mark on history join hands across the centuries, above our human cities; they invite us into a divine city. . . . We may not hear their voices distinctly but something answers from the depth of our soul . . . ; to this . . . society we bow down when we reverence the dignity of man within us.[78]

[78] Henri Bergson, *Two Sources of Morality and Religion,* p. 59.

POLITICAL OBLIGATION AND THE OPEN SOCIETY

ALEXANDER PASSERIN D'ENTRÈVES

Can political obligation exist except in an open society? The question, thus flatly put, may well sound, and probably is, somewhat rhetorical. And since rhetorical questions mostly expect to be answered by yes or no, I should not be surprised if my intention in raising it were interpreted as aiming at a restatement of some stale arguments in favour of modern democracy. Let me make it clear that this is not necessarily my purpose. All I intend to do is stress the importance of some peculiar, practical conditions, which seem to me to be required in a given society if we are to conceive of a duty, on the part of its components, to abide by the rules which hold that society together. By choosing to speak about practical, i.e., political conditions, I trust that I may ease my task, and leave the main philosophical question of the "essence" of the open v. the closed society (and vice versa) to more competent hands than mine. And if, in the end, my argument may appear to coincide on several points with those of modern democratic theory, let me hope at any rate that the manner in which I will have presented it may claim some originality, and leave the door open to a charitable view of systems which, in the current use of the term, would probably not be called democratic.

To begin with, what is meant by political obligation? Since I have discussed the question at length in many of my writings, I shall limit myself to giving a short summary of my conclusions. The crux of the matter lies in my view in the ambivalence of the word, obligation. To say that a man has an obligation may mean simply that he is compelled to perform, or to abstain from, certain actions, by the menace, or the likelihood, of a sanction. But it may also mean that, independently of that sanction, he has a duty to behave in a certain manner. In the first case – to resort to a distinction which is commonplace in modern philosophical jargon – obligation is used as a descriptive, in the second as a prescriptive term. Surely the phrase, political obligation – as it recurs in the language of political theory, in contrast, maybe, to that of political science – implies a prescriptive rather than a descriptive use of the word obligation. For indeed the very question, "why should laws be obeyed?" – which I take to be the basic question of political theory – is a question which refers to an *ought,* not to an *is,* to duty, not to compulsion. Political theory is not concerned with the fact that men obey or disobey, but with the reasons which justify and recommend obedience or disobedience. There is no denying that men can be forced to obey, and that the fear of sanctions may well be in most cases the ultimate cause of obedience. But can force be a source of duty? I am – on this point at any rate – a faithful disciple of Rousseau. "Force is a physical power, and I fail to see what moral effect it can have. To yield to force is an act of necessity, not of will – at the most, an act of prudence. In what sense can it be a duty? . . . Let us then admit that force does not create right, and that we are obliged to obey only legitimate powers."

I now turn to examine, on such assumptions, the question of the open society. Professor Germino, in the paper which he has had the kindness of submitting to us well in time for our discussion, has presented us with three different approaches to the notion of the open society: Bergson, Popper, and Voegelin. Since my own approach is, so to speak, from the backdoor – the backdoor of political obligation – and since, as I stressed from the start, the views which I propose to set forth before you are essentially of a practical nature, I shall begin by listing some aspects of that particular type of society where political obligation may be expected to arise. I shall refrain, for the time being, from calling that particular type by the name of an open society, although I certainly think it deserves it.

My argument, in fact, is a very simple one, one which may well sound very much like a truism. If political obligation can be said to arise only in a society which is not held together exclusively by force, I cannot see by what else that society can be held together except by consent: here indeed is the truth which, in my view, the old and discredited theory of the social contract contained, when it stressed that consent was the only legitimizing title of power. To put the matter in more modern terms I suggest that we say that the essential requisite of political obligation is freedom. Freedom in the positive sense, in the sense that consent be assured at least to the basic decisions and to the procedures by which further decisions be reached at: the great and decisive argument in favour of democracy. But freedom also in the negative sense – the liberal sense – which implies not only the respect and the guarantee of the fundamental rights of man, but the possibility for each member of the society to recede from the social contract. Yet positive and negative liberty, democracy and liberalism, may be a sham, if they are not accompanied and made possible by a third type of liberty. Freedom from want is the great case for socialism. How can an active participation of the citizen in political decisions take place, how can the respect for the rights of man have any meaning, where social conditions are such as to prevent individuals from giving their own, fully conscious contribution to the general will, and seek, if necessary, a new bond of allegiance in a different society? When we think that in our old countries of Europe millions of men were drafted and slaughtered in wars whose reasons they never understood, and that many are still herded about and forced to accept any sort of labour by hard economic necessity, surely we must admit that to speak of political obligation in their case sounds very much like a mockery. Force, not consent, is what prompts men to obey whenever they are excluded from playing their part, as free men, in the social and political process.

My conclusion then is, that there are several requirements which must be satisfied in order that political obligation exist in a given society: and democracy, liberalism and socialism all provide different, though not necessarily contrasting, ways for meeting such requirements. A society where the three basic freedoms are balanced and insured within apt institutions, and where the bond of political allegiance may therefore be expected to be strongly felt by most, if not all, of its members: should a society of this kind not be called an open society? This is the question which I prefer to leave for you to discuss: but I would like to end this short paper with a few comparative remarks about the vision of the open society outlined by two of the authors whom Professor Germino has chosen for his presentation.

There is no denying that my idea of a free society is much more akin to Popper's views than to Bergson's *société ouverte*. A free society, as I conceive it, does in fact set free, or should aim at setting free, to use Popper's words, "the critical powers of men." It is a society in which men can learn, or should be able to learn, "to base decisions on the authority of their own intelligence," "after discussion." My difference from Popper lies in the fact, that my concern is not so much with the philosophical premisses as with the actual conditions – the structural devices – which make that society possible. Popper's open society is a society of rational men, reminiscent of the idealized models of the age of enlightenment. My free society is a society which takes men as they are, but offers them the possibility of being free agents, responsible citizens. Its rise is connected, in my view, not so much with the "rise of philosophy," as with the constitutional struggles which mark the beginning of the modern era. This is not to say that free societies, where obligation was felt to arise from consent, were entirely unknown to earlier periods of history. Leaving the Greeks and the Romans aside, there certainly must have been a fair amount of consent, expressed through appropriate institutions, in medieval republics; and feudal monarchies, with their emphasis on a compact or covenant between rulers and ruled, certainly stressed voluntary acceptance as the basis of loyalty. But surely it is only thanks to the criticisms and the investigations of such men as Locke, Montesquieu and Rousseau, and also (why not?) thanks to the bitter denunciations of Marx, that modern man has become aware of the possibility of transforming a society dominated by force into one where consent, and consequently political freedom, should be possible. So much for Popper, and, incidentally, also for the view, still widely held, that the open or free society is but an ideological tool in the cold war between East and West.

My difference with Bergson goes much deeper. It is not only, as Popper points out about his own, a difference between a "rationalist" and a "religious" approach to the problem of politics. But first let me say that I have no intention of denying that obligation in general, of which political obligation is a subspecies, may assume a moral or even a religious overtone. Men may feel bound to obey the laws of the State on the ground of a moral imperative. Or they may do it because they believe that God commands them to do so: "Let every soul be subject to the higher powers. For there is no power but of God: the powers that be are ordained of God," etc. But this has little to do with the practical problem of political obligation: that problem, as I have already pointed out, is one of constructing a type of society where consent, not force, is the source of obedience. Now Bergson would like us to believe that we are drawn to the open society through some kind of mystical experience, or at any rate through love, love of mankind, which is the essential characteristic of openness. The call is indeed very grand and alluring. It echoes the greatest call that has ever been addressed to man, the call of Christian perfection. But love alas has not much say in political matters. Men are not likely to turn into saints overnight, and politics entail harsh realities. Yet these realities must be faced, and, where possible, controlled; to escape into a dream of universal love is to blind ourselves to the humble task that is within our reach, that of bettering the lot of our fellow creatures. And it is also exceedingly dangerous. For if the transition from "closeness" to "openness" implies a "qualitative leap" in man's moral experience, and if the way to that leap is best shown by "privileged persons" – prophets and heroes – then, clearly, it is on them, not on the institutions of a free society, that men's allegiance will focus. Besides, who is going to test the genuineness of the leap, how shall we beware of false prophets? Men are easily deceived, and we should know by experience how tempting it is for them to idolize their masters, and to discharge themselves of their political responsibilities in the hands of those who claim to "know better."

My preference for the rule of law rather than the rule of men should by now be fully apparent. And so will be my conclusion. Political obligation, I believe, is closely linked to the open or free society. It can in fact fully exist only in this kind of society. It may be fostered, and crowned as it were, by moral and religious obligation. But it remains at bottom a question of sound and viable institutions. This is why, from the start, I ventured to call our attention to the practical side of our problem. Unless it is peopled by angels, the open city is not, can not, and never will be, the city of God. Nevertheless, there would be no reason for working at it, for accepting the responsibility laid upon us for doing so, unless we perceived in the distance, however dimly, the towers and spires of the heavenly city which may perhaps be one day our reward – though in a world very different from the one in which we live at present. Let me end with a quotation from our greatest national poet, where this idea is set forth with an admirable image.

Esce di mano a Lui, che la vagheggia
Prima che sia, a guisa di fanciulla
Che piangendo e ridendo pargoleggia,
L'anima semplicetta, che sa nulla,
Salvo che, mossa da lieto Fattore,
Volentier torna a ciò che la trastulla.
Di picciol bene in pria sente sapore;
Quivi s'inganna, e dietro a esso corre,
Se guida o fren non torce suo amore.
Onde convenne legge per fren porre,
Convenne rege aver, che discernesse
Della vera cittade almen la torre.

Dante Alighieri, *The Divine Comedy.*
Purgatorio, XVI, 85-96.

Therefore, if the world to-day goeth astray, in you is the cause, in you be it sought, and I now will be a true scout to thee therein.

From his hands who fondly loves her ere she is

in being, there issues, after the fashion of a
little child that sports, now weeping, now laughing,
the simple, tender soul, who knoweth naught
save that, sprung from a joyous maker, willingly she
turneth to that which delights her.
First she tastes the savour of a trifling good;
there she is beguiled and runneth after it, if
guide or curb turn not her love aside.
Wherefore 'twas needful to put law as a curb,
needful to have a ruler who might discern at least
the tower of the true city.

(The Carlyle-Wicksteed Translation)

POLITICAL SOCIETY AND THE OPEN SOCIETY: BERGSONIAN VIEWS

ANTHONY PAREL

Henri Bergson must rightly be considered the father of the theory of the open society. His *The Two Sources of Morality and Religion* appeared in 1932, thirteen years before Karl Popper's *Open Society and Its Enemies*. It is only fitting that any comprehensive treatment of the notion of the Open Society should include Bergson.

We must begin with a general description of the meaning of openness in Bergson. Openness for Bergson is an active but not natural disposition of the soul to love man *qua* man and to render him absolute justice. It is an inventive, dynamic love of humanity that changes qualitatively the natural basis of one's social relations. The source or cause of this love is divine grace and not natural reason or instinct, and the mode of its acquisition is the mystical experience, not ratiocination.

The Bergsonian view of openness must be distinguished from the mere concept of openness, mystical love and absolute justice. Naturally, the experience of openness may give rise to the concept of it, but from the mere concept we do not arrive at the experience of it. Openness, therefore, is first of all a moral and spiritual virtue, and only secondarily an intellectual virtue. Put differently, Bergsonian openness is more than openness to an idea, or an argument, or a viewpoint or a political scheme: it is an openness to man, whoever he be. To be truly and fully human the soul must be open, not only to the rationality of things but also to the humanity of man which according to Bergson is possible only if man is open to divine grace. An open disposition of the Bergsonian kind does not shut off a priori the manifold sources of experience and knowledge. Philosophic reason has the tendency to identify the rational alone as real. For Bergson, this is folly. Bergson is as opposed to the rationalist variety of closedness as he is to the organic closedness of the natural society.

The methodical scepticism of the scientist and the philosopher is not opposed to Bergson's philosophy of openness. To arrive at truth a posteriori one must adopt a method of trial and error, of hypothesis and verification. St. Thomas, for example, adopts this methodological scepticism: to every issue at hand he invariably applies the test of *videtur quod non.* Far from opposing this type of openness, Bergson considered it a characteristic feature of his philosophy.[1] Jean Guitton's observation on this point is absolutely reliable.

There were two strong tendencies in Bergson, writes Guitton,[2] the scientific and the mystical; and it was his vocation to unify them. Like Darwin and Pasteur, he was devoted to scientific rigour, but unlike Spencer, he did not apply to the moral science the method which was successfully applied to the natural science. In his effort to unify science and mysticism, he was not like Comte and Durkheim: a man of science first, who allowed mysticism to enter into the study as it were surreptitiously, and gave a mystical quality to what was in fact positive science. Nor was he like Pascal who tried to give mysticism a positivistic foundation. Bergson approached reality without presuppositions. But a yearning for deeper understanding of reality made him realize that there were zones of experience which were related to man's moral destiny, where, unlike in natural sciences, tentative and probabilistic solutions did not satisfy experience itself, and which therefore impelled the mind to relate partial solutions to the higher and mysterious zones of life, namely mysticism. In short, Bergsonian openness,

[1] We may be excused for citing, despite its length, a résumé of Bergson's philosophy, written by himself in 1915 and revised by Edouard Le Roy in 1933. It gives the reader an idea of the peculiar flavour and method of Bergson's philosophy. "He tried to carry metaphysics onto the plane of experience, and by calling upon science and conscience, by developing the faculty of intuition, to make a philosophy capable of furnishing no longer just general theories, but also concrete explanations of particular facts. Philosophy taken in this way is capable of the same precision as physical science. Just like science it will be able to make boundless progress, adding one set of results to others once acquired. But over and above, it will aim, and it is in this that it differs from science, to widen more and more the spheres of understanding, even breaking against some others, and enlarge indefinitely human thought. Spurred on with these ideas, he set about the major questions of traditional philosophy one by one. Be it through analysing the original bases of (duration) and finishing by bringing to light what liberty in fact is. Be it by studying the problems of perception and memory, he was able to put his finger on the reality of the spirit and to define its relation to the body. Be it that in a perspective where the intrinsic substantiality of change is affirmed, he noted the evolution of life and discovered creation therein as a real fact. Be it in dividing the two sources of morality and religion and in recognizing the preeminence of the mystical source – his solution always stays on the same line; but always for each new problem, he states the need to make an entirely new effort of adaptation ... Philosophy thus remains a great synthetic effort, without pretending to be a grand synthesis."
French text is found in Bergson, *Ecrits et paroles,* 3 Vols., (1959), II, pp. 430-432. (Author's translation).

[2] Jean Guitton, *La Vocation de Bergson*, (Paris, Gallimard, 1960), pp. 23-25.

while faithful to methodological scepticism, was hospitable to moral certitudes and ethical absoluteness.

There is a natural impulse in man to expand the base of his community – a natural kind of openness if you will. But the natural means he employs to pursue this impulse is war and aggression, not love and justice. Thus the natural communities he creates, whatever they may be, rest on the principle of the inclusion of some and the exclusion of others. His natural regard for love and justice normally ends with the family or clan, caste or race, nation or state, or some other natural community. Even the most civilized notion of citizenship implies the notion of the alien. Bergson therefore rejects "innate sympathy" of man for man, and the "fraternity enjoined on us by philosophers in the name of reason," as the basis of his concept of openness. Such natural sympathies only increase conflicts between nations rather than unite them into one human family:

> With family, country, humanity appearing as wider and wider circles, they – philosophers – thought that man must naturally love humanity as he loves his country and family, whereas in reality the family group and the social group are the only ones corresponding to instinct, and social instinct would be far more likely to prompt societies to struggle against one another than to unite to make up humanity.[3]

The love which animates the open soul, and which is at the origin of the open society, is not natural sympathy or empathy, but the love which the mystic experiences in his contact with God, the Subsistent Love. It is the "love of God for all men. Through God and in the strength of God, he loves all mankind with a divine love." [4] Thus supernatural love of man for man is indirect, i.e., acquired through the medium of God. Like God's love, this received love is also creative: "What it wants to do, with God's help, is to complete the creation of the human species . . ." [5] The work of completion suggested here is the attainment of spiritual perfection, the ability to love every man as one's brother, the attainment of the open society. It is this contact with the living God that gives the mystic his moral certitudes, his prodigious dynamism, his will to serve others, and his mission to transform the natural man into divine man, and his attempt, as it were, to change the material universe into a "machine" for the making of gods.[6]

[3] Henri Bergson, *The Two Sources of Morality and Religion,* Translated by R. Ashley Audra and Cloudesley Brereton (Garden City, New York, Doubleday, 1956), p. 234. (Hereafter, TS).
[4] TS, p. 233.
[5] *Ibid.,* p. 235.
[6] *Ibid.,* p. 317.

Mysticism! Divinization of man! The Universe, a machine for the making of gods! Heady wine indeed! Assuming that what Bergson says is true, what is its relevance for political theory?

Bergson's theory of openness offers a critique of politics, and thus contributes towards the clarification of the nature and significance of the political life. Bergson himself believed that his metaphysics led to certain practical conclusions.[7] These conclusions, in our opinion, form the basis of his critique. His philosophy, based as it is on the evolutionary process taken in its entirety, sees the unity and mutual influences of the diverse elements of reality. As such Bergson is able to identify the nature and place that political activity occupies in the evolutionary ascent of man. Politics belongs to the sphere of instinct and intelligence, of nature and culture. It occupies a middle position between nature and grace, the closed and the open, but receives the influences from both. He does not believe that in reality reason is an autonomous faculty, at least as far as political ethic is concerned. All political values originate either in nature or in mysticism, reason either analyses and makes them practical or, if the reason involved is that of the philosopher, merely conceals the true origins of political values and makes instead reason itself appear as their origin. The resultant idea of the autonomy of politics for Bergson is an illusion created by reason acting in isolation of other spheres of experience.

Reason, from Bergson's evolutionary perspective, is neither autonomous nor able to comprehend the whole of reality, being itself but one product of evolution, and that too of a relatively later stage. It is a faculty of action devised to fit life to matter. Consequently, it feels at home in inert matter, and can understand the living only according to the categories used for the understanding of matter; and consequently without the aid of intuition, it will tend to understand the vital phenomena, whether psychological, social, political or moral, according to the laws of natural science, i.e., mechanistically and statically. It is Bergson's basic position that the vital phenomenon must be grasped from within by an act of intuition, as *durée*, which of course, reason, with its affinity for inorganic matter, is unable to do. We shall elaborate below Bergson's stand on reason and its bearing on his political theory. Suffice it to say here that reason, if it is to deal with values and ethics, must receive the original insights from either instinct or intuition. To that extent, in moral matters, reason is their handmaid.

In brief, Bergson's theory of the open society gives us a ready-made tool for examining certain key problems of political philosophy. Bergson

[7] *Ibid.*, pp. 271, 288.

himself concentrates on mainly three of them – namely, the nature of moral obligation, in so far as it is the inner principle of human societies; the nature of political regimes; and the nature of that political phenomenon par excellence – viz, war and aggression. We shall take these three in turn.

OBLIGATION

Obligation, "the bond between men," [8] holds the key to the understanding of society. Once we grasp the basis of obligation, how and why intelligent and free social beings obey rules and accept authority, we grasp the nature of the human communities. According to Bergson, there are two typical ways in which men relate to each other and constitute community. The first is infra-rational, and the bond of unity present there is social pressure. Bergson calls the resultant society the closed society. The second way of relating to others is supra-rational, which Bergson considers genuinely completely human; and its bond of unity is divine love and it generates the morality of aspiration. Bergson calls the resultant society the open society.

Now social life is an organic, vital necessity determined by the fact that man is a member of the species. Evolution, in endowing a social being like man with intelligence, introduces a certain degree of tension between his sociability and intelligence. On the one hand he feels the pull of organic necessity, yet on the other he also feels that he is free. How is this tension to be controlled? Bergson's answer is that society is immanent in each individual, and by numerous ways exerts an influence on the individual's behaviour and reinforces the natural bond. He uses the analogy of concentric circles to describe the relationship between the two:

> Society occupies the circumference; the individual is at the centre: from the centre to the circumference are arranged, like so many everwidening concentric circles, the various groups to which the individual belongs. From the circumference to the centre, as the circles grow smaller, obligations are added to obligations . . . Thus obligation increases as it advances . . . and is the more easily accepted. When it has become fully concrete, it coincides with a tendency, so habitual that we find it natural, to play in society the part which our station assigns to us.[9]

[8] *Ibid.*, p. 15. Bergson offers a somewhat more formal description of obligation on p. 14. "An individual forming part of a community may bend or even break a necessity of the same (organic) kind, which to some extent he has helped to create, but to which, still more, he has to yield; the sense of this necessity, together with the consciousness of being able to evade it, is none the less what he calls an obligation."

[9] *Ibid.*, p. 19.

The mechanism whereby society assures obedience to authority is habit, more accurately, the habit of forming habits. For habit is to civic community what instinct is to the anthill or the beehive, or necessity to inorganic matter.[10] It makes sure that the individual and the group maintain the necessary equilibrium. From the moment of birth, before and after he attains the "age of reason," society subjects the individual to a relentless process of socialization. Without the regularity which socialization assures, each of the countless choices which the individual must make daily would lack predictability for society and risk for the individual. The habit of forming habits, which is essentially pre-rational, does not destroy freedom, because it does not destroy the freedom to form or not form particular habits and to fulfill or not fulfill particular obligations. Hence the similarity and difference between instinctive and intelligent societies: "in the former each rule is laid down by nature, and is necessary: whereas in the latter only one thing is natural, the necessity of a rule." [11]

Compliance with habits is so natural to man that he fully realizes their power over him, not when he acts in conformity with them, but when he violently breaks with them.[12] Bergson uses the example of the remorse of the murderer which finally forces him to give up. He condemns himself for the crime. The feeling which haunts him is not so much fear of detection and punishment as the desire to wipe out the past. He wants to be reinstated as if he had not committed the crime. But his own knowledge persists, and this drives him to give himself up as the only way of reinstating himself. The point is that the very impulse of life, *élan vital*, ties us to society and we cannot break the tie except at our own cost. Thus each time we obey social rules, society stands behind us with the weight of the "totality of obligations," with the force of the accumulated mass of other obligations.[13]

It is this pressure which is immanent in us, and which is expressed through the habit of forming habits, and behind which society stands with "the concentrated extract, the quintessence of innumerable specific habits of obedience to the countless particular requirements of social life," [14] that Bergson considers as the source of one part of our social obligation, the obligation which underlies the closed society. Overriding concern for security, self-preservation, conformism, the feeling that the individual's welfare is indistinguishable from that of the group, lack of concern for one's obligation to members of alien groups, unless it be for attack and

[10] *Ibid.*, p. 83.
[11] *Ibid.*, p. 28.
[12] *Ibid.*, p. 18.
[13] *Ibid.*, pp. 23, 25, 26.
[14] *Ibid.*, p. 25.

aggression, these are some of the more manifest signs of the closed society.

The source of the other part of obligation is mysticism, the actual experience of the living God and the resultant charisma. We need not concern ourselves here with Bergson's epistemological description of the mystic experience nor with the distinctions which he draws between authentic and false, complete and incomplete varieties of mysticism. Our concern here is mainly with Bergson's thesis that mysticism or charisma is the source of the higher aspiration in social obligation, that in consequence mysticism influences the development of society, and that it enables man to break with the conditions of the closed society. The creators of this morality are charismatic, not political, heroes: the saints of Christianity, the sages of Greece, the prophets of Israel, the arahants of Buddhism, founders and reformers of religion, obscure heroes of moral life.[15] Bergson explicitly rejects any implication that his moral heroes are the same as Nietzsche's supermen: His are heroes by *nature*, whereas those of Bergson are heroes by grace. They do not will to power, but only to love and serve others whose well-being they identify with their own.[16] Grace is gratuitously given (*gratia gratis data*) to those who make the moral effort and who therefore have divested themselves of the natural will to power.

The most important effect of grace, i.e., of the open society, upon closed society has been the ushering in of true democracy and the transformation of social justice. The ideals of democracy, according to Bergson, are evangelical in inspiration. "Of all political systems,[17] it – democracy – is indeed the furthest removed from nature, the only one to transcend, at least in intention, the conditions of the 'closed society.' " Human rights, "in order to remain inviolate, demand of all men an incorruptible fidelity to duty. It therefore takes for its matter an ideal man, who respects others as he does himself, inserting himself into obligations which hold to be absolute . . ." [18]

Similarly the passage from relative justice to absolute justice has been made possible by the mystics. Relative justice, originating as it does in mercantile and utilitarian social practice, expresses the notions of social equilibrium, proportion and relativity. From this to reach 'the rights of

[15] *Ibid.*, pp. 34, 50.
[16] *Ibid.*, p. 16.
[17] The phrase, "political systems" does not, in my view, accurately translate the original French phrase, *des toutes les conceptions politiques*. See the French text, in the 164th edition, Presses Universitaires de France, 1967, p. 299. The point is important, because Bergson in this context is talking about the ideals, not institutions, of democracy. The ideals are evangelical in origin. The institutions, however, are social in origin, and therefore they pertain to the closed order.
[18] *Ibid.*, p. 281.

man' doctrine of justice required a mystical vision of man. Man, irrespective of his class or merit or status, is presented as incommensurable with any other social good. Such a change in attitude required a spiritual leap forward. Historically, the prophets of Israel according to Bergson, were the first to give justice "a categorical and transcendent" character. Even though they applied this justice only to the children of Israel, its essence transcended justice as derived from social practice. Christianity, with its universal mission of salvation, extended this justice to humanity as a whole.[19]

The open morality is dynamic; i.e., its bearers are consumed by missionary zeal. They want to ameliorate the conditions of historical existence of their hearers. They see in their "mind's eye a new social atmosphere, an environment in which life would be more worth living." [20] Moreover, the beauty of their lives, by itself, is able to evoke in others a desire for imitation. They activate and elevate man's capacity for imitation, which plays in open society a role similar to that played by habit in closed societies. A corollary of the mystic love of the moral genius is the ability of the non-mystic souls to respond to that love. The efficacious realization of the open society depends on both these factors, attraction of the ideal and the capacity for imitation. Bergson writes:

> The great moral figures that have made their mark on history join hands across the centuries above our human cities; they unite into a divine city which they bid us enter. We may not hear their voices distinctly; the call has none the less gone forth, and something answers from the depth of our soul; from the real society in which we live we betake ourselves in thought to this ideal society; to this ideal society we bow down when we reverence the dignity of man within us, when we declare that we act from self-respect.[21]

THE ROLE OF REASON IN SOCIETY

The question arises: if the foundations of morality are infra-rational and supra-rational, what is the role of reason in moral obligation? Bergson's critique of the role of reason in morality is perhaps the most challenging part of his theory of openness. He ascribes to reason only two valid functions consistent with its nature. They are, first, the organization of matter, particularly in the form of tool making (science and technology); and secondly, the organization and rationalization of social morality according

[19] *Ibid.*, pp. 76-77.
[20] *Ibid.*, p. 80.
[21] *Ibid.*, p. 68.

to the criteria of utility and need. It is in these ways that reason contributes to social progress. To this extent Bergson is not an anti-intellectualist. However, he rejects any other claims made on behalf of reason, particularly the rationalist claim that reason is the foundation of morality and of the open society. Indeed he considers this misrepresentation of the functions of reason as the chief obstacle to attaining the open society.

Reason occupies a middle position between instinct and intuition; and the city of reason – the world of technology, civilization, of utilitarian ethics – occupies the middle position between the closed and the open societies. The rational city is the city in the process of becoming open.[22]

Bergson's critique of reason is based on the empirical evidence of evolution as he sees it. In this respect the *Creative Evolution* is an extended elaboration of his fundamental thesis that evolution is the result of the confrontation between life and matter; that there is a mutuality between the two; that, in proceeding along divergent lines, evolution created intelligence and intuition, but that intelligence is the faculty of matter, while intuition is that of consciousness, *durée.*

Thus, the history of evolution shows that reason is only an "appendage of the faculty of acting," of adapting life to matter, "to think matter." Consequently it represents the relations of external things, feels at home only among inanimate objects, and forms concepts on the model of solids. Being a faculty meant to deal with matter, it triumphs in geometry and mathematics, in tempero-spatial thought; "whatever is geometrical in things is entirely accessible to human intelligence." [23] Its power of deduction and induction, of decomposing according to any law, and of recomposing into any system is unlimited. It manifests its theoretical accuracy in the system of tools it develops. From the point of view of evolution, tool making is the characteristic feature of reason (*intelligence fabricatrice*). Its success in tool making leads the intellect to treat the material universe itself as a mechanical system. It follows that "our thought, in its purely logical form, is incapable of presenting the true nature of life, the full meaning of the evolutionary movement." [24]

Reason makes its specific contribution to social life through its tool making ability. Bergson feels that the change in technology is the basic material force of social evolution: "our social life gravitates around the manufacture and use of artificial instruments." Technological changes will

[22] *Ibid.*, pp. 63, 266, 288.
[23] Henri Bergson, *Creative Evolution,* authorized translation, by Arthur Mitchell (New York, H. Holt and Company, 1923), p. 210. (Hereafter, C.E.).
[24] C.E., p. ix.

contribute more "to define an age" than "our wars and our revolutions," even supposing they are remembered in the future.[25]

Bergson's objection to reason does not stem from the objective contributions it makes towards social progress, but from the invalid inferences rationalists draw from them, and which lead to a mechanistic view of society and morals:

> The intellect bears within itself, in the form of natural logic, a latent geometrism that is set free in the measure and proportion that the intellect penetrates into the inner nature of inert matter.... Now when the intellect undertakes the study of life, it necessarily treats the living like the inert, applying the same forms to this new object, carrying over into this new field the same habits that have succeeded so well in the old; ... But the truth we thus arrive at becomes altogether relative to our faculty of action.... What must the result be, if it (philosophy) leaves biological and psychological facts to positive science alone, as it has left, and rightly left, physical facts? It will accept a priori a mechanistic conception of all nature....[26]

This is precisely what happened, Bergson feels, in the 19th century. The success of positive science in ameliorating the material conditions of life has been used as an excuse to tilt the balance between intelligence and intuition in favour of the former. There is no difference of kind, it was argued, but merely one of degree, between laws of physical bodies and human societies. Thus society is viewed as a system of force and morality itself as the stronger force. It follows from the above that strong nations conquer weaker nations, that a balance of power regulates their mutual relations. Treaties represent the will of the conqueror, i.e., the actual direction of force, and law is what is written in codes.

According to Bergson the opposition between natural sciences and social sciences is the artifical creation of the mechanistic philosophers who ignore the mutuality of science and mysticism and the immanence of norms and values in the social fact. The task of analysis, classification, verification, prediction, composing, decomposing and recomposing, and of introducing self-consistency in the various elements under investigation – all this is common to both sciences. But the facts they deal with, the experience which underlies them are as different as matter is different from life.

Even when the political scientist introduces self-consistency in the political facts, he is unavoidably dealing with norms and values in so far as they are inherent in such facts. Political science is value free only in

[25] *Ibid.*, pp. 138-139.

[26] C.E. p. 196. For Bergson's view on the connaturality between reason and matter, see C.E. pp. 186-200. And for his critique of the mechanistic interpretation of life see *ibid.*, pp. 304-363.

the sense that analysis and prediction do not create new values and norms. Political science merely makes existing values and norms more and more self-consistent. This rationalizing activity is necessary for attaining social progress: the more advanced a society becomes the greater its need for self-consistent rules and practices. Bergson fully recognizes this. What he rejects is that this activity is the source of new values.

If the mechanistic philosopher misrepresents the role of reason in society, the rationalist moral philosopher performs the necessary function of rationalization of social morality. For reason acts as the intermediary between the morality of pressure and the morality of aspiration. In the process of rationalization of morality instincts and ideals interpenetrate and intermingle. "The result is mental pictures, many of them of a compound nature, being a blend of that which is a cause of pressure and that which is an object of aspiration."[27] Basic principles and maxims are abstracted from this melange of infra-rational data, and they are made to appeal to the conscience. Thus the moral activity of civilized society appears as rational and as representing the highest ideal of man. We can see in J. S. Mill, for example, an illustration of this point. The spirit of the ethics of utility, he says, is in complete accord with the ethics of the gospel. "In the golden rule of Jesus of Nazareth, we read the complete spirit of the ethics of utility. To do as you would be done by, and to love your neighbour as yourself, constitute the ideal perfection of utilitarian morality."[28] According to Bergson, the basis of obligation according to Utilitarianism lies in the fact that it represents the morality of pressure, the immanence of common interests in individual interests, or at least the difficulty to point out where the limits of one end and those of the other begin. Intelligence sees that an "intelligent egoism must allow all other egoisms its share. And if the intelligence is that of a philosopher, it will build up a theory of ethics in which the interpenetration of the personal and general interests will be demonstrated, and where obligation will be brought back to necessity, realized and felt, of thinking of others, if we wish intelligently to do good to ourselves."[29] The rational theory of Utilitarianism takes obligation for granted, it merely demonstrates the fact of obligation which is already there and makes it apt for social organization of a certain kind. "If utilitarian ethics persist in recurring in one form or other, this means that it is not untenable, and if it is tenable the reason is precisely because,

[27] TS, p. 65.

[28] John Stuart Mill, *Utilitarianism, Liberty and Representative Government,* Everyman's Library edition (New York, Dutton, 1900), p. 16.

[29] TS, pp. 92-93.

beneath the intelligent activity forced in fact to choose between its own interests and those of others, there lies a substratum of instinctive activity, originally implanted there by nature, where the individual and the social are well-nigh indistinguishable." [30]

In rational systems of morality, what really takes place is the justification of either social pressure or individual aspirations or both for purposes of meeting the pragmatic needs of the individual or the group.[31] On the basis of need and utility, the rational morality selects from moral alternatives already present. Hence the many contradictions between the professed ideals and practices of the rational society. Reason is capable of justifying any line of conduct, for example, in war or in political contests such as elections, depending on the actual need of the time or of the person or of the task at hand. Reason provides only the *concept* of the moral imperative; the moral impetus itself, according to Bergson, comes either from pressure or aspiration.[32]

The error of the rationalists lies in the equation of the rationalizing activity with the motive or source of moral action itself. What reason does in such acts of justification, says Bergson, is merely remove its own initial hesitation to follow the moral rule or resist its own resistance and hinder its own hindrance. Thus the rational act does not add anything intrinsically to the moral act: "from the fact that we get back to obligation by rational ways, it does not follow that obligation was of rational order." [33]

There is an element of pessimism in Bergson's conclusions regarding the ability of pure intelligence to fulfill man's deepest yearnings. Bergson is a realist and has no illusions about the actual world of culture and politics, about the society in the process of *becoming* open. The intellect knows that its rationalizations are at bottom a sham, that man must pass from rationalization to the actual realization of the ideals. But this he cannot achieve on a purely rational basis. Hence the scepticism and the despair of the purely rational man.[34] Science and technology, the prodigious capacity of modern economic organizations, spell social progress, but they do not by themselves contribute to man's liberation from nature. In many respects, they tend to reinforce the elements of closed society, as witnessed by the increasing tensions between the races, between the rich and poor nations, and between the various ideological camps. Bergson's

[30] *Ibid.*, p. 37.
[31] *Ibid.*, p. 235; C.E., p. 155.
[32] TS, pp. 21, 93-94.
[33] *Ibid.*, p. 22.
[34] C.E., p. 196. See also Vladimir Jankelevitch, *Henri Bergson* (Paris, Presses universitaires de France, 1959), pp. 195-198.

analysis of the role of reason in society points out the nature of the existential predicament of the man who is satisfied with purely rational and political activities. He cannot carry out his rationally conceived high purposes unless he becomes a mystic. But even if he becomes a mystic, actual human societies will always remain natural societies, societies in the process of becoming open. And the fundamental law of natural society is war. Thus, as Raymond Aron has pointed out, in the final analysis Bergson is a realist, not an idealist or a utopian pacifist.[35] Or as Merleau-Ponty puts it in a less pessimistic light, Bergson is an optimist only as far as the individual is concerned and a pessimist regarding society.[36]

OPEN SOCIETY, WAR AND PROPERTY

The phenomenon of war, according to Bergson, is the incontestable proof that the political society retains the essential features of a closed society, and that the work of reason and culture does not and cannot make it really open. War defines the scope of the application of civil laws and civil rights. The doctrines of national security and vital interests are rationalizations of the instinct of group self-preservation. The law and the constitution, even though they may enshrine abstract principles of universal justice, in reality provide only the legal framework of a closed society. How little such abstract rights mean to us is shown in times of war: "Murder and pillage and perfidy, cheating and lying become not only lawful, they are actually praiseworthy. The warring nations can say, with Macbeth's witches: 'Fair is foul, and foul is fair.' "[37]

Now the most remarkable thing is that Bergson traces the origin of war to the structure of human communities and to the institution of property.[38] "The origin of war is ownership, individual or collective, and since humanity is predestined to ownership by its structure, war is natural. So strong, indeed, is the war instinct, that it is the first to appear when we scratch below the surface of civilization in the search of nature."[39] The structural necessity of property is inseparably tied to *intelligence fabricatrice* and its activities of tool making and politics. Man either makes his own tools or steals the tools which others make. Thus for Bergson intelli-

[35] Raymond Aron, "Notes sur Bergson et l'Histoire," in *Les Études Bergsoniennes,* IV (Paris, 1956), pp. 46-51.

[36] Maurice Merleau-Ponty, *Éloge de la philosophie et autres essais* (Paris, Gallimard, 1960), p. 301.

[37] *Ibid.,* p. 31.

[38] The word used in the French text is *propriété. Loc. cit.,* p. 303.

[39] T.S., p. 31.

gence, desire for property, the unjust mode of its acquisition and production, politics and war are all interrelated phenomena. Hence the struggle among classes within closed communities and the wars among them.[40] Man batten upon man,[41] and communities come into being for purpose of defense and attack of property.

The character of war changes accordingly as society becomes more rational, and the character of tool making, i.e., of industry and economy, changes. The wars of civilized societies are more rational – for gain, markets, territory, glory.[42] But there is nothing surprising in the alliance between industrialism and imperialism, and industrialism and militarism. Nearly half a century before President Eisenhower spoke of the industrial-military complex, Bergson warned us about the "résonance continué" between militarism and industrialism:

> A travers toute l'histoire que nous venons de raconter il y a comme une résonance continuée de militarisme et d'industrialisme, de machinisme et de méchanisme, de bas matérialisme morale.[43]

The foundation of this unholy alliance lies, then, in the mechanistic moral doctrine that science is the sole key to human progress, that political development is fundamentally identical with maximization of property. But for Bergson, political development, if it is to be beneficial to the society as a whole, must maintain a balance between the requirements of both material and moral needs. And if this balance is not maintained, technology, commerce, industry, positive science, organizational efficiency will put all the forces of nature at the service of barbarity.[44] In brief, the increased and increasing violence of war must be traced to the imbalance in our political theories between the rational and the spiritual.

War is natural and ineradicable. However, it can be circumvented.[45] Bergson bases this claim on the evidence supplied by evolution. According to Bergson there is no evidence in evolution supporting an "unescapable historic law," or any "paramount necessity," or "fatality of history." In the evolution of life in all its forms there are only biological laws.[46] And evolution proceeds "in divergent directions" and the only law discernible in social evolution is that progress results from oscillation between dichotomous tendencies. A tendency, "advantageous in itself, cannot be moderated

[40] *Ibid.*, p. 71, 73.
[41] *Ibid.*, p. 235.
[42] *Ibid.*, p. 286.
[43] H. Bergson, *La Signification de la Guerre* (Paris, Bloud et Gay, 1915), p. 19.
[44] *Ibid.*, p. 34.
[45] TS. p. 288.
[46] *Ibid.*, p. 293.

otherwise than by the action of a counter tendency, which hence becomes advantageous also." These tendencies cooperate, "the first intervening when circumstances require, the other restraining it when it threatens to go too far." [47] "Progress by oscillation," almost 'parliamentary' in its operation, is the law of human evolution discernible in creative evolution.

The primordial oscillation is between quantity and quality. Thus from Socratic thought, Bergson remarks, two divergent lines developed, the Cyrenaic and the Cynic, the first emphasizing quantity and the maximization of property, leading to Epicureanism, and the second emphasizing quality or asceticism, leading to Stoicism. Similarly the otherworldly view of the middle ages was followed by the wordly outlook of the bourgeois culture. The law of progress by oscillation is the reason why Bergson thinks that mechanism and technology will develop in man a yearning for mysticism and simplicity. Hence the Bergsonian dictum: "mechanism should mean mysticism," [48] and man must "use matter as a support to get away from matter." [49]

Accordingly the basic condition to be met for circumventing war and thereby increasing the openness of the political community would be restraint on the ethic of the maximization of property. Pleasure must be transcended by joy, "that simplicity of life diffused through the world by an ever spreading mystic intuition." [50] What in effect Bergson asks for is the end of Benthamite type of liberalism or what C. B. Macpherson has called "possessive individualism." [51] Bentham saw irreconcilable opposition between utility and asceticism. "Let but one tenth part of the inhabitants of this earth pursue it consistently," he wrote, "and in a day's time they will have turned it into hell." [52] There was to be no external restraint on the principle of maximization of utility. Yet Bergson believes that this ethic has only fostered luxury, favoured towns to the detriment of the countryside, and widened the gap and revolutionized the relation between employer and employed, capital and labour.[53] Utilitarianism has not become fully democratic, the maximization of utility has in effect meant maximization of the utility for some, not all. Thus, "mankind lies groaning, half crushed beneath the weight of its own progress." [54]

[47] *Ibid.*, p. 295.
[48] *Ibid.*, p. 310.
[49] *Ibid.*, p. 309.
[50] *Ibid.*, p. 317.
[51] See C. B. Macpherson, *The Political Theory of Possessive Individualism: Hobbes to Locke* (Oxford, Clarendon Press, 1962); and his recent book *Democratic Theory* (Oxford, Clarendon Press, 1973), esp. pp. 195-207.
[52] Jeremy Bentham, *Principles of Morals and Legislation,* Ch. 2, *passim.*
[53] TS., p. 307.
[54] *Ibid.*, p. 317.

Bergson feels that further opening of democracy to the disinherited would not come so much from the maximization of property as from the regard for the individual moved by love. No one expresses this idea better than Macpherson when he writes (although starting from a non-Bergsonian point of view) that "the societies which can best meet the demand of their own people for equal human rights, equal freedom for their own members to realize their essential humanity will be the ones that survive." [55] Bergson would add, of course, that in existential terms fraternity is prior to equality.

The circumvention of war or the enlargement of the degree of openness of democracies would require, in addition to change in moral attitude, the appropriate institutional changes as well. Reason yielding to natural impulses has perfected the institutions of war and maximization of property; the same reason must now listen to the promptings of aspirations and develop the institutions of peace. Hence Bergson's advocacy of "a central, organizing intelligence." [56] He regarded the Covenant of the League of Nations an institutional expression of man's supra-rational aspirations "de faire passer l'esprit évangélique dans les rapports entre nations." [57]

The conclusion is clear: war can be circumvented if society really becomes democratic, and this can occur only if man imposes self-restraint on war and property. But to bring this self-restraint about the political community needs vital contact with the open society. Bergson would say no more than this, he would not predict the future: "the future of humanity remains indeterminate, precisely because it is on humanity that it depends." [58]

TYPES OF REGIMES AND DEGREES OF OPENNESS

Bergson's critique of politics rests on the three-fold distinction between the open and the closed societies and the society in the process of becoming open. The genus of political society belongs to the latter. Leaving political societies at that without further distinctions might cause serious misunderstandings. It is precisely to remove such misunderstandings that

[55] C. B. Macpherson, *The Real World of Democracy* (Oxford, Clarendon Press, 1966), p. 66.

[56] TS., p. 306.

[57] Bergson, *Ecrits et paroles,* III, p. 496. It may be recalled that Bergson was the first president of the International Commission for Cooperation among Intellectuals, the parent body of the present UNESCO. He was also sent by the French Government on several diplomatic missions, including two to the U.S., in 1917 and 1918.

[58] TS., p. 299.

Bergson distinguishes between types of political regimes.[59] They differ among themselves in the degree of their openness.

The three types, corresponding to three types of political community, are those of the *chef* (monarchy), of the *dirigeants* and *dirigé* (aristocracy) and the people (democracy). The first two are closed in theory as well as in practice and the third, democracy, is open in theory and closed only in practice. That is to say, in a monarchy and an aristocracy, the king and the aristocrats at least in their origins are thought to be superior to the rest of the community, whereas in democracy, whose essence for Bergson is fraternity, all natural distinctions are made theoretically irrelevant.

Now Bergson offers an interesting explanation of why men who are in fact equal come to consider themselves either as politically superior or inferior. Naturally there is the process of culture – relations of property, myths, superstitions and the like – which inculcates these attitudes. But Bergson believes there is something deeper going back to the structure of sociality itself, or what he calls the natural dimorphism of the social man: no one by nature is fit only to rule; by nature man is fit to rule as well as to be ruled. Culture and the process of socialization build on this natural dimorphism, and over a period of time gradually make us accept our lot as if it was natural.

But potentially we are all chiefs, though actually we may be only subjects, or frustrated chiefs, *chef manqué*. We failed in the process of accumulating property and aggrandising over our fellows, and that alone is the reason why we are not chiefs or aristocrats. This is the deeper explanation of class divisions. Hence, argues Bergson, ferocity, actual or potential, is the natural virtue of the non-democratic political man: "Within honest and gentle men there rushes up from the depths a ferocious personality, that of the leader who is a failure (*chef manqué*). Here we have a characteristic trait of that 'political animal,' man." [60]

The class regime represents, at least in its more evolved forms (for Bergson believes that monarchy and oligarchy "are indistinguishable" in the rudimentary state: the chief needs the barons, and the barons, the chief),[61] a greater degree of openness than monarchy. But here too culture and property relations take full advantage of the natural dimorphism. Although it is economic and military tools that initially gave the aristocrats their superiority, gradually the plebeians themselves come to accept their inferiority as natural, and the aristocrats succeed in maintaining their

[59] Our discussion of the regime is based on TS., pp. 277-283.
[60] TS., p. 279.
[61] *Ibid.*, p. 277.

superiority, which is not natural, only by means of special codes of discipline. And as Bergson acutely points out, the self-induced inferiority of the lower classes is so strong that it is usually from disgruntled members of the higher classes that the leadership of the movement of reform or revolution initially comes. It was men of the educated classes who demanded education for all, and even Marx recognized that the proletariat needed the guidance, at least initially, of a dedicated vanguard.

Now the democratic élan transcends at least in theory the natural principle of dimorphism. The overwhelming idea of fraternity, which for Bergson is the essence of democracy, strikes at the very root of the illusion of superiority and inferiority. The moral basis of the regimes of the *chef* and the *dirigeants* are shattered. The fraternity of everyone in the community is achieved.

The distinction between the ideals and institutions of democracy is of capital importance in Bergson's thinking. Realization of ideals means their materialization, rationalization by criteria of need and utility. Besides, even the democratic regimes must fight wars. The president or the prime minister is also the commander-in-chief, the war leader. Consequently it will never attain full openness, it will forever be in the process of becoming open. Political activity by itself cannot lead us into the promised land.

The real distinction of the democratic regime, then, lies not so much in its organizational or governmental aspects as in its ideals and aspirations, in its conception of man as brother. Hence a purely positivistic approach to democracy does violence to its very essence. As Bergson remarks, the so-called science of politics has not yet been able to devise a programme of training for its democratic leaders. The princes receive special training to become princes. The aristocrats train themselves. But what about the democrats? Elections seem to be the only school of democracy. Bergson writes:

> The art of governing a great people is the only one for which there exists no technical training, no effective education, especially when we come to the highest posts. The extreme scarcity of political leaders of any calibre is owing to the fact that they are called upon to decide at any moment, and in detail, problems which the increased size of societies may well have rendered insoluble.... you will find plenty of great scientists, great artists, great soldiers, great specialists in every line – but how many great statesmen? [62]

There is only one conclusion: the real strength of democracy lies in its spiritual origins and moral concern for the individual as brother. As

[62] *Ibid.*, pp. 275-276.

Bergson puts it, there is "in the democratic mind, a mighty effort in a direction contrary to that of nature." [63] It is not by fostering the illusion of complete openness that democracy attains its object, but by fostering the moral ideal that man is a brother, not a rival or enemy of man. This as Bergson points out is attainable only through supra-rational means, especially since even the democrat has to come to terms with war and property.

CONCLUDING REMARKS

There is much that is acceptable in Bergson at least in the sense that others also have made essentially the same point. Thus he is not the first to point out the importance of great religious men for the development of political societies. Did not Machiavelli put founders and reformers of religion above founders of states? [64] As history has verified, mysticism and politics have sometimes mixed well, witness Mahatma Gandhi. The classical and medieval thinkers saw the necessity of virtue for restraining man's natural tendency for the maximization of property. Although St. Thomas Aquinas and Bergson may disagree on the nature of reason, they are agreed that in the final analysis, reason's proper role is to be the handmaid of grace (or intuition). No Weberian could take exception to Bergson's emphasis on grace and charisma, although he might differ from the Bergsonian critique of rational-legal morality.[65] Likewise Bergson differs from Rousseau on the place that nature occupies, or ought to occupy, in political life: the one demanding transcendence from it, while the other calls for a return to it. But in either case there is agreement that the accumulation of culture, the arts and the sciences, per se do not really liberate man from his existential alienation. Similarly both are agreed that democracy as an idea is quite different from democracy as a form of government. The first is fit only for angels, the other only legitimizes our social chains. On these and many other points of agreement there can be little quarrel with Bergson.

But agreement on particular details is one thing, acceptance of the philosophic system as a whole is quite another. In other words, is the

[63] *Ibid.*, p. 283.

[64] Niccolò Machiavelli, *Discorsi,* I. 10.

[65] In this connection the reader's attention may be drawn to two criticisms of Bergson's critique of rational ethic, of particular merit, though the authors are not Weberians. I refer to F.C. Copleston, S.J., "Bergson on Morality," *Proceedings of the Britisch Academy* (1955), pp. 247-267; and Jacques Maritain, "Sur l'éthique Bergsonienne," *Revue de Métaphysique et de morale* (1959), pp. 141-161; the same essay appears in English, in Maritain, *Moral Philosophy* (London, G. Bles, 1964), pp. 418-448.

Bergsonian system viable? [66] Is Bergson's synthetic approach to reality useful for political theory? Is Bergson's appeal to mysticism really credible? Does it undervalue politics? These are some of the questions which the student of politics might wish to put to Bergson, questions which we cannot adequately answer here. Suffice to say that appeal to mysticism means basically two things for political theory.

First, insofar as mysticism is a historical fact, and as a historical fact has influenced the course of politics, there is nothing objectionable a priori to taking it into account in political theory. This is the position which Maritain [67] and Gilson,[68] for example, have taken. Bergson's appeal to mysticism, it must be remembered, is not the same as appeal to theology, which he did not make.[69] (Hence Gilson's criticism of Bergson from the theological viewpoint.) In brief, a discipline which professes to ground itself on empirical evidence cannot arbitrarily dismiss certain types of empirical evidence, such as mysticism, even if it is supra-rational. This has been the great error of Auguste Comte and positivism.

Secondly, the acceptance of mysticism as a datum of experience would mean that Bergson undervalues only the liberal view of politics as competition for the maximization of property. He does not undervalue politics conceived as the harmonious development of intellect and intuition, technology and asceticism, under the inspiration of grace. He rejects the view that openness can be achieved through force or secret machinations of governmental agencies. It can be achieved only through love, i.e., volun-

[66] Merleau-Ponty opines that Bergson radically transformed philosophy and that the spirit of Bergson – the respect for facts, the search for the deeper meaning and the lack of fear of the supra-rational – is of permanent value and that his philosophy "gives as a principle to philosophy, not 'I think' [cogito] and its immanent thoughts but a 'Being-itself' [Etre-soil]." *Éloge de la philosophie,* pp. 40ff. An English translation of this essay is found in Thomas Hanna, ed., *The Bergsonian Heritage* (New York, Columbia University Press, 1962), pp. 133-150. Cf. also Jean Guitton's judgement that "Il se peut qu'un jour Bergson apparaisse comme ayant accompli en son temps ce qu'avait fait Socrate, selon lui." *Op. cit.,* pp. 218-219. On the specific point of Bergson's treatment of mysticism, Etienne Gilson feels that Bergsonian philosophy could do for modern theology what Aristotelian philosophy did for Thomism. However, the "New Aristotle has not found his Thomas Aquinas." Gilson, *The Philosopher and Theology* (New York, Random House, 1962), p. 144, *passim.* See also Gilson, in *Les Études Bergsoniennes,* I (1948), pp. 180-186, where he credits Bergson with putting an end to the anti-metaphysical tradition in modern philosophy and of reinstating the validity of metaphysics.

[67] Maritain, "Sur l'éthique Bergsonienne," *loc. cit.,* p. 145.

[68] Gilson, *The Philosopher and Theology,* pp. 107-174.

[69] Hence Gilson's criticism of Bergson from the theological viewpoint. He warns the student of Bergson, and quite correctly, against any attempt at considering him a theologian. See *op. cit.,* pp. 133ff. Also Gilson, "L'itinéraire d'Henri Bergson," *Les Nouvelles Littéraires,* No. 1795 (1962), pp. 1 and 9.

tarily, for the genuinely open city has no enemies, *pace* Karl Popper; and if there is a city that claims to be open and yet requires force and secrecy for its survival, well Bergson would say, 'forget it.' [70]

[70] I have avoided in this paper to deal with Popper's view of open society for the simple reason that it would require more space than I have at my disposal. However, it must be said in passing and for the record, that there is an irreconcilable difference between the two thinkers on the role of reason in open society. Popper seems to identify open society with the liberal democratic society, or what he calls "free society" as opposed to dictatorships. For him the U.S. is the model of an open society. See, Popper, "Reason and the Open Society," *Encounter* XXXVIII, No. 5 (May 1972), pp. 13-19. For Bergson, to repeat, the rational city, the city that must still wage war, can at best be the city in the process of becoming open, but not the open city.

THE OPEN WORLD AND CULTURE CHANGE: SACRED AND SECULAR TRENDS*

ALI A. MAZRUI

The Open World is a world in the process of enlarging its capacity for empathy. We may be the decisive generation in all this. The ultimate problem of the concluding decades of the twentieth century is not the problem of identity; it is this problem of *empathy*. Identity is one major problem, but not the most critical. Human bewilderment at this particular phase of the history of the species does not merely lie in the question "Who am I?" but in the question "Who is my fellow?" Some of the current discussions of the psychological problems of the age mistake a reflection for the reality of the problem. The problem of identity, of the question "Who am I?" is ultimately a mere reflection of the problem of empathy.

The crisis arises partly because mankind is on the verge of a great empathetic leap. The *communications revolution* in the world has promoted a level of mutual awareness unprecedented in human history. This is a central aspect of the concept of the open world. The villagization of the globe has sharpened our awareness of ourselves. There is indeed a crisis of identity – of a groping for self-recognition. We shall indeed be discussing that in passing. But that arises only because we are on the verge of an empathetic leap, and have not yet found the will to swing into motion in response to the hour.

But what is empathy? Our sense of the term is a combination of Theodore Lipps and Sigmund Freud. Lipps was the originator of the concept of empathy. His theory was first presented in his "Aesthetics of Space" (1893-1897). According to Lipps, empathy is an act of sympathetic projection into objects or persons distinct from the agent. He defined empathy as the "objectivated enjoyment of self" – meaning by that that the agent discovers and identifies himself with "something psychical" in another

* This paper is part of a larger study entitled *Towards a World Federation of Cultures: An African Perspective* (World Order Models Project, 1973).

human being or in the qualities of a subject of aesthetic contemplation.[1]

Our sense of empathy, therefore, definitely has connections with theories of aesthetic experience. We hope to demonstrate that the transformation of values in the world might in fact ultimately have to rely on an aesthetic revolution.

But the concept of empathy is both an aesthetic and a psychological concept. In our sense in this book we would prefer to fuse Lipps' idea with Freud's concept of *narcissistic identification.* Narcissism is Freud's term for self-love. As an idea it is of course based on the myth of Narcissus, who fell in love with his own image as he contemplated it in his reflection in a pool of water. In popular usage we think a person is narcissistic when he spends a lot of time admiring himself in the mirror, or in the anecdotes he contrives to relate in everyday conversation.

In Freudian terms narcissism lies in recognizing in others characteristics which one shares with them. Under normal circumstances two people in love are deemed to be, in some sense, involved in an act of self-recognition. Their love is partly based on their capacity to see in each other characteristics they share. As Calvin S. Hall once put it in his definition and simplification of Freudian psychology:

> Narcissistic identification is responsible for the ties that exist between members of the same group. Members of a fraternity identify with one another because they all share at least one common characteristic: every two or more people have something in common, whether it be a physical or mental trait, an interest, a value, a possession, membership in the same club, citizenship, or whatever, they tend to identify with one another. Two people might identify with one another because they both want the same thing, yet fight with each other over possession of the desired object. It may sound paradoxical to speak of an affinity between enemies or rivals, but there can be no doubt that such affinities do exist. Enemies sometimes become friends, and competition sometimes turns into cooperation. The policeman identifies with the thief, and the thief with the policeman.[2]

The linkage we have attempted to establish between the primarily psychological concept of narcissism promoted by Freud and the primarily aesthetic concept of empathy as formulated by Lipps is a conscious attempt

[1] One of the fullest accounts of Lipps' psychology in the English language is given in E. B. Titchner, *Systematic Psychology* (New York, MacMillan, 1929). See also Lipps, *Psychological Studies,* translated by Herbert C. Sanborn, (Baltimore, 1926).

[2] Calvin S. Hall, *A Primer of Freudian Psychology* (New York, The New American Library, 1954), pp. 75-76. The date of the publication of Freud's paper "On Narcissism: An Introduction" is significant. It appeared in 1914, the year of the First World War. Stanley Edgar Hyman sees in this paper another effort by Freud to enter into the domain of "metapsychology." See Hyman, *The Tangled Bank: Darwin, Marx, Frazer, and Freud as Imaginative Writers* (New York: The Universal Library, Grosset and Dunlap, 1966 edition), p. 368.

to reintroduce into discussions on world order the aesthetic dimension in relation to psychology.

In our own approach to aesthetics we define the term not merely in relation to concepts of beauty, but also to concepts of good taste and bad taste. In some spheres of human relations the revolution in values is a revolution from values rooted in morality to values rooted in taste. The physical dimension of *toleration* is at the heart of this transition from a culture of moral reprobation to a culture of aesthetic assessment. We shall discuss this especially with regard to freedom of the individual.

But in intergroup and international relations the shift may well be from a culture of judgments based on taste to a culture of judgments based on duty and morality. There was a time when aggression by one country against another was at worst a matter of "bad diplomatic taste." Whether one got along with people of other races, whether one was capable of admiring them or only of despising them, was again, very often, a matter purely of taste. The shift in intergroup relations and international relations is away from a reduction of all judgements in terms of taste and towards judgements in terms of duty, obligation and moral censure.

AESTHETICS: BEHAVIOURAL AND PERFORMATIVE

We might here, perhaps in an oversimplified way, reduce human judgements into three areas – legal judgements, moral judgements, and judgements of taste or aesthetics. Legal judgements are those which are subject to enforcement and judicial process. They presume a system of procedural interpretation whereby no man need be judge in his own cause. Legal judgements also imply sanctions following due process.

Moral judgements are derived from concepts of right and wrong, are rooted in social approval and disapproval, and imply the duty to do what is right and avoid doing what is wrong. Moral judgements differ from legal judgements in relation to the question of due process sanctions and enforcement. Where moral judgements are made by due process and are enforced by a system of sanctions, they are moral judgements that have been converted into legal judgements.

Judgements of taste are, by contrast, judgements of what is beautiful and what is ugly, sometimes what is good and what is bad – but not really what is right and what is wrong. When judgements of taste include concepts of "bad" and "good" they are sharing some area of terminology with both moral and legal judgements.

But what could all this have to do with problems of world order? In relation to the individual and his society the distinctions are really vital. The nineteenth century was, in the Western world, the century of the liberation of the individual in the political domain. That was the century which produced John Stuart Mill and the extension of the franchise to the working classes, Abraham Lincoln and the flowering of the novel as an art form preeminently designed to study individuals – either in isolation or in interaction.

John Stuart Mill produced the classic essay *On Liberty*, in which he made the critical distinction between self-regarding acts of an individual and other-regarding acts. The self-regarding acts are those which ultimately should concern only the individual, since in the final analysis they harm nobody else. The other-regarding acts, on the other hand, are those acts done by an individual or by a group of individuals, which have direct adverse consequences for people other than themselves. In Mill's words:

> . . . the only purpose for which power can be rightfully exercised over any member of a civilized community, against his will, is to prevent harm to others. His own good, either physical or moral, is not a sufficient warrant.[3]

In many ways John Stuart Mill was ahead of his time. The implication of his essay *On Liberty* was a plea not only for intellectual freedom in the sense of freedom to give and receive ideas; not only for political freedom in the sense of freedom of expression, political debate and political competition; but also for moral freedom in the sense of freedom to make moral choices and to determine one's moral conduct. What John Stuart Mill was asserting was that the individual had a right to be immoral if he wished to be, provided it was a form of immorality that would not harm others directly. His concept of harm was very much that which later came to be designated in American rhetoric as "clear and present danger." This was to be sharply differentiated from concepts of harm rooted in allegations of "corrupting the young" or "degrading the standards of the race of society." The danger to others in the moral misbehaviour of a particular individual could not be assessed merely in terms of bad influence on other adults; the adverse consequences had to be more tangible.

Out of the distinction between self-regarding and other-regarding acts emerged the whole debate on how far a person's sexual behaviour should be subject to the constraints of society. Take, for example, a man and a woman, unmarried but living together – if they harm nobody directly, has society a right to act against them? How about a man and a man living

[3] John Stuart Mill, *On Liberty*, especially Chapter IV concerning "The Limits to the Authority of Society over the Individual."

together in sexual intimacy, both adults and in full possession of their faculties, with due consideration for the freedoms of others – should these two be permitted to cohabit provided there is no evidence of a "clear and present danger" to some third party? On balance the eighteen-sixties in England were the great era of debate about the freedom of the individual to be moral or immoral without undue restrictions imposed by the law upon him. Constitutionalism and homosexualism became subjects of debate in the popular press, in Parliament, and by special commissions of enquiry, preeminently the Wolfenden Commission. Homosexuality between females was already permitted, but homosexuality between men was illegal. Was the illegality an invasion of the rights of the individual?

Church voices were heard arguing that the issue of sin was a matter for the Church and not for the state. Assertions were reactivated that what was immoral need not at the same time be illegal. The sexual deviant, or even the would-be suicide, could legitimately be an object of strong moral reprobation without the necessity of dragging him before the courts for prosecution as a criminal.

What was emerging was precisely the concept of the permissive society, to supplement the concept of a free society. The free society had been the creature of the nineteenth century and its liberalism, the freedom conceived there having been political and intellectual. But the permissive society is a society which goes beyond political and intellectual freedom – and extends the right to an autonomous moral identity.

The Scandinavian countries had already arrived fairly early at the idea of "free love." But the nineteen-sixties saw the extension of the permissive society to other parts of the West. Sexual "deviants" received a degree of toleration never before conceded in this part of the world. The idea of accepting homosexuality between two consenting adults had been an aspect of liberal freedom which did not conquer the land of John Stuart Mill till the nineteen-sixties, when at last the laws against homosexuality were abolished in England. Permissiveness for homosexuals had already started with discreet blindness, and then began to grow into its acceptance between two otherwise-respectable males, culminating in toleration of special homosexual clubs and societies.

The toleration extended across the Atlantic and the beginnings of a social acceptance of marriage between partners of the same sex began to appear in parts of the Western world. Certainly the concept of husband and wife is a residue of a biocultural differentiation of roles between the sexes. At last a challenge was being posed to this very tradition itself.

In October 1970 the American magazine *Newsweek* published a report which was itself profoundly symptomatic of such permissiveness. A church had started in California under the leadership of the Reverend Troy Perry. It was a church designed to cater to Christians whom other churches did not want or found it difficult to accept. Forty percent of the parishioners in Perry's church were baptised Roman Catholics, and another forty percent, like Reverend Perry himself, were Evangelical Protestants. "But all have joined his fold because they desire a conventional religious life – and a minister with a personal interest in homosexuality." Perry was himself an ordained Baptist preacher, and was married and the father of two children "before he discovered his real sexual preference."

A whole reexamination of Christianity was under way in this group, and links were being established with similar Christian groups in San Francisco, San Diego, Phoenix, Chicago, and other growing congregations in cities as distant from each other as Boston and Honolulu.

Questions raised in this kind of atmosphere have included: Was Jesus a homosexual? If not, did his religion at least imply an acceptance and toleration of love even if it was homosexual? Although some religious historians have acknowledged that Jesus was a homosexual, Reverend Perry did not agree with them, according to this report.

> But had Jesus lived in this age he at least would have been labelled a homosexual. After all, he never married, ran around with twelve guys and was even betrayed by a kiss from another guy.[4]

But the real point that the Reverend Perry wanted to make was that the logic of Jesus' teaching implied an acceptance and toleration of homosexuality, despite Biblical prohibitions. "As far as Christ is concerned, love in any form is permissible." [5]

But even more startling was the report about marriage services conducted in Reverend Perry's church. At the time of publication Reverend Perry had joined in wedlock thirty-six homosexual couples, eight of them lesbians. "We substitute the word 'spouse' for 'husband' or 'wife'," the pastor explained. "Do you accept John Smith as your lawfully wedded 'spouse'? – Do you in turn accept Tom Jones as your lawfully wedded 'spouse'?"

A legal point to which the magazine drew attention concerned the implications of California law on such marriages.

> California law recognizes all marriages between partners who can show a certificate from an ordained minister proving that their marriage has been

[4] "The Homosexual Church," *Newsweek* (Oct. 12, 1970), p. 57.
[5] *Ibid.*

solemnized in a church ceremony. This law does not stipulate that the partners must be a man and a woman, only a 'husband' and a 'wife.'[6]

What is often overlooked is that the permissive society is beginning to shift the whole domain of sexual behaviour not only away from legal considerations, but also away from moral considerations, and into the domain of taste and aesthetics.

This is where we might distinguish between behavioural aesthetics and performative aesthetics. Behavioural aesthetics concerns questions of ugly forms of human indulgence and beautiful forms of human indulgence, without implying moral reprobation or disapproval.

Bigamy in the West is still illegal, but not marriage between a man and a man. Bigamy remains within the realm of enforced sanctions, while marriage between a man and a man in Reverend Perry's church is to some citizens immoral, but to others merely a matter of taste. Sex before marriage might in the West have been at one time a question of legal control and sanctions; then it became a question of strong moral control under the Church. Sex before marriage by the nineteen-fifties, and certainly by the nineteen-sixties, was becoming not a matter for moral judgement but a matter of taste. Toleration of the individual in a self-regarding act could very rapidly reduce ethics to aesthetics.

Performative aesthetics, on the other hand, concerns the more usual issues of appreciation of art and nature in their respective forms of beauty and meaning. But nature here would be nature as enhanced and tended by human contrivance. A beautiful garden, a well organized park, a display of multicoloured birds at a zoo, are all instances of performative aesthetics in our sense. The performance in this case is by man, either utilizing colour and sound and material, or utilizing living elements of nature for aesthetic effect. The range of performative aesthetics is from Makonde sculpture to Beethoven's Ninth Symphony, from the Taj Mahal to *Hamlet*.[7]

EMPATHY AND IMAGINATION

There is a direct relationship between permissiveness and empathy. Societies capable of high moral reprobation of individual behaviour are societies which reduce the area of empathy between individuals. Societies which are shocked by sexual deviance are societies which pollute the pool of the

[6] *Ibid.*

[7] There is a third category of aesthetics apart from behavioural and performative – natural aesthetics. This is quite simply the appreciation of beauty in nature and the cosmos which is independent of human manipulation and enhancement.

reflection of Narcissus. Victorian England with its high principles prevented moral critics from recognizing themselves in the behaviour of others. Prudishness often keeps hypocrisy company on the high road to self-righteousness. The capacity to see one's self in the other man is reduced. Indeed in this sphere of the high moral reprobation of the individual behaviour of others, there is a conscious attempt to create a moral distance between the object contemplated and the subject contemplating.

Oscar Wilde, the tragic English dramatist of the nineteenth century, was one such victim of Victorian prudishness and dissociation from empathy. He served a term of imprisonment on being convicted of homosexuality, falling in the process from a pinnacle of social applause and dazzling intellectual preeminence to the dark nadir of ostracism and social shame. As he was serving his sentence, Wilde wrote *De Profundis*. The whole work is addressed to his former lover, Lord Alfred Douglas, datelined January to March 1897, Her Majesty's Prison, Reading. Alfred Douglas had once written to Wilde to say, "When you are not on your pedestal you are not interesting." In *De Profundis* Wilde reminds Douglas that in those very words he created a distance both from the true temper of the artist and from what Matthew Arnold called "the secret of Jesus."

> Either would have taught you that whatever happens to another happens to one's self, and if you want an inscription to read at dawn and at night-time and for pleasure or for pain, write up on the wall of your house in letters of the sun to guild and the noon to silver, "*Whatever happens to another happens to one's self*," and should anyone ask you what such an inscription can possibly mean you can answer that it means "Lord Christ's heart and Shakespeare's brain." [8]

Wilde here was in fact discussing the phenomenon of empathy in our sense, combining in it the aesthetics of Lipps and the psychology of Freud. The fusion of aesthetics and psychology is nothing less than the imagination itself. And it is the imagination that must form the springboard of the emphathetic leap. Oscar Wilde continued:

> Christ's place indeed is with the poets. His whole conception of Humanity sprang right out of the imagination and can only be realised by it. What God was to the Pantheist, man was to him. He was the first to conceive the divided races as a unity. He alone saw that on the hills of life there were but God and Man, and, feeling through the mysticism of sympathy that in himself each had been made incarnate, he calls himself the Son of One or the son of the other, according to his mood.[9]

[8] Oscar Wilde, *De Profundis,* with an introduction by Jacques Barzun (New York, Vintage Books, Random House, 1964 edition), p. 100.
[9] *Ibid.*

Wilde's conception of the poetic imagination of Jesus Christ, in relation to the fusion of man and God and of man and life, is what the concept of empathy in our sense means. The capacity of nations to see themselves in others, the capacity of races to identify the shared humanity of it all, the capacity of individuals to judge each other if they must by the yardstick of taste and not of the inquisition – all are captured in some sense in the golden rule of Jesus Christ and further beautified by the sensibility of an English dramatist serving a sentence for homosexuality in Her Majesty's Prison, Reading, in the year of his Lord 1897.

In a sense Jesus Christ was an intermediate moral stage towards Karl Marx's precept that "the supreme being for man is man." Oscar Wilde tells us that before Jesus there had been gods and men, but with Jesus God and man fuse, and the son of God and the son of man find abode in the same person.

But Karl Marx, the humanist, takes the stage further and deifies man. What Marx deifies is not a particular man, not a king, not an emperor of Japan, not a prophet, but the human person as such. As Robert Tucker has reminded us:

> Marx's atheism ... meant only a negation of the trans-mundane god of traditional Western religion. It did not mean the denial of a supreme being. Indeed, denial of the trans-mundane god was only a negative way of asserting that 'man' should be regarded as the supreme being or object of ultimate concern. ... [as Marx himself put it] the criticism of religion ends with the precept that the supreme being for man is man. ...[10]

With Karl Marx, perhaps more than with any other thinker before him, history moved from a God-centred system of values to a man-centred system of values. Things were right and wrong, virtuous or vicious, not in relation to the grand design of the Almighty but in relation to the purpose and well-being of man. It was as if the whole Judeo-Christian tradition was dramatically tilting the balance as between the commandment "Thou shalt love the Lord, thy God" and the commandment "Thou shalt love thy neighbour as thyself." The second one was assuming not only greater importance than the first; it was also beginning to push the first out of the realm of relevance.

What was involved in this case was the grand secularization of culture. It was Bernard Murchland who, in a symposium about the debate on "The Death of God," had occasion to say:

> Every culture is undergirded by a substratum of religiosity. ... What is happen-

[10] Robert Tucker, *Philosophy and Myth in Karl Marx* (Cambridge University Press, 1961) pp. 22, 11.

ing now is that the religiosity of Western culture is expiring and at last appears as what it truly is, namely, the paraphernalia of faith in God.... We have 'desacralized' the world, forgetting that ultimately culture is a consecration of the world.[11]

The very debate about the death of God concerns this profound theme of desacralization in Western culture. Nietzsche had started the debate in its new form by contributing the very phrase itself:

God is dead. God remains dead. And we have killed him. How shall we the murderers of all murderers comfort ourselves? What was holiest and most powerful of all that the world has yet owned has bled to death under our knives.[12]

Then there is Nietzsche's provocative image of that old saint digging for roots in the forest while from the mountain Zarathustra descends with fire. "Can it be possible? This old saint in his forest has not yet heard the news that *God is dead*?"

But Nietzsche was moving from the concept of the Supreme Being to his own preferred concept of Superman. He was indeed thrusting destiny into human hands, but was looking for a Superman to control the steering wheel.

Can you create a god? – Then be silent about all gods! But you could create the Superman. Perhaps you yourselves cannot, my brothers! But you can recreate yourselves to be the fathers and forefathers of the Superman: let that be your best creation! [13]

The impact of Nietzsche on mid-twentieth century theological thought was deep, and not always conscious. It affected schools of thought ranging from nihilism to existentialism. In the words of Jean-Paul Sartre, God "spoke to us and now is silent, all that we touch now is his corpse." [14]

But the secularization of culture in the West was moving not only from Supreme Being to Superman, but also from Superman to man. A theme of *homocentrism*, the centrality of the person, seemed to augur at long last a "transvaluation of values" more fundamental than even Nietzsche's conception.

[11] Bernard Murchland, "Editor's Introduction: The Meaning of the Death of God," *The Meaning of the Death of God: Protestant, Jewish and Catholic Scholars Explore Atheistic Theology* (New York, Vintage Books, Random House, 1967), p. 11.

[12] Friedrich Nietzsche, *Joyful Wisdom*, translated by Thomas Common (New York, Frederick Ungar, 1960), pp. 307-385.

[13] Friedrich Nietzsche, "Ecce Homo," *The Philosophy of Nietzsche* (New York, Modern Library), p. 18.

[14] Dietrich Bonhoeffer, *Letters and Papers from Prison* (London, SCM Press, 1953), Letters dated April 30, 1944; June 8, 1944. Cited by Murchland, *op. cit.*, p. 70.

What we in this analysis would emphasize is not only the tripartite distinction between values as ethics, values as aesthetics and values as law, but also the hypothesis that the trend in the transvaluation of values is towards a diminishing area of morality, an expanding area of law, and an expansion of aesthetics. The old domain of ethics implying rules of behaviour which may or may not be codified in law is losing out both to the realm of pure taste and to the realm of law. Those issues of ethics and virtue which were "other regarding" would now in any case be codified. Those issues of ethics which were "self-regarding" are on their way towards being diluted into questions of taste.

The expanding area of law has now to include welfare legislation and social services. Those self-righteous days when the poor were helped through the charity of the rich were in fact the days when a broad area of model behaviour was not necessitated by law. With the expansion of social welfare and social services the domain of voluntary charity from the rich to the poor is contracting, as the domain of enforced distributive justice expands.

In domestic arrangements we might therefore say that the process of the secularization of culture at once reduces both the penalties of vice and the opportunities of voluntary virtue. Lovers out of wedlock find wider boundaries of freedom; well meaning millionaires find narrower horizons of charity. The United States, that last bastion of voluntary charity, is beginning to put the squeeze on charitable foundations. A new tax law seeks to expand the sources of revenue for the state, in the wake of greater demands of welfare legislation and urban renewal – and that same tax law reduces the options of charitable initiatives by voluntary organizations. Once again the phenomena of expanding legislation, expanding aesthetic choice, and diminishing virtuous initiative, together add up to a new trend in the secularization of culture. This is now more true of the Western world than of any other, but the loosening social controls in tribal communities in Africa and the growth of impersonal forces in the wake of urbanization would seem to suggest that, in this secularization of culture, the West is once again anticipating a global trend.

THE SACRALIZATION OF INTERNATIONAL RELATIONS

But while the trend in domestic arrangements is in the direction of secularization, the trend in international politics is, by contrast, in the direction of a new sacralization. There was indeed a time when international politics were sacralized in the most literal of senses – they were profoundly influenced by religious factors. Wars were fought for religious reasons and diplomacy conducted beneath the supervising eye of an "omniplomatic" God. But Europe after the Thirty Years War, weary and receptive to the tidings of the Renaissance, gradually moved towards a secular diplomacy. And this secularization was in the direction of diplomatic aesthetics and propriety. Morality as a factor in international politics began to recede. Power and good taste moved to the centre as determinants of the behaviour of states.

It is, of course, an exaggeration to suggest this style of politics was absent until after the Thirty Years War. It was, after all, Machiavelli who first put into immortal formulations the whole dictum of secularized diplomacy. Machiavelli's advice to the Prince was based not on authority and theological prescriptions but on the concrete experience of history and observable political behaviour. Machiavelli as a political theorist took a great step towards isolating state policy from religious, metaphysical and ethical principles. By so doing Machiavelli initiated a grand process of desacralization in policy making.

Machiavelli was not so naive as to exclude the role of religion and morality as rationalizations of the pursuit of self-interest. He cited the example of an early invasion of Africa in the name of religion – the invasion by Ferdinand, King of Aragon, who later became King of Spain as a whole. Ferdinand extracted money from the Church in order to pay his soldiers, and the Church in return received the solace of knowing that Ferdinand's conquests were in the name of God. As Machiavelli himself put it:

> [Ferdinand] found out a way of maintaining his army at the expense of the church and the people; and by the length of that war he established such order and discipline among his soldiers, that afterwards they gained him many honourable victories. Besides this, to adapt him for greater enterprises (always making religion his pretence), by a kind of devout cruelty he destroyed and exterminated the Moors, than which nothing could be more strange or deplorable. Under the same cloak of religion he invaded Africa . . . and began many great things which always kept the minds of his subjects in admiration and suspense, wondering what the event of his machinations would be.[15]

Machiavelli himself was the first great rationalizer of hypocrisy and false pretences as a cornerstone of high policy in diplomacy and politics. He still allowed room for virtue and morality, but these were to be in the area of public relations and rhetoric. The real calculations which lead to decisions are to be conducted on an *amoral* basis, sometimes verging on

[15] Machiavelli, *The Prince,* Chapter XXI.

cynical immorality. In Machiavelli's terms:

A prince therefore, is not obliged to have all the ... good qualities in reality, but it is necessary he have them in appearance; nay, I will be bold to affirm that, having them actually, and employing them upon all occasions, they are extremely prejudicial, whereas, having them only in appearance, they turn to better account; it is honourable to seem mild, and merciful, and courteous, and religious, and sincere, and indeed to be so, provided your mind be so rectified and prepared that you can act quite contrary upon occasion.... Nevertheless, it is of great consequence to disguise your inclination, and to play the hypocrite well.[16]

More than four hundred and fifty years later another diplomatic realist, Kenneth W. Thompson, reminded his readers that nations were more inclined than individuals to follow their own interests; the imperatives of national security and survival forced the statesmen to distinguish between personal and public responsibilities.

There is no clearer and more poignant example than Lincoln's subordination of his private views on slavery to the goal of the preservation of the Union. Nations always pretend to have a purer devotion to morality than they actually have. They are not as pure in their actions as they claim to be in their intentions. Moral pretension arises from the claims of a nation that it has acted not from self-interest or national security but in obedience to some higher purpose like 'civilization' or 'justice.'[17]

A more controversial exponent of the realist school of international relations is Hans J. Morgenthau. Certainly his initial position in *Politics Among Nations* had strong echoes of the Machiavellian tradition of diplomacy.

The main signpost that helps political realism to find its way through the landscape of international politics is the concept of interest defined in terms of power. This concept ... sets politics as an autonomous sphere of action and understanding apart from other spheres, such as economics, ... ethics, aesthetics or religion....

A realist theory of international politics, then, will guard against two popular fallacies: the concern with motives and the concern with ideological preferences.[18]

The concepts of interest and power as determinants of behaviour are in this context preeminently secular. And much of the diplomacy of Europe in the eighteenth, nineteenth and first half of the twentieth centuries went

[16] *Ibid.*, Chapter XVIII.

[17] Kenneth W. Thompson, "Toward a Theory of International Politics," *American Political Science Review,* XLIX, No. 3 (Sept. 1955), pp. 739-742.

[18] Hans J. Morgenthau, *Politics Among Nations* (2nd ed., New York, Alfred A. Knopf, 1948, 1954), pp. 3-6.

a considerable way towards bearing out this realist school of international relations.

But three trends in the twentieth century began to reintroduce once again the sacred dimension in international politics, though still on a modest scale. These three trends are, firstly, the rise of internationalist ideologies; secondly, the rise of the United States to a superpower; and thirdly, the emergence of the new countries of Asia and Africa. The most important of the internationalist ideologies is communism, and its success in the Soviet Union heralded a new period of moral commitment in diplomacy. It is true that Stalin, after a period of hesitation, embarked on a policy of socialism in one country. But Stalin never completely broke away from the consequences of ruling the first country to be conquered by a new internationalist ideology. The imperative of proselytism and evangelical commitment was indeed regulated under Stalin but was also permitted to affect policy calculations. The triumph of communism in China in 1949, and the creation of a communist eastern Europe, added new layers of moralistic diplomacy to the arena of world politics.

A separate element in the remoralization of world politics was the rise of the United States. Here was a country which was born out of a transvaluation of political rhetoric, and deeply influenced both by moral bombast and by puritanic self-righteousness. The American phenomenon was not a simple case of an internationalist ideology; it was a case of a power steeped in the idiom of pioneering fervour. The Russians regarded themselves as missionaries not because they were Russians but because they were communists. After all, even the Czars had been Russians. But Americans regarded themselves as missionaries not because they were liberals but because they were Americans. Their evangelism was nationalistic first and foremost, rather than derived from the liberal tradition which they shared with Western Europe.

Within the nationalistic evangelism of the United States was a genuine charitable streak. There was a naive belief that every man was a potential American if only he were given the opportunity. But what was impressive was that this belief went with a readiness to expand the opportunities of others. The United States has probably more charitable institutions and foundations than any other country in history, and it has spent more on other nations and societies than is likely to be done by any other country for generations to come.

But this very belief in the potential Americanness of the rest of the human species, and the readiness of the United States to provide the opportunities for this Americanization of the world, made a contribution towards the resacralization of diplomacy. It is true that the United States is now undergoing that long awaited "agonizing reappraisal" with which John Foster Dulles had threatened Europe back in the nineteen-fifties. At the end of November 1971 the Senate of the United States made the historic decision to attempt a grand retreat from the policy of massive American aid to other parts of the world. The Senate decision was facilitated by President Nixon's own tactics following the expulsion of Taiwan, and the attempt by Nixon to appeal to American chauvinism in his denunciation of the ingratitude of those who received American aid and were ready to vote against the United States in the United Nations.

But even after we have made allowances for the isolationist tendencies shown by the United States in its military, fiscal, commercial and aid diplomacy under Richard Nixon, we may still be driven to conclude that some precedents in diplomatic styles which the United States has set are not completely reversible. The very diplomacy of aid, whatever the United States herself may decide to do, has become part of the world political system. The Marshall Plan and the subsequent methods of helping the Third World, ranging from funding world development to sending out peace corps volunteers, have influenced other rich countries in the world. On November 3, 1971 the *Uganda Argus*, for example, carried this headline: "U.S. Senate rejects foreign aid bill but British Queen makes promise." The report was from the London staff reporter of the *Argus* who was commenting on the speech of Queen Elizabeth II opening a new session of Parliament with a promise to maintain all economic and political friendships and alliances, while seeking a new relationship in Europe. The tone of the report was that no alternative aid could make up for losses sustained by the Third World following the Senate's decision to scale down the U.S. Administration's original aid from £1460 million to £1214 million. What is being suggested in our analysis is simply that the diplomacy of richer nations feeling some sense of responsibility towards solving the problems of poorer nations is probably here to stay, notwithstanding the fluctuations of America's own contributions. The United States helped to establish and consolidate a tradition of economic aid and technical assistance, and has itself played an important part in putting pressure on its allies to be active in this sphere. The survival of this kind of diplomacy as part of the world scene can now withstand changes in American contributions towards it. We cannot therefore escape the conclusion that the rise of the United States itself as a superpower, no less than the rise of internationalist ideologies, was a major factor towards the resacralization of international relations.

The third major trend which has resulted in this resacralization is the emergence of new states in Asia and Africa. By the time the United Nations was celebrating its 25th Anniversary in October 1970, the Organization had become more a weapon of war against certain forms of international immorality than a mechanism of peace among nations. As more and more countries from Africa and Asia joined the world body, the liberating role of the United Nations became more pronounced. What was happening was that the new members of the world organization were regarding it not so much as an organization primarily designed to ensure peace and security – as the big powers in San Francisco had originally intended it to be – but as an organization which should primarily be concerned with human rights at large. Those who framed the Charter in 1945 declared first their determination to "save succeeding generations from the scourge of war" and then only secondarily to "reaffirm faith in fundamental human rights, in the dignity and worth of the human person, in the equal rights of men and women and of nations large and small." [19]

But judging by their policies, attitudes and stands, the new states of Africa and Asia would have reversed the order of affirmation: they would have reaffirmed, first, "faith in fundamental human rights [and] in the dignity and worth of the human person" and only secondly their determination "to save succeeding generations from the scourge of war."

This had an important bearing on qualifications for membership in the United Nations as viewed by, on the one hand, countries like the United States which, until 1971, continued to oppose the admission of Communist China into the United Nations, and, on the other hand, countries like Tanzania which have sought South Africa's expulsion from the world organization. Those who used to be opposed to Communist China's admission interpreted Article 4 of the United Nations' Charter as restricting membership to those countries which were 'peace-loving.' This whole emphasis on peace was more characteristic of the big powers' conception of the United Nations' role than it was of the view of the new and smaller states.

Those who have sought South Africa's expulsion have indeed sometimes used rationalizations connected with international peace and security, but the main case against the continued membership of South Africa in the world organization has been deemed to lie in her racialistic political system at home.

In this trend towards the resacralization of diplomacy, we may say that the United Nations has been particularly important in casting a shadow of global disapproval on two phenomena which have been regarded as

[19] From the lines of reaffirmation opening the Charter.

legitimate for hundreds of years before – the phenomenon of colonial subjugation and the phenomenon of institutionalized racial prejudice.

On colonialism itself the United Nations' record must already be pronounced successful. In the course of the 1950's, if not earlier, the world body had already become the main forum of censure against colonial policies. The colonial powers first resisted these challenges from world critics. Even those countries being administered on behalf of the world organization as trusteeships had a difficult time persuading the administrative power to speed up the process of liberation. In 1954 a United Nations' Visiting Mission to Tanganyika recommended that a timetable should be drawn up for Tanganyika's independence within twenty to twenty-five years. In other words, the mission was envisaging the liberation of Tanganyika by 1974 and certainly not later than 1979. This timetable of the report was rejected by the Administering Authority, the United Kingdom. It was regarded as unrealistic and in any case it was presumptuous of the world organization to attempt to hurry up an Administering Authority in its responsibilities for trusteeship.

The impact of the United Nations on decolonization went of course beyond its own trusteeships. Sometimes the United Nations was implicated directly in other issues as well, as in the case of the argument between Indonesia and the Dutch over the control of West Irian. The United Nations interpreted the situation in favour of Indonesia – partly on the assumption that the Dutch were more alien in that area than the Indonesians.

In the Congo of Lumumba and Kasavubu the United Nations did try to be a mechanism for maintaining the territorial integrity of a newly independent African state, as well as for preventing the Big Powers from having a direct confrontation within the Congo. The UN Congo operation had its failures. Among them was the failure to save the life of Patrice Lumumba. But the operation did succeed in frustrating Katanga's bid to secede – and thereby helped to consolidate the principle of territorial integrity in post-colonial Africa.

The record of the United Nations as a liberating force became in 1965 one of the factors which inclined Harold Wilson's Government in Britain to favour the application of sanctions against Rhodesia, however ineffectual they might have turned out to be. There was a genuine fear in the United Kingdom that unless Britain acted firmly against Ian Smith, the initiative for action against Rhodesia would pass to the world body. A bipartisan policy in England in favour of a strong stand against Ian Smith was inspired precisely by this fear of this "red army in blue berets," intimating Russian participation in subduing the Ian Smith regime under the banner of the United Nations.

The regime of Ian Smith lasted much longer than might have been anticipated in 1965. And here then it is worth making the distinction between white minority rule and colonial rule. The United Nations does indeed have an impressive record in facilitating the end of colonial rule; but its success in ending white minority rule in independent countries has been much more modest. An alternative way of formulating this conclusion is to say that while the United Nations has to its credit important achievements in the fight against colonialism, the history of its participation in the fight against racialism has been characterized more by frustration than by accomplishment.

And yet the battle still continues, and is an aspect of the resacralization of diplomacy in the world. When the United Nations Organization was formed in San Francisco in 1945, South Africa was in fact the most influential African state present there. But history has come to indulge her ironic sense of humour once again. South Africa, which had been one of the architects of the world body in San Francisco in 1945, was destined to become one of the primary targets of the Organization's moral war. If the world body continues to survive it will not be a very long time before at last an African becomes the Secretary-General of the Organization. It is conceivable that when that time comes South Africa will already have been squeezed out of the world body, or will be considering withdrawing of her own accord before having to deal with a black Secretary-General.

The United Nations' influence has declined in the world in the last ten years; but the African influence within the world body has increased dramatically. Now that Communist China has entered the United Nations, it is conceivable that the Organization will receive a new lease of diplomatic life.

For the time being its mission in the fight against colonialism is virtually complete. That is in fact its most solid achievement. Its mission against underdevelopment through its specialized agencies may well be vastly strengthened before the end of the 1970's in spite of the present uncertainty concerning the American contribution. But for the time being the United Nations remains at its most helpless in dealing with problems of war – either a war within a member state, like the Nigerian civil war, or the massive danger of nuclear annihilation. Clouds of uncertainty continue to hang over the destiny of the world body and of the humankind it is supposed to serve. What is certain already is that the United Nations has been both a symbol of the resacralization of international relations and an instrument for promoting that fragile new morality in world politics.

And there is no doubt that the moral tone of international politics and the degree of commitment to moral causes implied by that tone are still delicate. All we can say is that the rise of new internationalist ideologies, the rise of the United States as a superpower and the emergence of the new nations of Asia and Africa have all converged as important forces behind the birth of a new *Pax Humana* in world affairs. It is precisely these forces which are beginning to give meaning to the concept of an Open World.

CONCLUSION

We have attempted to demonstrate in this paper two paradoxical trends in human relations, both of which are profoundly important both for the phenomenon of empathy as the essence of the Open World and for the role of culture therein. In relations between groups domestically, we have argued that judgements on human behaviour are moving from ethics to aesthetics. Large areas of the individual's active life, which before were fit for moral approbation or moral disapproval by others, have in the last few decades become areas of discretion according to *taste*. The range is from pre-marital sex to suicide, from milder forms of drug taking to homosexuality, from pornography to flamboyant modes of dress.

In relations between states, on the other hand, the trend has been from the diplomacy of propriety to the diplomacy of principles. The diplomacy of propriety was again an exercise in discretion according to taste, with some styles deemed as more civilized than others, in terms implying behavioural ugliness and behavioural attractiveness rather than good and evil.

An aesthetic judgement in our sense is of the kind which, for example, disapproves of a person turning up at a formal dinner party in shorts and an open shirt. He may incur serious censure from the other participants. But the judgement passed on him is fundamentally different from what we pass on someone who rapes a girl of fourteen. The latter judgement is still within the moral domain. What we have suggested here is that pre-marital sex according to Victorian morality belonged roughly in the same category as raping a girl of fourteen; pre-marital sex by the 1960's had moved from that category to the aesthetic category by the standards of which we also judge the man who turns up at a formal dinner party in shorts and an open shirt.

But there is a third category to be borne in mind – this is the category of legal judgements, distinct both from moral judgements and from aesthetic ones. In domestic relations there is an expanding area of legal judgements and legal obligations, an expanding area of aesthetic judgements, but a contracting area of moral judgements per se. Forms of personal behaviour which do not become outlawed specifically, very rapidly become matters of taste. On balance we are still talking about trends and tendencies, rather than about a world already aesthetically revolutionized. But the trend in domestic relations between individuals and between groups is towards expanding aesthetics, expanding law, and contracting morality.

Why is it that in interstate relations the trend is towards expanding international morality? The essential difference once again between the international and the domestic domain may hinge on the simple fact that the international dimension is not controlled by law in the same sense as the domestic is. There are no legal sanctions, as we know all too clearly, that can be applied against transgressors in the international system. There are no jails to which offending nations may be sent; and even economic sanctions and boycotts have been applied so half-heartedly that as often as not they have merely strengthened the transgressor.

Because the international arena does not have enforceable law, and because there is no legislature to bring international law up to date in conformity with changing norms, there cannot be at this level the equivalent of the domestic phenomenon of an expanding legal framework. In domestic relations, as we have indicated, morality is losing both to law and to aesthetics: but in international relations there is no law by which the new values of human obligation may be transformed into an authoritative allocation of values.

Both the domestic and the international trends we have discussed illustrate changes in the boundaries of empathy itself. In domestic relations law is expanding in those areas which manifest new social responsibilities and popular welfare. Behavioural aesthetics are expanding because of a new social permissiveness towards individual preferences. The widening frontiers of taste are in reality widening frontiers of toleration.

The world of the 1990's ought, therefore, to aim for the maturation of these two trends – increased social and welfare legislation, and diminishing moral self-righteousness with regard to the private behaviour of others thus widening horizons of personal choice and personal taste.

In the international system, on the other hand, the world of the 1990's should aim to consolidate the trend towards a new international morality, susceptible to the obligations of the strong towards the weak, the rich towards the poor, and of each towards a concept of *Pax Humana* and a man-centred system of values. Perhaps by that time a new concept of international law might also have matured, allowing for possibilities of enactment and enforcement. If that were indeed to be realized, the international system could continue to be, in important and defensible ways, different from trends in relations between national entities.

Behind both trends remains the phenomenon of culture. It is of course culture as a system of values that encompasses these changing balances between aesthetics, ethics and law. And in the notion of empathy and its connection both to psychology and to aesthetics we have a sense of culture that is narrower than the whole system of values, but one which could at the same time be richer and more symbolic of human creativity than other sectors of the normative world. Our concept of the Open World and its empathy is profoundly cultural in its roots, and our evaluation of world trends springs from an interpretation of changing cultural patterns behind both individual and national behaviour. We start in this perspective from the premise that, in the ultimate analysis, the problems of world order are concerned with the interplay between the sacred and the secular in human judgements, and these in turn find their origins in the world of values and cultural perspectives.

VISIONS AND EXPLANATIONS: FOUR PERSPECTIVES ON EDUCATION AND WORK

LEON BRAMSON

"Suppose that France suddenly lost fifty of her best physicists, chemists, physiologists, mathematicians, poets, painters, sculptors, musicians, writers; fifty of her best mechanical engineers, civil and military engineers, artillery experts, architects, doctors, surgeons, apothecaries, seamen, clockmakers; fifty of her best bankers, two hundred of her best business men, two hundred of her best farmers, fifty of her best ironmasters, arms manufacturers, tanners, dyers, miners, clothmakers, cotton manufacturers, silk-makers, linen-makers, manufacturers of hardware, of pottery and china, of crystal and glass, ship chandlers, carriers, printers, engravers, goldsmiths, and other metal-workers; her fifty best masons, carpenters, joiners, farriers, locksmiths, cutlers, smelters, and a hundred other persons of various unspecified occupations, eminent in the sciences, fine arts and professions; making in all the three thousand leading scientists, artists and artisans of France.

These men are the Frenchmen who are the most essential producers, those who make the most important products, those who direct the enterprises most useful to the nation, those who contribute to its achievements in the sciences, fine arts and professions. They are in the most real sense the flower of French society: they are, above all Frenchmen, the most useful to their country, contribute most to its glory, increasing its civilization and prosperity. The nation would become a lifeless corpse as soon as it lost them. It would immediately fall into a position of inferiority compared with the nations which it now rivals, and would continue to be inferior until this loss had been replaced . . . It would require at least a generation for France to repair this misfortune; for men who are distinguished in work of positive ability are exceptions, and nature is not prodigal of exceptions, particularly in this species.

Let us pass on to another assumption. Suppose that France preserves all the men of genius that she possesses in the sciences, fine arts and professions, but has the misfortune to lose in the same day Monsieur the King's brother, Monseigneur le duc d'Angoulême, Monseigneur le duc de Berry, Monseigneur le duc d'Orléans, Monseigneur le duc de Bourbon, Madame la duchesse d'Angoulême, Madame la duchesse de Berry, Madame la duchesse d'Orléans, Madame la duchesse de Bourbon and Mademoiselle de Condé. Suppose that France loses at the same time all the great officers of the royal household, all the ministers (with or without portfolio), all the councillors of state, all the chief magistrates, marshals, cardinals, archbishops, bishops, vicars-general, and canons, all the prefects and sub-prefects, all the civil servants, and judges, and in addition, ten thousand of the richest proprietors who live in the style of nobles.

This mischance would certainly distress the French, because they are kind-hearted and could not see with indifference the sudden disappearance of such a large number of their compatriots. But this loss of thirty thousand individuals, considered to be the most important in the State, would only grieve them for purely sentimental reasons and would result in no political evil for the State."

Henri de St. Simon, "The Organizer," (1819)

There is ample justification for considering education and work in the context of a conference on the open society. Sociologists have traditionally concerned themselves with the contrast between closed and open societies, and these contrasts are reflected in the typologies generated by 19th century social theorists such as St. Simon, Comte, Herbert Spencer, Marx, Durkheim, Sir Henry Maine, and Max Weber. Weber spoke of the "life chances" of individuals who were members of different groups, and modern sociologists have undertaken to try to determine the degree of social mobility in various societies, assuming implicitly that societies in which social mobility was possible were more open. Educational institutions are seen as crucial in modern industrialized societies because they provide a link between the family, on the one hand, and the occupational structure on the other. School is viewed as functioning as an intermediate institution in a way which was wholly unnecessary in pre-literate societies of the type which we can observe even today among, for example, the Bushmen of the Kalahari desert. The kinds of skills which are necessary to adult functioning in Bushman society for both males and females are skills which are learned quite readily by imitation, by association with adults and age-mates. Arrangements for learning the skills required in a hunting and gathering society like that of the Bushmen occurs within the context of the family and the band. Division of labor is so simple that there are really few if any alternatives for males or females to learn what they might do as functioning adults within such a society. The contrast with modern industrial society is dramatic. The *Dictionary of Occupational Titles* lists more than fifty thousand job descriptions, though this should not be taken to imply that all members of such societies as our own always have a wide range of alternatives available to them. But the possibility of such a range suggests why the school as an intervening institution might be crucial in determining the life chances of an individual. A person moves from the family setting, not directly into the occupational structure but into an institution which might provide some preparation for a place in that structure. Individuals are distributed into occupations in some measure according to what happens to them in schools. What happens to them, however, has been shown to vary tremendously according to a great many factors, including the very important five or six years of experience prior to the onset of formal schooling. We are becoming more sensitive to the fact that schools can function to confirm children's self-conceptions regarding their own stupidity or ineptitude as well as to develop their human potentialities. In spite of great variation, however, the experience of schooling seems to be fateful in all industrial societies, whether socialist, capitalist, communist or fascist. Indeed, it is the distinction of the functionalist theory of industrial society to emphasize the convergence of such societies in their fundamental characteristics regardless of political or cultural differences.

The paper which follows has four parts; in it I hope to outline some major alternative approaches to the phenomena of education and human resources which are relevant to the question of the open society. I will discuss the functionalist and the conflict theories of education, the movement toward de-schooling, and the steady-state society; and in each instance I will try to suggest the implications of these approaches for the idea of the open society.

THE FUNCTIONALIST CONCEPTION OF EDUCATION

The empirical literature on education and on the sociology of occupations is enormous. I shall be trying to abstract from this literature certain essential propositions which characterize an approach to modern industrial society, and in this section shall rely heavily on Robert Dreeben's recent book, *On What Is Learned In School*,[1] as an unusually concise statement of the implications of the functionalist approach. Dreeben's book takes as its fundamental starting point the notion that the most important things students learn in school (aside from reading, writing and arithmetic) have nothing to do with the curriculum as such. They have to do rather with their socialization for what he calls "stress-free psychic functioning" in an industrial society. Dreeben argues that there are certain orientations which must be assimilated by an individual for effective adult behavior in an industrial society. This emphasis reflects the view that "the main business of socialization is the training of infants, children, adolescents and sometimes adults so that they can ultimately fulfill the social obligations that their society and culture will place on them."[2]

[1] Robert Dreeben, *On What is Learned in School* (Reading, Mass., Addison-Wesley Publishing Co., 1968).

[2] Alex Inkeles, "Social Structure and the Socialization of Competence," *Harvard Educational Review,* Vol. 36, No. 3 (Summer 1966), p. 64.

Dreeben holds that it is impossible for the family to be the context of schooling in a modern industrial society, as it might be among the Bushmen. Exploring the differences between the family and the school as institutions, he emphasizes the very different structural properties of each. The character of a social setting varies according to its structural properties; pupils learn to accept principles of conduct or social norms and to act according to them. But the different tasks, constraints and opportunities which are available in the school by contrast with the family are crucial; and by coping with them, individuals derive principles of conduct or norms based on their experiences.[3] Adapting the theoretical work of Talcott Parsons to his purpose, Dreeben argues for the importance of the following four norms as an outcome of schooling. As principles of conduct, he regards these norms as "integral parts of public and occupational life in industrial societies or institutional realms adjacent to the school." [4]

1. Independence (vs. dependence)

Independence is viewed as the obligation to act by oneself (unless collaborative effort is called for) and to accept personal responsibility for one's conduct and accountability for its consequences. Dreeben is arguing that independence, as opposed to dependence, is something which children tend to learn in classrooms and which is reinforced by some of the structural qualities of school and schooling. (One example he uses is cheating.) Dreeben is here arguing that the school tries to function in such a way as to enable students to learn to work on their own, and a little reflection will indicate that although this norm is frequently violated, it is a very strong one associated with school performance. Even school systems such as that of the Soviet Union have not downgraded independence, even though stronger students are expected to help weaker ones and educators have tried to develop an orientation toward the success of the collectivity as opposed to the individual.[5] The ultimate goal is still that the weaker ones should eventually be capable of functioning in terms of the norm of independence.

2. Achievement (vs. ascription)

Dreeben here speaks of the obligation to perform tasks actively and master the environment according to certain standards of excellence, and the effort to foster this goal seems to be a widespread characteristic of schooling.

[3] Dreeben, *op. cit.,* p. 44.
[4] *Ibid.,* pp. 63-64.
[5] In spite of the inadequacies of the data base for Soviet schools, see Urie Bronfenbrenner. *Two Worlds of Childhood* (New York, Russell Sage, 1972).

Although there is no human society known in which statuses are assigned only on the basis of achievement as opposed to ascription, classical sociological theory has insisted (e.g., in Durkheim's early writings) that the individual should be liberated in pursuit of the career open to talent. This idea is so much a part of our own folklore in the United States that we are extremely embarrassed when we discover in our studies of education and life-chances that the system does not always work as it is supposed to work. This is a digression, however; Dreeben argues that achievement is one of the master norms associated with life in industrial society, and this is difficult to deny whether one is analyzing the process of schooling in capitalist or communist states.

3. Universalism (vs. particularism)

Universalism is defined as the obligation to acknowledge the rights of others to treat them as members of categories, and here Dreeben argues that schooling socializes individuals in a way which would be quite impossible within the bosom of the typical family. The student learns to define himself as a member of a category consisting of a large number of peers in a class of age-mates. Universalism is of course closely related to the ideal of the meritocracy and to the notion of objective criteria of merit or achievement, as opposed to (for example) kinship relations as a criterion for rewards.

4. Specificity (vs. diffuseness)

Dreeben defines specificity as the obligation to accept such treatment (as members of categories) on the basis of a few discrete characteristics, rather than on the full constellation of them that represent the whole person. Here we see again the emphasis on the segmentalized self – a person defined in terms of a particular role, by contrast with "the whole person" to whom we tend to respond in the context of the family. Dreeben's argument with regard to the differences between the family and the school as settings for the learning of these norms is that the family is a much more difficult context for learning them. There is an inconsistency between the nature of the family and the emotional relationships of the members, on the one hand, and the orientations reflected in the norms on the other. Although this might be taken as a brief for schooling as such, Dreeben argues that this would be a misinterpretation of his case. In typical functionalist fashion, he is saying that the learning of the four norms will be critical for effective functioning in an industrial society, and that schools are where these norms are being learned at present. But schools are not the only places where they might be learned, and of course he is not arguing that all students in all schools learn them either. But he is saying that until one can specify alternatives, in the context of which the norms might be internalized, one is left with schooling.

Dreeben's study is intended as a hypothetical and a theoretical approach; it has been criticized for the degree to which its application in particular empirical situations might be problematic.[6] Yet I introduce it here because it represents an approach which is characteristic of a point of view toward the relationship of education and society. When combined with a conception of the general characteristics of an industrial labor force, it becomes a typical functionalist argument about the pre-requisites of an industrial society. These characteristics include the following[7]:

1. Separation of the work place from the household
2. A distinction between the worker as a person and the position he occupies
3. Widespread employment in large-scale organizations of both bureaucratic and professional forms of authority
4. Individual accountability for the performance of tasks judged according to standards of competence
5. The affiliation of individuals to organizations through *ad hoc* contractual agreements.

The argument implies that the four norms are virtually required for the survival of industrial societies, and apply to industrial labor forces regardless of the political or cultural orientation involved. Such a theory emphasizes the convergence of characteristics of industrial societies; but it also emphasizes the importance of education for such societies. It has been demonstrated, for example, that the number of years a person has spent in school is a strong determinant of his level of occupational achievement in America, and that this is true even when social origins are held constant, thereby controlling for social class.[8]

[6] See the "Review Symposium," *Sociology of Education*, Vol. 43, No. 2 (Spring, 1970), which includes the comments of Campbell, Loubser, Etzioni and Stinchcombe.

[7] Dreeben, *op. cit.*, pp. 114-115.

[8] But social origins also affect occupational achievement after education is completed, as well as educational attainment itself. See Peter Blau and Otis D. Duncan, *The American Occupational Structure* (New York, Wiley, 1967); Bruce K. Eckland, "Academic Ability, Higher Education and Occupational Mobility," *American Sociological Review*, Vol. 30 (1965), pp. 735-746; William H. Sewell, Archibald O. Haller, and A. Portes, "The Educational and Early Occupational Attainment Process," *American Sociological Review*, Vol. 34 (Feb. 1969), Otis D. Duncan and Robert W. Hodge, "Education and Occupational Mobility: A Regression Analysis," *American Journal of Sociology*, Vol. 68 (1963), all cited by Collins, *infra*.

The general functionalist orientation, as elaborated primarily by American sociologists, holds that occupations in an industrial society call for certain kinds of skills; that in order to find people to perform the various occupational roles it is necessary either to train them or to locate people who already have the ability to do so; that some of these occupational roles are more important than others to the functioning of an industrial society; that the ability to perform these roles or to learn them in some kind of training context is not equally distributed among the members of a society; and finally, that the system rewards individuals who have special ability or training with income, power and status in order to fill the occupational positions and satisfy the demand for skill. Such a theory argues, of course, that differences in reward are therefore inevitable in modern industrial society.[9] To this analysis we may add a number of observations made by Dreeben concerning the extraordinary growth of education in the United States over time. He has pointed out [10] that schooling not only contributes to the performance of occupational roles, but also helps people to learn how to be "clients" in their many roles (as consumers, patients, passengers, bank depositors, renters, litigants, voters) which are not occupational. Dreeben regards the capacity to function as clients as part of competent participation for adults in industrial society. He also points out that the expansion of schooling is partly a result of the development of the rights of citizens in nation-states and a symbol of full participation in the larger national community. To anyone familiar with the history of education in the United States, not to speak of other countries, it is perfectly clear that the schools try to indoctrinate students in what Robert Bellah has called "the civil religion," [11] a secular nationalism which attempts to create common symbols and myths among members of various ethnic, religious, racial and class groups. There is reason to believe that the dissemination of "the civil religion" is one of the functions of schooling the world over, and that this tends to be true regardless of political or cultural orientation

[9] Kingsley Davis and Wilbert Moore, "Some Principles of Stratification," *American Sociological Review,* Vol. 10 (1945), and the debate between Davis-Moore and Tumin, reprinted in *Readings on Social Stratification* (Englewood Cliffs: Prentice-Hall, 1970). The statement that some occupational roles are more important than others, and the general theory of unequal distribution of rewards, have both been challenged by critics of functionalism. The critics assert that both statements are untenable unless accompanied by a specific reference to a particular level of functioning. The notion of "survival" or of "functional prerequisites" is said to be too elusive unless a particular state of the system is specified.

[10] Robert Dreeben, "American Schooling," in Bernard Barber (ed.), *Stability and Social Change* (Boston: Little, Brown, 1971).

[11] Robert Bellah, "The Civil Religion in America," in Donald R. Cutler (ed.), *The Religious Situation* (Boston, Beacon, 1968), pp. 331-356.

in modernizing societies attempting "nationbuilding," in industrial societies and even "post-industrial" societies.

Historically speaking, the general perspective we encounter in sociological functionalism with respect to education and occupations represents a tradition beginning with the parable of St. Simon and culminating in the concept of the meritocracy satirized by Michael Young in his social science fiction novel, *The Rise of the Meritocracy*.[12] In the century and a half which separates these two works, perhaps the most important figure for the development of the functionalist viewpoint is Emile Durkheim. In *The Division of Labor* (1893) Durkheim enunciated the basis of the concept of meritocracy by arguing that in the emerging industrial society "social inequality shall be a direct reflection of natural inequality." [13] Durkheim's discussion, at once remarkably sophisticated and remarkably naive, takes place in the context of an evolutionary argument concerning the transition in the sources of social solidarity. Solidarities characteristic of kinship-based pre-literate societies are giving way to the new form of society where status is based on achievement and in which individuals become more highly differentiated and specialized. *The Division of Labor* represents Durkheim's most optimistic vision of the new industrial society, for it celebrates the concept of the career open to talent and the importance of occupational specialization even as at the same time it questions where the new sources of solidarity are to come from, which will replace the kinship networks, primitive religions and tribal bonds of the pre-literate groups. Durkheim is more responsive to the potentialities of individualism and liberation in *The Division of Labor* than in any of his subsequent works. Individuals who are freed from traditionalism and from the context of local cultures will help to usher in the society in which "social inequality shall be a direct reflection of natural inequality." Obviously, what is involved here is not only an analysis of an evolutionary process, but also a justification – the new society would be one in which the individual can be rewarded for developing his occupational potentialities, and each man's striving will redound to the good of the whole. The only consideration marring this bright picture was Durkheim's concern for the source of social solidarity in the new society, a concern which emerges as the dominant feature of his thought in subsequent work (e.g., *Suicide*). In his later writings the social costs of the modern society are assessed and the paradoxes of *anomie* come to replace the optimism of "organic solidarity"

[12] Michael Young, *The Rise of the Meritocracy* (London, Thames and Hudson, 1958).

[13] Emile Durkheim, *The Division of Labor in Society* (New York, Free Press, 1960), p. 377.

achieved through the recognition of the interdependence of occupational and professional groups. Freedom of thought, the toleration of dissent, the creation of new sources of moral authority, a higher degree of individuality, greater involvement in economic life, the erosion of traditionalism, the increase in entrepreneurial activity, which are celebrated in *The Division of Labor*, all seem to be correlated with the highest rate of self-destruction, as documented in *Suicide*. Yet, in his orientation toward work, Durkheim is astonishingly modern. He argues for vocational commitment and specialization, brands over-specialization and the mindless labor of the assembly line as representing an "abnormal form" of the division of labor which cannot produce solidarity, and castigates "the forced division of labor" or lack of occupational choice as entirely without value for the creation of solidarity.

I have said that the functionalist tradition, beginning with St. Simon and moving through Durkheim, culminates in the concept of the meritocracy. It is important to see, however, that the functionalist tradition is not an egalitarian tradition. Michael Young notes this in his gracious acknowledgement to the socialists, to the effect that they broke down the old heredity principle of ascribed status. (This is somewhat analogous to Marx' acknowledging the beneficial role of the bourgeoisie in creating machine production and the modern industrial base for the socialist society to come.) The breakdown of the hereditary principle of ascribed status constitutes only Phase One of the meritocratic program. Phase Two is functionalist and efficiency-oriented, not egalitarian. The humanist concern of Michael Young for the impersonal operation of a system which creates vast differences of status based on the formula of "I.Q. plus effort equals merit" is a remarkably valuable critique of a tendency in modern industrial society flowing from the functionalist principle. At the same time, however, it seems to me important to recognize the degree to which industrial societies inevitably tend to become meritocracies, and to recognize those aspects of the meritocracy which represent models of the open society and appeal to us in our passion for some combination of efficiency and social justice. Both functionalism and the meritocracy, however, are under attack at the present time on both moral and empirical grounds. The conflict theory of education, to be discussed below, agrees on the importance of a "hidden curriculum" in the schools, but disagrees on its importance as a functional pre-requisite in contemporary industrial society. It is viewed rather as an important irrelevancy, a smoke-screen which helps to preserve the *status quo*. It conceals the fact that the real structure of society and of occupations is not determined by formulas such as "I.Q.

plus effort equals merit," but by the result of the conflict of interest groups. On moral grounds, the meritocracy is being severely criticized as representing a too narrow conception of merit and ignoring many valuable human qualities which are quite as important as academic achievement, even as qualifications for occupational roles. The ferocious debate among social scientists concerning the concept of I.Q. itself and the results of testing, the "cultural bias" of tests, and the hereditary component of ability may also be viewed in the light of these discontents. It is even being argued that meritocratic criteria favor some groups rather than others. It is now U.S. government policy that members of some American minority groups and women, heretofore underrepresented on university faculties, be actively recruited for vacancies on those faculties. Setting hiring goals based on race and sex is referred to as "affirmative action," mandated by a number of executive orders and by the Equal Employment Opportunity Act of 1972, even though the quotas it tries to establish are actually in violation of the Civil Rights Act of 1964. Record-keeping showing evidence of good faith is required and penalties for noncompliance include the threat of loss of federal grant funds in aid of research and instruction. (At Columbia University this amounts to $72 million.) Clearly the underpinnings for such policies and such views reflect a completely different conception of what constitutes an "open society" from the functionalist view discussed above.[14]

THE CONFLICT THEORY OF EDUCATIONAL STRATIFICATION

The conflict theory is derived primarily from the approach of Max Weber, although the influence of Mosca, Michels and Pareto as well as Marx-Engels are also important. It takes its point of departure from the idea that the basic material of political sociology may be found in the analysis of the struggles of interest groups striving to maximize their advantages and developing strategies for doing so. This type of analysis contrasts with the functionalist emphasis on society as a system of interdependent parts and by focusing on struggle and conflict of both individuals and organizations, it contrasts with the functionalist emphasis on consensus and division of labor. In its concern for domination and subordination, as a result of such struggles, it contrasts with the functionalist emphasis on internalization of

[14] Cf. Paul Seabury, "How Washington Enforces New Forms of Discrimination in the Name of Equal Opportunity," *Commentary,* Vol. 53, No. 2 (Feb. 1972); and "The Pottinger Papers," *Commentary,* Vol. 53, No. 5 (May, 1972).

societal values. Finally, in viewing change as the result of the struggle for advantage, it contrasts with the homeostatic emphasis in functionalism, the assumptions concerning equilibrium and the evolution of social systems.[15]

Conflict theory does not deny that the empirical linkages between education and employment in modern industrial societies are convincing; nor do they deny the evidence concerning the increased importance of education in such societies over time.[16] Collins, however, questions a number of propositions in terms of which functionalists *interpret* these linkages. He argues that in American society only about 15% of the increase in education of the labor force during this century is a result of changes in the occupational structure. These are the kinds of changes which reflect a higher proportion of jobs requiring high skill and a lower proportion requiring low skills. Most of the educational upgrading has taken place *within* job categories. Collins also challenges the concept that educational requirements of jobs in industrial societies rise because these jobs require increasing skill. The evidence available, although sketchy, suggests that the level of formal education required for many U.S. jobs is much higher than the skill requirements for those jobs would suggest.[17] Thus Collins might have pointed to the notorious example of the requirement of a high-school diploma for a member of the New York City garbagemen's union. He is generalizing this point and arguing that the phenomenon is widespread over American society as a whole. Collins questions the proposition that formal education provides required job skills particularly after the level of literacy has been achieved. He cites studies indicating a questionable relationship between secondary school and university enrollments and subsequent economic development. Berg's studies regarding the contribution of education to the productivity of individuals, particularly among better-educated employees, among samples of manual workers, department store clerks, secretaries, bank tellers, engineers, technicians, research scientists, military personnel and federal civil service employees are also cited. These studies tend to be skeptical concerning the contribution of education to productivity. Vocational skills of

[15] This discussion relies on an interesting summary of this approach by Randall Collins, "A Comparative Approach to Political Sociology" in Reinhard Bendix *et. al., State and Society: A Reader in Comparative Political Sociology* (Boston, Little, Brown, 1968), p. 67.

[16] In somewhat the same fashion as with Dreeben in the previous section, I have relied on Randall Collins, "Functional and Conflict Theories of Educational Stratification," *American Sociological Review,* Vol. 36 (Dec. 1971), pp. 1002-1019. And I have benefited from discussions with Randall Collins and Hans-Eberhard Mueller concerning conflict theory.

[17] Cf. Ivar Berg, *Education and Jobs: The Great Training Robbery* (New York, Praeger, 1970).

many manual workers are learned on the job as informal schooling, but Collins' argument does appear to fall down when confronting the training of professionals. Overall, Collins tends to interpret the data as indicating the inadequacies of the functionalist theory of education and stratification rather than as reflecting a fixed demand for skills of various kinds. He has viewed the requirements of many occupational positions as not fixed at all, but representing the results of bargaining between the persons who take jobs and those who try to control them. "Individuals want jobs primarily for the rewards to themselves in material goods, power and prestige. The amount of productive skill they must demonstrate to hold their positions depends on how much clients, customers or employers can successfully demand of them, and this in turn depends on the balance of power between workers and their employers." [18] Thus the requirement of a high-school diploma for a garbage collector is seen as the result of a complex negotiation involving unions and the municipal government, but the educational criterion involved has no relationship whatsoever to effective functioning on the job. Such extreme examples form part of the basis for a critique of functionalist ideas which have gained widespread acceptance among social scientists. Thus Collins concludes on the basis of his review of the literature that skill requirements of most jobs tend to be extremely vague, that most employees are not forced to work at maximum efficiency, and that standards of performance usually are reflections of a bargaining process of an informal nature, which in turn reflects the relative power of the groups engaged in the bargaining. Social origins do have some effect on occupational level and the American literature indicates widespread discrimination against Negroes and other minorities as well as standards for employment based on such elements of life-style as dress, manners, accent and sexual stereotyping. While functionalists would tend to regard such data as evidence of archaic survivals from a previous period that tend to put emphasis on ascribed status, Collins drives his argument much further by suggesting that "the power of 'ascribed' groups may be the *prime* basis of selection in all organizations, and technical skills are secondary considerations depending on the balance of power. Education may thus be regarded as a mark of membership in a particular group (possibly at times its defining characteristic), not a mark of technical skills or achievement." [19]

Collins argues that in order to understand the data one must introduce the general conflict theory of stratification which would emphasize the

[18] Collins, *op. cit.*, p. 1007.
[19] *Ibid.*, p. 1008.

competition of status groups based on economic situation, power or position, ethnicity, geographical origin, religion, education or cultural distinctions. These groups are viewed as engaged in a continuous struggle for advantage and the data on education and occupations is to be interpreted as the result of the struggle primarily between status groups rather than within them. Education is reinterpreted as an attempt on the part of schools to teach particular status cultures even including academic or vocational emphases where the results of such emphases may provide the claim for a particular basis for status. Collins makes an impressive effort to bolster his conclusions with data on education in the United States. But one of the most important pieces of evidence he introduces, his own study of California employers, seems to support the functionalist theory at the managerial and white collar levels.

Collins' paper represents a statement of a position and a review of the existing support for it; much of the data is not conclusive and there is a sense in which it represents an agenda for research rather than a definitive refutation of functionalism. Nevertheless, it must be said that the conflict theory represents a powerful alternative for the interpretation of the relationship between education and occupational achievement in the United States, particularly at the lower levels and after literacy has been achieved.

What are the implications of the conflict theory for the idea of the open society? In the first place, the conflict theory seems to present an obvious challenge to that aspect of functionalism which implies that the system itself results in a socially just occupational structure based on merit and ability. In the second place, it implies that attempts to justify particular structures or institutional arrangements are mere rationalizations or masks for privilege. These are viewed as having been institutionalized not as a result of technical requirements but as a result of the bargaining process of those competing interest groups. Yet it seems to me that insofar as the conflict theory of educational stratification is also a moral theory or a vision of the good society, it must ultimately end with the assertion of a principle resembling the meritocracy principle. The only alternative is a blind and amoral power struggle in which victory goes to the swift and the cunning, or a centralized authority which reserves all decisions concerning the allocation of human resources. For ultimately, even the conflict theorists face the problem of social order which is the central issue for functionalists from Hobbes to Parsons. Of course a conflict theorist could draw a sharp positivistic distinction between normative and analytical theory and refuse to be drawn concerning the desirable structure of society. But few if any conflict theorists today refuse to be drawn on such questions.

Most of them have specific prescriptions regarding the structure of society, visions as well as explanations. In this sense, both functionalist theory and conflict theory may be said to represent a combination of empirical and normative elements. In this they faithfully reflect the characteristics of their 19th century antecedents, whether they be St. Simon, Comte, Durkheim, Marx-Engels or Weber.

I have tried to suggest, in the first section of this paper that there is a relationship between a type of explanation – functionalism – and a vision of the good society – meritocracy. When we turn to conflict theory, we find that there is no such simple relationship between a particular explanation and a vision of the good society. Conflict theory has many sources. On the one hand, the work of Mosca and Pareto combines the conflict mode of explanation with an elitist vision of society. On the other hand, Marx and Engels and their numerous interpreters and followers have espoused an egalitarian vision, though often this has culminated in another kind of elitism in both theory and practice. Max Weber attempted to synthesize strands of conflict theory, but the vision of society which emerges from his work is infected with what one writer has called "metaphysical pathos," [20] the view of modern society as an iron cage.[21] Indeed, conflict theory is compatible with a number of visions of society, including an extreme view of "organic" authoritarianism and fascism, in which allocation of occupational roles is highly centralized and controlled. But in conflict theory there is an element of arbitrariness on the moral side, by contrast with the linkage between functionalism and meritocracy. It is this element of arbitrariness which accounts for the wide variety of visions of the good society which are associated with different versions of conflict theory.

What is "open" and what "closed" then turns on particular linkages between explanations and visions. The meritocracy, viewed by the functionalist as "open," is denounced as "closed" by the egalitarian conflict theorist. Yet the latter will probably end with some version of the meritocracy because of the very nature of modern industrial society. Does this mean that it is possible to speak of "the triumph of the meritocracy"? If a Chinese university professor earns several times the salary of an ordinary factory worker, does this signal the triumph of functionalism?

[20] Alvin Gouldner, "Metaphysical Pathos and the Theory of Bureaucracy," *American Political Science Review,* Vol. 49 (1955).
[21] Arthur Mitzman, *The Iron Cage* (New York, Alfred Knopf, 1970).

THE MOVEMENT TOWARD DE-SCHOOLING

In reviewing the massive literature on the sociology of education over time, a number of interesting shifts of emphasis are apparent. Observers of school systems all over the world have found many parallel phenomena including a very steep education pyramid. With the notable exception of the United States, a very small elite of individuals have access to higher education. Furthermore, there seems to be a strong relationship between social class background and academic achievement. In the decade of the 1950's, a primary concern among analysts of education was the fact that social class background and academic ability were not absolutely correlated, and that therefore societies with steep educational pyramids were suffering from a large talent loss. This was because many of the most able people in the schools (according to grades and testable achievement in academic skills) were not encouraged to go on to higher studies, or did not have the motivation to do so, or did not have the money which would enable them to do so. The theme of talent loss and "wastage" (as it was widely referred to in the literature of the period) was exacerbated in the United States by the remarkable achievement of Soviet scientists and engineers as symbolized by the development of the Sputnik. Post-Sputnik educational reforms at the secondary level in the United States were facilitated by this atmosphere of emergency and national interest generated by scientific advance in other countries. Sociologists of education, defining the issue in terms of talent loss, came to the conclusion that the structure of school systems was in part to blame for "wastage." As one of the leading scholars in this area declared, "In regard to organization, curriculum and staffing, the present trend in countries with rather developed school systems is to integrate the different school types that formerly ran parallel at the secondary level. A flexible school system where definitive choice between various educational paths is postponed as long as possible can take care of talent from all walks of life more readily than a rigid system with an early selection, which to a large extent depends on social background." [22] The notorious "eleven-plus" examinations in England which were the target of Michael Young's satire were also identified as inimical to the most productive development of the nation's resources. Early selection for the college or university preparatory course at ages 10-13 on the basis of test scores alone also gave rise to other related

[22] Torsten Husen, "School Structure and the Utilization of Talent," in George Z. F. Bereday (ed.), *Essays on World Education: The Crisis of Supply and Demand* (New York, Oxford University Press, 1969), p. 92.

questions concerning the effects of such "creaming." Far before the Coleman Report, many educators in Europe recognized that separating the more academically able children from the others at an early age had a depressing effect on the performance of those left behind.[23] And the potential talent loss in the sciences was great in countries where access to university training was based on examinations that emphasized linguistic or verbal ability, particularly classical languages.

By the beginning of the 1970's, the primary concern of analysts of education had shifted from the problem of talent wastage viewed from the standpoint of the system as already constituted, to the general phenomenon of inequality of opportunity. There has been particular interest in the question of access to university education. It is paradoxical that this should be true also in the United States, where more people are going to colleges and universities, both absolutely and relatively, than ever before in human history.

When adjusted for age, a 1965 comparison of the number of college and university students in the United States by contrast with other industrialized countries of Western Europe and Japan shows about 1.5 to 3 times as many attending institutions of higher learning in the United States. The unadjusted figure for students between the ages of 18 and 21 is far higher, with almost 50% of American youth aged 18 to 21 attending institutions of higher learning.[24] In spite of this, many American scholars have become exercised over continuing inequality of opportunity in higher education. Although this bears out Tocqueville's observation that the Americans would tolerate anything but that they would not tolerate inequality of condition, this concern for the continuing influence of social class and other "advantages" in determining whether or not people go on to higher studies regardless of their academic abilities and performance has led to a number of new developments. One of these has led toward the notion that people should be allowed to learn on their own, without benefit of professors in classrooms or ivy-covered buildings, through television and correspondence courses which might further democratize higher studies.[25] Another has led in the direction of special programs such as "Upward

[23] A basic source is A. H. Halsey (ed.), *Ability and Educational Opportunity*, (Paris, Organization For Economic Co-operation and Development, 1961), in particular the paper by A. H. Halsey, Jean Floud and Torsten Husen.

[24] Frederick Mosteller and Daniel P. Moynihan, *On Equality of Educational Opportunity: Papers Deriving from the Harvard University Faculty Seminar on the Coleman Report* (New York: Random House, Vintage Books, 1972), p. 58.

[25] Cf. Alan Pifer, "The Responsibility for Reform in Higher Education," Annual Report, Carnegie Corporation of New York, 1971; and Kingman Brewster, "The Future of Formal Education," in *Educating for the 21st Century* (Urbana, University of Illinois Press, 1969).

Bound," funded by the government, in which high school students from minority groups might be encouraged to study through special residential summer programs at local colleges, supplemented by continuing tutoring during the last high school years. More than 60% of the students in such programs in the United States have gained access to college, and their drop-out rate appears to be the same as that of the regular college-going population. Finally, this concern has led to an extraordinary movement in which schooling itself has been denounced and the first step toward reform of education has been advocated in terms of the abolition of schooling itself. The old emphasis on academic achievement is also questioned, particularly in terms of a critique of tests and testing, and the procedures of certification. Access to higher education has indeed become demonstrably important in the United States as a key to occupational advancement, as we have already seen. This represents a relatively new phenomenon in American society although such pressures exist in all industrial societies and may perhaps be predicted for those in the process of achieving industrialization. By 1970, almost seven million students were enrolled in institutions of higher learning in the United States, constituting 47.6% of the population aged 18 through 21. This movement has been accompanied by progressive differentiation among institutions of higher learning into more selective and less selective, more exclusive and less exclusive institutions. A survey of 2,320 American colleges and universities lists only 68 in the highest of seven categories of selectivity.[26] Colleges and universities inundated by applications have moved toward the use of standardized objective tests such as the Scholastic Aptitude Test administered by the College Entrance Examination Board, and one observer of that phenomenon concludes that "definitions of merit appear class-bound in our class stratified society, culture-bound in our multi-cultured society. There begins to be the suspicion that the allocation of economic, political and social resources by educational attainment is "a difference of degree, not of kind" from systems of inequality we would reject outright . . . Our use of the idea of equality of opportunity woven into a meritocratic social order rests on the premise that human beings are comparable and finite, that their use-value can be measured and that such measurement is a legitimate basis for stratification." [27]

On moral grounds, there is a rather complex question of distributive

[26] Alexander W. Astin, *Predicting Academic Performance in College* (New York, Free Press, 1971), cited by Schudson, *infra.*

[27] Michael S. Schudson, "Organizing the 'Meritocracy': A History of the College Entrance Examination Board," *Harvard Educational Review,* Vol. 42, No. 1 (Feb. 1972), p. 69.

justice related to the fact that there is evidence that existing subsidy programs for higher education which we would expect to try to offset the socio-economic disadvantages of the needy students do not, in fact, provide funds primarily for those students. "Not only do Federal moneys for training and research go mainly to institutions that are attended primarily by middle- and high-income students, but also most other forms of institutional aid go to high-prestige colleges and universities. Even student-aid moneys are not primarily concentrated in the community colleges, city colleges, and less prestigious colleges that serve the poor. Moreover in the recent analysis of the distribution of subsidy for public higher education in California, Hansen and Weisbrod argue that because higher income students are more likely to go to college, to attend the most expensive public institutions, and to stay in college longer, their families are in effect receiving a greater educational subsidy from the state than are low-income families." [28]

One element of discontent with schooling as presently constituted has culminated in the view expounded by Ivan Illich who argues, like Cato, that the schools must be destroyed.[29] Illich's book rages against the educational establishment and argues not only that schools as presently constituted do not teach what people need to know in order to live in an industrial society, but also that schooling as an ideal held out to the masses of newly-developing countries is utterly hypocritical. This is so, he argues, because there will never be enough money for those masses to be schooled, and since only a tiny elite will ultimately benefit from schooling. Illich argues that schools actually teach people to be consumers (a point with which Dreeben would agree, though he would evaluate it differently). He maintains that obligatory attendance at school offends civil liberties, that school is a manipulative institution which serves the educational bureaucracy and not the students, and that schools function primarily as agencies of social control rather than for educational purposes. There is much merit in some of Illich's critical comments on education, which has become a favorite target of social reform in the United States, and which Illich argues can be reformed now without waiting for structural changes in society. But Illich's analysis of schooling is primarily negative, and his attempts to

[28] William H. Sewell, "Inequality of Opportunity For Higher Education," *American Sociological Review,* Vol. 36, No. 5, (Oct. 1971), p. 801. The reference to California is documented in W. Lee Hansen and Burton Weisbrod, "The Distribution of Costs and Benefits of Public Higher Education: The Case of California," *Journal of Human Resources,* No. 4 (Spring, 1969), pp. 176-191; see also the debate in that journal during 1970 and 1971 when critics commented on their analysis and the authors replied.

[29] Ivan Illich, *Deschooling Society* (New York, Harper and Row, 1970).

delineate alternatives to schooling seem to me totally unconvincing. In some cases, as in his computerized matching networks for individuals with common interests, they rely on precisely the high technology against which he inveighs in his critical chapters. It turns out that Illich's argument is only incidentally concerned with education: his essential theme is the evil of established institutions as such. There is no understanding of the positive role of institutions or the ways in which they might help to support individuals' self-conception, their morale, or their continuity, or provide contexts for self-transcendence. Illich is expressing dissatisfaction with human society in its modern industrial form; his condemnation of "manipulated" institutions turns out to be a condemnation of institutions as such. The philosophical ground for Illich's argument rests on extreme individualism or anarchism. He argues for the same program in countries such as Brazil or Ghana as in the United States – the radical disestablishment of schools. Independently of Illich's arguments, however, the de-schooling movement (e.g., in China and Cuba) consists of an attempt to combine school and work in the effort to mobilize politically inert peasant populations, train technical and professional workers without losing their contribution to agricultural or industrial manpower, and serve political and ideological goals by avoiding the establishment of a bureaucratically entrenched intellectual, managerial and technical elite. While we know very little about the process whereby studies are combined with work among illiterate peasants, and what effect this has on the competencies necessary to an industrial society, there is some evidence that the Chinese are willing to pay the price of decreased efficiency in the use of their human resources in the interest of ideological purity. The familiar tension between "Red" and "expert" in the Soviet Union is also relevant to this issue although critics such as Illich would probably regard the Soviets as hopelessly bureaucratized and institutionalized in their commitment to schooling. We need to remain alert to the possibility that a new form of exploitation might be on the rise in many newly-developing countries – forced labor under the guise of "de-schooling."

Illich's discussion, in spite of its negativism, remains useful as a perspective on functionalism and as a critique of modern educational practices. It views an open society as one in which institutionalization should be minimized, and in which individuals might learn without being schooled. Given the agenda for modernization of the elites of newly-developing nations, it is highly unlikely that Illich's call for the destruction of schools will be heeded. But it is likely that because of the high costs of mass education, some institutional innovations in combinations of work experience and study will become more common during the next century. The recent orientation toward accountability in education, the realistic assessment of costs and benefits, of output as well as input, are part of the changing ideas concerning the economic base for the education establishment. Education tends to become an industry in modern industrial societies; it is estimated that 63,000,000 people are involved directly or indirectly in the education industry in the United States alone. But it has not been subjected to the same economic constraints as other industries, and has flourished as a government monopoly. The rising economic cost of education under these circumstances, as well as political considerations related to discontent with inequality of opportunity, are already affecting many industrial societies. It is tempting, in the context of a discussion of the de-schooling movement, to consider less drastic reforms which might encourage types of experience outside the school context such as voluntary national or international service. Such reforms are consistent with the idea of the open society as well as with the notion of individual self-development.[30] It seems to me that we could do more than we are now doing in this direction.

THE STEADY–STATE SOCIETY

It must have been seen, more or less distinctly by political economists, that the increase of wealth is not boundless; that at the end of what they term the progressive state lies the stationary state, that all progress in wealth is but a postponement of this, and that each step in advance is an approach to it . . . It is scarcely necessary to remark that a stationary condition of capital and population implies no stationary state of human improvement. There would be as much scope as ever for all kinds of mental culture and moral and social progress, as much room for improving the art of living, and much more likelihood of its being improved.

John Stuart Mill, *Principles of Political Economy*, 1857

As a *coda* to this discussion of the major approaches to the phenomena of education and human resources, perhaps it is appropriate to discuss briefly a recent movement of thought concerning the future of industrial society.[31] The authors of the MIT study on the limits to growth argue that:

"1. If the present growth trends in world population, industrialization, pollution, food production and resource depletion continue unchallenged,

[30] Leon Bramson, "The Social Impact of Voluntary National Service," in Donald J. Eberly, (ed.), *National Service: Report of a Conference* (Russell Sage Foundation, New York, 1968), pp. 105-130.

[31] D. H. Meadows, *et. al., The Limits to Growth* (New York, Universe Books, 1972).

the limits to growth on this planet will be reached some time within the next 100 years. The most probable result will be a rather sudden and uncontrollable decline in both population and industrial capacity.

2. It is possible to alter these growth trends and to establish a condition of ecological and economic stability that is sustainable far into the future. The state of global equilibrium can be designed so that the basic material needs of each person on earth are satisfied and each person has an equal opportunity to realize his individual human potential." [32]

The conclusions of the MIT group are based on the analysis of five elements – population, food production, industrialization, pollution, and consumption of non-renewable resources. Since the pattern of their increase involves exponential growth, the authors attempted to deal with the problem of projecting future trends by means of a complex computer program which attempts to anticipate the interaction of these variables. The intellectual foundation of the attempts at projection of the future may be found in systems theory and is ultimately based on biological analogies to the nature of organic metabolism which tends to view the steady-state as dynamic rather than inert.[33]

The MIT group tries to show that "the basic behavior mode of the world system is exponential growth of population and capital followed by collapse." [34] Their argument is a complex one that is based essentially on the compound interest or exponential growth feature in the five variables that they are using as a basis for their analysis. The steady state society which they recommend as an answer to the problems which emerge for the world population as a result of their predictions has the following characteristics:

"1. The capital plant and the population are constant in size. The birth rate equals the death rate and the capital investment rate equals the depreciation rate.

[32] *Ibid.*, pp. 23-24.

[33] The basic principles underlying this concept were stated by Ludwig von Bertalanffy, "The Theory of Open Systems in Physics and Biology," *Science* (1950). A rather abstract recent statement declares: "In general, steady state theory is an aspect of general system theory in which emphasis is placed on intervention in the interest of control over behavior variables of the system with a view to maintaining an optimum pattern of change. The master metaphor is cybernetic, in which variables are controlled and internal parts arranged according to some defined pattern of goals, values and norms of the system. In steady-state theory maximum growth is rejected for optimum change under a specified pattern of control over variables of the system." Paul Meadows, "The Steady State: Notes Toward A Theory," paper prepared for Symposium, Rensselaersville, N.Y. Institute on Man and Science (1971).

[34] D. H. Meadows, *et. al., op. cit.*, p. 142.

2. All input and output rates – births, deaths, investment and depreciation – are kept to a minimum.

3. The levels of capital and population and the ratio of the two are set in accordance with the values of the society. They may be deliberately revised and slowly adjusted as the advance of technology creates new options." [35]

The MIT group tries to argue that an equilibrium defined in this manner does not mean stagnation but simply means that within certain limits societies could make adjustments in a controlled way, guided by predetermined goals within a dynamic equilibrium. The authors find it very difficult to visualize what life would be like in such an equilibrium state and they find it very difficult also to imagine what kinds of new institutions might develop under these circumstances. The premium, they observed, would be "on any human activity that does not require a large flow of irreplaceable resources or produce severe environmental degradation . . . in particular those pursuits that many people would list as the most desirable and satisfying activities of man – education, art, music, religion, basic scientific research, athletics and social interactions." [36]

The projections of the MIT group and similar efforts by scholars in economics, biology, demography and related fields have created a sizable literature and generated a vigorous debate.[37] I shall touch on a few highlights of this debate which are relevant to the theme of the open society and the subject of this paper.

1. The steady state society concept attempts to deal with the world resources picture on a truly global basis. But an important feature of the world resources picture is also the imbalance between the development of industrial and "post-industrial" societies and newly developing countries still plagued by the "old" problems of poverty, ignorance, disease, and malnutrition. It is in the former societies that the threat, for example, of

[35] *Ibid.*, pp. 173-174. Although details of their computer program have been criticized by economists and others, it seems to me that their most important contribution lies in the central argument, which is not challenged by much of the criticism. Responses to the impact of resource depletion seem to be conditioned by ideology, especially in the case of optimists who believe that technological alternatives will emerge in time to forestall disaster.

[36] *Ibid.*, p. 175.

[37] Cf. Garrett Hardin, "The Tragedy of the Commons," *Science*, Vol. 162 (Dec. 13, 1968), pp. 1243-1248; "A Blueprint For Survival," *The Ecologist*, Vol. 2, No. 1 (January 1972), pp. 1-43; Peter Passell and Leonard Ross, "Don't Knock the $2 Trillion Economy," *New York Times Magazine* (Mar. 5, 1972); Barry Commoner, *The Closing Circle* (1971); Herman E. Daly, "Toward a Stationary-State Economy," in John Harte and Raymond Socolow, *The Patient Earth* (New York, Holt, Rinehart and Winston, 1971); "An Exchange on Man as Pest," *New York Review of Books*, Vol. 18, No. 3 (February 24, 1972).

industrial pollution to the character of the environment and to human health has been dramatized. The elites of newly-developing countries frequently feel that they can afford a certain amount of pollution in the process of their development; and in the cases of Brazil and India, officials have declared that economic growth which would help to solve short-run problems is far more important than long-run considerations. Thus the concern for the long-term results of growth is seen as an attempt to keep the poor countries poorer and to deal with the problems of the middle-classes; many Marxists have denounced the anti-growth movement as a new form of imperialism.

2. What will be the context for personal validation which until now has taken place in the industrialized countries in an occupational setting which is competitive and which has fostered social stratification and individual mobility? There are serious implications for the concept of the individual career, for the orientation toward work, and for the character of educational institutions. Even now in the United States we see that there will probably be less need for new capital expenditures in education because of population structure, particularly at the elementary and secondary levels. A large drop in the number of new teaching positions also seems to be predictable at a time when colleges and universities seem to be producing a larger number of qualified educators at every degree level. The U.S. Office of Education recently indicated an enrollment increase of only 2.4% in American colleges and universities in 1971-72, the smallest percentage gain in 10 years. Such phenomena are merely ripples on the surface but they give us an idea of what we may anticipate with regard to the steady state society. It seems fairly clear that elaborate manpower planning would be absolutely necessary, not to speak of the re-arrangement in the structure of motivation, which in turn has serious implications for the pattern of child-rearing practices. Personal identity focused on work might have to be re-defined though here it is quite possible that there will be a reorientation toward activities which do not deplete non-renewable resources, including organic agriculture and services. It could be argued that the structure of motivation is already changing in response to the perceived realities of life in post-industrial societies. Elements of the youth counter-culture, emphasizing natural foods, "organic" living, and a falling off of motivation for traditional work achievement might represent the wave of the future in a steady-state society which is not exclusively oriented toward economic growth, production and individual aggrandizement. Economists such as E. J. Mishan have argued that gross national product as an end in itself is extremely misleading and is not an adequate measure of human

welfare. The social costs incurred in the production of society's goods and services must also be assessed. Production of "bads" as well as "goods" results from treating values such as clean air, privacy and quiet as if they were free goods. We are now discovering that someone must pay for the "bads" and this would be taken into account in the equilibrium proposed by the steady-state theorists.

3. Even the slightest effort to visualize the character of such a society indicates that it would exacerbate the problem of individual freedom in an age of organization, and contribute to further centralization of control in both the economic and the social sphere. The apparatus necessary to guarantee population curbs and curbs on economic growth could mean the beginning of totalitarian rule in many places, or merely the realization of trends which are already under way. The steady state society might mean the creation of vast bureaucracies for the purpose of controlling individuals and abridging their freedoms, a more sophisticated form of tyranny in a technological age which has developed new forms of tyranny. Such bureaucracies as would be necessitated in the steady state society might ultimately end as self-serving and self-perpetuating bodies interested only in their own perquisites and survival. Civil libertarians might argue that the Draconian measures called for are not justified in terms of the price to be paid in the erosion of individual rights.

The concept of the steady state society has been introduced here as a *coda* to a paper on education and human resources in the effort to encourage the conference on the open society to confront the basic issues raised by a consideration of global, long-term trends. The effects of these trends are being felt even now in most of the industrialized countries and they may require drastic social, economic and political intervention within our own lifetimes. The doubling of world populations takes place in slightly more than thirty years. The depletion of non-renewable natural resources indicates that the crisis point of supply for most non-renewable resources which are crucial to industrial societies will occur within a hundred years based on current rates of consumption. The pattern of potential collapse has extremely important implications as mentioned above for the pattern of human resources as well as the question of motivation, self-conception and the idea of career open to talent. In assessing the implications of the steady-state society concept however, both the functionalist and the conflict theories discussed above will be indispensable. At the present time it is safe to say that neither of these two perspectives alone can help us to account for what we know about the structure of educational institutions and their relationship to patterns of work and occupations. It is a better strategy for the sociologist of education and work to utilize both perspectives without asserting priority for either one to the exclusion of the other. It may be that at some future time one of these two models will be demonstrated as superior in explaining the available data on education and work; that time has not yet arrived. Used together they can help provide an approach to the understanding of these phenomena which will aid in determining their role in shaping and maintaining a truly open society. Can such a society foster both equality and excellence? Can striving for competence and outstanding achievement be reconciled with a demand for social justice?

SOME VIEWS OF THE CLOSED SOCIETY

MELVIN RICHTER

In this paper, I shall argue that to no small extent, difficulties in the distinction between open and closed societies derive from unexamined assumptions about what constitutes a closed society. That concept has assimilated a family of concepts – tyranny, despotism, absolute monarchy, dictatorship, and totalitarianism – which has been far less subject to analysis and criticism than those polar concepts associated with liberty, consent, legitimacy, and obligation.[1] Concepts of total domination, as I shall refer to them, are political, deployed not only by theorists, social scientists, and philosophers, but also by statesmen and publicists. Such concepts may be applied in a partisan and polemical spirit, and directed to practical purposes: to identify, categorize, and discredit arrangements regarded by the theorists as antithetical to, or incompatible with those making for political freedom or some other good on which he places supreme value. Often the members of a state or of an alliance are mobilized against enemies by attributing to them the desire to impose total domination. Thus the Greeks stigmatized the Persians as despotic in much the same way as the Christians were to treat the Turks. What we need to know about every theory of total domination is its context. Is it framed by those claiming title to exercise total domination, or by political opponents who seek to fix upon their targets a name of sinister repute? If something is being condemned, what is being recommended?

In addition to incorporating such classifications of regimes by students and practitioners of politics, the concept of the open society derives from classifications of societies by the eighteenth and nineteenth century founders of political economy, sociology, anthropology, and conjectural history. Just as the classification of regimes is usually associated with their evalu-

[1] This point is developed and illustrated with regard to the concept of despotism in my article, "The History of the Concept of Despotism," in *Dictionary of the History of Ideas* (New York, Charles Scribner's Sons, 1973).

ation, so too social theorists have employed categories that merge description and prescription. At its inception social theory was linked to discrete stages as postulated by a philosophy of history, and by an attitude towards politics that is sometimes hostile and always deprecatory. It was by no accident that despotic rule was often associated with a low stage of development. It came to be an assumption of one kind of social theorist that among the most significant differences separating types of society is that contrast between a dynamic economic realm and a static political realm, between civil society and the state. From those founding fathers who figure in the special histories of economics, sociology, anthropology, and philosophical history to those who study modernization and development within a "neo-evolutionist" framework, a set of categories have been employed, usually if not invariably, set forth in terms of binary oppositions, or paired contrasts. What is at stake is the distinction between traditional and modern societies, in the following terms: primitive-developed, lower-higher, inferior-superior, superstitious-rational, militant-industrial, closed-open, status-contract, mechanical and organic division of labor, rules with repressive sanctions and rules with restitutive sanctions, *Gemeinschaft-Gesellschaft*.

Depending upon the position of the theorist, who could be reformist, conservative, or revolutionary, varied the characteristics, phases, value, direction, and inevitability of these alleged types of society. Such contrasts between and among types served a variety of purposes, not all of which were acknowledged any more than they were defended by intrinsic and explicit justifications. To identify the political realm with the stagnant, class-ridden, church-dominated, and mercantilist state was one means of arguing for the desirability of a relatively free market economy. To identify politics with that type of state created by the need to make war was to attack the legitimacy of the aristocracy and to assert the claims of newer classes. To identify religion with that stage of human development in which loyalty, obligation, and sacrifice could be secured only through the threat of supernatural sanctions derived from superstition rather than reason, was to attack the Church, as both its enemies and friends recognized. Depending upon whether the classifier was a conservative, revolutionary, or technocratic theorist, such classifications could be made to serve quite different purposes. Then it was the past, the future, or the necessary link between them that was the standard; and the present was that to be judged.

Such dichotomies as that between the open and closed society are best understood as variations of the schemas used by social, economic, and anthropological theorists who explicitly or implicitly depended upon conjectural history and tended to subsume politics under some other, and in their view, determining set of characteristics. Few of the themes employed by either Bergson or Popper fall outside the repertoire of the conjectural history or sociologized politics practiced by Adam Smith, John Millar, Adam Ferguson, and the other luminaries of the Scottish Enlightenment; De Bonald and De Maistre; Saint-Simon and Comte; Maine, Spencer, and the two Mills; and finally two sociologists who drew quite discrepant conclusions from very nearly the same distinctions, Tönnies and Durkheim. Although Popper does not share many, much less all, of the assumptions made by such theorists, he has chosen to use polar types based on little more than one or two of the paired opposites developed by this conjectural style. As for Bergson, he described himself as doing sociology, and his themes in *Les deux sources de la morale et de la religion* derive principally from Spencer and Durkheim. In both theorists, Bergson and Popper, the direct or residual influence of this style is most marked in their treatment of closed societies, which they place early in human history and development, although they attribute much to vestigial remains or revivals.

The term "conjectural history," coined by the Scottish writer, Dugald Stewart, is a method once much in vogue, but with rather few defenders or practitioners remaining. By comparing all known societies, and arranging them in stages, it was thought possible to reconstruct the history of our own society and that of all human societies. What is at stake is the belief that it is possible to construct "hypothetical scales of progress, at one end of which were placed forms of institutions or beliefs as they were in nineteenth century Europe and America, while at the other end were placed their antitheses. An order of stages was then worked out to show logically what might have been the history of development from one end of the scale to the other." [2] The objections to this method is that it assumes historical types, phases, or stages of civilization, rather than offering adequate evidence for their existence; it does not explain why changes occurred and in what direction; it assembles its materials and alleged evidence from a variety of societies at different points in space and time, as did Spencer, Tyler, and Frazer. The question was never put of whether a custom, institution, or practice may not mean quite different things in different contexts and structures. Often such stages or classifications represent a value-loading of a sort which puts together in an alleged set of traits all the institutions and beliefs cherished by the theorist, while its polar opposite contains all those detested by him. Nor is there any satisfactory way of

[2] E. E. Evans-Pritchard, *Social Anthropology* (London, 1951), p. 41.

resolving disagreements about how such traits are to be classified; Spencer, for example, makes military activity the distinctive characteristic of traditional society or less evolved society, but Durkheim simply does not place stress upon this point when dealing with societies organized on the principle of mechanical solidarity. Finally, it may be said by way of criticism that almost all such schemas were Europocentric and assumed that its culture and society represented the highest point of a continuing development, while even the high cultures of other continents, such as those of India and China were either of lower order or were to be regarded as fatally flawed because they were static or weaker than European societies. So-called primitive societies were all lumped together, whether it was their religions, social organization, or their alleged failure to become states of the modern European type. Political organization in general was identified with this European version of it. Subsequent investigation has demonstrated how great is the range of variations in almost every aspect of societies once considered as similar.[3]

One final point remains to be made about such theories: they have often served as a substitute for natural law arguments. That is, such a procedure derives recommendations and prescriptions from the alleged nature and succession of social and political things in a way that resembles the logic of natural law arguments, and is subject to the same criticisms. As Leon Bramson has phrased it:

> Both the sociology of conservation and the sociology of change have reference to a concept of 'natural order'... The ambiguity of the concept of natural law resulted in two persistent confusions of the idea by its exponents: they either invested the physical laws of nature with moral qualities or identified moral and ethical imperatives with the characteristics of physical laws of nature ... That is, these thinkers endowed the social hierarchy they studied with ethical qualities.[4]

Although Bramson was here referring to conservative theorists, the point that he makes is applicable to all such efforts as Bergson's and Popper's. In a recent article, John Goldthorpe has contended that our contemporary futurologists tend to repeat the errors of nineteenth century social theorists:

> ... it entails a striking failure, or deliberate restriction of the imagination. One manifestation of this is its ethnocentrism. It has often been remarked how the great social theorists of the nineteenth century tended to regard their own societies as being in the van of the historical movement which they discerned ...

[3] Georges Balandier, *Political Anthropology* (New York, 1970), p. 4. Balandier gives as the first aim of modern political anthropology: "A determination of the political that links it neither to 'historical societies alone, nor to the existence of a state apparatus."

[4] Leon Bramson, *The Political Context of Sociology* (Princeton, 1961), pp. 18-19.

> In quite similar fashion, . . . , liberal 'convergence' theorists of the present day envisage the 'pure form' of industrial society, on which the process of convergence is focussed, as in fact the ideal-type of western, democratic capitalism. The possibility of there coming into being a range of different types of advanced or post-industrial society with highly variable structural and cultural forms, is not seriously contemplated. Furthermore, there follows from this position not only a tendency to view present-day society with a blandness and optimism which, to others, is often staggering, but also the tendency previously noted to dismiss aspirations and programmes which stem from different perspectives solely on the grounds that they are incompatible with the way in which history or social evolution is destined to go.[5]

Before engaging in a brief discussion of Bergson and Popper, I should like to summarize what has been said about the notions of open and closed society. They derive from a period which derived its imperatives from alleged characteristics of the nature of things: social, historical, political. What I should hope has emerged is the necessity that proposed typologies be considered on the basis of explicit justifications for each of the details, and the internal compatibility of what is proposed for inclusion. Neither the philosophy of history nor the alleged sociological types should be accepted without close scrutiny.

In the case of Popper, it is remarkable that a philosopher of the social sciences should have been content with such a casual choice of terms. In a recent article, he wrote that "In England I found that I could at last breathe freely. It was as if the windows had been flung open. The term 'open society' derives from this experience." [6] But why should Popper have chosen the term "society" rather than "government?" As he himself states, what counts for him is not who rules, but what institutionalized arrangements govern politics.[7] He could have stated the case for those institutional arrangements in terms of their merits. But instead he chose to construct a typology based on two types of society, the open using reason; the closed based instead on superstition, magic, or taboo. In a remarkable passage, Popper stated the rationale of his two volumes, which is to show that totalitarianism is as old as our civilization. This is an indirect mode of justification and condemnation, to say the least. Its status as sociology, history, or politics is not clear:

> It attempts to show that this civilization has not yet fully recovered from the

[5] John H. Goldthorpe, "Theories of Industrial Society: Reflections on the Recrudescence of Historicism and the Future of Futurology," *European Journal of* (1972), p. 14.

[6] Karl R. Popper, "On Reason and the Open Society," *Encounter,* XXXVIII *Sociology,* XII (1971), p. 278.

[7] *Ibid.*

shock of its birth – the transition from the tribal or 'closed society,' with its submission to magical forces, to the 'open society' which sets free the critical powers of man . . . the shock of this transition is one of the factors that has made possible the rise of those reactionary movements which have tried and still try to overthrow civilization and to return to tribalism and it suggests that what we today call totalitarianism belongs to a tradition which is just as old or just as young as our civilization itself.[8]

What Popper has done is to construct a hypothetical history, and two types of society, the closed version of which he treats in the familiar style of nineteenth-century theory: civilization-tribalism, reason-magic, openness to change-resistance to change. Just as it is not necessary to condemn totalitarianism by reference to a conjectural history of the closed society, so it does not follow that all tribes display the same characteristics, or that societies which do not have a rationalist style are incapable of ruling themselves or are to be placed lower on some hypothetical scale of civilization. Can discussion based on such a theory help very much with political argument about the desirability of arrangements today or in the future?

As for Bergson's notion of the closed society, almost the first point to be established is that of the sense in which it is to be understood. Is it fair to represent Bergson as engaged in something like sociology? Or, is he to be understood as functioning in quite another mode, speculative metaphysics, philosophy of history, for example, in which case the quality of his evidence or the adequacy of his social types would not invalidate his argument, which might be defended on the basis of its internal coherence and capacity to take all of experience into account. Let me cite two documents which seem to show that Bergson thought himself to be doing sociology of a sort that took all of experience into account, and indeed that the categories he used were based upon Durkheim, especially that of the closed society. Durkheim himself had based much of his analysis upon Herbert Spencer's distinction between militant and industrial societies. In his treatment of the closed society, Bergson restored Spencer's identification of a society centered on making war and the lower or inferior state of society.

Bergson thinks that Durkheim's conception of morality is accurate with respect to the 'closed morality,' but not with respect to the 'open morality.' This opinion has only confirmed the impression I have had while reading *The Two Sources (of Morality and Religion)* that Bergson in distinguishing closed from open morality wished also to react against Durkheim and sociologism in general.[9]

[8] Karl R. Popper, *The Open Society and Its Enemies* (2 vols; 4th ed., revised; London, 1962), I, 1.

[9] I. Benrubi, *Souvenirs sur Henri Bergson* (Paris, 1942), pp. 126-127. Cited and translated by Steven Lukes, *Emile Durkheim* (London, 1973), p. 505n.

Let me now thank you especially for not having treated me as an adversary of sociology, as has been done by one or two critics . . . I believe that my book on the two sources of morality and religion is from beginning to end a sociological book [*un livre de sociologie*], and I cannot permit my work to be treated as 'scientific' when I speak of collectivities, and as 'literary' (this is to say, 'arbitrary') when I study the role of exceptional individuals [*individualités exceptionelles*]. When indeed shall we decide to take *all* experience into account? [10]

Bergson's characterization of the closed society is a repetition of the familiar distinctions, modeled once again in terms of binary oppositions. The closed society has a type of morality and religious experience peculiar to itself; it is the focus of loyalties. The closed society is like an organism or like an anthill, that is, an organization in which the individual is fixed in his function by the general structure; more specifically, he is subject to a relatively unchanging ensemble of rules or laws.[11] Such a static and monolithic form of social cohesion or solidarity is due in large part to the society's need to defend itself. It is produced through that pressure which Bergson calls moral obligation, and communicated through a religion that is static, and teaches that the members of a group owe nothing to those outside it. Within a closed society the morality that is operative must also be static, enforced by sanctions that emanate from the necessities of the common life.[12] Almost all of this is derivative from either Spencer or Durkheim.

When Bergson seeks to explain how men could develop societies larger than the small anthill-like communities natural to them, he again turned to conquest and war as the explanation. This he derived from Spencer, who saw in despotism the key to development within the militant society from its simplest to its more complex form of organization. "The militant type is one in which the army is the nation mobilized while the nation is the quiescent army, and which therefore acquires a structure common to army and nation." [13] This "social structure adapted for dealing with surrounding hostile societies is under a centralized regulating system to which all the parts are completely subject." [14] Under such a system there is a marked tendency for the military chief to become the political head as well. It is in this way, despotism is established. Its support is religion:

[10] Written to thank Celestin Bougle for his book, *Bilan de la sociologie Française*. Ms. Letter, Henri Bergson to Celestin Bougle, May 10, 1935. The reference: to Henri Bergson, *Les deux sources de la morale et de la religion* (Paris, 1932).

[11] Bergson, *Deux sources* . . ., p. 22.

[12] *Ibid.*, p. 286.

[13] Herbert Spencer, *The Principles of Sociology* (5 vols; 2d ed., London, 1877), I, Ch. X, p. 577.

[14] *Ibid.*, p. 584.

"During the militant phase of activity, the chief god is conceived as holding insubordination the greatest crime (as it is then legally considered the greatest offence), as implacable in anger, as merciless in punishment." [15]

Bergson sketches the phases of his conjectural history in a way that refers to "oriental despotism." [16] These larger societies he asserts were formed by conquests, as the result of which the victors appropriated the lands and populations of the defeated. This casually reproduced the western image of oriental despotism. Bergson then discusses two further modes of political integration and disintegration, that found in the Roman Empire, and that characteristic of feudalism. But the regime of a society that has emerged from the hands of nature is always dependent upon absolute command on one side, and absolute obedience on the other. Such a society is barbaric, remarks Bergson, invoking the Greek epithet for non-Greeks, and its form may be either monarchic or oligarchic, or both, combined.[17] In the closed society, man's original nature is adapted to that blind obedience which is necessary to meet the prerequisites of self-defence; at the same time pitiless cruelty is required on the part of chiefs.

I have reproduced Bergson's characterization of the closed society in detail, and indicated its resemblances to the portrait drawn in the grand conjectural style of Spencer. Bergson refers once to Spencer – by way of criticizing him. This is generally Durkheim's way with Spencer as well, a curious method of acknowledging intellectual debts. It would not be difficult to demonstrate how in the case of all four theorists mentioned in this section – Spencer and Durkheim, Bergson and Popper – the characteristics of the closed society correspond closely to what they dislike. As for the functions performed by the image of the closed society as the binary opposite to the open society, this can be seen by observing the one similarity and the several differences between Bergson's concept of the open and closed society and Popper's. The one similarity, as Popper observes, is Bergson's characterization of the closed society as "human nature fresh from the hands of nature." [18] But Popper goes on:

> The main difference, however, is this. My terms indicate, as it were, a *rationalist distinction*; the closed society is characterized by the belief in magical taboos, while the open society is one in which men have learned to be to some extent critical of taboos, and to base decisions on the authority of their own intelligence (after discussion). Bergson, on the other hand, has a kind of *religious distinction* in mind. This explains why he can look upon his open society as the product

[15] *Ibid.,* p. 580.
[16] Bergson, *Deux sources,* p. 294.
[17] *Ibid.,* pp. 294-295.
[18] *Ibid.,* p. 295.

of a mystical intuition, while I suggest (in chapters 10 and 24) that mysticism may be interpreted as an expression of the longing for the lost unity of the closed society, and therefore as a reaction against the rationalism of the open society.[19]

Bergson identifies the closed society with self-defence and war; Popper has little to say on this score. Bergson refuses to consider Athenian democracy as authentic, because like other ancient city-states, it was built upon slavery, and thus avoided by this fundamental iniquity the necessity to resolve other and more pressing problems. Popper, on the other hand, not only defends some wars as necessary, but provides a qualified justification of Athenian imperialism.[20]

If both are discussing types of society, what sort of method are they using? Why is it that some characteristics are included in Bergson's types, and excluded from Popper's, and vice versa? The point to observe here is that both are engaged in an exercise of the same order. As historical sociology its method cannot be justified. And in both cases it illustrates the dangers of constructing types of this sort. For two consequences, it may be argued, are apt to ensue from thinking in such terms; any time two societies are contrasted in a way that makes one superior in nearly every trait to the other, the first may be led to dominate the second on the basis of its alleged superiorities. The second potential disadvantage is that a society which has ranked and compared itself on the basis of a number of traits which are said to comprise a system or structure is apt to resist criticism by taking the attitude that it cannot deal with any one of its defective parts because it may be indispensable to the functioning of the whole. This is especially true of a society alleged to be free or open, for free societies have generally been assumed to be complex while unfree societies are assumed to be simple.

The terms "open and closed societies" share the obscurity and tendentiousness of such notions as "total" in the term totalitarianism. Such general terms are applied to politics and society despite the difficulties of finding any precise meaning for them. Indeed the fuzziness of such concepts along with their persuasive qualities, may be the secret of their attraction for theorists. For as Ernest Gellner has pointed out, the general adoption of a concept "may depend upon its lack of meaning, its possession of wholly different and incompatible meanings in different contexts,

[19] Popper, *The Open Society* . . ., I, 202.
[20] *Ibid.*, I, 181.

and on the fact that, at the same time, it . . . emits the impression of possessing a consistent meaning throughout." [21]

[21] Ernest Gellner, "Concepts and Society," in Bryan R. Wilson (ed.), *Rationality* (Oxford, 1970), p. 45.

AUTHORITARIAN REGIMES – DEVELOPING OPEN SOCIETIES?

KLAUS VON BEYME

Some of the papers in this round table foresee a decline of openness and pluralism in our society and ascribe the absence of openness and pluralism to all authoritarian societies. From a normative point of view it seems to be sufficient to take the empirical evidence of differences in pluralism between democratic Western and authoritarian societies as a justification to condemn in toto the underlying political ideologies of the less-open societies. The models of empirical research for European authoritarian systems, the most notable of which were the concepts of "totalitarianism" and "fascism," were usually rather static. Even possibly valuable ideas of authoritarian corporatism on one hand and socialist systems on the other were considered futile, since there seemed to be no chance to develop them in a ideologically closed society. Liberal conservative students in the fifties and sixties usually used the concept of totalitarianism to explain both fascist and socialist societies, whereas leftist dialectical critics usually refuted totalitarianism as a valuable concept for socialist countries except for the Stalinist period, and used the concept of Fascism for the explanation of almost every reactionary system from the first Austrian Republic to Portugal and some South American regimes. In spite of the differences, these two schools had one thing in common: they did not believe in the possibility of peaceful change in authoritarian regimes. Only in the second edition of their famous analysis of a novel form of autocracy did Brzezinski and Friedrich [1] admit that there might be a development of these autocracies by internal transformation, though they stuck to the affirmation that none of the totalitarian dictatorships disappeared unless as a result of war and foreign invasion. Leftist critics of fascist dictatorship are still more reluctant to recognize any chances for development in fascist autocracies: "A fascist system, once it is established, does not develop any

[1] C. J. Friedrich - Z. Brzezinski, *Totalitarian Dictatorship and Autocracy* (Cambridge, Mass., 1965), p. 378.

tendency for internal liberalization from within." [2] Marxists even tend to assume that there is an inherent tendency of capitalist systems in their last stage to become more and more violent, and they see the opposite of evolution, an inevitable process of decline, which continental Marxists call "Involution," derived from the Italian notion "involuzione." [3]

The author of this paper does not try to prove that there is a unilinear evolution of authoritarian regimes toward an open society, but there is certainly in the long run a development towards greater openness and pluralism in all modern autocratic systems, in fascist as well as in socialist systems. The most spectacular deviant cases from the static models for the explanation of authoritarian regimes are Spain on the one hand – the only fascist system that did not collapse by force from outside – and the CSSR on the other hand, the liberalization of which was initiated by internal forces within the Communist party and interrupted by the hegemonial power of the Communist bloc. Spain is also a deviant case in many other respects: the weaker the falangist ideology grew within the decision-making elites, the more centralized it became in other respects, such as in economic planning.

The Soviet Union and Spain are the two oldest species of socialist and fascist dictatorship which survived. By the end of the sixties both had seen the first signs of internal upheaval and are now in a stage of new repression, but nevertheless there are processes which create, with certain relapses, tendencies towards openness and pluralism. The means of social control have been liberalized and the mechanisms of steering a society have become more indirect. The reasons for this development in dictatorships were not uniform – sometimes even very different elements within the system created functional equivalents that accounted for a similar development.

MARKET VERSUS PLANNING

In socialist countries this was brought about mainly by the growing importance of market elements within the economy – especially 1) in the sectors of employment, 2) in the exchange between land and cities through the intermediary activities of the state acquisition companies and 3) the introduction of rentability analysis for the individual enterprises in the planned economy. A good deal of the discussion among Marxist econo-

[2] R. Kühnl, *Formen bürgerlicher Herrschaft. Liberalismus-Faschismus* (Reinbek bei Hamburg, 1971), p. 147.

[3] See: J. Agnoli - P. Brückner, *Die Transformation der Demokratie* (Frankfurt, 1968).

mists in socialist countries is concerned with the question of how far these elements of market economy deprave socialism into a new kind of bureaucratic state capitalism; and, paradoxically, several Western Marxists such as Dobb, Szweezy or Bettelheim are less tolerant towards the pluralistic tendencies of this new kind of socialist "mixed economy" than economists in the socialist countries such as Lange and Brus in Poland or Ota Sik in the Soviet Union (CSSR).[4]

Socialist countries have tolerated in different degrees the inclusion of market economy elements which have strengthened tendencies towards liberalism. Formerly fascist regimes which relied instead to an overwhelming degree on direct repression – which in Spain in comparison to other fascist regimes was extremely high [5] – have reluctantly accepted planning methods which were partly condemned as being socialist, and were able, in face of the advantages of a growing economy, to liberalize the political and cultural sectors of society. In both cases the process of economic development caused a differentiation in the channels of interest articulation, a development of a kind of technocratic counter-elite against the ideologically legitimated elite of the founding fathers of the regimes, and a structural differentiation of the formerly monolithic regimes. Market elements in socialist economies guarantee a certain social differentiation, and the competition of the two elements enforces the maintenance of presocialist methods to increase the economic output, such as the principle of material incentives (material 'naya zainteresovannost') and of socialist competition which is mostly a collective competition rather than an individual one, and frequently is more suppressive than the competition among workers in early capitalism. The differences of planning in the two authoritarian systems were not always flattering for the Soviet Union. The Spanish plans since 1964 were badly prepared and were conceived with the aid of insufficient statistical material and data, planning staff and control for the realization of plans, and without coordination with the budgetary policy of the country.[6] Nevertheless the fulfillment of the plans was higher than

[4] Cf.: Ch. Bettelheim, *Calcul économique et formes de propriété* (Paris, 1970); and the controversies between Huberman, Sweezy, Dobb and Bettelheim in the *Monthly Review* since 1964. O. Lange *Ekonomia poliyczna* (Warsaw, 1963), Vol. 1; W. Brus, *Ogólne problemy funkcjonowania gospodarki socjalistycznej* (Warsaw, 1961).

[5] K. von Beyme, *Vom Faschismus zur Entwicklungsdiktatur. Machtelite und Opposition in Spanien* (Munich, 1971), pp. 102 ff.; G. Jackson, *The Spanish Republic and the Civil War 1931-1939* (Princeton, 1965), pp. 533 *et seq.*

[6] A. Waterston, *Development Planning. Lessons of Experience* (Boston, 1965), p. 193; The Economic Development of Spain. Published for the International Bank for Reconstruction and Development (Baltimore, 1963), p. 70; R. Tamames *Estructura económica de Espana* (Madrid, 1969 [4]), pp. 744 *et seq.*

in the first years of planning in the Socialist countries (between 87 and 99%) and, in some sectors, spectacular overfulfillment of the plan could be claimed, especially in tourism and housing. In spite of the more or less speculative character of Spanish plans, planning prognoses had an immense importance for the development of the system toward a more open society: 1) The double opposition against planning by speculating industrialists of the former laisser-faire-Neocapitalism, who made enormous profits in a period of rapid inflation, and the rightist opposition of the Falangists were rolled back by the technocratic elite, mostly stemming from the enlightened circles of the Opus Dei organization.

2) The planning elite transformed the predominant patterns of conflict resolution. The authoritarian-bureaucratic tradition of conflict resolution of the forties and fifties was replaced by a complex system of consultation of organized interests, which created "consultative authoritarianism" for socialist countries to a much greater extent than Alfred Meyer and Peter Ludz have stated.[7] We know from a former official in the higher East German bureaucracy how the consultative process even in the Socialist system works on a pre-decisional stage of ideological policy formulation. Subsystems, interest organizations and groups try to get their postulates mentioned in the main speeches of the party leaders – especially during party meetings – and later try to derive from these claims concrete allocations of resources and manpower.[8] The planning authorities in consultative authoritarian regimes tend to become a functional equivalent for the legislatures in democracies as an addressee of lobbying and pressure.

IDEOLOGY

Whereas the older models of explanation of authoritarian regimes tended to overrate the impact of ideology, modern explanations became more Marxist in the respect that changes are mostly explained by the dynamics of economic development. Even scholars who formerly contributed strongly to the elaboration of a theory of totalitarian control, now discovered that the totalitarian elements of socialist societies have become dysfunctional. Totalitarianism involves a merger of the political and the social systems within society. In all the modern authoritarian regimes with a rapidly developing economy, the distinctiveness of the two subsystems is increasing.[9] Daniel Bell's "End of Ideology" hypothesis was developed for the West,

[7] P. Ch. Ludz, *Partei-elite im Wandel,* (Cologne Opladen, 1968), p. 324.
[8] F. Schenk, *Im Vorzimmer der Diktatur* (Cologne Berlin, 1962), p. 144.
[9] Z. Brzezinski, "Dysfunctional Totalitarianism," in, K. von Beyme (ed.), *Theory and Politics: Festschrift für C. J. Friedrich* (The Hague, 1971), p. 389.

but has been extended to the East as well during the sixties.[10] The hypothesis proved to be premature not only for the West – in an age of re-ideologization by leftist protest movements and the revival of interest in all kinds of more or less laicist religious sects – but also for the East. Deviant thinkers today are persecuted more severely than at the beginning of the sixties and there are still the four degrees of persecution of ideological dissent in socialist countries: 1) imprisonment (the case of Harich or Amalrik); 2) dismissal from office and seclusion (the case of Solzhenyzin and the Czechoslovakian intelligentsia that collaborated with Dubcek, as far as it does not live in exile); 3) thc middle range persecution of exclusion as a party member which was taken in the first stage of dissent with Havemann or Kolakowski; 4) and the everyday kind of social control by an ideological war on the nerves.[11] But especially in the peoples' democracies ideological discussion is no longer so controllable as in the Stalinist time. The more technical and scholarly the discussion grows, the greater is the impact of the "secret positivism" which has been discovered in the late work of Marx [12] and this apparently strengthens the development towards greater openness of the society. But for quite some time this development has not been more than "pragmatism" and certainly not de-ideologization, even if politicians only pay lip-service to the formula of the official dogmas in their Sunday speeches.[13] Certainly the ideological legitimation of the early elites is no longer without competition from the technical skills of the new intelligentsia – which is not counted among the creative intelligentsia (tvorcheskaya intelligentsia as the Russians call it in a touch of old-fashioned thinking in ontological terms).

Paradoxically enough, even certain elements of the socialist ideology which proclaim the future disappearance of the two spheres – since everything after the withering away of the state becomes self-regulating and autonomous society – help to enforce the differentiation of the social and political systems. The tendency toward greater openness is strengthened not only by the increasing ritualization of its ideology and the routinization of its inspirational appeal [14] but also by those elements which are still taken seriously by the Communist leadership in their periodization theory, which forces them from time to time to show that certain steps on the way to communism – such as withering away of the state and reduction of re-

[10] Cf. M. Rejai (ed.), *Decline of Ideology?* (New York, 1971).

[11] Cf. for the latter: K. Marko, *Dogmatismus und Emanzipation in der Sowjetunion* (Stuttgart, 1971), p. 16.

[12] Cf. K. v. Beyme, *Die politischen Theorien der Gegenwart* (Munich, 1974), p. 66.

[13] G. Kiss, *Marxismus als Soziologie* (Reinbek, 1971), p. 265.

[14] C. J. Friedrich, in C. F. Friedrich - M. Curtis - B. R. Barber, *Totalitarianism in Perspective* (New York, 1969), p. 154.

pression – have been taken. Much more unilinear is the impact of the "withering away of ideology" in the process of liberalization in Spain. Ideology in Spain has never played as dominant a role as in the Socialist countries or in Nazi Germany. Franco was a fascist *malgré lui,* who always tried to keep the balance between orthodox Falangists and the technocratic military and Catholic groups. Corporatism – the only element of fascist ideology which showed a way to the institutional realizations of the idea – was introduced in a more efficient way by the Ley Orgánica in 1966 only after the end of the clearly fascist period of the Spanish system, whereas in Italy only with increasing totalitarianism were the corporativist devices carried through.[15]

The weaker the ideological isolation of Spain became the more frequently institutional devices of integration were introduced, but failed to create mass loyalty or even interest among the majority of citizens. Thus the de-ideologization made the dictator – unlike the socialist dictatorship in the period where the cult of personality was unpopular in the parties – the only integrative force in the system, and Franco was even rather successful in binding the groups and partial oppositions that grew in the system by means of personal ties and gratitude. In Spain there never existed a persecution of intellectuals to the extent known in socialist countries – except for the cruelties during the Civil War. Later in the liberalization period Franco proved to be a master of using a kind of "brutal magnitude" and only reluctantly used direct physical persecution such as ousting intellectuals from their posts (with the notable exceptions of Aranguren and Tierno Galvan). Members of the oppositions were occasionally exiled, but after a while were readmitted and lived unhampered in civil life as far as they refrained from political activities. In the case of partial Christian Democratic opposition Franco even managed to conserve a certain personal respect for the dictator as can be seen by the statements among the oppositional leaders of Gil Robles, Ruiz-Giménez, Emilio Romero, José Maria de Areilza, or Ridruejo.[16] There are even quite a few elements of the despised fascist ideology in the ideas of the moderate opposition.[17] Similar experiences have been had by students of German anti-fascist oppositions [18] and even the radical and communist opposition

[15] Cf.: P. C. Mayer-Tasch, *Korporativismus und Autoritarismus* (Frankfurt, 1971), pp. 229 *et seq.*

[16] S. Paniker, *Conversaciones en Cataluna* (Barcelona, 1970 [7]), p. 305; S. Vilar, *Protagonistas de la Espana democrática. La Oposición a la dictatura 1939-1969* (Barcelona, Madrid, Paris, 1969), pp. 456, 489.

[17] Cf. v. Beyme, *op. cit.,* p. 113.

[18] See H. Mommsen, "Gesellschaftsbild und Verfassungspläne des deutschen Widerstandes." In H. Buchheim – W. Schmitthenner (eds.), *Der deutsche Wider-*

has no idea of continuous development of ideas and movements under Franco. Even the leader of the Secretariat General of the Communist Party, Santiago Carillo expounded his plans under the title "After Franco What?" [19]

Socialist Systems and the eroding fascism in Spain have at least one thing in common as far as ideology is concerned: they do not tolerate other ideologies which try to replace the hegemonial claims of the party, but they tacitly admit the existence of competing ideologies as long as they remain on the level of interest articulation in the sphere of promotional groups. The rubicon which cannot be stepped over is the attempt of ideologies to serve as a vehicle for interest aggregation or interest articulation which defies the monopoly of the party in the definition of the common good for the society.

PLURALISM OF INTEREST GROUPS AND ELITES

Within these limits the development towards greater openness is supported by a greater independence of the interest groups, which goes far beyond the only form of subsystem autonomy which Friedrich and Brzezinski admitted in the fifties: "islands of separateness." [20] Only the Yugoslavian Communists went so far as even to renounce the claim to ideological leadership,[21] but even the other socialist regimes tolerate and occasionally encourage the extension of activities for social organizations for ideological reasons.[22] Interest representation is increasing in its importance even in the Soviet Union, but it has certain traits which distinguish it from Western lobbyism.

a) Addressees of lobbyism are not so much the institutions of the state as the steering committees in the party.

b) Since state and society are much more narrowly linked than in capitalist countries, subunits of the party are to give much more consideration to the pressure groups than is the case for governmental institutions in Western democracies.

c) The ideological stage of policy formation is more interesting for

stand gegen Hitler (Cologne, 1966), pp. 73-167.

[19] S. Carillo, *Après Franco - quoi?* (Paris, 1966).

[20] Friedrich - Brzezinski, *op. cit.*, pp. 279 *et seq.*

[21] For the first time abroad very cautiously: J. Djordjevic, "Interest Groups in the Political System of Yugoslavia," In H. W. Ehrmann (ed.), *Interest Groups on Four Continents* (Pittsburgh, 1960), p. 201.

[22] Cf. A. I. Lukynaov - B. M. Lazarev, *Sovetskoe gosudarstvo i obshchestvennye organizatsii* (Moscow, 1960), p. 879; A. V. Mitskievich: *Rasshirenie roli obshchevennych organizatsii v period razvernutogo stroytel'stva kommunizma. Sovetskoe gosudarstvo i pravo* No. 9 (1969), p. 30.

socialist lobbyists than in Western countries, though even there is a certain manipulation of the public-opinion part of the lobbying process.

d) Increasing economic development leads to a differentiation of the governmental structure which entails an increasing number of consultative organizations and institutions (for instance, the technical and economic council of the Sovnarchozy under Khrushchev, the societies of inventors and rationalizers, the production conferences and so on).

e) "Shot-gun pressure" by mass petition and the use of the interventional powers of the "prokuratura" have an increasing importance for the development of openness and the protection of law.

f) Most conflicts of interest groups are solved within the political elites. Pressure comes more from within than from outside of the organization – as is the case in authoritarian organizations in the West.[23]

The erosion of fascist authoritarianism enabled a much more rapid development of pluralism in Spain. Informal groups became the functional equivalent of parties, the admission of which was discussed within the "National Movement" in the form of so-called "associations," but which exist in a more or less formalized way in the Communist factions and various other groups which collaborate within the new and more pluralist form of a "Soviet System," the "comisiones obreras." Pluralism of elites goes much further than in any socialist countries since parts of the older pillars of the regime, the left wing of the Falange, the Carlist traditionalists, parts of the Christian Democrats within the Church and other groups live in partial opposition to the regime. This leads to a regime which may be subsumed under the type of "reconciliation system" elaborated by David Apter,[24] which is pluralist and consultative but not democratic. Thus Spain went back to the mediterranean type of "syndicalist pattern of politics" which is typical for many South European states [25] and the state as a strong superstructure is no longer able to fulfill its function as a universal mediator. Violent opposition is growing much faster in Spain than in any Socialist country. But the fact that the first upheavals in Socialist countries led to changes in politics and sometimes even in government (Czechoslovakia 1968, Yugoslavia 1969/70, Poland 1970) shows that the monopoly of ideological definition of what is good for the state and the monopoly of

[23] Cf. K. von Beyme, "Gesellschaftliche Organisationen und Interessenpluralismus in der Sowjetunion." In: R. Loewenthal - B. Meissner (Eds.), *Sowjetische Innenpolitik* (Stuttgart, 1968), pp. 39-49; G. Skilling (ed.), *Interest Groups in Soviet Politics* (Princeton, 1971).

[24] D. Apter, *The Politics of Modernization* (Chicago, London, 1967), p. 397.

[25] Cf. K. Silvert, *Expectant Peoples* (New York, 1963), pp. 358 et seq.

legitimate force, which is much more rigorously claimed by socialist than by most Western capitalist states, is in a process of decline.

NEGATIVE CONVERGENCE OF HEGEMONIAL PARTY SYSTEMS?

Marxist ideology, which has been misused for some time for legitimation of a closed society, is becoming one of the strongest vehicles of pluralization. Neomarxist theories in the peoples' democracies – most highly developed in Yugoslavia and Poland – and in the Western capitalist countries contribute to fighting the "statism" of bureaucratic socialism and criticize the new class society in Monopoly Socialism.[26] The most interesting view in these debates is the hypothesis that Socialism is not only compatible with pluralism and open society, but that Socialism is even the necessary prerequisite for authentic pluralism in society since true competition among individuals and groups is impossible in a society characterized by the dominant cleavage between owners of the means of production and workers who sell their labour.[27] Modern democratic theory influenced by Marxist thought no longer believes that the question of who owns the means of production is the decisive question for an open society, since the tendencies toward state capitalism and the development of monopolies in close connection with state agencies create rather comparative conditions of economic and political concentration of power in socialist and in capitalist countries. The decisive question instead is how decisions in the subsystems and organizations are brought about and to what extent self-determination of all groups participating in the process of production and the autonomy of subsystems is realized. In this respect capitalist countries – and even some authoritarian regimes – seem to have better roots for development of an open society than bureaucratic Socialist countries with the hegemonial one-party system, which led at all stages of the development to the discrimination against new ideas – from psychoanalysis to cybernetics – as tools of the pretended "class enemy." The chance for internal democratization of mass organization and parties, which is considered since the studies of Lipset and others in "Union Democracy"

[26] Cf. S. Stojanovic, *Izmedju Ideala i Stvarnosti* (Beograd, 1969); J. Kuron - K. Modzelewski, *List otwarty do partii* (Paris, 1966), quoted from the German edition: *Monopolsozialismus* (Hamburg, 1969), pp. 79 *et seq.* General Surveys for the Impact of Neomarxist Theories: A. von Weiss, *Neomarxismus* (Freiburg, 1970); A. Langner: *Neomarxismus, Reformkommunismus und Demokratie* (Cologne, 1972).

[27] Cf. L. Lombardo-Radice, *Pluralismus in einer sozialistischen Gesellschaft* (1966) reprinted in H. Nuscheler - W. Steffani (eds.), *Pluralismus. Konzeptionen und Kontroversen* (Munich, 1972), pp. 291-301.

as a competitive organization of party wings,[28] is less likely to be used in one-party systems where no competition from outside the organization can enforce internal competition of groups. Not even the small roots for a competitive internal party structure in Soviet Russia, Khrushchev's proposal to divide the basic party units into agrarian and industrial units, were developed. Socialism today still suffers from the original sin of having destroyed the group pluralism which existed in the Soviet organization until 1917 among Bolsheviks, Mensheviks, Social Revolutionaries and Anarchists; factionalism and "krugovchina" is still the greatest "party sin" in the Soviet Union.

In this respect the people's democracies which still preserve rudimentary party pluralism and a more developed participation of mass organizations in the decision-making process have better chances to become an open society than the Soviet Union itself. Chances for an open society, even in partially competitive multi-group and party systems, depend on the extent to which opposition is recognized. In most of the modern states opposition is only partially recognized; and even Western democracies, for instance, France, West Germany and Italy, practice a policy of "defensive democracy" which controls the extremist groups and occasionally even outlaws groups and parties. The recognition of partial opposition in all socialist countries is narrowly limited and does not include the right to fundamental criticism on ideological grounds. But political scientists in Socialist countries, such as Wiatr and Przeworski in Poland, emphasize correctly, that even nonfundamental criticism has, in the long run, important impact on the decision makers who try to anticipate potential criticism,[29] though the elections still have no real competitive function but rather the character of a referendum initiated by the government and where citizens have to answer "yes" or "no," although the Polish electoral system enables the electors to express certain preferences on the party list. If Robert Dahl's basic assumption for the development of polyarchies is correct,[30] it cannot be excluded that socialist systems will also tolerate oppositions more as the expected costs of toleration decrease – since groups which are interested in a restoration of capitalism are not very likely to appear.

Similarities in the development between Socialist and Capitalist countries have frequently been stated in the form of theories of convergence. None of these theories of convergence has been made sufficiently operative and most prognoses on the basis of convergence theories are valueless, since

[28] F. Naschold, *Demokratie und Organisation* (Stuttgart, 1969), p. 38.

[29] J. J. Wiatr - A. Przeworski, "Control without opposition," in *Studies in Polish Political System* (Warsaw, 1967), p. 132.

[30] Cf. R. Dahl, *Polyarchy* (New Haven, London, 1971), p. 15.

tendencies of development are indicated without exact indication of the conditions and prerequisites, but are usually given unconditionally from Sorokin to Tinbergen. But exact functional comparisons which no longer claim to find substantial similarities in the development of the First and the Second World but only look out for functional equivalents in the development of both forms of societies, which may differ in many points, lead us to the statement of certain negative tendencies of convergence. One of these is the structural differentiation of developing systems which makes oversteering of societies and overorganization of states by a single party more and more dysfunctional. Modern dictatorships are functional equivalents to certain stages which most modern democracies have run through, i.e., bureaucratic absolutism in Europe.[31]

With progressing modernization, the autonomy of subsystems and competition within the organizations of interest articulation and aggregation develops even in formerly monolithic systems. Perhaps it is too early to speak of a Mexicanization of the Socialist Systems,[32] but there are undoubtedly similar tendencies in Socialist countries towards a system with increasing fragmentation of interests within the national party, and a weakening influence of the old "revolutionary family" towards elite competition and tolerance of small and partial oppositions as in the Mexican party system under the hegemony of the PRI.[33]

These negative tendencies towards a convergent erosion of authoritarian systems must lead us to a partial revision of the predominant ideas about the open society. The antimetaphysical and antihistorical assumptions of Karl Popper have led to a rejection of all ideologies, though even Popper in his "logic of scientific discovery" and some of his continental pupils have always admitted that ideologies have an importance not only for the formulation of hypothesis but also for action, since values are not to be "proven" scientifically but can be subject to scientific discussion.[34]

An open society does exclude the fact that the state has a monopoly of the definition of values and the interpretation of the meaning of a fictitious historical process, but does not exclude the fact that all of the participant groups are more or less motivated by ideological assumptions about the

[31] S. P. Huntington, "Social and Institutional Dynamics of One-Party Systems," in S. P. Huntington - C. H. Moore (eds.), *Authoritarian Politics in Modern Society* (New York, London, 1970), p. 12.

[32] See M. Coban, "Is Mexico the Future of East Europe?" in Huntington-Moore, *op. cit.*, pp. 452 *et seq.*

[33] R. Furtak, *Revolutionspartei und politische Stabilität in Mexico* (Hamburg, 1969), p. 59.

[34] K. R. Popper, *Logik der Forschung* (Tübingen, 1966, 2nd revised edition, p. 12); H. Albert, *Traktat über kritische Vernunft* (Tübingen, 1968), pp. 55 *et seq.*

values which should be realized in the near future. Thus even Marxist socialism is capable of an open society and the existing distortions in Socialist countries are the consequence of the premature attempt to take over the power of the state by tiny minorities without the active collaboration of the masses, and we should be careful not to restrict the principles of the "open society" to the actual forms of bourgeois pluralism which were never complete and symmetric for most of the groups. In a "post-industrial society" where the states become more and more laicist – even if certain subsystems undergo a rapid re-ideologization – the open society, even in capitalist countries, cannot but include the admission of ideological groups as long as they acknowledge the mechanisms of open intellectual conflict and try not to fall back into the substitutionalism of the older Marxist and Fascist groups which tried in the name of a historical "telos" to act as representatives of the unenlightened masses by means of force.

LIBERALISM AND THE OPEN SOCIETY

JOHN H. HALLOWELL

The word liberal defies precise definition since its usage includes a variety of meanings in a number of different contexts. The word liberal has at least three connotations: (1) personal, (2) political and (3) economic. The difficulty of precisely defining liberalism is further compounded by the fact that it has somewhat different meanings in different historical periods. Nor is there agreement among scholars as to its historical origins since its convictions derive both from ancient and modern sources. Thus one scholar describes liberalism as "the modern embodiment of all the characteristic traditions of Western politics," [1] while another would define it more narrowly as the embodiment of the political aspirations of a bourgeois middle-class society, as the political counterpart of capitalism.[2]

Frequently the word liberal is used to designate a personal attitude of mind and spirit. In this sense it is used, as Thomas M. Greene suggests, to signify "an open, receptive and generous attitude. . . . It signifies a critical rather than a subservient attitude to tradition and convention. . . . It points to the life of the spirit and its ultimate values without committing us to any dogmatic formulation of these values or to any specific means for their realization." [3] In this context the word liberal is used to describe the way in which a person holds his opinions rather than the opinions themselves. Its meaning is relative to each situation. It signifies a person who is of a sceptical frame of mind, ever ready to discard old ideas and to embrace new ones, who is inclined to view tradition as something to be overcome and transformed rather than preserved and who welcomes change both in intellectual modes and institutional forms. From this perspective, as Ramsay Muir expresses it, "Liberalism is a habit of mind, a point of view, a way of looking at things, rather than a fixed and unchanging body of

[1] Frederick Watkins, *The Political Tradition of the West* (Cambridge, Mass., 1948), p. ix.
[2] Harold J. Laski, *The Rise of European Liberalism* (London, 1936).
[3] *Liberalism: Its Theory and Practice* (Austin, Texas, 1958), p. 23.

doctrine. Like all creeds it is a spirit not a formula. It gets expression from time to time in formulae and programmes of policy, but these are always and necessarily determined by the circumstances of the time in which they are framed; they can, therefore, have no permanent validity; they need to be continually revised and recast, or they become mere shackles on the spirit which they try to express." [4] While agreeing that liberalism is an attitude of mind, William Ebenstein suggests that it does nevertheless embody certain doctrinal positions. As the reflection of the spirit of individualism in all spheres of life and thought the liberal attitude embodies: "agnosticism in religion, empiricism in philosophy, utilitarianism in ethics, laissez-faire in economics, anti-authoritarianism in politics, pacifism, anti-imperialism and free trade in international relations, equality for all regardless of sex, class, religion or race." [5]

Despite the variety of usage and its relative meanings scholars do seem to agree that the essence of liberalism is to be found in its primary attachment to the concept and practice of individual freedom. Although the word liberal is not used until the early decades of the nineteenth century (it appears to have been used first in Spain around 1811), liberalism is a product of that climate of opinion which emerged in the Western world between the fifteenth and seventeenth centuries. The Renaissance, the Protestant Reformation and the rise of modern science all contributed to the emergence of a kind of individualism which was unknown either in the Middle Ages or in ancient times.[6] While the new concept of individuality derived in part from Stoic and Christian sources it also represented a modification of Greek and Christian ideas. The respect for human personality which is embodied in the new concept of individuality derives from Christian sources but the emphasis which is placed upon the *autonomy* of individuality is something known neither in classicism nor Christianity. The assertion of individual autonomy involved the rejection of traditional sources of authority and the affirmation of the sufficiency of individual reason and conscience. This individual autonomy finds dramatic expression in Martin Luther's famous words before the Diet of Worms: *Hier steh' ich: ich kann nicht anders.* And it leads to the attempt of Descartes to found

[4] *Liberalism and Industry* (London, 1920), p. 15.

[5] *Introduction to Political Philosophy* (New York, 1952), p. 207.

[6] "The individual human being, with his interests, his enterprise, his desire for happiness and advancement, above all with his reason, which seemed the condition for a successful use of all his other faculties, appeared to be the foundation on which a stable society must be built.... Not man as a priest or soldier, as the member of a guild or an estate, but man as a bare human being, a 'masterless man,' appeared to be the solid fact." George H. Sabine, *A History of Political Theory,* (2nd ed.; New York, 1950), p. 432.

an entire philosophy upon the premise *cogito, ergo sum*. The assertion of the autonomy of individual reason culminates in the eighteenth-century Age of Enlightenment. To be enlightened means, according to Immanuel Kant, to think for one's self, "to seek the highest touchstone of truth in one's self, i.e. one's own reason." [7] According to Ernest Cassirer: "The basic idea underlying all the tendencies of enlightenment was the conviction that human understanding is capable, by its own power and without any recourse to supernatural assistance, of comprehending the system of the world and that this new way of understanding the world will lead to a new way of mastering it." [8]

This new way of understanding the world derives from modern science. The "useless" knowledge yielded by the speculative philosophy of the Middle Ages is contrasted with the "practical" knowledge yielded by the experimental physical sciences. As Descartes expressed it: "It is possible to attain knowledge which is very useful in life, and instead of that speculative philosophy which is taught in the schools, we may find a practical philosophy by means of which, knowing the force and the action of fire, water, air, the stars, heavens, and all other bodies that environ us, as distinctly as we know the different crafts of our artisans, we can in the same way employ them in all those uses to which they are adapted, and thus render ourselves the masters and possessors of nature." [9] Science, it was hoped, would unleash powers and provide the kind of knowledge that would make men the masters of their own destiny.

This climate of opinion produced a demand for individual freedom in every aspect of life: intellectual, social, political, economic and religious. Liberalism embodied these demands. It was at once a theoretical intellectual attitude and a practical expression of rebellion against specific restraints upon individual freedom. It culminated in many countries in political revolution. Specifically it was directed against the restrictions imposed by a feudalistic society. Some, but not all, liberals regarded the Church as the greatest institutional and intellectual barrier to the attainment of individual freedom and equated religion generally with obscurantism and superstition. The alliance of the Church with absolute monarchies and with the feudal hierarchy made it a prime target for those liberals who were determined to wrest political power from the formerly privileged ruling class.

[7] *Was ist Aufklärung?* 1784, Werke, ed. by E. Cassirer (Berlin, 1922), Vol. 4, p. 169.

[8] "Enlightenment," in the *Encyclopedia of the Social Sciences* (New York, 1937), Vol. 5, p. 547.

[9] *The Philosophical Works of Descartes,* transl. by Haldane and Ross (Cambridge, 1931), Part 6.

It was the rising commercial class which felt these restraints most keenly and which sought most actively to resist them. It was this class which universally led the political revolutions of the seventeenth and eighteenth centuries and transformed absolute monarchies into constitutional ones. The liberal political theory which accompanied these revolutions was at once a protest against feudal privileges and institutions and an affirmation of the rights and liberties of individuals. The political liberal of this time typically ascribed the origin of society to a social contract, insisted that government should rest upon the consent of the governed, espoused a belief in the rule of law as opposed to the arbitrary rule of persons, and described the principal function of government as one of preserving and protecting the individual's natural right to life, liberty and property. This political theory found classic expression in Great Britain in John Locke's *Two Treatises of Civil Government* (1690) and in America in the writings of Thomas Jefferson and the *Declaration of Independence* (1776). Political liberalism found practical expression in the Glorious Revolution in Great Britain in 1688, in the American Revolution of 1776 and the French Revolution of 1789. These revolutions were all accompanied by the proclamation of Bills of Rights which demanded recognition of freedom of speech and press, freedom of worship, freedom of assembly, freedom from arbitrary arrest and imprisonment, fair and speedy trials by one's peers, the protection of the rights of private property. Political liberalism found expression in the writings of Kant, Schiller, Fichte, von Humboldt and in the reforms proposed by the Prussian Baron von Stein. It found expression in Italy in the writings of Vittorio Alfieri, Pietro Verri and Giuseppe Mazzini. But liberalism as a political movement was probably most succesful in Great Britain, the United States, and France.

The Glorious Revolution of 1688 marked the beginnings of the liberal tradition in Great Britain. It ushered in the two-party system and transformed the absolute monarchy into a constitutional one. Political power passed from the crown to Parliament and until the nineteenth century was exercised by the landed gentry. With the coming of the Industrial Revolution and the emergence of vast property in forms other than land, there came into being a new social class that demanded political recognition and protection. Industrialists and businessmen began to claim the freedom necessary to follow their economic self-interest, an interest which they equated with the national interest. The Liberal Party in Great Britain came into being following the Reform Act of 1832, an act which extended the franchise to the property-owning middle classes and gave the industrial cities representation for the first time in Parliament. Bourgeois liberalism remained dominant in Great Britain throughout the greater part of the nineteenth century subordinating both the working class and the landed gentry to rule by the industrial and business class.

Unlike the British liberals, American liberals did not have to contend against an established aristocracy nor wrest political power from an entrenched ruling class. So pervasive were the liberal doctrines in America that they seemed to almost everyone to be "self-evident." There was no need for a liberal party as such since the major parties subscribed to the fundamental tenets of liberalism. Liberalism in the United States has tended to be equated with "the American way of life." [10]

Although the early liberals in all countries were distrustful of democracy and sought to restrict the exercise of political power to members of the property-owning middle class, the logic of their doctrine, especially the principle that government should rest upon the consent of the governed, could be and was used successfully against them by a working class that became more numerous, more articulate and better organized for collective action. By the end of the nineteenth century a liberal was one who advocated the universal franchise and political democracy. And the individual rights which were originally advocated to give the bourgeoisie greater freedom of action and political power were now claimed by all segments of society.

Political and economic liberalism are closely related and it is difficult in classical liberalism to distinguish between them. Yet it is important to make a distinction since many persons in the twentieth century would subscribe to many of the tenets of political liberalism while repudiating the doctrines of economic liberalism. Economic liberalism found its clearest expression in the classical school of economics which flourished throughout the greater part of the nineteenth century but it had its root in the eighteenth-century utilitarian ethics of Jeremy Bentham and the economic theory of Adam Smith. In the nineteenth century Bentham's hedonistic ethic was merged with the biological theory of evolution to produce a belief in inevitable social progress.[11] The idea of progress which was born in the eighteenth century and conceived then as being confirmed by history was transformed in the nineteenth century into a "scientific" law imbedded in the biological nature of man himself. A social Darwinism emerged which spoke of the "survival of the fittest" and of free competition as the engine of social progress.

[10] Cf. Louis Hartz, *The Liberal Tradition in America* (New York, 1955).
[11] Cf. Herbert Spencer, "Progress: Its Law and Cause," *Illustrations of Universal Progress* (New York, 1864).

Through the spontaneous action of millions of individuals following their own self-interest Smith contended in his *Wealth of Nations* (1776) that natural economic institutions are produced which are not only good but Providential. "It is not from the benevolence of the butcher, the brewer, or the baker that we expect our dinner," he wrote, "but from their regard to their own interest. We address ourselves, not to their humanity, but to their self-love, and never talk to them of our necessities, but of their advantage." [12] An innate propensity in human nature to truck, barter and exchange one thing for another leads to the division of labor. Money is invented to facilitate this exchange. Through self-interest individuals are spontaneously urged to save a part of their earnings and this leads to the accumulation of capital. The greater the capital available the greater the division of labor and the larger the stock of exchangeable commodities. A natural and spontaneous mechanism assures that there will be a balance between the quantities of goods produced and of goods effectively demanded. The public interest is best served by each individual pursuing his own self-interest. The individual, Smith explains, "neither intends to promote the public interest, nor knows how much he is promoting it. . . . He intends only his own gain, and he is in this, as in many other cases led by an invisible hand to promote an end which was not part of his intention." [13] The assumption underlying economic liberalism is the conviction that there are certain natural laws of economic production and distribution which, if not interfered with, will naturally produce wealth, reward the industrious and punish the indolent. As a consequence that government which governs least governs best. The motto of economic liberalism is *laissez-faire, laissez-passer, le monde va du lui-même.*

The most extreme distrust of government and the most extreme defense of individual liberty was expressed in the writings of the nineteenth-century English sociologist, Herbert Spencer. He firmly believed that society, if left unregulated by government, would make inevitable progress towards a state of perfect harmony, peace and plenty through the operation of immanent laws of nature which would eliminate the unfit and perpetuate those fittest to survive. Spencer was widely read in the United States and no one appreciated him more than the American sociologist, William Graham Sumner. "The social order," Sumner wrote, "is fixed by laws of nature precisely analogous to those of the physical order. The most that men can do is by ignorance and self-conceit to mar the operations of social laws." Let nature alone and eventually she will cure, through free compe-

[12] *Wealth of Nations,* Book I, Chap. IV.
[13] *Ibid.,* Book IV, Chap. II.

tition, the evils that now plague society. "Let it be understood," he continued, "that we cannot go outside of this alternative: liberty, inequality, survival of the fittest; non-liberty, equality, and the survival of the unfittest. The former carries society forward and favors all its best members; the latter carries society downwards and favors all its worst members." [14] Alfred North Whitehead has summarized the creed of economic liberalism by saying: "What the notions of 'form' and 'harmony' were to Plato, that the notions of 'individuality' and 'competition' were to the nineteenth century. God had placed his bow in the skies as a symbol; and the strip of colours, rightly read, spelt 'competition.' The prize to be competed for was 'life.' Unsuccessful competitors died; and thus, by a beautiful provision of nature, ceased from constituting a social problem." [15]

The *laissez-faire* system envisaged by its most extreme proponents did not in fact ever exist nor did the unsuccessful competitors lay down and die, at least not without protest. But the attempt to realize the ideal of the *laissez-faire* state in practice did result in widespread human misery. And the more sensitive liberals began towards the end of the nineteenth century to modify their original beliefs. John Stuart Mill, for example, argued in his later writings that a distinction should be made between the laws which govern economic production and those which govern distribution. Only the former partake of the nature of physical laws; the latter are conventional laws subject to change by human legislation. Accordingly he urged the abolition of the wage system, the adoption of a tax on land that would eliminate rent, the restriction of the rights of inheritance and the formation of associations of laborers collectively owning the capital of the enterprise and working under managers elected by themselves. In his own lifetime Mill moved from economic liberalism to a form of socialism.

Freedom of contract had been proclaimed throughout the nineteenth century to be a cardinal tenet of economic liberalism but it soon became apparent in practice that if the bargaining power of the parties to the contract were not approximately equal that freedom of contract meant no more than the freedom of the strong to impose their will upon the weak. The social consequences of a theory which insisted that the state may not legitimately act in a positive way to promote human welfare or to alleviate human suffering forced many liberals to recognize that the power of government is often necessary to provide the conditions under which individuals may freely realize their potentialities as human beings. Freedom, accordingly,

[14] "The Challenge of Facts," in *Essays of William Graham Sumner,* ed. by A. G. Keller and M. R. David (New Haven, 1934), Vol. II, pp. 87ff.

[15] *Adventures of Ideas* (New York, 1933), p. 39.

was conceived in more positive terms, less in terms of freedom from this or that restraint and more in terms of freedom of opportunity. Twentieth-century liberals, accordingly, favor an active role for the state in regulating the economy in the public interest, in providing economic security in the form of unemployment insurance, old age pensions, health insurance and other measures designed to alleviate human suffering. Those in the twentieth century who advocate the doctrines of economic liberalism are now described as reactionary or conservative. While repudiating the tenets of economic liberalism twentieth-century liberals reaffirm their belief in political liberalism (constitutional democracy, the rule of law, protection of the civil rights of individuals). They claim a kinship with classical liberals by saying that they, too, believe in individual freedom as the primary value but they recognize, as the classical liberals did not, that the state must play an active role in removing obstacles to the full enjoyment of that freedom and that it is a freedom not for the few but for all. The open society for the liberal is the free society. The question is whether freedom conceived as as end in itself can perpetuate itself, whether the philosophical basis of even a more humane liberalism is not too shallow to provide the convictions necessary to sustain what we call the free society.

It was a characteristic belief of nineteenth-century liberalism that in the absence of governmental restraint each man pursuing his own self-interest would somehow mysteriously promote the good and harmony of all. Experience has shown that instead of promoting the common good such a belief has led to the wanton destruction of natural resources, exploitation of the weak, fraud and deception. Freedom conceived simply as the opportunity to pursue one's own self-interest has proven inadequate.

The liberal conception of freedom is as old as Callicles. What people conventionally call "the good," says Callicles, is simply the gratification of desire and what men call "freedom" is the ability and opportunity to get what they want. "He who would truly live ought to allow his desires to wax to the uttermost and not to chastise them; but when they have grown to their greatest he should have the courage and intelligence to minister to them and to satisfy all their longings." It is because the many are not sufficiently courageous to attain this kind of life that "they praise temperance and justice out of their own cowardice." [16] The first law of nature is that might makes right and no man or society can stand up against it. Justice is simply the will of the stronger; law is what the stronger commands.

This view of freedom presupposes that the desire for self-satisfaction is

[16] *Gorgias,* 492.

the supreme law of all human actions, that man is responsible to no one but himself and that reason has no role to play except to minister to desire. From this point of view there is no such thing as a community or brotherhood of man. Men live naturally not in society but in a state of anarchy. In that state, as Hobbes describes it, life is "solitary, poor, nasty, brutish and short." In this condition life is a kind of warfare of man against man where force and fraud everywhere prevail. Fear of death, says Hobbes, is what drives men to enter society and form governments and the sole justification of civil society is that it makes possible physical survival. The predicament from which men require deliverance, in Hobbes' view, is the lack of any authority among men, the lack of any understanding of what constitutes the common good, the impossibility of communicating with one another. If one denies the authority of reason and of God, as Hobbes does, then the only way out of this predicament is the substitution of an artificial authority created by individual acts of will and embodied in an absolute sovereign will whose will determines what justice shall mean. This is not only Hobbes' problem but the problem posed by an extreme individualism that regards society as composed of discrete, autonomous, self-seeking individuals motivated solely by the wish to gratify their own desires. Curiously enough it is the affirmation of a kind of "freedom" that eventually calls forth despotism as the only way of preserving peace among men. Hobbes would appear to have faced the problem posed by individualism more consistently than Locke and to have foreseen the "solution" to the problem once the common conscience of the liberal evaporated under the impact of secularism and positivism.[17]

THE ACHIEVEMENTS OF LIBERALISM

As a political weapon liberalism proved to be much more effective than as a political philosophy. Locke was in search not of a universally valid political philosophy but of a justification for the "Glorious Revolution" of 1688. Consent of the governed meant for Locke consent of the landowners and merchants and individual freedom was interpreted to mean primarily the right to acquire and increase property. The dogma of natural rights that proved effective in the seventeenth century in destroying political privilege became in the nineteenth century the justification for economic privilege. The shallowness of Locke's philosophy of man and society did not at the time affect its efficacy as an ideological weapon with which to

[17] I have described this process in some detail in *The Decline of Liberalism as an Ideology* (Berkeley, 1943). Reprinted by Howard Fertig (New York, 1971).

attack absolute monarchy and to assert the right of the people to participate in government.

While most of us today recognize the shallowness of the liberal views of man and society, the superficiality of its optimism and its unwarranted belief in an impersonal mechanism that would "providentially" promote the public interest, we also recognize that its affirmation of freedom of thought and conscience and its identification of other civil liberties has done much to promote an appreciation for the inviolability of human personality. It rightly emphasized that the spirit of man grows best when it is persuaded rather than coerced. The liberals who fought for the establishment of constitutional government, for the supremacy of the rule of law binding alike upon sovereign and citizen, for the principle that the ruler is responsible to the people for the excercise of power and holds legitimate title to rule only so long as he serves their common good strengthened those institutions that serve as restraints upon would-be tyrants. But those institutions were not the sole creation of the liberal mind; they had their origins and their roots deep in the Middle Ages.[18] Although the English and American revolutions were strongly affected by the ideas of Enlightenment both countries had remnants of classical and Christian culture that opposed too consistent a reliance upon liberal ideology alone. "In this situation," Eric Voegelin has remarked, "there is a glimmer of hope, for the American and English democracies which most solidly in their institutions represent the truth of the soul are, at the same time, existentially the strongest powers. But it will require all our efforts to kindle this glimmer into a flame by repressing Gnostic corruption and restoring the forces of civilization. At present the fate is in the balance." [19]

If we now live, as some suggest we do, in a post-liberal age, the question is: how can we salvage the achievements of liberalism from the shallowness of its ideology?

Our liberal, democratic institutions are designed individually and collectively to preserve and enlarge the area of freedom within which individuals may fulfill their potentialities as human beings. But however essential to the enjoyment of this freedom these institutions are not identical with that freedom. All democratic institutions are subject to misuse and to the perversion of their inherent purpose. Free elections may be used by demagogues as well as statesmen. Popularly elected legislative assemblies may neglect their deliberative role and degenerate into playing the role of

[18] Cf. C. H. McIlwain, *Constitutionalism: Ancient and Modern* (Ithaca, N.Y., 1940).

[19] *The New Science of Politics* (Chicago, 1952), p. 189.

a broker among competing interest groups. Freedom of speech, press and assembly may be used to promote the intelligent discussion of significant issues or to pander to the lowest human passions. They may be used to deceive as well as to enlighten, to engender prejudice and inflame hatred. It is the way in which democratic institutions are conceived and used that will ultimately determine their efficacy as instruments of freedom. Government by persuasion and consent can very easily degenerate into government by manipulation. The democratic way of doing things is not self-validating nor self-perpetuating.

There is a truth in liberalism, according to V. A. Demant, which modern liberal thought has tried to preserve without its foundations:

The truth of the liberal idea is that man cannot be confined to his political relationships. He is more than a brick in the social edifice. 'The Christian revolution' in the ancient world was an affirmation of this truth based upon the positive doctrine of man as a creature of God, with his life reaching out to an eternal world, thereby affecting his life in this. . . .

Modern liberal thought tried to preserve the truth without its foundations. It affirmed the dignity of the human person, not in the name of something larger than his social relationships would warrant, but of something smaller. It claimed liberty for the individual man, not on the ground that man is a creature with one part of his being in the eternal world, but on the ground that as a political atom he has a right to exist in himself. . . . Instead of claiming liberties *for* the pursuit of positive social purposes directed by man's spiritual relationships, it encouraged demands for liberty *from* this or that encroachment. . . .

In consequence of liberalism's emancipation from the religious basis of freedom for positive ends, the modern world has earned, not a secular freedom, but a drift towards social disintegration that is sending men in self-protection into the arms of oppressive collectivisms.

Our task is therefore to recover in the conditions of the present world, that positively religious concept of human life that will alone save us from the consequences of the assumption that the State is the source of community instead of an instrument of it. . . . It has been for want of an organic relation between man's secular and spiritual life that the natural social functions of industry, commerce, education, family and regional politics have lost a sense of purpose. . . .

The 'primacy of the spiritual' must be upheld, not as a retreat from the secular tasks of life, but as a condition of handling them aright.[20]

In a similar vein Eric Voegelin declares that:

The death of the spirit is the price of progress. Nietzsche revealed this mystery of the Western apocalypse when he announced that God was dead and that He had been murdered. This Gnostic murder is constantly committed by the

[20] *Theology of Society* (London, 1947), pp. 64-66.

men who sacrifice God to civilization. The more fervently all human energies are thrown into the great enterprise of salvation through world-immanent action, the farther the human beings who engaged in this enterprise move away from the life of the spirit. And since the life of the spirit is the source of order in man and society, the very success of a Gnostic civilization is the cause of its decline.[21]

GNOSTICISM

The phenomenon which Voegelin identifies as gnosticism is to be found not in any doctrinal position but on the level of experience. In fact, on the level of doctrine we find various types of gnosticism opposing one another. Nevertheless gnostic movements do share certain common attitudes: namely, the belief that salvation from the evil of the world is possible, that the order of being will have to be changed in an historical process and that this change in the order of being lies within the realm of human action. The method of altering being is the central concern of the gnostic. In short, gnosticism is characterized by a search for a formula that somehow will guarantee salvation both for oneself and the world.[22] Gnosticism has manifested itself not only in political movements such as Marxism and National Socialism, but in intellectual systems [23] and religious movements. To the extent that liberals subscribe to the attitudes described above, liberalism is itself another form of gnosticism.

Those who encounter Voegelin's conception of gnosticism for the first time sometimes assume that the term as used by him is unique and that the phenomenon has never been noticed before. As a consequence there is a tendency to regard his analysis as eccentric. But interest in the phenomenon goes back at least to the 1930's when Hans Jonas published the first volume of *Gnosis und Spätantiker Geist* and Hans Urs von Balthasar published his study on modern gnosticism entitled *Prometheus*. Their work was followed by Henri de Lubac's *Drame de l'Humanisme Athée* (1950), Jakob Taubes' *Abendländische Eschatologie* (1947), Albert Camus' *L'Homme Revolté* (1951), and Norman Cohn's *The Pursuit of the Millennium* (1957).

Gnosticism is not a modern phenomenon alone. Its roots, according to Voegelin's analysis, are in the Revelation of St. John which predicted the coming of the millennium in which Christ would reign with his saints on this earth. St. Augustine in *Civitas Dei* dismissed literal belief in the millennium

[21] *The New Science of Politics,* p. 131.
[22] Cf. *Science, Politics and Gnosticism* (Chicago, 1968).
[23] See Eric Voegelin, "On Hegel: A Study in Sorcery," *Studium Generale,* Vol. 24 (1971), pp. 335-368.

as a ridiculous fable and declared that the realm of the thousand years was to be understood as the reign of Christ in his church in the present that would continue until the Last Judgment. The only true republic in which mutual love reigned supreme and in which there was perfect peace and justice was the *Civitas Dei*. "The one Christian society was articulated into its spiritual and temporal orders. In its temporal articulation it accepted the *conditio humana* without chiliastic fancies, while it heightened natural existence by the representation of spiritual destiny, through the church." [24] This Augustinian conception of the two cities remained effective until the end of the Middle Ages.

It was towards the end of the twelfth century that a significant break with the Augustinian conception of a Christian society occurred in the doctrines of Joachim of Flora.[25] It was Joachim of Flora who invented a philosophy of history in which he "discovered" three periods of history corresponding to the three persons of the Trinity. The Kingdom of God, which up to this time was declared "not of this world" but "within you," was transposed into a symbol that promised its fulfillment on earth in the course of time. History could now be conceived as the journey of mankind towards a perfect society in this world. In Voegelin's terms the Christian de-divinization of the world gave way to its re-divinization. This re-divinization finds expression in modern gnostic movements even when Christian symbols are no longer employed. After the eighteenth century the favorite word identified with history is "progress."

From the Joachitic immanentization a theoretical problem arises which occurs neither in classic antiquity nor in orthodox Christianity, that is, the problem of an eidos in history. In Hellenic speculation, to be sure, we also have a problem of essence in politics; the polis has an eidos both for Plato and for Aristotle. But the actualization of this essence is governed by the rhythm of growth and decay, and the rhythmical embodiment and disembodiment of essence in political reality is the mystery of existence; it is not an additional eidos. The soteriological truth of Christianity, then, breaks with the rhythm of existence; beyond temporal successes and reverses lies the supernatural destiny of man, the perfection through grace in the beyond. Man and mankind now have fulfillment, but it lies beyond nature. Again there is no eidos of history, because the eschatological supernature is not a nature in the philosophical, immanent sense. The problem of an eidos in history, hence, arises only when Christian transcendental fulfillment becomes immanentized. Such an immanentist hypostasis of the eschaton, however, is a theoretical fallacy. Things are not things, nor do

[24] *New Science of Politics,* p. 109.

[25] Voegelin is not alone in appreciating the importance of Joachim of Flora. See Herbert Grundmann, *Studien über Joachim von Flora* (Leipzig, 1927), Ernesto Buonaiuti, *Gioacchino da Fiore* (Rome, 1931), Karl Löwith, *Meaning in History* (Chicago, 1949).

they have essences by arbitrary definition. The course of history as a whole is no object of experience; history has no eidos, because the course of history extends into the unknown future. The meaning of history, thus, is an illusion and this illusionary eidos is created by treating a symbol of faith as if it were a proposition concerning an object of immanent experience.[26]

The search for meaning in history, despite the fallacy of looking for one, is motivated by men who cannot endure the uncertainty of knowing their place in history, uncertainty about the significance of their own existence. Christians who succumb to the fallacy do so, Voegelin suggests, because they can no longer endure the uncertainty that is the very essence of Christianity. For faith in the Christian sense is precisely the substance of things hoped for and the proof of things unseen.

Ontologically, the substance of things hoped for is nowhere to be found but in faith itself; and, epistemologically, there is no proof for things unseen but again this very faith. The bond is tenuous, indeed, and it may snap easily. The life of the soul in openness toward God, the waiting, the periods of aridity and dullness, guilt and despondency, contrition and repentance, forsakenness and hope against hope, the silent stirrings of love and grace, trembling on the verge of a certainty which if gained is loss – the very lightness of this fabric may prove too heavy a burden for men who lust for massively possessive experience.[27]

In more recent writings Professor Voegelin speaks of "tension" as characteristic of human existence:

Not the possession of his humanity but the concern about its full realization is the lot of man. Existence has the structure of the In-Between, of the Platonic *metaxy*, and if anything is constant in the history of mankind it is the language of tension between life and death, immortality and mortality, perfection and imperfection, time and timelessness; between order and disorder, truth and untruth, sense and senselessness of existence; between *amor Dei* and *amor sui*, *l'âme ouverte* and *l'âme close*; between the virtues of openness toward the ground of being such as faith, love, and hope and the vices of unfolding closure such as hybris and revolt; between the moods of joy and despair; and between alienation in its double meaning of alienation from the world and alienation from God. If we split these pairs of symbols, and hypostatize the poles of the tension as independent entities, we destroy the reality of existence as it has been experienced by the creators of the tensional symbolisms; we lose consciousness and intellect; we deform our humanity and reduce ourselves to a quiet despair or activist conformity to the 'age,' of drug addiction or television watching, of hedonistic stupor or murderous possession of truth, of suffering from the absurdity of existence or indulgence in any divertissement (in Pascal's sense) that promises to substitute as a 'value' for reality lost. In the language of Heraclitus and Plato: Dream life usurps the place of wake life.[28]

[26] *New Science of Politics,* pp. 119-120.
[27] *Ibid.,* p. 122.
[28] "Equivalences of Experience and Symbolization in History," unpublished ms.

Life is existence in tension. To describe this, as Dante Germino has done, as succumbing to pessimism or as an expression of "conservatism" seems to me to be beside the point.[29] Rather the question is: is the fact of this kind of tension a common human experience? Voegelin has sought to document it with considerable empirical evidence. "Can Augustine's two cities become one city?" Professor Germino asks. It is not only Voegelin who would deny the possibility but Augustine himself. To recognize the fact that "enmity, war and violence" have played a prominent part in "recorded history" is not pessimism but realism. To be sceptical of the possibility of doing something in the future which the human race has never succeeded in doing in the past is not to condone "enmity, war and violence" though it may be to acknowledge that man does not have the capacity to establish the Kingdom of God on earth. It is a dream that dies hard.

> Lenin was surely right when the end he sought for was to build his heaven on earth and write the precepts of his faith into the inner fabric of a universal humanity. He was surely right, too, when he recognized that the prelude to peace is a war, and that it is futile to suppose that the traditions of countless generations can be changed, as it were overnight.[30]
>
> The power of any supernatural religion to build that tradition has gone; the deposit of scientific inquiry since Descartes has been fatal to its authority. It is therefore difficult to see upon what basis the civilized tradition can be rebuilt save that upon which the idea of the Russian Revolution is founded. It corresponds, its supernatural basis apart, pretty exactly to the mental climate in which Christianity became the official religion of the West.[31]
>
> It is, indeed, true in a sense to argue that the Russian principle cuts deeper than the Christian since it seeks salvation for the masses by fulfillment in this life, and, thereby, orders anew the actual world we know.[32]

Russian attempts to improve upon the sorry creature of God's making by creating the new Soviet man have not been reassuring nor do they seem to have advanced mankind to a state of existence in which "enmity, war and violence" are nothing more than bad memories of a distant past. There are

[29] "Preliminary Reflections on the Open Society: Bergson, Popper, Voegelin," p. 21.

[30] Harold J. Laski, *Faith, Reason and Civilization: An Essay in Historical Analysis* (New York, 1944), p. 184.

[31] *Ibid.*, p. 51.

[32] *Ibid.*, p. 143. Voegelin is by no means alone in recognizing the phenomenon of gnosticism. See Michael Polanyi, *The Logic of Liberty* (Chicago, 1951). In part he says, "Modern totalitarianism is a consummation of the conflict between religion and scepticism. It solves the conflict by embodying our heritage of moral passions in a framework of modern materialistic purposes. The conditions for such an outcome were not present in the age of antiquity before Christianity had set alight new vast moral hopes in the heart of mankind." p. 110.

those, of course, who say the fault was Stalin's who betrayed the Revolution and they now look to Chairman Mao.

Despite the failures men still persist in pursuing the impossible dream. One of the more recent puts its faith for self-salvation not in the outworn language of the Marxist but in the language of contemporary social science.

> Physical and biological techniques have alleviated pestilence and famine and many painful, dangerous, and exhausting features of daily life, and behavioral technology can begin to alleviate other kinds of ills. In the analysis of human behavior it is just possible that we are slightly beyond Newton's position in the analysis of light, for we are beginning to make technological applications. There are wonderful possibilities – and all the more wonderful because traditional approaches have been so ineffective. It is hard to imagine a world in which people live together without quarreling, maintain themselves by producing the food, shelter, and clothing they need, enjoy themselves and contribute to the enjoyment of others in art, music, literature, and games, consume only a reasonable part of the resources of the world and add as little as possible to its pollution, bear no more children than can be raised decently, continue to explore the world around them and discover better ways of dealing with it, and come to know themselves accurately, and therefore, manage themselves effectively....
>
> Early versions of environmentalism were inadequate because they could not explain how the environment worked, and much seemed to be left for autonomous man to do. But environmental contingencies now take over functions once attributed to autonomous man. Is man then 'abolished?' Certainly not as a species or as an individual achiever. It is the autonomous inner man who is abolished, and that is a step forward....
>
> A scientific view of man offers exciting possibilities. We have not yet seen what man can make of man.[33]

Now "man," of course, is an abstraction. When Skinner suggests that we have not yet seen what "man can make of man" what he must mean is that we have not yet seen what some particular men through manipulation of the environment and armed with knowledge yielded by social science research can do to other particular individuals. Man's conquest of Nature leads many contemporary men to dream of extending that conquest to the very last frontier, to the conquest of *human* nature.

> The battle will then be won. We shall have 'taken the thread of life out of the hand of Clotho' and be henceforth free to make our species whatever we wish it to be. The battle will indeed be won. But who, precisely, will have won it?
>
> For the power of Man to make himself what he pleases, means ... the power of some men to make other men what *they* please. In all ages, no doubt, nurture and instruction have, in some sense, attempted to exercise this power. But the situation to which we must look forward will be novel in two respects. In the

[33] B. F. Skinner, *Beyond Freedom and Dignity* (New York, 1971), pp. 213-215.

first place, the power will be enormously increased... the man-moulders of the new age will be armed with the powers of an omni-competent state and an irresistible scientific technique: we shall get at last a race of conditioners who really can cut out all posterity in what shape they please. The second difference is even more important. In the older systems both the kind of man the teachers wished to produce and their motives for producing him were described by the *Tao* – a norm to which the teachers themselves were subject and from which they claimed no liberty to depart. They did not cut men to some pattern they had chosen.... This will be changed. Values are now mere natural phenomena. Judgements of value are to be produced in the pupil as part of the conditioning. Whatever *Tao* there is will be the product, not the motive, of education.... The Conditioners... are to choose what kind of artificial *Tao* they will... produce in the Human race. They are the motivators, the creator of motives. But how are they going to be motivated themselves? [34]

They are not likely to be motivated, at least for very long, by traditional conceptions of Humanity since they conceive of their task as determining henceforth precisely what Humanity shall mean. Skinner tells us that they will be motivated by a desire to preserve the species. But why should they want to preserve the species? "One of the questions before them is whether this feeling for posterity... shall be continued or not. However far they go back, or down, they can find no ground to stand on. It is not that they are bad men. They are not men at all. Stepping outside the *Tao,* they have stepped into the void. Nor are their subjects necessarily unhappy men. They are not men at all: they are artefacts. Man's final conquest has proved to be the abolition of Man." [35]

MORAL CONSENSUS AND MORAL INVERSION

What C. S. Lewis refers to for brevity's sake as the *Tao* is what others have called natural law, traditional morality or the first principles of practical reason. It has been nurtured not only by Plato and Aristotle but by the Decalogue, by the Babylonian *Hymn to Sama*, the *Analects of Confucius*, the *Bhagavad gita*. It expresses the conviction that there is a kind of conduct appropriate to man simply by virtue of his humanity. Refusal to conform to this code of conduct is to act in a way that is less than human, to deform our humanity. It presupposes that man is a member of an order created by God, that we live in a cosmos not in chaos, that we live to realize purposes inherent in our nature, a nature we did not make and cannot change. Unlike animals who respond to the order of nature by instinct men endowed with reason conform to this order only by an act of

[34] C. S. Lewis, *The Abolition of Man* (New York, 1947), pp. 37-39.
[35] *Ibid.,* pp. 40-41.

will. Men are free to acknowledge the obligations imposed upon them by the existence of this moral order or to reject them. This freedom is the source both of man's glory when used well and of his degradation when abused. When applied to political life it requires the exercise of practical reason (Aristotelian prudence) by mature men of common sense (Aristotle's *spoudaioi*). It recognizes the legitimacy of individual rights but derives these rights and understands them as expressions of obligations laid upon men as human beings. It does not speak of absolute rights but emphasizes the correlation of rights with corresponding duties.

Within such a climate of opinion the freedom championed by classical liberalism can flourish and is constructive. When the conviction in the existence of a transcendent moral order, however, disappears that freedom rapidly degenerates into a license that is appropriately described as nihilism. The intellectual climate of opinion out of which liberalism grew was not supportive of this conviction but fortunately remnants of the classical and Judaeo-Christian tradition lingered in Anglo-Saxon liberalism and liberals in England and America never consistently acted on the intellectual presuppositions of their ideology.[36] Continental liberals were more inclined to be consistent. They were not restrained by the English predisposition to follow the teachings of "common sense." John S. Mill, for example, was never a consistent utilitarian and when the principles of Benthamite utilitarianism conflicted with common sense, Mill came down on the side of common sense. His appreciation for the principles of traditional morality

[36] "American society, like the great vital societies of the past, was created and maintained by the belief in the universal validity of... objective standards.... Society had not created these standards and, hence, could not abolish them.... The standards were the human formulation of the objective nature of things.... In brief, society was believed to be embedded in, and guided by, self-evident truths, rational and moral, from which society derived whatever truth was to be found in its thought and action....

"It is emphatically not the conception that prevails in America today. In the prevailing view of social life, nothing precedes and transcends society.... A society conceived so as to find the standards for its thought and action only within itself becomes the final arbiter of all things human. The objective criteria of excellence through which civilized man has learned to distinguish a work of art from trash, craftsmanship from shoddiness, scholarship from pretentious sophistication, a good man from a scoundrel, a statesman from a demagogue, greatness from mediocrity – these vital distinctions are blurred if not obliterated by the self-sufficient preferences of the crowd... what the crowd desires and tolerates becomes the ultimate standard of what is good, true, beautiful, useful and wise. What you can get away with, then is morally permitted; what you can get accepted in the market place... becomes the test of truth; art is what people like; what can be sold is useful; and what people will vote for is sound. The honest man and the scoundrel, the scholar and the charlatan, the artist and the hack, the statesman and the demagogue live side by side, and it is not always easy to tell which is which." Hans Morgenthau, *The Purpose of American Politics* (New York, 1960), pp. 223-225.

are apparent in his writings despite his efforts to explain them in language alien to their meaning.

Under the impact of positivism, however, the moral consensus has all but disappeared and the destructive implications of the intellectual presuppositions of the liberal ideology are more apparent. The so-called Age of Reason ushered in by the Enlightenment felt impelled to challenge tradition and authority, not only the authority of Christianity but the authority of the classical tradition as well, and to proclaim the scientific method as the only authority to which men could reasonably submit. The scientific method could not, and was not designed, to arbitrate questions concerning the meaning of human existence and questions which were not susceptible to inquiry by the methods of science were thought to be either illusory or irrelevant. The more positivism has come to dominate the contemporary intellectual climate, the more readily men have abandoned the convictions that constituted the original moral consensus. But being men they have not lost their moral passions.

We are thus confronted with a curious phenomenon which Michael Polanyi has identified as "moral inversion." Moral perfectionism seems to have grown in the contemporary world in almost inverse proportion to scepticism concerning the reality of a moral order. This scepticism which is linked with perfectionism scorns the traditional morality as "banal, second-hand, hypocritical." The individual in this situation is divided against himself and

> seeks an identity safe against self-doubt. Having condemned the distinction between good and evil as dishonest, he can still find pride in the honesty of such condemnation. Since ordinary decent behaviour can never be safe against the suspicion of sheer conformity or downright hypocrisy, only an absolutely a-moral, meaningless act, can assure man of his complete authenticity. All the moral fervour which scientific scepticism has released from religious control and then rendered homeless by discrediting its ideals, returns then to imbue an a-moral authenticity with intense moral approval. Today we have a whole literature, much of it of high quality, in which absurdity, and a sombre, fantastic obscenity are presented as tokens of unflinching honesty.[37]

Moral nihilism united with moral fury, such as was exemplified by Raskolnikov, is what Polanyi means by moral inversion. In private life it leads to gratuitous crimes committed in the name of moral authenticity. In public life it leads to totalitarianism. Polanyi explains this in his analysis of Marxism:

> Marxism . . . predicted that historic necessity would destroy an antiquated form of society and replace it by a new one, in which the existing miseries

[37] "On the Modern Mind," *Encounter,* XXIV (May, 1965), p. 8.

and injustices would be eliminated. Though this prospect was put forward as a purely scientific observation, it endowed those who accepted it with a feeling of overwhelming moral superiority. They acquired a sense of righteousness, which in a paradoxical manner was fiercely intensified by the mechanical framework in which it was set. Their nihilism had prevented them from demanding justice in the name of justice, or humanity in the name of humanity. . . . But, silenced and repressed, their moral aspirations found an outlet in the scientific prediction of a perfect society. Here was set out a scientific Utopia relying for its fulfillment only on violence. Nihilists could accept, and would eagerly embrace, such a prophecy, which required from its disciples no other belief than that in the force of bodily appetites and yet at the same time satisfied their most extravagant hopes. Their sense of righteousness was thus reinforced by a calculated brutality, born of scientific self-assurance. There emerged the modern fanatic, armoured with impenetrable scepticism.[38]

More and more in contemporary society we hear it said that only violence is honest. Hannah Arendt confirms the insight of Polanyi when she says that totalitarianism is "a form of government whose essence is terror and whose principle of action is the logicality of ideological thinking."[39] In the preface which Sartre wrote to Fanon's *The Wretched of the Earth* he speaks of the "irrepressible violence" by means of which man "is recreating himself." It is, he says, only through "mad fury" that the "wretched of the earth" can "become men."[40]

Can a revulsion against the consequences of modern totalitarianism restore a set of beliefs, on the logical weakness of which the doctrines of totalitarianism itself were founded? . . . Can we face the fact that no matter how liberal a free society may be, it is also profoundly conservative?

For this is the fact. The recognition granted in a free society to the independent growth of science, art and morality, involves the dedication of society to the fostering of a specific tradition of thought, transmitted and cultivated by a particular group of authoritative specialists, perpetuating themselves by cooption. To uphold the independence of thought implemented by such a society is to subscribe to a kind of orthodoxy which, though it specifies no fixed articles of faith, is virtually unassailable within the limits imposed on the process of innovation by the cultural leadership of a free society. If this is what Lenin meant by saying that 'The absence of party spirit (partinost) in philosophy is nothing but despicable and disguised servility towards idealism and fideism,' we cannot deny the charge. . . .

Unjust privileges prevailing in a free society can be reduced only by carefully graded stages; those who would demolish them overnight would erect greater injustices in their place. An absolute moral renewal of society can be attempted

[38] *The Logic of Liberty, op. cit.*, pp. 105-106. It is impossible to do justice to the profundity of Polanyi's analysis in such a brief reference to his work. Readers are referred to his *Personal Knowledge: Towards A Post-Critical Philosophy* (Chicago, 1958), for an important attempt to overcome the contemporary epistemological crisis.

[39] *Totalitarianism* (New York, 1968), p. 474.

[40] Quoted by Hannah Arendt, *On Violence* (New York, 1969), p. 12.

only by an absolute power which must inevitably destroy the moral life of man.
This truth is unpalatable to our conscience. Does it follow that we must suppress our conscience, or else accept the totalitarian teaching that violence alone is honest? . . . The attempt made in this book to stabilize knowledge against scepticism, by including its hazardous character in the condition of knowledge, may find its equivalent, then, in an allegiance to a manifestly imperfect society, based on the acknowledgement that our duty lies in the service of ideals which we cannot possibly achieve.[41]

There is such a thing as the intemperance of moral aspiration. Recorded human history is replete with examples of armed fanatics who wanted to serve Humanity by waging war upon individual men. It is surely not an indication of lack of compassion for the suffering of our fellowmen nor indifference to injustice if we suggest that the exercise of prudence (in the Aristotelian sense) is a surer road to the improvement of our social environment than violence. It is surely realistic to accept the fact that we must deal with human beings as we find them rather than as we would like them to be. We might wish that God had created us in some better way, but to assume that some men can now do better what God "failed" to do is not only to indulge in impiety but in make-believe.

[41] *Personal Knowledge, op. cit.*, pp. 244-245.

THE LIBERAL THEORY OF THE OPEN SOCIETY

C. L. TEN

Whenever liberalism is attacked today, Mill's name will almost certainly be mentioned. Often indeed the conservative and radical critics of liberalism have seen in Mill's essay *On Liberty* [1] the embodiment of all the liberal errors and vices they wish to expose. Thus when Willmoore Kendall speaks of the fallacies of the open society, it is Mill's alleged fallacies on which he dwells.[2] Similarly, when Robert Wolff attacks the poverty of liberalism, he devotes a great deal of his time to laying bare the purported confusions, inconsistencies and gross inadequacies of Mill's essay.[3] Like Mill's critics, I too regard this essay as the most eloquent expression of the liberal theory of the open society. The foundations Mill provides for his liberal theory have some flaws, but a careful study of the essay will reveal that these are quite different from those which conservative and radical critics of his have been inclined to stress.

As Kendall sees it, the issues are as follows: "Ought there to exist in organised society – the United States, e.g. – that 'fullest liberty of professing and discussing' that Mill argues for? On what theoretical grounds can that liberty be defended? Is openness of the kind Mill's society would possess one of the characteristics of the *good* society?" [4] He rightly emphasises the fundamental importance of freedom of expression to Mill's open society. It is therefore appropriate to begin with a consideration of Mill's justification of this freedom.

Superficially Mill's arguments for freedom of expression are simple enough. He himself summarizes them as follows: "We can never be sure

[1] John Stuart Mill, "On Liberty" in Ernest Rhys (ed.), *Utilitarianism, Liberty, and Representative Government* ("Everyman's Library"; London, J. M. Dent & Sons Ltd., 1926). All subsequent references in the essay are to this edition.

[2] Willmore Kendall, "The 'Open Society' and Its Fallacies," in Peter Radcliff (ed.), *Limits of Liberty: Studies of Mill's On Liberty* (Belmont, California, Wadsworth Publishing Co., 1966).

[3] R. P. Wolff, *The Poverty of Liberalism* (Boston, Beacon Press, 1969).

[4] Kendall, *op. cit.*, p. 29.

that the opinion we are endeavouring to stifle is a false opinion; and if we were sure, stifling it would be an evil still." (p. 79) But if one examines the way in which these arguments are elaborated, one soon discovers that Mill's summary of them is in fact oversimplified. One of his central arguments is based on the notion of human fallibility. But this argument is ambiguous, and, depending on how it is interpreted, it in fact establishes two very different connections between human fallibility and the allowance of freedom of expression, and corresponding to these two connections, there are two different notions of the value of the search for truth.

Sometimes Mill points to human fallibility as a reason for not suppressing an opinion because we may be mistaken, and in suppressing a purportedly false opinion, we may in fact be suppressing what in future will be shown to be true. Thus he points to the mistakes, arising out of human fallibility, which led to the deaths of Socrates and Jesus and to the persecution of the early Christians. Those who engage in mistaken acts of suppression are often sincere men who believe in the rightness of what they are doing. Indeed in the Roman emperor Marcus Aurelius we had a man who was intellectually and morally far superior to the average person. Yet if such a man could make mistakes, how much more likely are ordinary persons to do so. Sincerity and nobleness of purpose, intellectual and moral wisdom do not rule out the fallibility which is shared by all human beings. Even when our beliefs are generally and widely accepted by the rest of our society, and indeed by the whole age, this is no guarantee that we are not mistaken. We are not justified in accepting the optimism of Dr. Johnson that persecution will not suppress the truth forever, that the truth will always survive the ordeal of persecution and has the intrinsic ability of ultimately triumphing over error. This is "idle sentimentality": "History teems with instances of truth put down by persecution." (p. 89) The absence of freedom of expression also creates an atmosphere in which men fear to pursue their opinions to unorthodox and socially unacceptable conclusions. Instead they will trim their beliefs to suit the existing orthodoxies, and in such an atmosphere of intellectual timidity and conformity, no new true beliefs will emerge to challenge prevailing views.

Let's call this the *Avoidance of Mistake Argument.* Its central claim is that human fallibility makes necessary freedom of expression if we are to avoid suppressing true beliefs. This first argument should be distinguished from what may be called the *Assumption of Infallibility Argument.*

The latter is put forward by Mill when he considers an objection to the Avoidance of Mistake Argument. According to this objection, from the fact that we may act mistakenly in suppressing a true opinion, it does not follow that we should not act at all. If we genuinely, and on good grounds, believe that an opinion is false and that its expression will have pernicious consequences, we should not be deterred from suppressing it by the mere possibility that our views may be mistaken. At this point Mill replies: "Complete liberty of contradicting and disproving our opinion is the very condition which justifies us in assuming its truth for purposes of action; and on no other terms can a being with human faculties have any rational assurance of being right." (p. 81) The reply tries to undercut the claim that we could have good grounds for believing that our opinion is true in the absence of freedom of discussion. Unlike the earlier argument for freedom of expression which stresses the dangers of making mistakes, this new argument emphasises the lack of rational assurance of fallible men in the truth of their beliefs. According to the Assumption of Infallibility Argument, the opinion we desire to suppress may very well be false, as we claim it to be, but, as fallible beings, we can have no rational assurance that it is false unless there is freedom to discuss it. In the absence of freedom of discussion we are not *entitled* to believe that it is false, even though it may in fact be false. To claim that we know it to be false is to make an implicit claim to our own infallibility. So unless there is freedom of expression fallible men can have no rational grounds for believing that their opinions are true. Mill is no longer referring to the benefits of holding true beliefs. He has now shifted his attention to the rationality of our beliefs, and freedom of expression is defended as an indispensable condition for the holding of rational beliefs.

The Assumption of Infallibility Argument is closely related to a third argument of Mill's that, even if an opinion is false, it would be wrong to stifle it. Let's call this the *Necessity of Error Argument*. It maintains that in the absence of freedom of discussion one will not appreciate the full meaning of the opinion. The true belief will be held as a "dead dogma." By this Mill means that the person who holds such a belief will not be properly influenced by it. He will not appreciate to any considerable degree what he is committed to when he accepts the opinion. At the same time his acceptance of this belief will prevent him from accepting other beliefs that appear to oppose it, but may in fact be no more than complementary to it, or perhaps a refinement of it, or even completely unrelated to it. The absence of freedom of discussion also prevents us from knowing "the grounds of the opinion." Men will hold on to a belief quite independently of the balance of arguments and evidence for and against it. Their belief will therefore be held in a rigid and dogmatic way, and they are unable to adapt it to changing circumstances. If, for example, there are strong arguments limiting the area of application of a rule, they will not appreciate them. They will apply the rule indiscriminately, overlooking what may well be proper exceptions to it. They may even insist on applying it in situations where the rule was not meant to cover. Mill goes on to say that the effort to know the grounds of an opinion cultivates the intellect and judgment. On the other hand, the absence of freedom of discussion leads to the atrophy of these faculties.

Once again it is not simply the having of true opinions that Mill values. Rather, it is the way in which the truth is held. He wants people to hold their opinions in a rational manner, with a knowledge of the significance of these opinions and the grounds for them, and with a willingness to change or modify them in the light of new arguments and evidence. Referring to those who hold a true opinion without knowing the grounds of the opinion, he says that the true opinion "abides as a prejudice, a belief independent of, and proof against, argument." (p. 96) There is therefore for Mill a distinction between *having true opinions* and what he calls "*knowing the truth*." Whereas the Avoidance of Mistake Argument stresses the value of having true opinions, both the Assumption of Infallibility and the Necessity of Error Arguments emphasise the importance of trying to know the truth.

The value of having true beliefs lies in the good consequences produced by the beliefs. True beliefs promote progress and improve the welfare of men. But a man's views about morality, politics and religion are intimately linked to his personality. The beliefs he has, and the way he holds them, help to define the sort of person he is. The mere fact that he has true beliefs is not enough. We do not think much of a person who simply holds on to true beliefs but has no clear understanding of them or of the reasons for holding them. In assessing the type of person he is, or whether his life is worthy of imitation, we will look at his personal qualities, and these include the way he holds his views about what is and what is not desirable, the influences these views have on his daily life as displayed in the manner he applies them to particular situations and the way he reacts to changing circumstances. For Mill, it really is important not only what beliefs men hold, but also what manner of men they are that hold them.

Now true beliefs may be acquired in all sorts of ways – through revelation, indoctrination, manipulation of the sources of information and the media of communication, as well as through freedom of discussion. If a person's ultimate value is that all men should have true beliefs, no matter how these beliefs are generated, then he will cherish freedom of discussion only insofar as it promotes such true beliefs. Freedom of discussion then becomes simply a means to the promotion of true beliefs, and if it is not the most efficient and economical way of attaining this goal, there appears to be no reason why other means should not be adopted. In certain actual, and in many imaginable situations, it is for example possible that the cultivation of specific true beliefs in as many people as possible is best achieved through indoctrination. In these cases one who values freedom of discussion only as a means to the establishment and propagation of true beliefs will be prepared to ditch freedom. Mill in fact believes that true opinions are most likely to emerge through freedom of discussion. But some critics of his have pointed out that if he is wrong on this, he is committed to abandon his liberal belief in freedom of discussion. Alternatively, it is maintained that it is only because Mill is sceptical about the truth of, for example, competing religious doctrines that he preaches religious toleration. All these objections overlook the importance that Mill attaches to trying to *know* the truth instead of merely having true opinions. Mill's critics tend to concentrate on his first argument for freedom of expression and to ignore his other arguments.

Consider the case of religious toleration. One argument for it is the optimistic belief that though persecution can change men's outward behaviour, it cannot affect their views about what is true or false. Thus Locke argued that "Neither the profession of any articles of faith, nor the conformity to any outward form of worship . . . can be available to the salvation of souls unless the truth of one, and the acceptableness of the other unto God, be thoroughly believed by those that so profess and practice. But penalties are no way capable to produce such belief. It is only light and evidence that can work a change in men's opinions; which light can in no manner proceed from corporal sufferings or any other outward penalties." [5] In a similar vein, Mill's disciple, John Morley, wrote: "Here is the radical fallacy of those who urge that people must use promises and threats in order to encourage opinions, thoughts, and feelings which they think good, and to prevent others which they think bad. Promises and threats can influence acts. Opinions and thoughts on morals, politics, and the rest, after they have once grown in a man's mind, can no more be influenced by promises and threats than can my knowledge that snow is white or that ice is cold. You may impose penalties on me by statute for saying that snow is white, or acting as if I thought ice cold, and the penalties may affect my conduct. They will not, because they cannot, modify my beliefs in the matter by a single iota. One result of intolerance is to make hypocrites.

[5] John Locke, *A Letter Concerning Toleration* (New York, Bobbs- Merrill, 1955), p. 19.

On this, as on the rest of the grounds which vindicate the doctrine of liberty, a man who thought himself infallible either in particular or in general, from the Pope of Rome down to the editor of the daily newspaper, might still be inclined to abstain from any form of compulsion." [6] But against this type of argument, even long before the awareness that modern techniques of propaganda and subtle manipulation of the social environment can radically change the beliefs of men, Pascal had already argued that the "sickness" of religious disbelief can be cured if a man acted as if he believed in God. In the end he can work his way into genuine belief. (Whether genuine belief generated in this way will win him a place in Heaven, as Pascal thought, is more debatable, and I am inclined to think that a good God would, when confronted with such a man in the afterlife, tell him bluntly, "Go to Hell.") I doubt that we can now be as confident as Locke was that only "light and evidence" can change men's opinions, and consequently the argument from the ineffectiveness of persecution and intolerance in changing men's beliefs rests on dubious foundations.

Hence if freedom of discussion is supported solely by Mill's Avoidance of Mistake Argument, it will cut no ice with those who believe that they have the truth from some infallible source, and who further believe that it is easier for them to share the truth with others if freedom is not accorded to opposing false beliefs. Although he tries to forge a strong link between freedom of discussion and the true beliefs which in turn lead to the progress that men value, it is clear that as far as Mill himself is concerned, the ultimate defence of freedom of discussion lies elsewhere – in his Assumption of Infallibility and Necessity of Error Arguments. Though he thinks that in the end there would be a consensus of opinion on many currently contentious matters, he believes that this state of affairs is only desirable if it resulted from freedom of discussion. He does not regard peace and tranquility, which the absence of conflicting and contentious views gives rise to, as intrinsically desirable, irrespective of how they were attained. In this he differs from so many of his critics who share the view of Fitzjames Stephen that if all men could be made, without too great cost, to have true opinions, this will be "the greatest of all intellectual blessings." [7] Whereas Stephen merely wanted men to have true beliefs, Mill wishes them to know the truth.

Mill admires rational and intellectually active men, and freedom of discussion is necessary for raising "even persons of the most ordinary

[6] John Morley, *Compromise* (London, Macmillan & Co., 1891), pp. 247-248.
[7] Fitzjames Stephen, *Liberty, Equality, Fraternity* (London, Cambridge University Press, 1967), p. 86.

intellect to something of the dignity of thinking beings." (p. 95) For him thinking beings are those who seek to know the truth, and who are not afraid of pursuing a view to whatever conclusions it leads. They do not hold a view dogmatically. They adopt a certain attitude towards evidence and arguments which commits them to accept freedom of discussion so that all those who disagree with them will be allowed to state opposing views. A free atmosphere is necessary if there are to be thinking men, and thinking men would want freedom both for themselves and for others.

It is sometimes maintained that Mill cherishes freedom of discussion only for the elite. Certainly he recognises that the intellectual powers and abilities of men differ greatly, and he believes that the intellectual elite of society has a special contribution to make. In an early essay he quotes with approval the remark, "Some are wise, and some are otherwise." [8] and in the essay *On Liberty* he sees the elite as pioneers who will break through the barriers of custom to new and better ways of life. But freedom is not for them alone, and indeed he goes so far as to say explicitly that the chief benefit of freedom of discussion lies in what it can do for average human beings: "Not that it is solely, or chiefly, to form great thinkers, that freedom of thinking is required. On the contrary, it is as much and even more to enable average human beings to attain the mental stature which they are capable of. There have been, and may again be, great individual thinkers in a general atmosphere of mental slavery. But there never has been, nor ever will be, in that atmosphere an intellectually active people." (p. 94)

Mill, then, has a number of different arguments for freedom of expression. But he believes that these arguments are connected. Rational and thinking men who seek to know the truth are more likely to arrive at true opinions than those who wish to suppress false opinions. So, though in a particular case, false opinions may prevail over true ones if freedom of discussion is permitted, in the long run many more true doctrines will be discovered in a free atmosphere which breeds thinking men than in an atmosphere where there are restrictions on freedom of expression.

Mill intends his powerful case for freedom of expression to apply to the important areas of "morals, religion, politics, social relations, and the business of life." (p. 96) However, there are flaws in the details of his arguments.

He considers an objection to his Assumption of Infallibility Argument that fallible beings cannot have a rational assurance that their opinions are true unless there is freedom of discussion. The objection tries to get round the Argument by avoiding the making of truth claims about an

[8] John Stuart Mill, "Pledges," *The Examiner* (15 July 1832), p. 449.

opinion. There are certain beliefs so useful to the well-being of society that it is the duty of government to protect these beliefs and to suppress the expression of opinions contrary to them. Such suppression would not, it is argued, be based on an assumption of infallibility since it rests on the claim that the belief is useful, and not on the claim that it is true. Mill makes two points against this objection. First, he says that the usefulness of an opinion is itself something about which men may dispute. We therefore can have no rational assurance that our view concerning the utility of an opinion is correct unless there is freedom of discussion, or unless we assume our own infallibility. Second, Mill maintains that no false belief is really useful, and so it is not possible to avoid making truth claims after all. To assess the usefulness of an opinion we have first to know whether or not the opinion is true.

Mill's first point does not in itself satisfactorily answer the objection. Consider the two statements p and q:

p = Members of race R are all incurably stupid.

q = The expression of statements about the stupidity of the members of any race will, in the present situation of racial tension and antagonism, lead to race riots.

In other words, q is a second-order statement about statements like p. Now if q is true, it provides a reason for suppressing the expression of p in certain contexts. Mill's point can be met so long as we remain free to dispute q. But q can be freely disputed even if p is suppressed. However, Mill's second point tries to rebut this. By claiming that the truth of an opinion is part of its utility, he in fact tries to undermine the two-level analysis above. Mill would say that in order to find out whether q is true, one has to know whether or not p is true. One can't have a rational assurance that q is true unless one is free to discuss the truth or falsity of p. So one has to allow freedom to discuss *both* p and q. But surely Mill goes too far now. For it is possible, and perhaps even likely, that in the sort of situation under consideration, *whether or not* p is true, dangerous consequences will result from its expression.

Mill himself recognizes the dangers of free speech in certain situations. He says that "even opinions lose their immunity when the circumstances in which they are expressed are such as to constitute their expression a positive instigation to some mischievous act." (p. 114) Thus one may prevent the opinion that corn-dealers are starvers of the poor from being delivered orally to an excited crowd assembled in front of the corn-dealer's house. But the same opinion should be permitted to be expressed in the press. Again he believes that the instigation to tyrannicide "in a specific case, may be a proper subject of punishment, but only if an overt act has followed, and at least a probable connection can be established between the act and the instigation." (p. 78)

Although Mill uses the same term "instigation," his two cases are different in some important respects. In the tyrannicide example, it would appear that the resultant harm, the killing of a particular person, must be intended by the speaker or the writer. But in the corn-dealer case, the "positive instigation" is not of this type: the speaker may neither intend nor even welcome any harm to the corn-dealer, and yet, in the given circumstances, his speech would be a causally relevant factor in bringing about the harm. He need not be urging the excited crowd to commit any "mischievous act," but nonetheless harmful acts were very likely to result. The most that one could infer from Mill's description is that the speaker was carelessly indifferent to the fate of the corn-dealer, or that he was unusually stupid in not foreseeing that harm would result from the expression of his view in the given situation.

Because the notion of "instigation" in the corn-dealer case is a causal and not an intentional concept, it appears that Mill is not confining restrictions to freedom of expression merely to contexts where someone urges others, with the probability of success, to commit specific harmful acts. But there is now a real danger that the restrictions on freedom of expression that are permitted by Mill's remarks in the corn-dealer example may be far greater than he supposes, or would be prepared to accept. As Watkins has argued, "But suppose that the publication of a certain book may reasonably be expected to lead, after a time-lag, to much more serious damage than would have been caused by the speech outside the corn-dealer's house: would not society be justified, on Mill's principles, in suppressing such a book? Or consider the series of scientific papers which made possible the construction of an atom-bomb: should not they have been suppressed?" [9]

The way out for Mill is to insist, as his corn-dealer case suggests, on the immediacy of the harm done by the expression of an opinion before that opinion can be legitimately suppressed. This rules out an appeal to harm that may arise in the long run, and thereby confines restrictions on freedom of expression to a relatively small class. But what considerations favour this proposal?

First, there are the familiar uncertainties about making long term predictions. Again, where no immediate damage is likely, we have the oppor-

[9] J. W. N. Watkins, "John Stuart Mill and the Liberty of the Individual," in D. Thomson (ed.), *Political Ideas* (London, C. A. Watts, 1966), pp. 173-174.

tunity of bringing into play the good effects that discussion generally has: dangerous opinions can be argued against and countered with other views. Even if there is every reason to believe that serious long term harm will result from the expression of an opinion, our very awareness of this, and our continued attempts to argue against the opinion or to avert the harm, may be enough. This at least would be the belief, or sometimes perhaps merely the hope, of a Millian liberal.

In certain cases his hope will indeed prove to be too optimistic. But the alternative policy of allowing the state the right to suppress free speech, whenever it can put up a reasonable case that such expression will cause long term damage to society, is highly undesirable. Even when the state allows its decisions to be openly challenged, this will not be enough to remove the grave threat to the atmosphere of free inquiry inherent in the conferring of such a right. In the nature of the case, new and bold, as well as old and unpopular, ideas are likely to look dangerous to most people, and the state will have no difficulty in putting up a reasonable case, acceptable to the majority, that serious harm will be caused by the open espousal of such ideas.

Part of the apparent reasonableness of the state's case will depend on the fact that the harmful ideas may threaten a change in the existing legal rights of persons, and thus be subversive of the current social order.

Furthermore, a man's conception of what constitutes harm tends to be partly determined by the prevailing framework of accepted ideas. And this raises a fundamental difference between, on the one hand, the claim that immediate harm will result from the expression of an opinion, and on the other hand, the claim that serious long term harm will be caused. In the short run, if free speech leads to a violation of accepted legal rights of persons, this will constitute the damage done. But the violation in the distant future of current legal rights need not be regarded as harm viewed at from the perspective of a changed legal and social order. The legal rights of persons change with time, and some of these rights may cease to exist, and hence cannot be violated. So there is a conceptual problem in predicting that certain types of damage would result in the long run from the expression of particular opinions. Consider Mill's own example of someone expressing the view that private property is theft. If this is delivered before an excited crowd which immediately proceeds to steal the goods of wealthy people, then these acts of theft would be the harm resulting from the expression of the opinion. But if, on the other hand, it is claimed that no such immediate effects are forthcoming, but that far more serious cases of theft will result in the long run from the constant utterances of this opinion, one may object that if the run is indeed a very long one, private property may by then have been abolished by constitutional changes. No "stealing" is possible without the institution of private property, and no harm of this type can be inflicted. One has, however, to be careful not to exaggerate this point. It applies to certain types of damage or harm that are closely bound up with the violation of a particular system of values embodied in a definite social or legal order. It does not equally apply to harm that consists in the violation of the physical integrity of the person, for here the concept of harm seems to be tied to something more general and fundamental than variable social orders. Unless human beings become very different from what they now are, physical assault will cause harm in any social system, and hence speech that leads men to assault other persons physically will be harmful in the same sense, whether or not the harm is caused in the immediate or in the distant future.[10]

Again, where the harmful effect follows immediately from the expression of a certain view, the expression is often so closely connected with the act as to be properly considered part of the act. Any description of what happened would be incomplete unless it incorporates the expression. This is particularly so in the case of verbal expressions urging an immediate and specific harmful act, and delivered to a live audience on a face to face basis.[11]

Finally, the further away the harmful consequences are from the time of the expression, the more likely it is that there are other intervening causal factors which contribute to the harm. The imputation of responsibility cannot then be fairly laid on the agent's expression. The intervention of other factors lets him off the hook.

Though the likelihood of immediate harm is a necessary condition of justifiable legal intervention, it is not always a sufficient condition. There are other relevant factors. It matters, for example, whether the agent was responsible for the resultant harm, or whether he was a victim of a deliberate and organized disruption of public order by an intolerant section of his audience who wished to prevent his unpopular view from being heard.[12]

[10] For an instructive discussion of the connection between the concept of harm and men's general wish to survive, see H. L. A. Hart, *The Concept of Law* (London, Oxford University Press, 1961), pp. 186-189.

[11] Cf. Thomas I. Emerson, *The System of Freedom of Expression* (New York, Vintage Books, 1970), pp. 328-336 *et passim*. This is a detailed and valuable discussion of "the legal foundations for an effective system of freedom of expression" in the United States of America.

[12] This raises "the problem of the hostile audience." For illuminating discussions, see Thomas I. Emerson, *op. cit.*, pp. 336-342, and Geoffrey Marshall, *Constitutional Theory* (Oxford, Clarendon Press, 1971), pp. 160-167.

Mill himself pays little attention to the circumstances under which freedom of expression may justifiably be restricted. The corn-dealer example is mentioned only in passing, and the incitement to tyrannicide is discussed in a footnote. He is much more concerned with putting forward the theoretical grounds for freedom of expression in general. His liberal theory is incomplete unless it is supplemented with a more detailed examination of the types of restrictions which it would allow. But such a detailed examination should follow from a clearer appreciation of the nature of the general theory. For Mill the chief justification of freedom of expression is that it enables even persons of ordinary intellect to strive to know the truth and thereby to attain "the dignity of thinking beings." This ideal of what a worthwhile human life should be is, he feels, within the reach of ordinary persons in many areas of their lives. In the chapter on "Individuality" he develops and defends the ideal which is now described as "the free development of individuality." (p. 115)

Individuality is opposed to the blind submission of oneself to the customs and traditions of one's society. Customs may have developed within too narrow a range of experience, and even within that range, what is embodied within customary practices may not be the best interpretation of that experience. Again, the knowledge and wisdom contained in the traditions of one's society may be suited to the needs of ordinary men living in ordinary situations, but not all men are so placed. A particular person may be very different from others, and he may also find himself in highly untypical circumstances. For such a person customary styles of life may have little to offer. Human beings are not machines to be built after a model. They are more like trees which grow and develop from inward forces. Just as not all plants can survive in the same physical atmosphere, so too not all human beings will grow up healthily in the same moral and social atmosphere. Some modes of life will cultivate the potentialities of some individuals, but they will at the same time crush those of others. Different persons require different conditions for their development, and there is no one pattern of life that will suit everybody. The attempt to force, by customary and other pressures, essentially different people into a uniform mould will stunt and warp them, thus preventing them from realizing their different potentialities.

But Mill's central objection to blind conformity to custom is that if a man accepts custom simply because it is custom, then he does not make a *choice*. To that extent he is less of a human person, for he has failed to develop in himself "any of the distinctive endowments of a human being." (p. 116) These distinctive human faculties of "perception, judgment, discriminative feeling, mental activity, and even moral preference, are exercised only in making a choice." (p. 116) Those who are unable, or who refuse to exercise their human capacity for choice, Mill compares with apes, with cattle, with sheep, and with steam-engines. They have lost or surrendered that which is distinctively human, that which marks them out from the rest of nature and from the artifacts of human creation which cannot have aims and purposes of their own but are designed by human beings to serve the purposes of human beings. Once one has succeeded in building a good machine for a particular purpose, one can multiply it many times, and each additional machine, so long as it is a faithful copy of the original, will be just as good as the original. But with human beings the matter is different. Even with human beings who are very similar in potentialities, and who are similarly placed, it is not the case that they would all have the same human worth if they were all forced to copy a good model of their kind. It is possible that a person "might be guided in some good path, and kept out of harm's way" without his making choices of his own. "But what will be his comparative worth as a human being? It really is of importance, not only what men do, but also what manner of men they are that do it." (p. 117) What is lost in the forced imitation by human beings of good models of conduct is the conscious choice between alternatives, and all that this involves. The act of choice brings into play various faculties. "He who chooses his plan for himself employs all his faculties. He must use observation to see, reasoning and judgment to foresee, activity to gather materials for decision, discrimination to decide, and when he has decided, firmness and self-control to hold to his deliberate decision. And these qualities he requires and exercises exactly in proportion as the part of his conduct which he determines according to his own judgment and feelings is a large one." (p. 117) Men who make choices develop what Mill called a "character": their desires and feelings are the products of their own conscious choices and are not the passively generated products of external factors.

Individuality for Mill, therefore, consists in part in the readiness to make deliberate and considered choices between alternative beliefs and patterns of life, and in part in the direction and content of such choices. The right choice for each individual depends on the sort of person he is, and hence varies from individual to individual. Each person should choose that pattern of life which develops to the fullest extent his potentialities, subject only to the condition that in so developing himself, he does not harm others, and so does not hamper their development. Mill does not go further to specify how one can discover what one's potentialities are. He believes that freedom and variety of situations are the necessary conditions for this discovery.

A common criticism of Mill's notion of individuality is that he equates mere eccentricity with individuality. This point of view is well put by R. P. Anschutz who accuses Mill of substituting "bohemian nonsense for bourgeois nonsense." [13] Mill, he says, is guilty of "the error of assuming that a man is only himself when he succeeds in being different from other men, as if individuality meant peculiarity and idiosyncracy. Hence – and this is the greatest weakness of his position – he is led to ignore the fundamental part played by tradition in providing a context for the empty form of individuality." [14] But the objection is mistaken. Mill is not opposed to tradition and custom as such. Either to reject or to accept customary practices, without first considering their claims as opposed to those of alternative patterns of behaviour, is equally to refuse to exercise choice. In fact Mill believes that there is much that men may learn from the customs of their society. To reject them out of hand is foolish, for customs embody past experience which may well be relevant to the present problems of many men. Customary practices can furnish useful guides as to how we should choose, but it is the necessity for choice from which we should not run away. If a person, in exercising choice, decides that a customary style of life is the one that most suits him, there is nothing that Mill need find objectionable. However, at the time when he wrote, he felt that the sway of custom was too great. There was a "despotism of custom," and this is manifested in two different ways in which the lives of men are affected. First, the demands of custom were *imposed* on many. Men were forced to act in the same way and to hold the same beliefs. Second, even when customary rules were not imposed, men willingly and unthinkingly accepted them. It never occurred to them that there could be alternative ways of doing things. Mill praises eccentricity in this context because it is a means of breaking through the tyranny of custom. Eccentricity provokes thought. It shows men that alternative ways of life are possible. It shakes men out of their unthinking complacency, and thereby encourages them to accept or reject custom as an act of conscious choice. His hostility toward the uniformity of human behaviour should also not be taken as an expression of his love of variety and eccentricity as such. He in fact believes that human beings are different from one another, and that if they are left alone to pursue their own plans of life, individuals would behave differently. Uni-

[13] R. P. Anschutz, *The Philosophy of J. S. Mill* (London, Oxford University Press, 1963), p. 25.
[14] *Ibid.,* p. 27.

formity of behaviour is an artificial state of affairs created by the tyranny of prevailing fashions. Uniformity of human behaviour is therefore for him a *sign* that human nature has been suppressed and forced into a narrow range of preconceived directions and patterns. Certain avenues of self-development have been blocked. So he values variety and eccentricity not in themselves but because he believes that the free development of individuality will in fact produce variety and eccentricity in human conduct, and these are welcomed as expressions of individuality.

The ideal of individuality is one that Mill thinks is within the reach of all men, and it is therefore not an elitist notion. But here, as elsewhere, he sees a special role for the elite. He believes that only a few men are capable of *initiating* new practices. The rest are, however, capable of realizing their individualities too because they can choose for themselves among a range of alternatives which they have not initiated. Like so many other political thinkers, Mill sees the prevailing state of human affairs as highly undesirable and the life of men in such a state as lacking in dignity. But, unlike many other thinkers, he does not put forward an authoritarian solution. He relies in the end on the processes of reasoning and on the therapeutic shocks to complacency which new ways of life are likely to have. To force ignorant and complacent men to realize their individuality is for him a contradiction. The element of free choice is necessary, though not sufficient. So the elite have only "the freedom to point out the way," but not the right to coerce others. "The power of compelling others into it is not only inconsistent with the freedom and development of all the rest, but corrupting to the strong man himself." (p. 124) Here he displays the characteristic liberal fear of the corrupting effects of vesting too much power in the hands of men, no matter how enlightened or morally good they may be. The elite should persuade others not to remain in their present undesirable state and should set examples of how men may "grow up to the mental, moral, and aesthetic stature of which their nature is capable." (p. 125)

The significance of Mill's notion of individuality is that he has in fact paved a middle way between the doctrines of Benthamite utilitarianism and those of later British idealist philosophers. A Benthamite utilitarian is not primarily concerned with how people come to have certain desires; he takes men's existing desires as the given data, and he concerns himself with trying to satisfy as many of these desires as possible in such a way that the greatest amount of happiness is produced. The idealist philosophers, on the other hand, are more interested in what a man ought to do than in what he currently desires to do. A man's true self is taken to be a rational self, and not the person we meet everyday. When Mill speaks of the importance of having a "character" and of cultivating desires of "home growth," or of desires that have grown out of one's free choices, he is very much concerned to provide a basis for the criticism of the existing desires of men and of the way in which they come to engage in various activities. The barriers to freedom of thought and action are not exhausted in prisons and in threats of punishment, all those things that try to prevent a person from carrying out what he wishes to do. In a closed society where the sources of information are very limited, and only prevailing views are easily accessible, men tend to come under the unquestioning sway of these views. They do not hold views different from the prevailing ones or seek to conduct themselves differently from customary practices. There is, therefore, no need for them to be restrained by threats of punishment and by prison bars. Yet such men are, as Mill would say, in a state of "mental slavery," unaware and therefore unconcerned with alternative conceptions of what is worthwhile doing or of what is true or desirable. They remain conditioned and docile creatures without any beliefs and desires which are the products of the deliberate choices they have made. They have merely passively assimilated what is in their limited social environment.

Mill's emphasis is on the cultivation of active rather than passive persons. Men are not to be viewed simply as passive instruments for the reform and reconstruction of society by a few enlightened men: "there are as many independent centres of improvement as there are individuals." (p. 128) The plea for individuality is also a plea for a society that is open to a variety of influences and ideas and that does not seek to control and manipulate knowledge, for it is only in such a society that men can discover what they really regard as valuable and important and what views and plans of life they are prepared to accept. To take the existing views and desires of men as the ultimate basis of political calculation, without regard to the way in which these views are formed, is to surrender to the tyranny of current orthodoxies. On the other hand, to disregard such views and desires completely, and to seek to impose enlightened standards on all against their clear wishes, is to practice paternalism. Mill's ideal of individuality provides an alternative to these two influential traditions of social and political thought.

Mill claims quite explicitly and clearly that individuality is both valuable "on its own account" and that it has instrumental value. (p. 115) But in what sense does he believe that individuality and freedom are valuable in themselves? Robert Wolff explains that for Mill "individual expression is *itself* a satisfying experience and hence one of the ends of life, not merely a means to some end." [15] However, on Mill's account, the notions of freedom, individuality and happiness do not appear to be contingently connected in the way that is suggested by Wolff's analysis. As we have seen, individuality *consists* in part of choosing for oneself. Hence the connection between freedom and individuality is internal. There seems to be a similar relation between individuality and some kinds of happiness. Mill is of course well known for his claim that "some *kinds* of pleasure are more desirable and more valuable than others." [16] The connection between individuality and happiness depends on the kinds of pleasure one has in mind. As far as the qualitatively lower pleasures are concerned, the connection is purely contingent. But Mill seems to envisage a more intimate connection between individuality and some kinds of qualitatively higher pleasures. Thus he urges men to cultivate "native pleasures" or the pleasures of "home growth," pleasures that result from the making of free choices between alternative patterns of life. (p. 119) These "native pleasures" cannot be attained except through the pursuit of individuality and the exercise of freedom that it involves. Indeed Mill sometimes seems to imply that these pleasures are identical with the exercise of free choice, though in general he adopts the position that free choice is a logically necessary condition for their attainment.

Those who have rejected Mill's claim that freedom and individuality are important as ends in themselves have often misunderstood the nature of the claim. They take Mill to be asserting that all freely chosen acts are good or valuable, and they have no difficulty in rebutting this. Alternatively, the claim that freedom is valuable as an end is said to have the absurd implication that there is some value in an immoral act simply in virtue of its being freely chosen.[17] But Mill is not arguing that all freely chosen acts are valuable, nor that freedom reduces the badness of an immoral act, nor yet that good consequences cannot flow from coerced and unfree acts. Mill's emphasis is on the worth of the *agent* – "his comparative worth as a human being." (p. 117) Freedom for him is a precondition of the worth of the agent. Unless a person's conduct is freely chosen, he cannot be regarded as a good or worthy person even though good results may have been achieved by the denial of his freedom.

What is the relation between the acceptance of freedom as an end in

[15] Wolff, *op. cit.*, p. 26.

[16] Mill, *Utilitarianism, op. cit.*, p. 7.

[17] J. D. Mabbott argues that Mill's treatment of liberty as valuable in itself has this implication. Mabbott's argument is quoted and critically discussed by S. I. Benn and R. S. Peters, *Social Principles and the Democratic State* (London, George Allen & Unwin, 1959), pp. 200-222, and by Basil Mitchell, *Law, Morality, and Religion in a Secular Society* (London, Oxford University Press, 1967), pp. 95-97.

the sense advocated by Mill and the belief in objective truths? This is an issue that has been excellently discussed by Basil Mitchell.[18] He distinguishes between different varieties of liberalism, and in particular between what may be called "the old liberalism," which claims that only in a free society will men be able to discover true answers to moral and other related questions, and what he calls "the new liberalism" which values freedom because it denies that there are objective truths. According to Mitchell, the new liberalism is represented by P. F. Strawson in his paper, "Social Morality and Individual Ideal," [19] where he argues for the freedom of individuals to bring into effect a variety of different and conflicting ideals of life within the framework of a common social morality. Freedom is valued not on the ground that it is the best, or perhaps even the only, means of promoting the discovery of new truths, for the new liberal does not believe that there is a truth about life, but rather freedom is valued because it promotes ethical diversity which is regarded as intrinsically good. On the other hand, according to Mitchell, Mill is an advocate of the old liberalism although "the seeds of the new liberalism" are to be found in his defence of individuality. Mill never embraces fully the new liberalism because, even when he praises individuality, he is not indifferent to the question of truth. He sees the importance of individuality in the discovery of new truths that it makes possible and in setting the example of "more enlightened conduct and better taste and sense in life." [20] With Mill as the notable exception, Mitchell argues that there is in general a tension between the belief that one already has the truth and the belief in the importance of freedom. So those who claim that there are objective truths, already known, feel constrained to deny toleration, while those who wish to vindicate freedom feel obliged to deny objectivity. However, a middle path between the old and the new liberalism is possible: there is "a liberal case which does not rest on the premise that the truth is not known or not knowable." This case rests on the belief that "a man cannot live the life of a moral and rational being unless he is able to make his own choices, so that restriction of this power by fear of punishment is in itself an evil." [21]

If my account of Mill's notion of individuality is correct, then Mitchell's middle path lies in the very heart of Mill's case for freedom. Mill, of course, also subscribes to some version of the old liberalism, as his Avoidance of Mistake Argument for freedom of expression indicates. There is

[18] *Ibid.*, chap. vi.

[19] P. F. Strawson, "Social Morality and Individual Ideal," *Philosophy; The Journal of the Royal Institute of Philosophy,* XXXVI, No. 136 (January, 1961), pp. 1-17.

[20] Mitchell, *op. cit.*, p. 92.

[21] *Ibid.*, p. 97.

no inconsistency here for Mill recognizes that freedom has instrumental value and is also to be valued as an end in itself. The old liberalism merely captured the instrumental value of freedom. On the other hand, the significance of freedom as an end is given expression in both the new liberalism and in Mitchell's middle way. In saying that Mill subscribes to the latter rather than to the former, it is still necessary to account for "the seeds of the new liberalism" to which Mitchell has alluded.

There is first no necessary incompatibility between the new liberalism and the middle path. What is distinctive of the middle path is that, unlike the new liberalism, it does not *presuppose* the absence of objective truths. But this is quite compatible with there being *in fact* no objective truths. Whereas the new liberalism collapses if there are objective truths, the middle way remains equally viable whether or not there are in fact such truths.

Mill believes that there are objective truths in many areas, and his discussion of freedom of expression makes this clear. But in the area of personal ideals concerning the sort of life a person should lead, or the sort of person he should strive to be, his view is complex, and it is here that the seeds of the new liberalism seem to be sown.

It is, however, very odd to claim in the alleged spirit of the new liberalism that there is an area of life where it is a matter of indifference to what ideals one subscribes. One may indeed, as Strawson says, experience sympathy "with a variety of conflicting ideals of life," but I doubt that he wants this to be taken as suggesting that one sympathizes with *every* ideal of life that men happen to accept or that they may be persuaded to accept. One's sympathy extends to a certain range of conflicting ideals, and within that range, no question about one ideal being truer or better arises. But there is, or should be, a limit beyond which ideals of life are rejected because they are regarded as degrading, or because they do violence to one's most general conceptions of what human life should be.

It is against this background that Mill's notion of individuality can be further elucidated. Within a certain range Mill undoubtedly accepts different ideals of life as equally valid for different men. "There is no reason that all human existence should be constructed on some one or some small number of patterns. . . . Such are the differences among human beings in their sources of pleasure, their susceptibilities of pain, and the operation on them of different physical and moral agencies, that unless there is a corresponding diversity in their modes of life, they neither obtain their fair share of happiness, nor grow up to the mental, moral, and aesthetic stature of which their nature is capable." (p. 125) This sounds like the new liberalism, but Mill's range of sympathy is not unrestricted. He still recoils, for example, from the ideal of polygamous marriages which he views with deep disapprobation and as "a retrograde step in civilisation." (p. 148) The institution of polygamy falls outside his range of what is attractive or captivating, though not of course outside his range of what should be tolerated.

More generally, it may be said that to the question, what sort of life a person should lead or what sort of person he should become, Mill does not believe that there is one objectively true answer applicable to all men. But at the same time he does not think that so long as the agent's choice is freely and deliberately made, it is to be welcomed no matter what its content may be. The free and deliberate choice of a way of life is only one component in his ideal of individuality. The other component is that the choice should be such as to develop a person's potentialities. Now no matter how different the potentialities of different persons may be, there are still some basic resemblances between them simply in virtue of the fact that they are human beings. They have "the distinctive human endowments," and it is part of every man's potentialities to develop these endowments.[22] Depending on what their other and more specific potentialities are, different men will find different plans of life most conducive to their self-development. But certain limits are set to the type of conduct which will be compatible with the ideal of individuality. For if a chosen plan of life is such as to destroy to a large extent, or to arrest the growth of these endowments, it would retard a person's potentialities, and hence run foul of Mill's second component of individuality.

Again, a person may also fail to develop fully his more specific potentialities, his special talents and abilities, because of a lack of knowledge and guidance. The traditions of one's society and the experience of others can therefore be very helpful if only they are taken account of intelligently. But changing circumstances call for adjustments in one's plan of life. What may have been an ideal form of life for a certain type of person under one set of circumstances may cease to be so when new circumstances arise. Hence, "There is always need of persons not only to discover new truths, and point out when what were once truths are true no longer, but also to commence new practices, and set the example of more enlightened conduct, and better taste and sense in human life." (p. 122) For a variety of reasons, Mill can not be indifferent to the question of truth, and must therefore subscribe to Mitchell's middle way rather than to the new liberalism.

[22] Cf. R. S. Downie and Elizabeth Telfer, *Respect for Persons* (London, George Allen & Unwin, 1969), pp. 71-76.

Nonetheless he seems to come closer to the new liberalism when he is putting the case for individuality than when he is arguing for freedom of expression, and this calls for some explanation.

In defending individuality, Mill is concerned with those personal ideals of life which, if they are carried out, do not cause harm to others, whereas in discussing the case for freedom of expression he emphasizes interpersonal questions of concern to all about what is right or wrong, true or false, good or bad in "morals, religion, politics, social relations and the business of life." Many of these latter issues are about our common social duties and responsibilities, the merits and demerits of social institutions, and the pursuit of appropriate social policies. In these areas the analogy with choosing a coat or a pair of boots (p. 125), which Mill uses in the context of personal ideals, is inapplicable. The correct answers in these areas do not vary, as they do in the case of personal ideals, with the individuals to whom we are speaking: it would be inappropriate to say here that a size of boots or a coat which fit perfectly well one person would not fit another.

Mill believes that freedom and variety of situations are indispensable conditions for the flowering of individuality. Freedom is necessary because individuality consists in part of choosing for oneself. Variety of situations is necessary because the genuineness of one's choice is to a great extent dependent on the range of alternatives one can visualize. Though it is of course possible for a man who has not been presented with alternative modes of thinking to conceive such modes and to reject them critically in favour of the way of life prevailing in his society, this possibility is considerably reduced for most men if they do not have the opportunity of knowing about different "experiments in living," or of listening to and reading about views which propose such alternatives. Variety of situations enlarges the range of alternatives available for choice and also puts alternatives more vividly before us.

Mill's notion of individuality does not, however, exhaust the goals of political action. The good life involves more than the realisation of each person's individuality. As the title of the chapter on "Individuality" indicates, individuality is "one of the elements of well-being." This perhaps puts it too modestly, for Mill certainly regards individuality as the *central* element of the good life. But the point remains: there are other goals to be pursued as well. The ideal of individuality guides the manner in which these other goals are to be fulfilled. The framework of the political life is set by this ideal, and the pursuit of other goals is to be carried out within this framework. Mill's liberalism does not seek to provide solutions to every contemporary political problem. But individuality furnishes a positive guide to political action in two ways. At a rather general level, it sets limits to what may be done in the attainment of other positive goals. It is not an ideal that is to be put aside and forgotten while we get down to the business of seeking other things. Secondly, it itself makes more specific claims by insisting that opportunities for its realization should be provided. The protection and improvement of the institutions which allow and encourage free discussion where they already exist, and the building up of these institutions where they do not yet exist, constitute a permanent part of the aims of political action.

IMPERFECT LEGITIMACY *

GEORGE KATEB

1. In the last few years there have been a number of serious assaults on the political institutions of the United States. The very idea of the open society – as Karl Popper has made it famous – has been put in jeopardy. Among the assaults, there was, first, the wide receptivity to quasi-Marxist and neo-Marxist critiques of democratic government in an advanced capitalist society. Marxism had never died; but what was new in America was the readiness of large numbers of people to pay attention to those who espoused it in some form or other, and then perhaps to borrow a few elements from it or use it as a kind of general sanction for feeling that something was very wrong with America. There was, second, the willingness to look upon democratic law as something a good deal less than sacred: the politics of civil disobedience, non-compliance, active confrontation, exemplary violence against property, massive coercive non-violence, and other forms of illegal and irregular political activity was practiced. It may be that even more important than the practice of this politics was the large amount of first-rate writing that the practice called forth, writing aimed at the philosophical defense of the practice. Such writing was another intellectual tendency, besides Marxism, which worked in the direction of questioning the conventional understanding of the nature and status of the institutional life of the open society.

There was, third, the seeming erosion of the value of individuality. New forms of human association, new ways of breaking isolation, new conceptions of players and audiences, new exultation in mutual dependence, a revived recklessness concerning possessions and boundaries, a disregard for names, titles and roles, a joy in confusion and unnameable experience, a thirst for communities that were intense and evanescent – all these and other related expressions signalled at least a temporary alteration in the

* I wrote this paper on a sabbatical leave made possible by a grant from the Guggenheim Foundation for the academic year 1971-72. I wish to express my appreciation to the Foundation.

middle-class ethic, the ethic supposedly of the open society. Fourth, there was the regular assertion of executive power (often with legislative approval or acquiescence, less often with judicial) at the expense of the rule of law, the guarantees of the Bill of Rights, the independence of the judiciary, and the separation of state and society. Thus the spirit of limited government, another aspect of the open society, grew fainter.

It is undeniable that the story of recent times cannot now be told. So many events were elusive or inconclusive. Things changed so fast and then changed again that it is too easy to feel that there was no change at all. The power or will of the actors and movers to speak their minds with a scholarly thoroughness or even with plain honesty was only fitful: the worst offenders were the liars and deceivers in government. We are still dazed by what we witnessed, so that the job of analysis is almost as imperfect as the job of interpretation. But it seems that the open society endured a tough siege; and it may be that – it is likely that – it is in for worse.

At the same time, there have been tendencies working to strengthen the spirit and practices of the open society. In some respects, government in America is more of an open government than it was, say, twenty years ago. The Warren Court made immense contributions to square American reality with American professions. Various movements for greater rights, or for participation, constituted a revivification of the open society. Indeed, often on closer examination, the best types of an open society, types that only an open society nurtures or nurtures best, were leading the assault on the open society. That is to say, some of the attack was not attack at all: it was deliberate and exaggerated defense: shock therapy. The Marxism was sometimes a clumsy disguise for populism; illegal politics was often the only appropriate answer to government lawlessness; the new communitarianism sometimes appeared as simply the necessary next step for a more subtle individuality. So, the story of the open society in these few years is desperately ambiguous. The effort to foretell the next moment is hazardous.

Still, we can see clearly enough to say that the open society in America has been in crisis. Whatever the outcome in daily and institutional life may turn out to be, a challenge – though often inchoate – has been thrown down to the theory of the open society. More narrowly, a challenge has been thrown down to the legitimacy of the democratic state. In executive prerogative, on the one hand, and in Marxism, irregular politics, and communalism, on the other hand, we find assumptions and feelings surely not compatible with an untroubled belief in the legitimacy of established democratic states. There are, of course, other sources of trouble than the ones just named. It is now commonplace to say that there has been, and continues to be a crisis of authority, a crisis of *legitimacy*. I think the commonplace has enough truth in it to warrant our paying some attention to it.

2. When we say that a state is legitimate, let us mean that it deserves the obedience and support of a good person. The state *deserves* such obedience, and support, *is worthy of* such obedience and support, when it meets certain criteria to the satisfaction of a good person. One must specify these criteria. I say *obedience and support* to indicate that a putatively legitimate state deserves not mere acquiescence: it certainly deserves better than indifference: it deserves an active engagement of the affections. By a *good person* I mean, quite simply, one who cares for those around him, whether he can see them or not; one who takes into account the well-being of others, as well as his own, when he acts in the world. This is not general self-sacrifice, though it may sometimes come to that. Rather, the good person does not obey and support the state *only* because it preserves him in his proper claims, but also because it preserves others in theirs. Furthermore, if he decides to withdraw inwardly, or to disobey, or to resist, or to emigrate, he wants to do so not only because his proper claims are denied, but also because others' proper claims are being denied. (Even when he wants to go against the state, he may still rightly decide not to do so, nor to encourage others to do so. That it is better, from the point of view of others, to keep the peace, may be enough reason, in many situations, to keep the peace. By definition, only legitimate states *deserve* obedience and support; but there may be a moral duty to obey and support an illegitimate one: out of concern for, say, the safety of others.)

The criteria of legitimacy, in the opinion of a good person, would pertain to the tendency of the state to preserve people in their proper claims. What are these claims? Without going deeply into the matter, we can say intuitively that they are claims to certain kinds of *relations* between persons and the state, and to certain kinds of *treatment* received by people from the state. The state is legitimate if and only if these kinds of relations and treatment exist. The concept of consent covers the relations. The concept of justice covers the treatments. The state is legitimate if and only if it rests on consent and promotes justice. It promotes justice because it rests on consent. What I am doing is reaching the conclusions of the contractarian tradition on legitimacy, but by way of the mind of the good person rather than the enlightened self-interest of everyman. I also assume that consent and justice are intrinsic to the idea of the open society.

Leaving the world in which the contractarian tradition began, we ask: What would consent be in the modern world? It would be principled acceptance of basic political institutions, of a Constitution (with a capital C). This kind of consent is, except for a founding generation, largely after-the-fact – even if we take notice of change or amendment of the Constitution. The test is: Would a good person choose freely what he has inherited? If he had a chance, would he re-create what has already been created? It is a matter of more or less, not of an exact "fit" between what he accepts and what he would help to call into being.

What would a good person give his principled acceptance to? It would be a Constitution, a system of political institutions, a form of government which did its work with the consent of the governed. Here we must distinguish between the *fundamental* consent accorded the Constitution and the *continuous* consent given to the men who hold offices specified by the Constitution and to the laws and policies they make and carry out. For the second kind, continuous consent, to exist, there must be a system of elective and representative government. The good person would consent to only that Constitution which gave form to continuous consent.

What would justice be? What kinds of treatment are due people? What have they the right to except? What rights have they, which the state must guarantee? Within its jurisdiction, the state promotes justice by adhering to the essential features of the American Bill of Rights (provided the Warren Court's principles of interpretation are followed); by preventing or abolishing poverty and other politically corrigible degradations; by striving to narrow inequalities of power and fulfillment; and by working to satisfy other human rights which the sense of the community may, as time goes on, deem implied in or contiguous with justice.* The state must also recognize that it owes certain kinds of treatment to people outside its jurisdiction: its foreign policy must also be just, though with a justice necessarily less strict and altogether less formal and rule-governed. Here, justice is obviously not guaranteeing certain rights or trying to prevent or correct all major ills: that is beyond the power as it is beyond the obligation of a single state. Rather, the state's justice in its dealings with foreign peoples consists primarily in remembering their humanity, and avoiding therefore, the transgressions and enormities which the Nuremberg law names. Domestic justice is a matter both of action and forbearance; international justice is a matter mostly of forbearance. I think it right to say that, at the present time, there is a growing understanding that a state's legitimacy depends, in part, on the nature of its foreign policy: on the degree of justice it shows. A good person cares for everyone, not only his

* I acknowledge that the ability to give or withhold consent of either kind can be described as a right required by justice, and that justice may be the inclusive term.

fellow citizens; though he may properly care a little more for his fellow citizens.

3. It is transparent that by the criteria we have cursorily discussed, the legitimacy of the democratic state in America is imperfect. The legitimacy of the political institutions, laws, and policies in the greatest open society is imperfect. This is not to say that the democratic state in American lacks legitimacy *tout court*, or is illegitimate. I think that legitimacy exists in degrees. There are, however, minimal requirements that have to be met if a state is to have any legitimacy at all. The requirements cannot be quantified. But one can say that if a good person would never have freely chosen a given Constitution because it did not institutionalize continuous consent; and if therefore there were no continous consent; and if the idea of a right is absent from the minds of those who govern, then there is no legitimacy. For there to be even a minimal legitimacy, the criteria of consent and justice must be met to a certain degree. The degree varies with time, with changes in the attainments and expectations of people, with their demands and passions. In any case, just as it is transparent that legitimacy in America is imperfect, so it is also transparent that the charge of illegitimacy is false. Certainly that charge is false if it is made by reference to any other open society. If the democratic state in America is illegitimate, then all other such states must be. The argument applies *a fortiori* to all closed societies. It is only by reference to some higher potentiality that such a charge could be sustained.

The important point is that the legitimacy of the democratic state in America is imperfect. Consent and justice are imperfectly realized. That is no revelation, to be sure. Then, too, we should never expect perfection on earth. It may also be quite appalling to be faced with a state so fully legitimate that it left no room for double-mindedness or alienation, for criticism and complaint. Saying all this, however, does not suffice to calm the discussion, or to avoid an inference. The inference is that there ought to be a crisis of legitimacy in America and other open societies. The distance from full consent and justice is great enough to justify militance and irregularity, though (I would say) not so great as to justify revolutionary violence. One must add that militance and irregularity are justified if they are carried out in the name of a more perfect legitimacy: in the name of greater consent or greater justice or both. Obviously (as we have already said) some of the militance and irregularity meet that test. The aim has sometimes been the improvement of the democratic state in America and elsewhere. Just as its rigidity made irregularity necessary, so its imperfection made irregularity justifiable. To the degree that legitimacy is imperfect, by that amount is the burden of apology lessened on those who use illegal but non-violent methods, provided the reason for such methods is to secure greater legitimacy.

4. So far all I have done is to rehearse platitudes. The plain fact is, however, that this rehearsal, or some other presentation of an argument similar to mine, would not necessarily strike everyone as platitudinous. Some would be shocked by the notion of imperfect legitimacy. Or if they nodded their assent to it, they would perhaps still insist that the inference I have drawn from it – on militance and irregularity – is invalid. The question is, How has it come about, as I think it has, that there has been so much amazement and chagrin at the assault on the political (and other) institutions of the open society? I mean especially among political scientists and other students of society. There is oddness here. For, what has American political science been teaching for the past thirty or forty years, if not the lesson of imperfect legitimacy? You need only the standard supplied by the *common* understanding of legitimacy – consent as the instrument and justice as the consecration of enlightened self-interest – to draw the lesson. Consent and justice were present only intermittently, or only on some matters, or only for some people. The labor of post-war political science is radically deflationary. Its gravamen has been that American democracy (and *mutatis mutandis* other democracies) is not really a democracy but a "polyarchy," or is a democracy but not in all the ways people think, or is a democracy in spite of itself, or some other equally radical assertion.

American political science should have been the ideal preparation for a compassionate understanding of some of the extraordinary political tendencies of recent times. Much of their justification can be found, before the fact, in that political science. The puzzle is that the connection has not been made. Why have many of those who contributed to political science, or read it had been influenced by it, not seen that if what they wrote and read were true or approximately true, then the system was already in crisis. It would only be a matter of time before the undemocratic reality was challenged, that it had a day of reckoning in store for it. Or, if there were nothing inevitable about the crisis, then should a crisis occur political science had already shown that it would be fitting if one did.

Or have I misstated the case? Perhaps I have; perhaps there really is nothing odd about the fact that those who knew what political science was teaching still felt amazement and chagrin at the recent assault – even at those aspects of it powered by a desire for greater legitimacy. The key consideration may be that a deflationary attitude towards consent and justice was present or implied in much of the deflationary political science. Not only was the reality not what conventional expectations held out for it; there was something wrong about conventional expectations. This same deflationary attitude was also present among a number of influential political theorists whose work encouraged or vindicated political scientists, or prepared the way for them among interested audiences. The deflationary attitude – fed from a number of sources – is suitably called, I think, proceduralism. This is the attitude which helped ward off sympathy to the political and cultural efforts that were made as if in response to the findings of political scientists. Thanks to proceduralism, these political scientists were horrified not by their findings but by the struggles of those who knew from their lives the reality of the findings, but were intent, nevertheless, on changing that reality. Proceduralism did not inhibit *them*.

5. What is proceduralism? It is a moral attitude which holds that the procedures (the means and methods) of democratic political life * embody or express moral values. These means and methods are to be esteemed not only because they are instrumentally indispensable. After all, means could be esteemed for their indispensability and still be considered morally indifferent or neutral. But democratic means would be esteemed morally even if they were not indispensable, and men could live anarchically without political means and methods. There are possible varieties of this attitude. An adherent could say that the moral values in procedures are at least as important – they count as much – as the moral ends or purposes which the procedures serve. Or that they are more important. Or, the procedures are morally prior to ends or purposes: only those which the procedures permit to emerge are worthwhile; in Camus' phrase, the means justify the ends. Or, most strongly, the procedures alone matter: the means *are* the ends: only procedural values should be taken into account when a moral estimation is made of a political system: ends are too problematic to discuss. My belief is that any version of the proceduralist attitude works to take the sting out of the findings of post-war political science.

I wish to add that by proceduralism I do not mean the view that regularity is the supreme value; and that, therefore, any procedure is better than no procedure at all; or that strict compliance with a bad procedure is better than loose compliance with a good one; or that it is better that harm be done according to a procedure than that good be done on impulse. Proceduralism is a doctrine of the inherent value of certain specific procedures.

* The attitude can perhaps be extended to non-democratic political life, though with a much diminished intensity. It can also be extended to many areas of social life which are not strictly political.

The original locus of proceduralism is, of course, due process of law. In America, the prestige and prominence of the law and lawyers, and the practice of politics through litigation in the form of judicial review, have combined to help make legal procedure a political model. Proponents have sought to make proceduralism an entire moral attitude about political life in a democracy. My aim is not to belittle the doctrine, but rather to indicate that its unqualified extension is unacceptable; and how it does harm by clouding perception of the imperfect quality of present-day democratic legitimacy.

6. The end or purpose of a legal system is justice: to render correct verdicts or judgments. It is best to distinguish between legal justice and justice *simpliciter*: the latter includes the former, but it also includes many other kinds of treatment which government owes to people. So I shall say, for the purposes of my argument, that the end or purpose of a legal system is legal justice (clumsy as that sounds). A proceduralist would say that certainly the legal system must do legal justice, but that it must do justice in accordance with certain forms or means or methods. The general name of these methods is due process of law, some of which are specified in the Constitution of the United States, especially in the Fourth, Fifth, and Sixth Amendments. The belief is that these methods will, in most cases, yield legal justice. In discussion of legal systems, I assume that no proceduralist would go so far as to say that the end of legal justice is morally inferior to the values contained in legal methods, or that the methods render the end morally negligible. Instead, the proceduralist would say that despite occasional errors of legal justice, despite even the possibility that some other kind of legal system would make fewer errors or do its work more quickly or cheaply, American due process of law is still morally preferable and should therefore be retained.

The basis for this position is that due process of law has a high moral value, that there are a number of moral values embodied in it. From the proceduralist point of view, it is seen primarily as a system of inhibitions on government in its treatment of suspects, accused persons, and criminals. It is besides a system in which there is a principled avoidance of the molestation of the innocent, no matter what benefits would accrue therefrom. The constraints include the prohibition against self-incrimination; the right to be judged by one's peers, the concept of judge as umpire rather than interrogator; the concept of inadmissible evidence; and many other practices and explicit or implicit principles.

When these inhibitions are accepted, when these forms are followed, what moral values are thereby present? Most importantly, government is expressing respect for the person. It goes beyond legal justice to the larger concept of justice. When, for example, it enforces to the full the prohibition against self-incrimination, it expresses that respect to the point of delicacy. It is *unclean* to implicate a person in injury to himself; it is *mean-spirited* or *unfair* to want to triumph over a person largely through his own coerced acts rather than through the deployment of some superiority of one's own. Hobbes would have said that by nature no person can ever be obliged to renounce any part of the right to self-preservation. To put it yet another way, to force a person to hurt himself is to invade the very integrity of his being. Most simply, it is to treat him unjustly: justice belongs to procedure as much as to verdict.

Thus, if we took only one of the practices incorporated in due process of law, we see that it is involved in deep moral significance. We approach that significance when we acknowledge, first of all, that it is possible for so seemingly a narrow and instrumental thing as a legal practice to embody one or several moral values. Then we spell out its moral significance by reference to principles that lie at hand and that have traditionally been discussed in American and British political and legal thought. Then we may look at the practice this way and that; we interpret it. Through interpretation we coax further moral significance out of it. We hope to give it alternative (thought not far-fetched) descriptions. At the same time, we can see that when government treats people in accordance with such a form it is teaching its people certain general (though perhaps amorphous) moral lessons with applications in all sorts of social relations. Or, it could be said that government solidifies and strengthens pre-existing moral sentiments in the community when it treats people in certain legal ways rather in others. I believe that other elements of due process of law would lend themselves to a full proceduralist mode of perception. Taking due process as a whole, we could say that some of the values embodied in it caused men to fight for it and install it; some values were discovered or recognized in it as time went on; some values one finds only when challenged to offer a defense; some values are so weighty that one would be almost unhappy to see the need for a system of justice disappear (in some Utopia): the embodied values would disappear with the need. We thus assimilate (legal) procedures to institutional life in general. It is hardly surprising that ends are almost lost sight of, when methods are so rich in meaning, so suggestive of influence and connections beyond themselves.

Political procedures, means, and methods are also rich, and will give much to an interpreter who adopts the proceduralist mode of perception. It would be hard to imagine a rationale of the open society which did not seize upon the moral values embodied in such democratic methods as competitive elections and majority rule. My complaint is that some advocates of proceduralism go to the length of denying that anything matters in democratic politics except democratic methods. While no proceduralist would say that it is immaterial whether or not due process of law regularly leads to a legally just outcome, there have been some proceduralists who maintain that the end results of democratic politics are out of the reckoning because the moral significance is in the methods. As long as elections are free and contested, and laws come from the will of the majority of those elected, democratic morality is served. To use a word they rarely use, legitimacy is present.

But how much legitimacy is established by free and contested elections and majority rule? It is not possible to answer that question in the abstract, as proceduralists are wont to do. Only if certain background conditions are met, could we say that these democratic methods would go a long way towards solving the problem of legitimacy. By "background conditions" I do not mean criteria as formal as universal adult suffrage and complete freedom to publish all views on issues and candidates. These are major historical achievements: but our discussion must take them for granted.

The background conditions I refer to must be such as to make consent genuine and (social) justice likely. The proceduralist mode of perception (and defense) is much more adequate when the system within its purview can be counted on to get its job done. If it gets its job done, more or less, or most of the time, then the observer can point to the qualities of the method and find cause for praise in them. In the case of due process of law, as we have said, proceduralists expect that legal justice will be forthcoming. The background conditions are such that the system of rules, principles, conventions, and mannerisms moves in the direction of legal justice. Among the conditions are: acceptance, even admiration, of the system by the professional participants; high competence and knowledge; their dependable rationality; some consonance with the moral sentiments of the community; some deep and thorough similarity to the general canons and methods of truthful inquiry; enough wealth to float the system in its immense complexity; and so on. When these conditions are met, the system of due process of law – the moral heart of the legal system in America and Britain – will achieve the great moral end of legal justice in ways which are themselves morally superb. Proceduralists may not talk too much about the background conditions of due process of law. But then the need is much less: legal justice is done: the system *works* as it is supposed to work. If, in case after case, things went wrong, observers would start studying the background conditions to see if that is where the trouble comes from.

It seems, however, that in regard to the political system, proceduralists have been so enchanted by the methods that they have not thought it necessary or appropriate to examine the purposes or ends which the system promotes, deliberately, unconsciously, or accidentally; and the background conditions which account for the tendency of the methods to promote those ends. Certainly no system can be devoid of roots or results in fact. A political system is crucially implicated in determining the shape of reality, whether it is energetic or timid, capable or stupid; as it is determined crucially by forces external to it. Its essence is power in its many forms. It uses and is used. What is so enchanting about democratic method that political scientists can treat democratic politics as a self-enclosed activity, a kind of art-form or intricate exercise about which it would be crude to ask: What does it grow out of? What does it lead to? Particularly: Does it earn legitimacy? Does it grow out of consent? Does it lead to justice? What is its persistent tendency?

Let us try to give the proceduralist position its due; let us try to account for the enchantment. There is no great strain in speaking of the values embodied in the procedures, means, and methods of democratic politics. Writers like Walter Lippmann, Ernest Barker, T. V. Smith and Eduard C. Lindeman, S. I. Benn and R. S. Peters, Henry Mayo, Henry Kariel, and Frank Sorauf (to name only a few, recent examples) provide elements, which we can add to. Looking at democratic politics abstracted from its role as the agency which makes laws, rules, decisions, and policies against the background conditions of social reality, we find practices which we can subject to the same kinds of moral interpretation used in connection with due process of law. When people go through these motions, take part in these procedures, what are they doing? What are they expressing, illustrating, symbolizing, teaching, suggesting, implying? What are they achieving beyond their specific purposes? What variety of descriptions can we offer of their involvement? Let us simplify by concentrating on the practices of free and contested elections with universal adult suffrage and majority rule in the elected legislature. With these practices in mind, I shall speak of the methods of democratic politics as a whole.

Democratic politics is the politics of choice. Choice is itself good. It shows up the problematic nature of social reality: at least two contending approaches may possess a substantial plausibility to rational people, whether they formulate the choices or are entitled to decide between them. The politics of choice permits the public display of human divergence in the persons of candidates and political workers: a diverse population is given the opportunity to see themselves or parts of themselves magnified and made heroic or villainous, but at least the object of serious and perhaps impassioned attention. Vicarious experience and oblique vindication inhere in the politics of choice.

Democratic politics is the politics of rational choice. It takes place in public, in the open, in a transparent medium of publicity. Things get talked out. Most viewpoints have interested spokesmen, thus insuring an advocacy that will not be tepid or overlook good favorable arguments. On the other hand, publicity guarantees that viewpoints must address each other. Adversaries can learn from each other: a general sense of the benefits of self-criticism may come to pervade a society with democratic politics. Or, if adversaries remain locked in their positions, others, outsiders, neutrals, may be stimulated into making some new synthesis or into discarding all the old elements. The politics of publicity demystifies politics; it makes a salubrious irreverence possible, and with it, a collective sanity not to be found in non-democratic countries. Because of these features, democratic politics more closely approaches the general criteria for rationality in decision-making than any other kind of politics.

Democratic politics is the politics of human dignity. Everybody counts, is counted, is taken into account. More than any other political system, it wars on self-contempt; and does so by institutionalizing equality. At the same time, it goes as far as modern mass life permits in institutionalizing fraternity, the fraternity of equals who realize their common humanity and common interest are the same thing and are served by the political methods of a democracy. Democratic politics is a school of public warmth. It teaches that some of the best qualities of domestic life can be re-created in public life.

Democratic politics is the politics of energy. It elicits, employs, and rewards alertness, vigor, and ambition, while civilizing all these otherwise raw characteristics, and turning them to public use. It imposes on men the understanding that they must associate to compete, and that competition is also a form of association. The politics of energy is the politics of regulated conflict, much like a game. Virtuosity and fair-play, a sense that playing is more important than winning, and that winning is more important than exploiting victory, are all heightened when men engage in practices that constrain important contests with almost sacred rules. The very concept of game is enhanced by absorbing the activities included in democratic politics. The politics of energy is the politics of limited conflict. Compromise is of its essence. Besides, or beyond, compromise is the acceptance of the spirit of inconclusiveness: no result, good or bad, is final, frozen, complete, or unambiguous. The mutability of life receives a humanly distorted political reflection. Change is welcomed, not feared. Democratic politics is a school of courage. Defeat is seen to be inescapable for every cause or movement, sooner or later; yet the soreness of defeat may be overcome by a contemplation of the beauty of the means or procedures which led to defeat, and which will survive any particular victory or defeat. And there is always tomorrow. Democratic politics consecrates difference, contrast, variety: each tendency stretches itself to the limit in order to define itself and so become publicly recognizable. The developed tendencies are numerous and amazing in their juxtaposition, but they hold each other in place. People in a democracy are thereby taught, or are confirmed in their belief, that homogeneousness is unhealthy, that enormous complexity can turn out to be manageable, and that freedom has little meaning unless it is used extravagantly.

Democratic politics is the politics of accountability and continuous consent. It establishes the right to an answer. The political actor must explain himself to those to whom he owes his power. He is chastened by the possibility of rebuff. Those who go high can be thrown out, and revert to a level of equality with the anonymous mass. No tenure is so long as to implant the feeling that power belongs to an office-holder as a matter of unearned right or inherited privilege. Thus, one of the most coveted prizes of life (official power) is made obedient to the most bitterly resented law of life: the dependence of great things on chance, the fragility of great things.

Democratic politics is the politics of limits. All its practices, not only due process of law, conspire to instill scruples, inhibitions, leniency, indulgence in those who hold power. The state is strictly separated from society. Fences are placed around the personal, the domestic, the vocational, the fraternal.

Democratic politics is the politics of social prophylaxis. By permitting tendencies self-expression, it may prevent their festering. By giving them publicity, it may embarrass them out of some of their worst excesses. By granting them access to the arena, it spares society the horror of action spurred by buried rage. It spares society the further horror of catastrophic surprise. It teaches the lesson that if you seek, you shall find, and that if you knock, it shall be opened. It prevents societal disease by institutionalizing hope.

Obviously much more could be said along the lines indicated. It is no wonder that a sympathetic mind will feel enchantment when such descriptions and interpretations of democratic methods can be given. Much of the tone and spirit which differentiate the open society from the closed society is embodied and expressed in the methods of democratic politics. Moral, esthetic, and spiritual values inhere in them. If it is right to say, as I have, that the practices of due process of law embody (social) justice (even as they lead to (legal) justice), then it would be right to say that democratic methods embody continuous consent and (social) justice. These are not the only values they embody: there is more to praise democratic methods for than their contribution to legitimacy. One almost wants to say that if government were not necessary, we should want to invent it in its democratic form, so fine are the values inherent in it, and so unlikely would it be to find other, non-political frameworks that could contain them. In any case, democratic methods are in themselves just; and in their representative form, make some kind of continuous consent possible. But as I have tried to suggest, the matter of legitimacy cannot be exhausted by consideration of methods alone, no matter how elaborate that consideration.

7. Proceduralists must face questions. Most generally, there are two questions that go with the two aspects of legitimacy. First, Is the continuous consent genuine? (I assume here that when continuous consent is genuine, the good person consents to the Constitution which gives form to continuous consent.) Second, is (social) justice realized as fully as it could be given the level of cultural and economic development and sophistication? The two questions are obviously connected. In a just, or nearly just, society popular involvement will be of a higher quality, and hence consent will be more genuine. Reciprocally, popular involvement will usually place its weight behind measures which deepen and enrich justice, or which preserve it from inevitable tendencies to deterioration. But let us artificially keep the two aspects apart, and say that the quality of consent is a summary term for the background conditions against which the democratic methods function, and that the amount of (social) justice is the summary term for the characteristic pattern of outcomes over time. Put another way, what is the democratic game really like? Is it rigged or honest? Does it come as close to meeting the expectations of legitimacy as due process comes in meeting the standards of (legal) justice?

The two questions can be broken down into a series of questions, all of them familiar. On consent: How extensive is participation? How rational is it on the average? How informed is it? What goes into the making of the public mind on the succession of issues? How equal are the capacities to participate? What sorts of people typically enter public life? What virtues and vices in them does the system encourage and discourage? How wide is the range of choice which the system regular offers? What possibilities remain submerged? What voices dominate? How thorough is the accountability?

On justice: Are the worst off as well off as they could be made to be? Is the long-term trend in the direction of reducing inequalities of power and fulfillment? Do the guaranteed rights mean much to most people? Are they able to use them, and use them in pursuit of fuller personal development? Are the sorts of treatment included in justice accorded to all equally? How safe is society from the state?

The answers are as familiar as the questions. Thanks to what we have called the deflationary political science of the last generation (at least), we know, or think we know, that the questions would have answers leading us away from trust in the electorate, from belief that the system is rational, that it is democratic because the people make it democratic. We see more and more that the political system avoids or represses certain issues, like fundamental inequalities; and thus presents a very narrow range of choices. We observe the rapacities of men who seek office, and the corruptions they carry, spread, and sanctify. We see the appallingly mindless uses to which much guaranteed freedom is put. And so on.

The basic point is that whatever the findings of political science, they establish the true meaning of the game of democratic politics. That is, the extent to which the values supposedly embodied in and expressed by democratic methods are in fact embodied and expressed *depends on* the background against which the game is played and the consequent general tendency of the results of the game. We could not speak of democratic politics as the politics of choice unless the conditions of genuine choice were met. Similarly, certain conditions must be met before we could speak of the equation of democratic politics with rational choice, the acknowledgment of human dignity, the best channel for and expression of humane energies, preventive and curative social medicine, the principle of accountability, or the principle of limit.

All these values are attained in more or less degree. But one can speak of gross differences. It is impossible to say clearly and definitely to what degree these values are attained in America or in any other open society. They exist, however, to a morally significant degree only if the great mass of people are responsible for the functioning of the methods as they are supposed to function, and if the result of their functioning is the promotion of (social) justice. Unless these *external* criteria – the criteria of legitimacy – are satisfied (also to a morally significant degree), we could not say that the inherent values of democratic methods were sufficiently attained. The methods would no longer be democratic, or democratic enough to count a great deal. The reasons for being enchanted by them would not obtain. Democratic methods lose their moral sense unless they grow out of consent and issue in justice; just as due process of law would lose its sense unless it grew out of the competence, desire, and rationality of policemen, judges, and lawyers, and issued in (legal) justice.

The findings of recent political science should, then, confirm us in the will to ask how much legitimacy the American political system has. It would be illicit, it would be to misconstrue the meaning of proceduralism, to know the findings and still not be troubled by the question of legitimacy. Political methods do not constitute *merely* an art-form or an intricate exercise. Proceduralism is a doctrine about a *political* system: the metaphor of game should not be allowed to conceal that fact. Proceduralists should go back to the original locus of their doctrine, due process of law, to see how misconceived it is to base a defense on proceduralist reasons without at the same time realizing that these reasons cannot stand by themselves. Those reasons vanish when isolated.

8. If, however, proceduralism is only a disguised form of positivism, then what I have said does not apply. Suppose that someone believes that there is no way of showing that one thing is better than another; that it is not possible for reason to adjudicate between competing claims; that all contestants are equally "good," "bad," or "indifferent," because the entire vocabulary of judgment is arbitrary and not governed by any rules or conventions in its employment. If someone believes all this or something like it, he then may go on to say that he merely has a personal preference for democracy, and that he prefers it because it lets people fight without letting them really get hurt; that there really is no way of knowing which side deserves to win; that, in any case, by letting people fight limited battles, greater battles, lethal ones, are avoided. Democratic methods preserve the peace: peace is not so much a value as the precondition of values and the contest between them. One prefers democracy because it tends to preserve the peace. Democracy is the politics of positivism.

If that is what proceduralism amounts to, then of course it would lead away from any concern with legitimacy, and with the question of the degree to which democratic methods serve it. If one thinks it philosophically wrong to assert the moral superiority of one condition or one form or one outcome to another, then he simply accepts what is, provided there is peace. With that attitude, political theory disappears. This entire discussion is then nugatory: positivists are no more interested in the inherent values of democratic methods than in any other values.

9. If proceduralism is, on the other hand, only a disguised form of pessimism or realism, then, once again, what I have said does not apply. The findings of political science may conduce to abandoning total commitment to democracy, and a consequent feeling of relief that democratic politics is not really or fully democratic. By making methods and procedures primary, the disguised pessimist or realist may find a way of philosophically blocking further inquiry into what the methods and procedures truly signify. Confident that prevailing democratic procedures involve most people only formally or minimally; and relieved that that is the case, because the findings of political science paint such an awful picture of the electorate, the pessimist or realist embraces semi-democratic politics, or "mixed" democratic politics. He may think that the best disguise which suspiciousness of the people may wear in an open society is proceduralism. Proceduralism is thus the politics of imperfect democracy, with the imperfection welcomed.

When proceduralism is a disguise for this attitude, the moral values of procedures are not especially prized. Rather, procedures are seen mostly as obstacles to popular action: their justification is purely practical, and conservative in motivation. But then the disguise is off: we depart from proceduralism as a moral attitude, as a contribution to the theory of democratic legitimacy. The subject is changed. When we take up proceduralism in order to praise it for alerting us to the inherent worth of democratic methods, and to criticize it when it claims to be solely sufficient as an account of democratic legitimacy, we assume that its adherents are democrats. It is interesting, more than interesting, that both positivism and anti-democratic sentiment find it possible and useful to wear proceduralist disguise. But in all fairness we should sort out insincere from sincere espousal. We assume that some proceduralists (anyway) are looking for the strongest possible case to justify democratic politics over any alternative; and that they do so because they believe that a strong case can and should be made.

10. The full glory of proceduralism will be disclosed only when the people involved in the procedures are better than they are now. By "people" must be meant the adult population; spectators and partisans, occasional participants and steady activists, voters and officials. It would not be quite true to say that procedures are only as good as the people involved in them. After all, good people, if they conform to bad or mediocre rules, act worse than they could; while obedience to rules, if the rules are good, may induce a mechanical or mimetic goodness in mediocre or bad people. It is nevertheless clear, I think, that in the long run there must be

some close congruence between feelings and behavior. And until the people of a democracy are better than they are now, consent and justice will remain as imperfect as they are now, and therefore the moral values inherent in democratic methods will remain as incompletely realized as they are now. It is not only that inherent values cannot compensate for deficiencies in consent and justice: it is that the quality of consent and justice determine the democratic worth of the methods.

11. To repeat an earlier point: some of the recent assaults on the political (and other) institutions of democratic society have been inspired by the wish to improve the quality of consent and justice. In the course of these assaults, democratic procedures have sometimes been ignored. Activists have said that these procedures are too slow, or too complex, or not democratic enough, or not responsive enough, or were rooted in an insufficiently informed or even manipulated public, or were dominated by those with disproportionate power of one kind or another (especially wealth), or were dominated by people who had a too feeble will to justice, or did not seem to extend to some of the most important decisions affecting the people as a whole (especially in foreign policy). Some of the radicals, some in the New Left, would, I think, have accepted some version or other of what I have maintained. Namely, that the political system was imperfectly legitimate, and that in order to make it more perfect, people had to go, on occasion, outside the procedures, and break the rules. The procedures were not the procedures of *democracy* – with sufficient directness. (Howard Zinn and Christian Bay can stand for their number.)

I should wish to stress, however, the similarity between proceduralism and some of the currents in recent leftist politics. At first sight, it may seem odd to link a doctrine so legalist in its inspiration with one that seems so lawless in its effects. What can a doctrine that cherishes regularity and correctness have to do with impatient and impulsive practice? I think, a fair amount. Adversary as proceduralism and the Movement appear to be, and, in truth, to a great extent, are, the fact remains that some in the Movement carried the moral outlook of proceduralism into their agitations, confrontations, and displays. The radicalism of the last few years is or was many things, some of them new, some of them revivals of things past, some of them the fruition of things past, some of them the natural continuation of permanent things. But one thing the Movement was for certain: it was the latest form of the moral idea that inherent in politics are important values, and that these values must count for a lot when a general assessment is made of political life. It would seem that the underlying assumption is that it is the politics of the open society which contains these values. But a great gap existed between the real aspiration of an open society and its political procedures. The procedures could not contain the democratic surge: they were oligarchic in practice: they were not adequate to the altered moral complexion of advanced elements in society. If political methods were to bear moral value, they would have to change dramatically. Their inspiration could no longer be legalism, even a generously interpreted legalism. Their inspiration would come from a theory of experience, a theory of the value of activity, of action, of participation. In that theory the ends of action would matter little or not at all; the action itself would be all or nearly all. It is the journey not the arrival that matters. You do for the sake of doing; therefore you play. If you make a revolution, said one clown-philosopher, make it for the hell of it. Do it, said his twin. Life is process, and the best politics shows fidelity to that truth.

A part of the Movement believed, then, in *intrinsic politics*. Here, from a formal point of view, is the similarity between it and the company of proceduralists. It is also true, less formally, that one can find in our proceduralist re-statement of the inherent value of democratic methods several propositions that could as easily fit in a re-statement of the processive position. The praise of energy, and the joining of human dignity with political inclusion figure in the talk and writing of such activists as Hayden, Lynd, Rubin, and Hoffman; not to mention the countless shouts, petitions, manifestoes, and pieces of occasional writing which the world-wide student movement engendered. I do not mean that one sums up that movement in the phrase "processive politics" or in any other phrase. Substantive aims were often there; and sometimes, the substantive aims were clearly those of non-procedural justice in the sense of expanded human rights or narrowed inequalities or forbearance from indecent treatment of foreign countries and peoples. (It was also true that less often the substantive aims were crazy or dumb.) But I do not think it can be denied that a salient aspect of the Movement was a delight in political action – action that is publicly visible, fraternally undertaken, concerned with problems outside oneself and one's routine, and able to be talked about in the categories of glamor, heroism, spontaneity, sport, martyrdom, free conscience, self-expression, self-forgetfulness, and, of course, play. The rewards of action are psychological and spiritual, not those of self-interest conventionally defined.

It was wonderful to see old, even ancient, ways of valuing political action and of preferring it to other human possibilities suddenly be enacted before one's eyes. Politics made life more vivid. The participants lived more intensely; observers observed more intensely. The tonic or therapeutic or prophylactic effects of politics were clearly in evidence. Allowing for severe adjustments in meaning, we could say that the motives for action seemed – in their populist, democratic, open spirit – more Homeric than Aristotelian, more Machiavellian than Rousseauist, more Sorelian than Marxist. That is to say, energy and extravagance seemed more important than wisdom and strict virtue, even though enlightened conscience, enlightened subjectivity, was sometimes placed foremost. The means were the ends, action was valuable apart from results, intrinsic politics was championed. A never-ending and always-changing process was held up as the design of the good life.

To say all that, however, is not to say enough. Indeed it may serve to belittle the Movement in the minds of those who find such an esthetic rationale either too precious or potentially immoral. If we go back to the beginnings of the Movement, to such sources as the Port Huron Statement, we will see that a dominant consideration was not esthetic; nor was it to praise action for action's sake, for the sake of the opportunities it alone gives for certain kinds of experience. What was at issue was the praise of action because it was interaction, and interaction that issued in individual and group self-determination or self-mastery. The traditional equivalence of continuous consent and representative institutions was questioned with severity, and typically denied. The nature of this tendency as a species of intrinsic politics survives my characterization. It was clear that as significant as any outcome was the process, the human interaction of talk and gesture which led to the outcome, provided all interested parties were personally involved.

The moral basis of this position is profoundly democratic, as numerous writers have pointed out. This position was, at its heart, Rousseauist (after all). One should have a part in deciding what the rest expect one to do; one ought to do what one with the rest have decided that all ought to do. Real democracy is direct democracy, participatory democracy. Only, Rousseauist strictness was absent. It was not a question of laws and infrequent general assemblies, but rather of sense of the meeting in daily gatherings. The good life was in talking things out: that was the cure for alienation from one's own feelings and from the institutions of power massed against one. Representation was hopeless to prevent alienation: it failed the greatest test which twentieth-century moralists have put life to. Insofar as representative institutions saved souls, the souls they saved were very few – that lucky minority who had a serious role in the procedures of supposedly democratic government.

Looked at from the perspective I suggest, processive politics can be described as a reaction against proceduralism. But the point of that reaction is not to deny the supreme worth of means, methods, procedures, but rather to deny that present-day democracies could claim supreme worth for the radically imperfect ones in existence. To use our language: the Movement asserted that the quality of consent in America and elsewhere was bad to the extent of vitiating any claim for the system's legitimacy.

It was further implicit in the thought of the founders of the Movement that when participation replaced representation, not only would consent become genuine, but the justice of substantive outcomes would grow greater. At its best, the spokesmen of the Movement rejected the idea that process alone counts, magnificent though it could be. The worry over poverty, discrimination, and war was not feigned – at least not in the early days, the pre-Yippie days. Thus, to put it most grandly: The Movement knew that democratic methods were rich in moral meaning, and also knew that without genuine consent and likelier justice the methods were not democratic, or adequately democratic, and could not therefore deserve the praise conservatives and liberals heaped on them. Processive thought is a corrective to its kin, proceduralist thought.

12. I do not deny that just as positivists and anti-democrats may wear a proceduralist disguise, so relativists and nihilists may wear a processive disguise. Some may not believe in anything beyond one's own pleasure, the pleasure taken in one's act (in both senses), and find in interaction another way of avoiding interaction. Ritual may come to prevail over reality, self-display over the common play. In formless participation, it may be easier to be solipsistic: in the noise you may just talk to yourself. Each tolerates everybody else's act: they are all equally good. Or, some may hate calm, and feel alive only when there is confusion. They live among symbols: all action is outrage or mischief. Such would find formless participation the best medium for their fury.

Relativism and nihilism are the degradations of the recent doctrine of action. Naturally we should take notice of what a doctrine lends itself to, as well as what it is at its best. Our concern here is with the doctrine of action at its best, just as it was with proceduralism. Each at its best is a contribution to democratic theory. We must not let either blind us to the democratic merits of the other or to its similarity to the other. If we are to have a discussion of democratic legitimacy, we must ignore the relativist and nihilist degradations of action as we ignored the positivist and elitist degradations of procedure.

13. There is a great shortcoming in processive thought to which I would like to refer. Just as the original source of proceduralism is non-political (due process of law), so the model of processive thought is non-govern-

mental. The emphasis on participation is most at home in social organizations and institutions which are local and delimited in nature. Schools were first and foremost; and then gradually the spirit spread to religious services and hierarchies, and to theatrical and musical audiences, and now to the army, mental institutions, and jails. Can the spirit spread much beyond these face-to-face situations? Obviously, there is still some life in local government, as there seems to be new participatory life in precinct caucuses of the Democratic Party (to take examples from America). But what of places of work? More important yet, can the great powers of state and national government be truly made more amenable to participation? Can the spirit of participation go from success to success, annexing greater areas of control as it goes, and eventually by accretion absorb the high national powers? How could the answer be yes? How can there be much plausibility in a vision of pervasive decentralization? Do not the conditions of modernity kill that vision? I mean numbers, distances, heterogeneousness, mobility, technological change, rising expectations, dire necessities. What can come to terms with such phenomena? Surely not maximum decentralization? And is it not a snare and a delusion to fall in love with participation when real power is out of its reach? More upper middle class fantasy and self-indulgence: is that what processive politics, politics as play, amounts to?

Are we not necessarily left with representative politics as the only practicable politics of continuous consent? Should not the major aim of democratic theorists be to search out ways of improving representative institutions, rather than dwelling on participation? It is doubtless good for local and delimited institutions to accommodate the demand for participation. But do not let the discontinuity between these institutions and the primary political institutions be obscured. Processive thought is a useful critique of the pretensions of proceduralist thought, and of democratic theory in general. I do not see how we could make more of it in political discussion. It is close to anarchism in its unreality.

To express it more generously: it is a utopian doctrine. The world would have to be almost wholly different from what it is now for the participatory ethic to be able to pervade all the important relations of life, including political ones. There would have to be maximum decentralization to insure maximum participation. Political institutions would be differentiated from non-political ones not so much by an absolute qualitative difference but by perhaps a trait like scope of consequences. Somehow small scale and sizable scope would be compatible. There would have to be controversies for political interaction to retain its savor; but the controversies could not be fraught with ruin or damage if the pleasure taken in participation were to be taken with a good conscience. Playing with lives is not play. Somehow safety and seriousness would be compatible. All the people (in small groups) would deal with all major issues; else participatory democracy would be, politically speaking, participatory frivolity. Politics would become the model for all human relations; but politics proper would continue in recognizable status. Private life would be politicized and political life would be communal. In these conditions, the full glory of processive politics would be disclosed. But until that time, processive doctrine may constitute as great an impediment to understanding the true condition of democratic legitimacy as proceduralist doctrine.

14. The worst is now to come. The two doctrines of intrinsic politics share an immense omission, and hence are implicated in a common failure. Neither doctrine can deal with – even when it tries – the undemocratically wielded power of making foreign policy. On this point, C. Wright Mills has not been answered, even when he has been understood; and that has not been often enough. Our age is one in which the decisions of greatest scope, actual and potential, are decisions of foreign policy. These decisions are mortal: life and death on an inconceivable scale. America combines possession of nuclear weapons with a global reach. The legislative and judicial agencies seem incapable of restraining a determined executive. It is not clear what precise shape such resistance could take, if the legislature or judiciary were to be as determined as the executive. The fears, the uncertainties, the secrets, the magic which inhabit the realm of foreign affairs daunt the will and the imagination of those outside the small executive circle. It makes almost no sense to speak of the operation of consent.

I do not bear new tidings. I do feel, for all that, that the theoretical importance of the matter has been neglected – not only by those who expound proceduralist or processive politics. The full measure must be taken of the question: What does it mean for the possibility of legitimacy when the most important *public* power is undemocratic? * The question is probably rhetorical. What *could* it mean except that, at the least, only with the destruction of all nuclear weapons and massive world-wide disarmament could there be a restoration of (approximate) legitimacy. I do not know whether the further step of abolishing national sovereignties would complete or complicate the task of attaining an ever fuller or more perfect legitimacy.

* I emphasize "public" in order to separate this question from the subject of undemocratic private power: this latter kind is not usually mortal. Must every great power be public and democratic whether or not life and death are at stake? But I may be wrong to make this distinction.

A derivation from these remarks is that irregular politics, the politics of conscientious disobedience, becomes all the more defensible. With the inclusion of foreign affairs in our discussion, we are ever more distant from ascribing such a degree of legitimacy to democratic governments that we could discountenance the political illegality of good persons altogether. As long as we live in a world in which human powers are so heavy with consequences, the good person must be on his guard constantly to avoid doing or lending himself to awful harm, whether he is a soldier, scientist, bureaucrat, office-holder, or voter. Obedience to law or authority may mean implication in or tolerance of enormity: enormity can be routinized, so that even good persons stop seeing what they do. In a condition of awareness disobedience may be the only moral response. The concept of *citizenly discretion* must be elaborated in the face of such dangers. What alternative is there when the discretion of a few office-holders is gigantic?

15. The existent procedures of representative government are seriously imperfect because only partially democratic. They could not become appreciably more perfect as long as war and peace is the gravest issue. If war and peace were no longer an issue, they would still be seriously imperfect because representation is in its nature incapable of being anything more than partially democratic, despite differences of degree. The participatory alternative to representation is infeasible in large societies and does not touch the issue of war and peace. It would remain infeasible if war and peace were no longer an issue.

We must therefore be wary of pretentiousness when we speak for democracy. We may be right in believing that democratic institutions are better than any others in the world, that they come closest to deserving the obedience and support of good persons. Still we cannot say that they are good enough to make obedience automatic or regular. At the same time they are good enough, more or less, to invalidate any justification of revolutionary violence proposed so far. Until utopia comes there is much improvement which democratic representative institutions need, as there are severe limits to how far we can expect improvement to go.

THE REVOLT AGAINST THE OPEN SOCIETY AND THE PHENOMENON OF DELEGITIMIZATION: THE CASE OF THE AMERICAN NEW LEFT

EHUD SPRINZAK

On Monday night, October 7, 1969, at 11 : 10 p.m. a dynamite blast destroyed the police officers' monument in Chicago. On Wednesday, posters headed "SDS Handwriting on the Wall" were circulated by a small radical organization, the Weatherman. The posters bore the slogan, "Bring the War Home," and announced four days of "national action" against the war in Vietnam. Chicago, the site of violent riots at the National Convention of the Democratic Party in August, 1968 and the place where the trial of the "Conspiracy 8" which were charged with organizing these riots had been proceeding for some time, was informed in the posters that the following four days were to witness both a rally to commemorate Che Guevara and Nguyen Van Troi (a Vietnamese revolutionary) and an attack on the Chicago Armed Forces Induction Center by the "Women's Militia." In addition, demonstrations at high schools were promised for Thursday; a "move on the courts" for Friday; and a massive march through Chicago's Loop on Saturday.[1] The posters proclaimed:

> We move with the people of the world, to seize power from those who now rule, we . . . expect their pig lackeys to come down on us. We've got to be ready for that. This is a war we can't resist. We've got to actively fight. We're going to bring the war home to the mother country of imperialism. AMERIKA: THE FINAL FRONT.[2]

From the beginning the hundreds of "Weathermen" and "Weatherwomen"

* This article is based on my doctoral dissertation, "Democracy and Illegitimacy; A Study of the American and the French Student Protest Movements and some Theoretical Implications," submitted in 1972 to the Department of Political Science at Yale University. I am greatly indebted to Professor Joseph Lapalombara who supervised this project and to Professors Charles Edward Lindblom and David Price for their friendly advice and fruitful criticism throughout.

[1] For a description of the "Days of Rage," see Tom Thomas, "The Second Battle of Chicago," in Harold Jacobs (ed.), *Weatherman* (Berkeley, Ramparts Press, Inc., 1970), pp. 196-226.

[2] *Ibid.*, p. 197.

who arrived that Wednesday in Chicago behaved differently from any other white demonstrators in America. As soon as they arrived, they organized themselves in a military fashion. Security guards were immediately stationed and no one was allowed to participate in the gathering who did not belong to the Weatherman, not even the photographers and correspondents of the "underground" media. In the meetings themselves, briefings and instruction by the "Weather Bureau," the national leadership of the Weatherman, were conducted in a military fashion. "Affinity groups" of five or six members who were to be the basic fighting units in the forthcoming battle with the police were formed by local leaders. Surprised new left members and veterans of previous confrontations with the police could not quite understand what was happening. When they tried to approach the Weatherman members to find out, they were told:

> You can't talk about the Movement, because we have to crush the Movement to build the revolution . . .
>
> We start to build a Red Army by fighting in the streets now. We're going to knock the pig on his ass in those streets. Sure there's going to be pigs hitting people like before, but this time there's going to be people hitting pigs. . . .
>
> The focal point is here in Chicago. We've got to show people that white kids are willing to fight on the side of black people and on the side of revolution around the world. If you're not going to fight, then you're not part of us. It's as simple as that. . . .[3]

These words did not remain just words. Violence occurred as soon as the Weatherman march began. Totally unprovoked by the police, the Weatherman members first attacked the North Federal Savings and Loan Building, breaking its large plate glass windows with rocks. As they moved down Clark Street they started to run and systematically smash the windows of buildings and parked cars on both sides of the street. People trying to protect their cars were beaten and left bleeding on the streets. The police, caught totally by surprise, did not interfere. Later, when a police line formed, the demonstrators charged straight into it and the line was broken.

Assessing the first evening of what became known in the history of the American protest movement as the "Days of Rage," Stephen Zicher, a Chicago assistant corporation counsel, said, "We never expected this kind of violent demonstration. There always has been a big difference between what they say and what they do." Deputy Superintendent of Police, James M. Rochford, Jr., said, "We were faced with revolutionaries."[4] Tom Hayden, a central figure in the protest movement of the 1960's and alleged-

[3] *Ibid.*, p. 199.
[4] *Ibid.*, p. 204.

ly a member of "Conspiracy 8," later commented on the Weatherman action:

We never did what the government accused us of in 1968, but the Weathermen did it in 1969. What we did in 1968 prefigured Weathermen; a few karate and snake dance exercises, some disruption, a lot of running in the streets, and at the end of Convention Week, a prediction that a fighting force would be created which would bring the war in Vietnam home. It remained for the government to develop this seed into a paranoid image of crazy, unruly, drug-ruined, club-carrying, Communist-inspired mobs rampaging in the Loop, and for Weathermen to fulfill the image one year later. Many Weathermen leaders were shaped by the events of Chicago '68. When our legal protest was clubbed down they became outlaws. When our pitiful attempts at peaceful confrontation were overwhelmed, they adopted the tactic of offensive guerrilla violence.[5]

As on other occasions, Tom Hayden was not attempting to make a detached and theoretical observation as to the behavior of radicals in time of national crisis; but in his acute and peculiar way he managed to do so. What he observed and described was the development of a *crisis of legitimacy* in a democracy. Like Zicher, Hayden noticed that rhetoric and symbols expressing an attitude of illegitimacy vis-à-vis the regime were now being matched by overt and intentional illegal behavior and that the gist of this behavior had become the readiness to challenge openly not only the elected authorities but also their agencies of physical coercion.

American observers of the student protest movement had witnessed worse scenes of violence originating in student protest before those in Chicago in October 1969. The violence in those previous scenes had not been planned, but had been shaped to a large extent by the unintended interaction of committed activists ready to apply tactics of direct action, uncommitted observers, and the appearance of the police. The violence of Chicago was planned and intended. Soon after the "Days of Rage," the Weatherman leaders, at that time in command of the national headquarters of the Students for a Democratic Society (SDS) in Chicago, closed the offices of that organization and entrusted its massive archives to the State Historical Society of Wisconsin in Madison. They went underground, declaring open war on the government of the United States and stating their intention of building a Leninist vanguard and a red army.[6] Splitting itself into small and secret action-oriented "affinity groups," subject to the hierarchical command of the "Weather Bureau," it now armed itself to the

[5] Tom Hayden, *Trial* (New York, Holt, Rinehart and Winston, 1970), pp. 91-92.

[6] Karin Ashley, Bill Ayers, Bernardine Dohrn, John Jacobs, Jeff Jones, Gerry Long, Howie Machtinger, Jim Mellen, Terry Robbins, Mark Rudd and Steve Tappis, "You Don't Need a Weatherman to Know Which Way the Wind Blows" in Jacobs (ed.), *op. cit.*, pp. 87-90.

teeth, enforced strict rules of secrecy upon its members and appeared in public again only after its members had committed illegal acts of violence against public institutions.[7] Through anonymous telephone calls and letters to the underground press, it claimed responsibility for otherwise unsolved cases of illegal and subversive behavior.

Shreds of information surfacing from the American underground have further suggested an untold story of personal transformations undergone by the members of Weatherman whose previous behavior had been marked by the use of antiregimist symbols and active dissent. However, they were now becoming self-proclaimed revolutionaries, acting illegally, and following in deeds what for years they had been merely saying.[8]

In a historical and theoretical perspective, what appears so intriguing about the activities of the Weatherman is not so much its attitude of illegitimacy towards the regime and the illegal behavior of its members in 1969, but the fact that it was the direct offspring of a student organization, the Students for a Democratic Society (SDS), which in 1962 constituted itself as a very liberal and democratic collectivity in order to promote the value of a "democracy of individual participation." [9] It is true that in its founding manifesto, the Port Huron Statement, the SDS severally criticized the Democratic and Republican parties. It accused them of becoming equally conservative and of denying to American citizens the possibility of choosing between real ideological alternatives regarding problems of great concern, such as the Cold War, the proliferation of nuclear armaments, relations with the Third World, racial discrimination, and domestic economic policies. It accused the national parties of sustaining an "organized political stalemate." [10] However, the structural conclusion of this totalistic critique was not a call for antidemocratic revolution nor a quest for a political system guided by one revolutionary party representing the true interests of the "proletariat." Rather, it projected a system of "Two genuine parties, centered around issues and essential values. . . . 'with' sufficient party disagreement to dramatize major issues, yet sufficient party overlap to guarantee stable transition from administration to admini-

[7] Cf. Harold Jacobs, "Inside the Weather Machine: Introduction," in Jacobs, *op. cit.*, pp. 302-303.

[8] Very little is known about the Weathermen. Harold Jacobs' collection of the best articles and reports written about the Weathermen and its leaders up to July 1970 is very useful.

[9] "SDS: Port Huron Statement," in Massimo Teodori (ed.), *The New Left: A Documentary History* (New York, Bobbs-Merrill, 1969), p. 167. References to the complete text of the Port Huron Statement, which is a rather rare document today, will be made only when the texts referred to are omitted by Teodori.

[10] *Ibid.*, p. 170.

stration." [11] Indeed, the SDS saw itself as a spearhead of a "new left" concentrated in the American campus. Yet this new left was very peaceful and nonviolent. It did not try to "out-revolutionize" the old left but to "under-revolutionize" it. Commenting on Marx, Tom Hayden, the cofounder of the SDS, maintained that although "Marx, the humanist, has much to tell us . . . his conceptual tools are outmoded and his final vision implausible." [12] He was equally unhappy with the "nonideological" thinking of revolutionary leaders of the rising nations, as for example, that of Che Guevara.[13]

Not only did the SDS of the early sixties reject the traditional solutions of the extreme left of the pre-World War II era, but it also refused to grant membership to members of Communist and, in general, "totalitarian" organizations. Section 2 of Article III (membership) of the SDS constitution maintained:

> SDS is an organization of democrats. It is civil libertarian in its treatment of those with whom it disagrees, but clear in its opposition to any totalitarian principle as a basis for government or social organization. Advocates or apologists for such a principle are not eligible for membership.[14]

Reflecting the impact of another student organization – the black Student Nonviolent Coordinating Committee (SNCC), an organization which fought for civil rights in the South and thereby became to the SDS a subject of great admiration and respect – the Port Huron statement insisted on a basic commitment to a philosophy of nonviolence.

> We find violence to be abhorrent because it requires generally the transformation of the target, be it a human being or a community of people, into a depersonalized object of hate. It is imperative that the means of violence be abolished and the institutions – local, national, international – that encourage nonviolence as a condition of conflict be developed.[15]

Commitment to nonviolence was conceived by the SDS not as a useful tactical means to be applied temporarily against a resourceful and powerful rival but as a normative ethical principle. Violence as a political means was to be abolished because it was basically a dehumanizing pattern of behavior. Politics could do well without violence and institutions encouraging nonviolence had to be devised. The SDS's commitment to nonviolence was thus fully congruent with its idealistic vision of the desired performance of

[11] *The Port Huron Statement* (New York, SDS Pamphlet, 1964), pp. 46-47.

[12] Thomas Hayden, "A Letter to the New (Young) Left," in M. Cohen and D. Hale, *The New Student Left* (Boston, Beacon Press, 1968), p. 3.

[13] *Ibid.*

[14] *SDS Constitution* (Mimeographed pamphlet, 1963).

[15] "SDS: Port Huron Statement," in Teodori, *op. cit.*, p. 168.

liberal democracy as well as with its criticism of the actual performance of this system in America.

It is when we consider the behavior of the Weathermen of 1969 in view of the vision of the SDS in 1962 that a reexamination of our conception of the open society comes to mind. An observation of the almost incredible behavioral transformation of the SDS between 1962 and 1969 appears to justify the conclusion that *the friends of the open society have become in a very peculiar way its sworn enemies.* In order to realize fully this peculiar process, I would like to suggest that we leave for a short while the SDS and examine some usually unnoticed aspects of Karl Popper's *The Open Society and Its Enemies.*[16]

Many charges could and should be raised against Karl Popper and his book, *The Open Society and Its Enemies.* To mention that Popper did great injustices to some of the political philosophers on which he wrote is to understate the case. Not only did Popper misread Plato and Hegel on many points of fact, but he also read into their writings political facts of the twentieth century of which they could not even conceive and for which they could not be held responsible.[17] By trying to *unmask* the intentionally concealed political purposes of these philosophers, Popper, paradoxically, used the same methods of intellectual totalitarianism that he so keenly identified in his analysis of the sociology of knowledge of Karl Mannheim.[18] Indeed, Popper did not try to "psychotherapise" or "sociotherapise" either Plato or Hegel. But by injecting heavy doses of accusatory biographical details into a critical examination of their teaching, he clearly tried to "biogratherapise" them, not for their own sake, which he considered lost, but for that of the reader.

Nevertheless, when we consider the unexpected student protest of the nineteen sixties – a protest that occurred in the flourishing academic centers of the postindustrial democracy and that caught observers, theoreticians, and social scientists alike by surprise – we can hardly avoid acknowledging the historical significance of Popper's analysis as well as his contribution to postwar social theory. A rereading of Popper in the wake of the last

[16] K. R. Popper, *The Open Society and Its Enemies* (4th ed. rev.; London, Routledge & Kegan Paul, 1962).

[17] Cf. John Wild, *Plato's Modern Enemies and the Theory of Natural Law* (Chicago, University of Chicago Press, 1968); Ronald B. Levinson, *In Defense of Plato* (Cambridge, Harvard University Press, 1953); Richard Robinson's review of Popper's book, *Philosophical Review,* 40 (1951); Shlomo Avineri, "Hegel and Nationalism" in Walter Kaufmann (ed.), *Hegel's Political Philosophy* (New York, Atherton Press 1970); Shlomo Avineri, *Hegel's Theory of the Modern State* (London, Cambridge, University Press, 1972), ch. 10; and Dante Germino, "Hegel as a Political Theorist," *The Journal of Politics,* 31, No. 4 (November, 1969), pp. 885-912.

[18] Popper, *op. cit.,* Vol. II, Ch. 23.

decade suggests that he not only tried to recast the intellectual tradition of the West in grayer shades in order to reveal the deep intellectual roots of modern totalitarianism, but that he also tried to demonstrate the everlasting relationship between the closed and open societies. By reconceptualizing (some would say misconceptualizing) Bergson's open and closed society to mean roughly liberal democracy versus totalitarianism, Popper tried, I believe, to achieve two major purposes: to present the two societies as mutually exclusive, traceable to two different intellectual schools; and to demonstrate the process that might lead the followers of the former to become proponents of the latter. The driving motive in Popper's effort seems to have been an attempt, so fashionable later in the nineteen fifties, to create an *intellectual warning system* against the pitfalls of modern totalitarianism. Such an attempt was signified, for example, by Arendt's *The Origins of Totalitarianism,* Talmon's *The Origins of Totalitarian Democracy* or Aron's *The Opium of the Intellectuals.* Popper's great eagerness to debunk Plato's credibility as an honest philosopher and to discredit Hegel as a philosopher of any merit substantially weakened his efforts to present the relationships existing between the closed and the open societies in their teaching and in the life time of the movements attached to them. Regarding the understanding of these relationships in Marx and the Marxist movement, Popper did, however, a great service. He identified clearly the social logic by which the earlier humanitarian elements of the Marxian theory – intensely related to the open society – were bound to bring about proponents of closed societies. A closer look at Popper's analysis of Marx may demonstrate the case.

Popper did not charge Marx with being a direct enemy of the open society. Assessing Marx's moral theory, he mentioned that "Marx's faith ... was fundamentally a faith in the open society." [19] Marx, according to this analysis, identified the cruelty of the capitalist system and wanted to correct it. He "attacked the eulogists of liberalism because of their self-satisfaction, because of their identification of freedom with the formal liberty then existing within a social system which destroyed freedom. Thus, by implication, he admitted his love for freedom ... he was certainly not a collectivist for he hoped that the state would 'Wither away.' " [20] But Marx, according to Popper, became indirectly a great enemy of the open society. His critical appraisal of the democratic liberalism of his time had led him to develop false theories of society and of science, and he "misled scores

[19] *Ibid.,* Vol. II, p. 200.
[20] *Ibid.*

of intelligent people" [21] and converted them into sworn enemies of the open society.

According to Popper, Marx and Engels produced this effect by discrediting the legitimacy of constitutional democracy as a genuine representative of the values of the open society. At the time when they wrote, political participation was denied the workers and it seemed unlikely that it would be granted. This discrediting had produced enormously damaging effects. Becoming a social force in itself in the form of a dogmatic ideology, it was maintained even after political participation was granted to the workers and when the social democratic movements developed patterns of *democratic behavior* like participation in the electoral and parliamentary processes. Democracy as a set of institutions, procedures, and principles of behavior could not, because of Marxist discrediting, be taken seriously. It was repeatedly presented as illegitimate.[22] Ultimately, such an approach has contributed to the emergence of modern totalitarianism in two ways. Refusing to take constitutional democracy seriously, the Marxists have done almost nothing to stop the fascists – who did not subscribe to the moral postulates of the open society in the first place – from ascending to political power. They also developed practices alien not only to the false democracy of the first half of the 19th century but also to the ideals of the open society in the name of which that democracy was criticized.

Believing deterministically in the final victory of the "real" open society, the followers of Marx have come full circle. They did not defend the democratic procedures, under which they themselves had flourished, as *minimal* conditions for the existence of the open society; and they did not try to *maximalize* these procedures even in their own organizations to safeguard their own home from the encroachments of the closed society. Maintaining an attitude of illegitimacy vis-à-vis liberal democracy, they eventually became the enemies of the open society.

The illuminating remarks of Popper regarding the conversion of the believers in the open society into its enemies appear all the more impressive in view of the fact that he wrote his book during World War II when Soviet Russia was at the peak of its prestige and before the full scope of Stalinism and its horrendous effects became known in the West.

Had the second volume of the *Open Society and Its Enemies* been written after 1956, very little would have had to be added to the logic of

[21] *Ibid.*, p. 82.

[22] *Ibid.*, pp. 151-65. Note especially Popper's comment regarding this analysis: "It is this prophesy of a possibly violent revolution which I consider, from the point of view of practical politics, by far the most harmful element in Marxism" (p. 151).

the argument. But a huge amount of evidence could have been used to support it empirically.

While it is true that Popper never tried to present the revolt against the open society as a discernible social and political phenomenon, his remarks and insights regarding this phenomenon appear significant and worth studying. A fuller exploration of the developments in the American new left may provide us with some further clues to help us identify features of this phenomenon.

If we observe the development of the American new left, focusing on its relation to the prevailing authorities and emphasizing *its practices* and *its symbolic behavior*,[23] we can hardly avoid the conclusion that the new left had initiated in the nineteen sixties, a *process of delegitimization*, marked by an increasing rejection of the legitimacy of American democracy.[24]

As early as 1963 young theoreticians of the new left started to discern their activities as "insurgent politics" and to refer to themselves as "new insurgents."[25] Reflecting the experience of the extra-parliamentary direct actions applied by the civil rights and peace movements – sit-ins, protests, and demonstrations, the new linguistic coin indicated a conscious attempt to conceptualize a new type of political action that would defy the rules of the prevailing American game without being illegal or unconstitutional. At the same time these new left theoreticians started to portray the system against which they were acting as "corporate liberalism" implying a gap between liberal progressive ideology and action in accordance with the interests of big corporations.[26] This portrayal introduced another key symbol into the terminology of the new left (already mentioned in the Port Huron Statement)[27] – "the military-industrial complex," a term borrowed from a famous speech of President Eisenhower. A change also started to emerge in the concept of "participatory democracy" (which appeared in the Port Huron Statement in the form of "democracy of individual participation") as fully congruent with the two-party model of representative de-

[23] The methodological justification for the emphasis on these two behavioral dimensions as indices of delegitimization cannot be expounded here in greater detail. It can be found in E. Sprinzak, *Democracy and Illegitimacy, op. cit.*, chapters 1, 3.

[24] For an identification of the development among the American new left of a process of delegitimization, see Jerome H. Skolnick, *The Politics of Protest* (New York, Ballantine Books, 1969), p. 100. See also Richard Flacks, "Revolt of the Young Intelligentsia," in Roderick Aya and Norman Miller (eds.), *The New American Revolution* (New York, The Free Press, 1971), p. 241.

[25] "SDS: America and New Era," in Teodori (ed.), *op. cit.*, pp. 180-182.

[26] This image was coined by the editorial board of *Studies on the Left*, a new left journal. See James P. O'Brien, "The Development of a New Left in the United States 1960-1965" (unpublished doctoral dissertation, University of Wisconsin, 1971), p. 237.

[27] *The Port Huron Statement, op. cit.*, p. 17.

mocracy. As a result of their bitter experience with the most brutal representatives of American policies – the sheriffs of the rural South and the northern political machines controlling the urban ghettos – and as a result of their discovery of the acquiescence of liberal politicians with these phenomena, the activists of the new left started to present "participatory democracy" as a key image to an *alternative* type of democracy, rejecting thereby party and interest group politics.[28] This tendency greatly deepened in the summer of 1964 when the young radicals failed to outsit the official Mississippi delegation to the Democratic National Convention held in Atlantic City. They clearly proved the discriminatory practices of the official Democratic party of Mississippi and came out with the newly created Mississippi Freedom and Democratic Party (MFDP) as an alternative delegation. This alternative, however, was rejected for obvious partisan considerations of Southern politics.[29]

Soon thereafter, in February 1965, the bombing of North Vietnam started. It was at this time that the language and imagery of illegitimacy first entered the vocabulary of the new left. Associated with the idea of "alternative institutions," it made its appearance in a discussion of the meaning of revolution in an article by Staughton Lynd, a historian and self-styled ideologue of the new left:

> So long as revolution is pictured as a violent insurrection, it seems to me both distasteful and unreal. The traditional alternative, the social Democratic vision of electing more and more radical legislators until power passes peacefully to the left, seems equally illusory. However, the events of the past year – the creation of the MFDP and the protest against the war in Vietnam – suggest a third strategy. One can now begin to envision a series of nonviolent protests which would, from the beginning, question the legitimacy of the Administration's authority where it has gone beyond constitutional and moral limits and might, if this insane foreign policy continues, culminate in the decisions of hundreds of thousands of people to recognize the authority of alternative institutions of their own making.[30]

Although Lynd cautiously avoided a comprehensive presentation of the system as illegitimate and did not attack democracy in principle, he went beyond the charge that the government was acting unconstitutionally. He

[28] Cf. Staughton Lynd, "The New Radicals and Participatory Democracy," *Dissent* (Summer, 1965).

[29] The MFDP was offered by the Credentials Committee of the Democratic Party two "delegates-at-large," an offer that was bluntly rejected. The story of the conflict regarding the MFDP can be found in Stokeley Carmichael and Charles V. Hamilton, *Black Power, the Politics of Liberation in America* (New York, Random House, 1967), pp. 86-97.

[30] Staughton Lynd, "Coalition Politics or Nonviolent Revolution," in Teodori, *op. cit.*, p. 199.

charged it as being immoral and suggested that the charges of unconstitutionality and immorality could be first steps in questioning the *legitimacy* of the administration's authority. Those first steps could then lead to the recognition of alternative (legitimate) institutions. What Lynd did, apart from his explicit argument, was to *introduce* the *terminology* and *imagery* of illegitimacy into the discussion. Tom Hayden, the past president of SDS, presented the case for alternative institutions in even stronger terms:

> The Movement is a community of insurgents sharing the same radical values and identity, seeking an independent base of power wherever they are. It aims at transformation of society led by the most excluded and unqualified people. Primarily, this means building institutions outside the established order which seek to become the genuine institutions of the total society, community unions, freedom schools, experimental universities, community-formed policy review boards, people's own antipoverty organizations fighting the federal money. . . . Ultimately, this movement might lead to a continental congress called by all the people who feel excluded from the higher circles of decision making in the country.[31]

In spite of its constant concern with national politics and with the total political system, the new left was a phenomenon motivated and directed by students. The students' growing sense of illegitimacy towards the prevailing political authorities was bound to affect also their attitude towards academic authorities who appeared to them as part of the same system against which they were protesting. In the fall of 1964, student activists of the Free Speech Movement (FSM) at Berkeley, many of whom participated earlier in civil rights actions in the South, sent waves of shock into the American academic world when they first demonstrated by stopping a police car for thirty-two hours and later took over the administration building at their university. Mario Savio, one of the leaders of the FSM, clearly indicated that what was happening in Mississippi was, in the self-consciousness of the new left, closely connected with what was going on at Berkeley:

> In Mississippi an autocratic and powerful minority rules, through organized violence, to suppress the vast, virtually powerless, majority. In California, the privileged minority manipulates the university bureaucracy to suppress the students' political expression. That "respectable" bureaucracy masks the financial plutocrats; that impersonal bureaucracy is the efficient enemy in a "Brave New World."[32]

[31] Tom Hayden, "The Politics of the Movement," *Dissent* (January-February, 1966), p. 87.

[32] Mario Savio, "An End to History," in S. M. Lipset and S. S. Wolin (eds.), *The Berkeley Student Revolt* (New York, Doubleday and Co., 1965), p. 216.

Soon a demand for "student power" was raised by the SDS.[33] This demand not only indicated a growing attitude of mistrust vis-à-vis academic authorities in the universities but also reflected another process of delegitimization taking place in the United States, that carried on by the black liberation movement. The SNCC (Student Nonviolent Coordinating Committee) had also been undergoing a profound transformation. In 1966 it had dropped its previous liberal identity and its commitment to non-violence to become a militant antiregimist organization. It now adopted *black power* as its key symbol and developed an ideology of national liberation.[34] Accordingly the government of the United States was projected as an illegitimate colonial ruler necessitating an anticolonial struggle of the "black colonies."

In its 1965 national convention, the SDS dropped from its constitution the "exclusionist" clause which had denied eligibility for membership to "advocates or apologists" of "totalitarian principle." It did so out of the growing feeling of mistrust in the prevailing system which was allowing the intense intervention in Vietnam to take place and out of their felt need to join forces with those who were rejecting the war in principle.[35] Members of the Maoist Progressive Labor Party (PLP) were now eligible for SDS membership. They streamed *en masse* accepting formally the libertarian non-organizational idea of "participatory democracy" but intending informally to take over control of the SDS. The Maoists then started a process of *marxization* of the SDS. Many of the SDS veterans were aware of the PLP's organizational intentions and of its demands to put students in the service of the American "working class," and they fiercely resisted these changes. They could not, however, resist the growing pressure from the local branches of their loose organization[36] to implement these ideas nor could they reject the *unmasking* character of the Marxian categories. Convinced that the system which allowed racial discrimination, poverty, and now war to take place was structurally corrupt, the veteran SDS members searched independently for a new, symbolic frame of reference that would express their sense of illegitimacy toward the regime without succumbing to the growing pressures of the PLP.

Early in 1967, an influential group within the SDS published a paper,

[33] Karl Davidson, "Toward Student Syndicalism," *New Left Notes* (September 9, 1966).

[34] *Black Power, SNCC Speaks for Itself: A Collection of Statements and Interviews* (Boston, New England Free Press Pamphlet).

[35] On the issue of nonexclusionism, cf. Alan Haber, "Nonexclusionism: The New Left and the Democratic Left," in Teodori, *op. cit.*, pp. 218-228.

[36] For an analysis of the struggles within SDS, cf. Andrew Kopkind, "The Real SDS Stands Up," in Jacobs, *op. cit.*, pp. 15-28.

entitled "Towards a theory of social change in America," [37] in which a theory of the "new working class" was formulated, and Gregory Calvert, the president of SDS, elaborated on this new theory in a major policy speech at Princeton University. It was now suggested that students were *themselves* part of a "new working class" created and exploited by "this super-technological capitalism." [38] The former image of "corporate liberalism" was replaced by "corporate capitalism." ("American corporate capitalism is an incredibly brutal and dehumanizing system whether at home or abroad.") The system was now challenged not by "new insurgents" and "alternative institutions" but by the working class heading towards revolution. The gist of the new theory was that modern society has created a new proletariat composed of middle class and professional workers. This "new working class" was presented as *a class* not because of its peculiar relation to the means of production – a unifying relation depriving it of a decent means of living – but because of conditions of "unfreedom" [39] in society, conditions affecting deprived minorities, high-salaried, middle-class professionals, and students living in "factory-like multiversities."

Had Karl Marx ever heard Calvert's speech and his claim to be a Marxist, he would have probably screamed aloud what it is told he once said, "I am not a Marxist." For indeed the new theory and especially its conceptualization of a "new working class" which would bring the inevitable revolution had no analytical relation with classical Marxism nor any considerable empirical support. How could one seriously create *a class* out of such diverse groups and believe earnestly that such a class could carry out a revolution? The Marxian conceptual tools remained indeed, as Tom Hayden noted in 1962, highly "outmoded" for diagnosing the American social, economic, and political realities as well as the position of students in this world. *But in 1967 and 1968 the new left did not need an analytically valid and reliable social theory. It needed a cultural system of symbols expressing a deep mood of illegitimacy vis-à-vis the regime.* In the late nineteen sixties, Marxism as a *Weltanschauung* had come to provide the most prestigious system of this kind. When in the summer of 1969 the SDS split into three factions – each presenting a different tactical and strategic perspective – they all had one thing in common: they presented

[37] David Gilbert, Robert Gottlieb and Gerry Tenny, "Towards a Theory of Social Change," *New Left Notes* (January 23, 1967).

[38] Gregory Calvert, "In White America: Radical Consciousness and Social Change," in Teodori, *op. cit.*, p. 417.

[39] *Ibid.*, p. 415.

their case in a militant Marxist language[40] directed at a totally discredited and illegitimate political system.

The *marxization* of many segments within the new left indicated an acceptance of a cultural system of symbols rejecting in principle the legitimacy of liberal democracy. It was not, however, matched automatically by *intended* illegal behavior and, in its most extreme form, by intended violence. Draft card burning, for example, was presented in the courts as a constitutional act falling well within the First Amendment as a case of symbolic speech expressing legal dissent.[41] The tactics of confrontation with public authorities and the police recommended by the SDS and other radical groups after 1967 were also not clear cases of illegal action. They indicated rather an extreme application of previous tactics of extra-parliamentary direct action.[42] If intensive violence occurred, and it did increasingly after 1967, it was usually not planned in advance but was a result of interaction between impatient police and passionate demonstrators. However, the experience of violence and the intensive use of symbols of illegitimacy have their own logical development. The increased bombings of induction centers marked the direction toward which the logic of an intense process of delegitimization was heading. It remained for the Weatherman to bring this process to its peak, a *crisis of legitimacy,* indicated by the use of symbols of illegitimacy and intended illegal action.

What is the theoretical lesson to be drawn from our analysis of the radicalization of the American new left and of Popper's critique of the teaching of Marx?

It appears to me that both lead to the conceptual identification of a political phenomenon and a discernible field of empirical research that might be called "delegitimization in a democracy." Operationally speaking, the phenomenon of delegitimization can be identified and studied, as I have tried to demonstrate, along two major dimensions of behavior: the use of symbols and images of legitimacy (or illegitimacy) and the application of legal (or illegal) practices vis-à-vis the prevailing political order. There are various possibilities of interplay between the symbolic dimension and the dimensions of legal action, and they must be studied empirically before a complete theory of delegitimization can be established. Seen in a historical perspective we should be able to identify and classify processes of delegitimization of leftist groups, rightist ones (mostly fascists), as well as

[40] Cf. *Debate Within SDS* (Detroit, Radical Education Project pamphlet, summer, 1969).

[41] Lawrence R. Velvel, "Freedom of Speech and the Draft Card Burning Cases," *Kansas Law Review,* 16 (1968).

[42] Cf. J. H. Skolnick, *op. cit.,* pp. 105-109.

religious and ethnic groups. However, in general there seems to be an inherent logic of development in the processes of delegitimization which is derived from the following propositions:

a. Established political authorities tend to consider themselves just and their practices legitimate. They do not change unless forced to do so by effective action.

b. Repeated structural criticism and pacific rejections of the prevailing rules of the game, which remain without response, are likely to develop into an intensive use of symbols of illegitimacy vis-à-vis the established order, as well as to tactics of physical confrontation with its agencies (especially those of law enforcement).

c. Repeated use of such symbols and experience of direct confrontation are likely to lead to intended illegal action, the highest stage of which is the application of antiregimist violence.

According to this logic, which may of course be expounded in greater detail, I suggest defining the process of delegitimization as: the historical transformation that takes place when a political collectivity which is behaving legally and is using symbols of legitimacy to denote public authorities is moving in time toward a political action characterized by illegal behavior and a use of symbols of illegitimacy vis-à-vis public authorities.

The essence of this definition in relation to democracy is that it presents the process of delegitimization not as an undemocratic phenomenon but as a special pattern of group political behavior that occurs within a democracy as a historical regime. The definition focuses on the fact that *in order to question the legitimacy of the open society one does not need to be in principle its enemy: one often begins as a friend and in a very peculiar process becomes an enemy.*

Two more reasons seem to justify the generalization of the cases dealt with in this paper into a distinct political phenomenon. The first is the repetition of such cases in the political history of democracy in spite of the good wishes of many constitutional democrats and democratic theoreticians. The second is my conviction that in spite of all its virtues, constitutional democracy, unless proven otherwise, must be held incapable of solving the problem of conflicts involving its own legitimacy. The ultimate rationale for this conviction is that no one has as yet shown convincingly that democracy – the political skeleton of the open society – takes an exception to Lord Acton's universal rule that "power tends to corrupt . . ." Processes of delegitimization are ultimately *one type* of reaction to such corruption. Corruption, or abuse of power, need not be personal. It may very well be, and in the case of democracy usually is, *institutional.* Without necessarily agreeing with all the details of their social criticisms or their suggested programs, we cannot fail to recognize that the Marxist labor movement and the new left identified major areas of abuse of power.

The conditions of the industrial proletariat of the nineteenth century, like the conditions of the blacks and the poor in the United States today, were not just a result of uncontrollable objective social forces. They were also due either to the unwillingness of the political authorities to resolve those problems or to the fact that the authorities were not disturbed by their existence.

Processes of delegitimization, to be sure, should not be seen as inevitable or unavoidable. They may not provide the best means for coping with cases of abuse of power and sometimes they may clearly be unreal or unjust. But such processes must be identified as a historically common pattern of group behavior. Given this fact such processes cannot be ignored. They must be *expected* and, consequently, be *studied* from a comparative perspective. A better understanding of these processes may greatly help in our understanding of the working of democracy as a historical regime.

MARXISM AND THE OPEN SOCIETY

MAREK SOBOLEWSKI

A considerable part of Popper's book, *The Open Society and Its Enemies*, is devoted to criticism of the social theory of Marxism. It is impossible to leave this criticism out of the question. Yet it is possible neither to attempt a broad and deep analysis of Popper's arguments nor to enter into any lengthy dispute with his thesis in this paper. Therefore, I shall present in the first and second parts only some polemical remarks referring to the selected and more essential questions of Popper's criticism of Marxism. My intention is to show only why Marxists reject the interpretation of the theory of Marx presented by Popper. In the third part of my article I shall present, though again very briefly, a critical analysis of the political doctrine of Popper himself. For the political estimation of Popper's ideas seems to be more important than the polemic around the proper interpretation of Marxism.

I

In 1974 a reader of Popper's book about the open society can not help feeling that, despite many interesting remarks and ideas it contains, its fundamental theses are out of date. This refers, first of all, to the methodological starting point of Popper – his criticism of historicism. The violent attack against the prediction of the future as well as against the idea of general reconstruction of the social order has already lost its force. No wonder: these are the times of the dynamic development of futurology and, at the same time, of sharp social conflicts and controversy in the Western world of the times of revolutionary ideas. In the dispute with Marx, which he carries on in the book, after thirty years it is Marx who seems to be the winning side.

The presentation of the social theory of Marx in Popper's book has not been considered proper by contemporary Marxists. If they were asked to express their objections, they would probably concentrate on two problems: 1. Popper deals with the ideas of Marx in a very brief and schematic way. One can hardly help receiving the impression that he consciously intends to put these ideas in a more rigid form than that which emerges from a careful reading of Marx. He is limiting the possibilities of the interpretation of Marx's thesis and is trying to formulate them as stiff dogmas. 2. Popper fails to differentiate clearly enough between the theses of Marx which bear the character of scientific laws and those which have the character of strictly historical diagnosis and generalizations valid only for a definite epoch, that is, for Marx's times. He deals with all the anticipations of Marx in the same way, regardless of their degree of circumstantiality. If an anticipation of a particular question has not proved true, Popper assumes the general anticipation, as well as the whole theory, to be false.

This narrow and, at the same time, stiff approach to Marxian theory excludes the possibility of its evolution. According to Popper, the authors who, on the basis of new facts unknown to Marx, attempted to supplement and develop his theory and put new theses in place of the falsified ones, ceased to be Marxists. They are believed to have abandoned Marx's theses under the pressure of reality.

I have always disliked the idea of entering the discussion on the "true" views of this or any other thinker. Fragments out of tune with one another as well as the evolution of opinions are to be found in the heritage of every great philosopher. The importance of a philosopher consists in the fundamental thesis of his doctrine and the new directions of thought (or activity) born out of it. The critical arguments of Popper hit only the details of Marxist theory – its fundamental assumptions remaining unassailable. At many points, however, his criticism misses the point nowadays. The development of capitalism took a different course, in many fields, than could have been foreseen by Marx. This, however, does not change the principal theses of his theory, which together with the methodological directions, are still being used by contemporary Marxists for the analysis of social relations.

To be brief and to the point, I shall indicate at random only two examples of the false interpretation of Marx. As one example, Popper writes that according to Marx's theory of the state, "all politics, all legal and political institutions as well as political struggles, can never be of primary importance. Politics are impotent." [1] This thesis recurs several times at different points of his book. It is, moreover, the natural and obvious result

[1] K. R. Popper, *The Open Society and its Enemies* (London, Routledge & K. Paul, 1945), vol. II, p. 147.

of his similarly simplified and schematic approach to Marx's thesis of superstructure – base correlation. Thus he writes: "This, however, is only a minor example of the danger of over-stressing economism. Often it is sweepingly interpreted as the doctrine that all social development depends upon that of economic conditions, and especially upon the development of the physical means of production. But such a doctrine is palpably false. There is an interaction between economic conditions and ideas, and not simply a unilateral dependence of the latter on the former." [2] Popper's conclusion is, of course, right; the interaction between the relations of production and the ideological superstructure is obvious. Never, however, has the thesis of vulgar economism been proclaimed by Marxism; the influence of ideas upon the base has never been questioned. The best proof of that is Marx's "Thesis on Feuerbach," to which Popper refers several times: "the philosophers have only interpreted the world in various ways; the point, however, is to change it." [3] Popper's criticism misses the point here.

Let us return to our definite example, to the assumption that, according to Marxism, "Politics are impotent." Attributing the first rate importance to economical factors does not lead to such a conclusion at all. For these factors and the economic situation constitute only the conditions of man's activity which may be favourable or unfavourable to certain changes. These changes, however, are, as was emphasized by Marx, brought about by people and this is the political operation. Indeed revolution is a political operation; "the destruction of the apparatus of the bourgeois state" in Marx's writings is a political activity which determines the whole further development of revolution and socialism-building. The "Civil War in France" does not create the impression of the impotency of politics. The analysis of the Commune's errors, carried out by Marx, makes explicit that the fall of the Commune was brought about by political mistakes. The Commune neglected certain reforms as, for example, the nationalization of the Bank of France; it did not pursue the opponents escaping to Wersal, etc. Thus Marx's thesis concerning the dependence of the super structure on the base receives in Popper's book a limiting interpretation, Marxist dialectic being simplified and historical materialism being changed into vulgar economism.

And here are several examples illustrating how Popper fails to differentiate between the principal theories of Marx and his particular, historical hypotheses. The conception of the classless society is derived by Popper

[2] *Ibid.*, p. 100.
[3] *Ibid.*, p. 189.

from the fact that, according to Marx, the development of capitalism is supposed to leave only two classes in the battlefield: proletariat and bourgeoisie, the latter being subsequently destroyed in the revolution. In this way, according to Popper, Marxism substantiates the formation of the classless society. Then he poses the question: "Is it true that the workers' victory must lead to the classless society? I do not think so. From the fact that of two classes only one remains, it does not follow that there will be a classless society." [4] That is right; however, this is not the motivation of the classless society in Marxist theory. The classless society is formed not as a result of the fact that only two classes are left before the revolution – the number of classes before the revolution is not important. According to Marx, it is the abolition of the private property of productive means that accounts for the rise of the classless society. This is the main point of Marx's theory. The thesis of the reduction of the number of classes in the course of the development of capitalism is particular and secondary and its verification or falsification does not effect the value of the principal thesis.

A similar case is Popper's interpretation of Marx's thesis of the advancing pauperization of workers under capitalism. As it is held by Popper, this is the main and principal premise of Marxist theory or the socialist revolution. The cause why workers aim at the revolution is that capitalism brings about an utmost misery for them. Popper could, therefore, easily assert that the improvement of the living conditions of workers in modern capitalism has invalidated the Marxist theory of revolution. I shall return later to the question of Popper's optimism in the evaluation of modern capitalism and the chances for peace between the classes. What I want to stress here is only that the Marxist theory of revolution is based not on the argument of workers' misery but on the thesis of workers' exploitation. A well-paid worker may be exploited too, if he is not rewarded according to his work. The feeling of exploitation and harm may spread among workers even though they do not suffer poverty any longer and have more to lose than "mere fetters." Marx's hypothesis of the advancing pauperization of workers in the course of the development of capitalism did not prove true. But its falsification did not shake any other fundamental theories of Marx, for though the misery decreased, the character of capitalism remained the same. The recurrent increase of class struggles, particularly in the highly developed capitalistic countries, confirms Marx's thesis.

[4] *Ibid.*, p. 127.

II

I do not intend to debate Popper's thesis concerning historicism. Historicism has been discussed by Polish scholars several times, though it has never attracted a special interest. The common opinion of the most outstanding contemporary experts concerning the methodology of the social sciences and history is that Popper's conception of historicism arouses serious doubts. It is too general and the features of historicism established arbitrarily by him are incoherent. J. Szacki writes: "The historicism of which Popper writes does not refer to any reality of the history of social thought. Neither is the separation of antinaturalistic and pronaturalistic conceptions of any good, for Popper treats them as the components of one model . . . Among the representatives of historicism so conceived there are to be found with Popper such diverse thinkers as Marx, Spencer, J. St. Mill, Spengler, Toynbee and Mannheim." [5] J. Topolski, who holds the same view, adds that the reconstructed model of historicism impugned by Popper is alien to Marxism; therefore, "the struggle is pointless." [6]

I do not want to dwell upon these comments any longer for it would require a deeper inquiry into methodological problems. I shall confine myself to one question only, which is the crucial point in Popper's arguments and his attacks against Marxism. Namely, Popper's thesis is that Marxism as the "peak form of historicism" denies any scientific laws in the social sciences which would be of a non-historical character. The only "scientific laws" formulated, according to Popper, by Marxist theory are those of social development, defining the "inevitability" of the occurrence of certain events – revolution, new systems, etc. Starting from these very arguments, Popper evolves the thesis that Marxism, as any historicism, is hostile to social engineering and unable to apply it in practice: "The task that Marx set himself in *Capital* was to discover inexorable laws of social development. It was thus not the discovery of economic laws which would be useful to the social technologist." [7]

Popper denies the possibility of science establishing the laws of social development. He proclaims "the immediate improvement of the world we live in" and is for "a method for piecemeal engineering" and "democratic intervention." Thus he writes: "Marxists would, of course, contend that

[5] J. Szacki, "On So-called Historicism in the Social Sciences" (in Polish) in S. Newak (ed.), *Methodological Problems of Sociological Theories* (Warsaw, 1971), pp. 72-73.

[6] J. Topolski, *Methodology of History* (in Polish, Warsaw, 1968), p. 125.

[7] Popper, *op. cit.*, p. 187.

this kind of intervention *is impossible* since history cannot be made according to rational plans for improving the world." [emphasis added] [8]

Marxists believe that, despite future forecasting which is one of the tasks of the social sciences, their functions consist in finding out and establishing certain constant social correlations and regularities. In the opinion of Marxists, the theory of historical materialism proclaimed by Marx formulates such very general but extremely principal relationships. They bear no traits whatsoever of "prophecies" concerning the future course of history. They ascertain, for example, a close correlation between the structure of property and the class stratification of society. They state a general correlation between life conditions and diverse forms of ideologies, the relation being neither simple and direct nor unilateral only. The majority of those general correlations have been quite commonly approved of by contemporary sociological theory and there is no need to dwell upon these matters at any greater length.

Besides those common laws, valid according to Marxists, in all epochs of the social development of humanity, Marxist historiography also formulates general historical laws, i.e., the laws valid within certain epochs. Those laws are not of the "prophetical" character either, but they fulfill Popper's conditions of the scientific laws. Let us quote one example of such a law, given in the last Polish book on the methodology of history by Professor J. Topolski: "the situation in which the serfdom of peasants coincides with an easy sale of farm products is a necessary and sufficient condition of the serf-farm system." [9] Therefore, Popper's thesis that Marxism excludes the formulation of scientific laws which are not of historical character comes out of a misunderstanding and is not true. Popper's argument that Marxism is not able to apply partial technologies leading to the improvement of social relations is also questionable. As before this is denied by social practice as well as by Marxist activities in both capitalist and socialist countries. In the socialist countries we observe the dynamic development of applied sociology undertaking the classical themes of social engineering. On the grounds of establishing certain correlations, attempts are being made to predict social development in the field of demography, urbanization, etc. In the capitalistic countries the Communist parties, inspired by the theory of historical materialism, struggle not only for revolution but also for partial reforms and for the partial and gradual improvement of the working class living conditions.

Popper's thesis that Marxism is against social engineering implies that

[8] *Ibid.*, p. 132.
[9] Topolski, *op. cit.*, p. 436.

Marxism is against the democratic transformation of the capitalistic state. According to Popper, the policy of Marxist parties "can be characterized as one of *making the workers suspicious of democracy*." [emphasis added] [10] This thought has been also raised by Professor Ehud Sprinzak who writes in his paper that Marxists, instead of making use of democratic institutions for themselves, for their own good refused to participate in them and thereby contributed to the delegitimization of democracy, a situation that helped to foster fascism.

This argument finds no backing in any of the writings of Marx and Engels. Marx very sharply criticizes the police-bureaucratic state, precisely for the lack of democracy. Well known is his passionate fight against censorship. A crucial argument here may be the unmistakable opinion of Engels in his introduction (1895) to the work of Marx, "Class Struggles in France." As we know the text had been greatly expurgated by the first editors, German Social-Democrats, and was published unabridged only in 1918. Since it is a fairly well known text, I shall confine myself to reminding only that in it Engels points out the value of democratic institutions for the working class interests and recommends making use of them and fighting for their preservation and expansion.

Similar is the case of Engel's introduction (1891) to Marx's "The Civil War in France." There one finds the famous words: "Well, gentleman, do you want to see what the proletariat dictatorship looks like? Have a look at the Paris Commune. This was the proletariat dictatorship." [11] However, reading Engels' opinion on what new and important contributions the Paris Commune had brought, we find that we have not departed far from the ideas of representative democracy. In the opinion of Engels, the Commune was desirous of preventing what was "unavoidable in all the hitherto existing states – the transformation of the state and its organs from the society's servants into its masters." Thus, the question involved was that of fighting off the phenomenon of isolation of the political elites – which sounds very contemporary. The means proposed by the Commune were not in the least contrary to the principles of constitutional democracy; these were the cligibility and recall of officials and representatives as well as the reduction of their salaries. Perhaps these postulates sound Utopian and naive now, but one can hardly assume they could have led anybody to totalitarianism.

One can also hardly agree with the argument that the criticism of the

[10] Popper, *op. cit.*, p. 150.
[11] Marx-Engels, *Selected Works* (in Polish; Warsaw, 1949), Vol. I, p. 455.
[12] *Ibid.*, p. 454.

shortcomings and limitations of bourgeois democracy, indications that it is incomplete and imperfect, were discrediting democracy itself. Popper refers to the opinion of Engels that even a republic is a "machine for the oppression of one class by another." [13] The same view, however, is held by contemporary French socialists concerning the regime of the Fifth Republic; the same is the opinion of the left-wing Social Democrats in West Germany. One can hardly consider such views a persistent mass superstition. If, in a certain transitory period of history, communists neglected the value of bourgeois democracy, in spite of Lenin's warnings expressed in his well-known paper, "The Infantile Disease of Leftsidedness," they paid a high price for that neglect and quickly withdrew from the wrong position. No encouragement to reject democracy is to be found in Marx's work; what is found is the effort to supplement political democracy with social democracy.

III

Popper's conception of the open society is not only a theoretical model in the field of sociology or in the history of human societies. It is also a political ideology addressed to contemporaries and enclosing univocal estimating opinions. This is a confession of faith of a liberal engaged in the fight against fascism and communism. We are free, therefore, to deal with it in the way we deal with political ideologies, as with a collection of opinions and norms of conduct for people who love freedom.

Poppers' book is for the most part a polemic. One can hardly find in it a full and exhaustive description or characterization of the open society, a list of features by which that society should be characterized. In particular, no answer has been given to the question regarding the borderline dividing an open society from a closed one, though the transition from one to another is, in Popper's account, a long historical process. When, then, shall we be able to talk of an open society?

One may say, to be sure, as does Professor Dante Germino in regard to Bergson, that the open society is merely an ever-alive ideal, a goal for which one should always strive but which can never be fully attained by humanity. Still, even in such a case, there arise some practical problems, linked with the question concerning the features of the open society, which need to be solved.

I find in the work of Popper two basic features of the open society. 1. "The society in which individuals are confronted with personal decisions";

[13] Popper, *op. cit.*, p. 150.

consequently "many members strive to rise socially and to take the places of other members." [14] In other words, people are free, not hampered a priori with the norms restricting their freedom of action and choice. 2. The development of society is accomplished by the way of evolution, through "piecemeal engineering." [15]

1. It seems that we turn back here to a very old and thorny dispute between the "advocates" of revolution and evolution in social development. I say "advocates" for, in fact, nobody, or almost nobody, wishes personally a revolution or prefers it to evolution. I think that both every average man in all the epochs of history and a majority of philosophers would prefer social progress to take a gradual and mild course – without unnecessary and excessive sacrifices. Some statesmen, from Attila to Hitler, perhaps held other opinions but we treat them as pathological individuals.

But then what of our good wishes when reality appears to be different? The great progressive changes in past history were, for the most part, achieved in a violent way. Studying history, one learns that the ruling classes hardly ever had the intention of improving, of their own will, the lot of their subjects. Even relatively minor changes and improvements usually took place under great threats. It is enough to mention here only the history of the social reforms of capitalism in the second half of the nineteenth century. Popper perceives and praises the social reforms of capitalism and counterposes them to revolution. He does not, however, raise the question concerning the causes of these reforms. Why had they not been introduced earlier? Why even nowadays in a democratic capitalistic country does the maintenance of social reforms and the extension of privileges require such hard fought battles, often passionate and violent? I also believe that a great many welfare state reforms after World War II were prompted by a threatening, serious growth of Communist influence. The "piecemeal engineering" takes advantage of the great revolutions.

The first attempt at carrying into effect the ideas of an open society was the Athenian democracy. Later, however, came a period of regression lasting two thousand years. Another attempt at creating an open society were the bourgeois revolutions – English, American and French. All of them were carried out violently, not by the way of slow and minor reforms. The democracy which Popper defends was formed in such a way, contrary to his conception, for it developed not only through a great violent change but also as the result of the mobilization of the masses by great revolutionary Utopias – holistic plans of rebuilding the society. Those great Utopian

[14] *Ibid.*, pp. 153-154.
[15] *Ibid.*, p. 139.

visions of a perfect future, of a thorough reconstruction of society and of creating a happy humanity became the motive power for human activities and great changes accomplished in the past.

If we approve of social progress in the sense of the improvement of the conditions of human existence and the perfection of human individuality, we can condemn neither revolution nor great Utopias. Could we renounce them in the future? I would be careful in formulating such an assertive thesis. One should bear in mind the fate of those pacifists who in the name of their noble idea opposed the war against fascism.

On the other hand, I am inclined to admit that Popper was right saying that the great Utopian visions also contain great risks. They easily become transformed from goals serving man into goals man himself is forced to serve. Ardent followers of some ideas often enough did not hesitate to spread the new faith with fire and sword; such was even the part of Christianity. Should one because of that condemn the faith itself? These are the questions which I purposely leave without an answer.

Contemporary Marxist theory admits the possibility of a peaceful transition to socialism without violent revolution. Popper combats this thesis assuming it a departure from the conception of Marx. I do not want to return to the analysis of the views of Marx himself. Let us assume that if Marx really denies the possibility of peaceful transition to socialism, such a view is easily explained by the political situation of his times. In what way, however, is the conception of the peaceful transition to socialism contrary to the assumptions of Marx's theory?

For Marx, the revolution is not the act of violence or armed uprising. The revolution is the change of the relations of production, the transition to another epoch, regardless of the form assumed by this transition. A peaceful revolution is not a contradiction, therefore. Popper makes a different argument. He assumes that the gradual reforms of capitalism lead to the decrease of class discrepancies. The workers who attain some profit under capitalism will not want, he asserts, to risk their welfare. The workers who have more to lose than "their fetters" will not want to expropriate the capitalists.[16] The evolutionary interpretation of social revolution he concludes, breaks the whole Marxist theory.

One can hardly agree with this attitude. It obviously did not prove true in reality. In the richest countries of the welfare state workers still crave for the socialization of property and support the expropriation programmes. The more they own, the more they struggle for living conditions equal to those of the bourgeoisie.

[16] *Ibid.*, p. 144.

Nor is this theoretically contradictory to Marxist theory. As I have already mentioned, according to Marx's theory, it is not poverty that is supposed to be the revolutionary motive but rather the existing oppression of hired labour as well as the relations of production creating the alienation of human labour. The rise of the living standard in capitalism does not eliminate either the former or the latter. Thus the revolutionary premises still remain.

The theory of revolution and the conception of democratic intervention are not contradictory nor do they exclude each other, as it is held by Popper. Marxists presume the possibility and appropriateness of society's improvement through piecemeal engineering in regard to bourgeois society. However, the full liberation of labourers and the attainment of full democracy is possible, according to Marxists, only through overcoming capitalism, through the elimination of this social order: this is what is called revolution. So far such revolutions have required the use of force. It is quite possible, however, that nowadays in some countries they can take place without the use of force through the accumulation of fundamental social reforms.

2. I should also like to consider the question: who is supposed to belong to an open society. The question may appear odd but one has to be aware of the fact that for many centuries people belonging to one society lived in greatly differentiated conditions. The conditions in which a great part of the nineteenth century bourgeoisie lived correspond probably with what Popper means by an open society. The middle and small bourgeoisies looked in turn for their place in the economy and politics, and they accomplished successive gradual reforms and improvements, removing the consecutive obstacles on their way to social advancement. At the same time, however, workers were doomed to a hopeless existence in miserable workmen's conditions, similary as in Plato's time slaves were doomed to slavery. Neither the workers nor the slaves participated in the open society.

There is no doubt that the idea of an open society applies to all the people. Thus, an open society will be such a society which realizes the features assumed by Popper but in regard to all. We may agree with the opinion that liberal democracy, in particular after World War II, created relatively very good facilities for realizing what Popper understands to be an open society. Yet such a system exists in only a few very highly developed capitalist countries. And even in those countries the legitimization of that system happens to be questioned again and again by numerous groups of people. If we reject the "conspiracy" theories – for conspiracy succeeds only there where the conditions are favourable for it – then there is only one explanation left. Highly developed, democratic societies of the West are not yet sufficiently "open" to a great part of their citizens.

And such was precisely the basic thesis of Marxism. Since the time of Marx this theory has been assuming that a total liberation of man, and this is the equivalent of Popper's open society, needs the carrying into effect of the principle of equality. This equality must not only be equality in the legal sense but also equality in regard to living conditions. This does not involve full equalization, "*Gleichschaltung*." But according to Marxism, in a just society too great differences in wealth cannot exist nor is there place for too rich or too poor people.

This conception is very old and has been many times renewed in history. Although it may seem Utopian to us it appeals very strongly to people, for it well agrees with their sense of justice, their aspirations. Yet it is very difficult to actualize, not for technical reasons – today in particular this would be possible – but because of the exceptional reluctance of rich people objecting to the limitations on their rights and privileges.

If we, however, do not realize those aspirations of the masses, can one say we will build a society open to all? Can we convince the people that for the sake of preserving present freedom they should give up equality? Can one make a proper use of freedom, do whatever he likes if he still lives in the conditions of economic limitations? Marxism answers these questions negatively and here lies the origin of its conflict with liberalism. Not that Marxism is by its nature an antiliberal doctrine; on the contrary, this is not the case. Nevertheless, to Marxists egalitarianism comes before all the other rights, for otherwise those rights would have no real value to the majority or to a considerable part of the people.

IV

The discussion of the individual theses of Popper could be still continued at a great length. However I will not dwell upon them any longer. There remains only one question that I would like to pose finally. How can one evaluate Popper's theory of the open society – this great and impassioned polemic for the gradual non-revolutionary improvement of the Western world?

The answer is enclosed in the remark made earlier in this paper. The world which Popper is willing to improve, only without thorough alteration, arose in the make of the bourgeois revolutions. Those revolutions constituted the foundations of the order which are accepted by Popper. He does not consider it necessary to change them. An advocate of gradual small and partial steps must accept the principles of status quo. No one wants to improve tyranny – tyranny is to be combated and demolished. It is the good government and good social order that are to be improved.

Popper's conception is a moderately conservative doctrine. It recommends the preservation of the existing society. It is the wise and rational conservatism which recommends keeping to the spirit of the age, introducing necessary small changes in order to counteract the opposition. It resembles the conception of the end of the ideology age, which is proclaimed, first of all, by those who dislike the existing ideologies. Popper does not want revolution for he considers the stage of social development attained by capitalism satisfactory.

Popper's conception is liberal conservatism. Similar to classical liberalism it defends the rights of an individual, his autonomy and freedom. Similar to classical liberalism, it wishes to limit the intervention of the state into the life of the individual to the minimum necessary in a given time; being afraid of power, it is distrustful of the state organization of individuals' life. Similar to classical liberalism, Popper's doctrine is based on belief in the rationalism of human beings people's ability to be guided with their own reason in organizing their lives. Popper believes in the possibility of reasonable compromises and in the idea of the golden mean and moderation. The method of piecemeal engineering which Popper recommends in reforming the society is the classical example of the method of moderation and of the golden mean.

There can be applied the same measures to the doctrine propagated by Popper as to liberal conservatism. This doctrine is a significant constituent of human progress; it relieves the tension of social struggles, it attempts to preserve the undeniable and important human values – the freedom and autonomy of the individual. However, without the effects produced in history by the ideas of the general revolutionary transformation of the world, the progress claimed by Popper could never be attained.

IDEOLOGY, OPENNESS AND FREEDOM

BERNARD CRICK

In the 1950s and the early 1960s it was believed that political theory in a learned sense was dead and that the practical influence of political ideas was dying. This was the time of Daniel Bell's book, *The End of Ideology*, of which it is fair to say that the title was more influential than the contents. It was widely believed that ideological motivations in politics were happily on the wane, that "new technocrats" had come to positions of political power, not merely in the Western world, and that political philosophy had become purely academic and historical. But this has proved an illusion, or rather it always all depended on what one meant by "ideology." Certainly there was a decline in ideology of the total and comprehensive kind typical of social thought as influenced by Hegel and Marx and typical of the actual politics of the 1930s. But ideology in that sense has not been replaced by purely technological, empirical or pragmatic thought – if such things could ever have been said to exist in purity.

For pure practicality is as much a myth as is "totality," either of explanation or action. They are powerful and influential myths, but they conceal particular and precise values. One task of political theory is to study the preconceptions and presuppositions of those who claim to be "purely practical" and "to have no time for ideas," and another rather similar task is to show how arbitrary and limited are most of the claims to have a total explanation of society (and how excessively abstract are the rest). But more than that, political doctrines have become more important as belief in total ideological solutions has collapsed and pure practicality has everywhere proved as impractical as pure coercion. Even the new or student Marxism believes that ideas can effect events (by creating a mythical "Young Marx" who never grew up), no longer that ideas are simply products of circumstance. Far from political thought having become a dry desert, it has become a tower of Babel. But if few people now act as if ideas either do not matter or are simply products of circumstance, still fewer (though some) would return to the somewhat naive pre-sociological era in which ideas can be seen as autonomous causes. We now accept a very complicated mental world in which ideas must be interpreted as having their meaning conditioned by social circumstances (though not caused by them), even while their significance or truth can again be a matter of moral reasoning. Thus political theory must be concerned with the double claim of political doctrines to point to something that is desirable but which is also possible. All that is possible is not desirable and all that desirable is not possible. Truly stated and sensibly studied, there is no conflict, rather a necessary complementarity, between political philosophy and political science.

Such an introduction is necessary, if only to make the formal point that the idea of an "Open Society" must be specified in both moral and empirical terms. I see an "open society" as one that depends upon moral freedom but also seeks to maximize the communication of possible truths.

Freedom I conceive as a category of action. To be free means that one *is* acting freely, without constraint and therefore unpredictably, not merely that one can act freely. It is not acting in any direction which can, in advance of the event and an evaluation of its consequences, be said with certainty to be right – except that it can always be said that a "free action" is wrong if it limits the free actions of others for no good reason (that is, just because I feel like it, or think that I have a right to do what I please). Here I agree with both Karl Popper's criticism of "historicism" and with Isaiah Berlin's criticism of what he calls "positive liberty" ("the truth shall set you free" or "in thy service, Lord, is the only perfect freedom").[1] But I disagree with Berlin (in his "Two Concepts of Liberty"). I think it important, of course, to stress that for there to be freedom there must be genuine, alternative courses of action and a genuine capacity for choice by individuals, and that freedom is not choosing the one that will, in fact, guarantee bliss or happiness. Yet it is equally important that the free man must, in fact, choose. It would be an unfair parody of Berlin himself to say that his ideal of freedom is delicious indecision when faced by beautiful alternatives, but his failure to specify the social conditions for free actions (when can real choices be made?) leaves his argument open, at the worst, to this uncharitable accusation of triviality or, at the best, to being simply a logical distinction, philosophical certainly, but not political at all without much more specification of institutions and circumstances. Elsewhere I

[1] Sir Karl Popper, *The Poverty of Historicism* (London, Routledge, 1957) and Sir Isaiah Berlin, *Four Essays on Liberty* (Oxford, Oxford University Press, 1969) which includes his "Two Concepts of Liberty."

have stressed the social context of the concept of freedom in criticism of Berlin's too narrowly analytical approach.[2] We need to look not just to the logical possibility of choice or choosing, but to the character, historical, social and psychological, of men who actually choose. When one actually chooses, of course, as distinct from mere contemplation of choice, some alternatives are then closed; but it is characteristic of a free action that the range of possible future choices is then narrowed, but never eliminated utterly.

An "open society" I conceive not as a category of action, like freedom, but as a category of communication – that we can know what we are all up to, not necessarily in the sense of knowledge as truth, more often only of opinion, but it is likely that in the long run no society can be both stable and just (reasonably stable and reasonably just) unless opinions are advanced in a manner and a form that are subject to refutation and correction by research and by reasoning – to follow closely the argument of Popper's great second volume of *The Open Society and Its Enemies* and his *The Logic of Scientific Discovery*. So I would apologise if my use of this term is more modest, empirical and commonsensical than some of the leading spirits in this symposium. A minimal definition of an open society is one in which the truth can be told about how the society is actually governed without thereby harming the system of government (although particular Governments may be hurt) – as cannot be done in most, possibly all, autocracies. All autocracies have some irrational element in their published claims for legitimacy which they cannot allow to be publicly and rationally discussed. A maximum definition of an open society is one in which it is typical for individuals to understand the true motivations of their behavior towards others and of others towards them without being harmed, in terms of mental health, or insulted in terms of human dignity.

Logically it is conceivable that an enlightened autocracy or a benevolent despotism, as envisaged by Voltaire or the young Bentham, could be an "open society" without being, in a political sense, a "free society." The practical and human difficulties, however, of being a genuinely enlightened autocracy are overwhelming, although there may be (again to follow Popper) an objection in principle in that the fallibility principle requires some external check or monitor, not simply a lofty "duty of doubt" in the heart of the ruler. But it is contradictory to say that society could be a free society without also being, at least to some considerable extent, an

[2] See my "Freedom as Politics" in Peter Laslett and W. G. Runciman, eds., *Philosophy, Politics and Society,* (3rd ed., Oxford, Blackwell, 1969) or as reprinted in my essays, *Political Theory and Practice* (London, Allen Lane, 1971).

open society. And it is likely that, as a cultural norm, free societies generate a seeming imperative towards ever more openness.

I wish in the main part of this paper simply to consider the main set of constraints on openness which arise not from coercion but because of arguments freely adopted. These seeming rational arguments which in fact restrain reason are no longer primarily religious, they are a distinctively modern belief-system: the belief in ideological necessity. Ideology demonstrates both that we are not free when we think we are free and that openness is an illusion at the service of class or elite oppression. The bird believes that the heavens are the air within the cage. To examine the concept of ideology closely is to begin to show how far it is, indeed, in its very variety, "the opiate of the intellectuals," and a closer of doors of choice rather than an opener. And at the end of the paper I will add a short note on different usages of "open" which I noted during the talks which gave rise to this volume – some of which sounded remarkably closed.

So oppressive to freedom of thought is ideology – and hence to the possibility of arriving at truths of an ever higher degree of probability about moral conduct and society – that I would draw a formal contrast between the idea of an "open society" and the idea of an "ideological society."

Such a formal contrast, however, needs two clear qualifications if what follows is not to be misunderstood from the very beginning. Firstly, "ideology," if it is used simply as a synonym for doctrine, is unobjectionable. Doctrines are true or false, plausible or implausible, good or bad in so far as they relate to the *possibility* of some *specific* actions or policies based on some *specified* principles or beliefs. They are about particular things. A man may be doctrinaire, either in the sense that he is inflexible and holds his beliefs with little or no regard to objections about their applicability, or in the sense that he is obsessive and would push his good doctrine into areas where it has no possible relevance. The folly of such doctrinaires is precisely that they think that their few good principles can be applied to the exclusion of all other considerations; but at least they – strictly speaking – exaggerate more than universalize and allow much human activity to escape their attention as simply trivial or irrelevant to their preoccupations. But the ideologist believes and an ideology states that *everything* is relevant to and explained by the principles.

There are general philosophical objections to "ideology" in this sense, but there can be no possible general objections to holding a doctrine. Each doctrine must be considered on its merits. I have argued elsewhere that, indeed, there is necessarily a doctrinal element in all political theories: in politics generalization and evaluation can never be fully separated.[3]

My second qualification concerns "open." While I endorse and follow Popper's great synthesis of liberal moral philosophy and of scientific method, stressing trial and error, hypothesis and deduction and then research to try to *refute* or *falsify* – neither inductivism nor final proof, indeed the plain commonsense of being "open to argument" – yet I do not share his views on "essentialism" and do not think that they are logically involved in his views on fallibility and falsification. "Essentialism," as he defined it in his *Poverty of Historicism*, may constitute a class of logically invalid and scientifically meaningless-because-unrefutable arguments, but it is logically invalid to pass from that to assuming terrible effects from holding beliefs in this form – as he did when he dedicated his *Poverty of Historicism* to the dead of the concentration camps "who died because of a belief in essentialism." Leaving aside that they died for many other reasons besides, it can only be accurate to say that they died because of a particular essentialist idea. But some "essentialists" are pacifists, theosophists, vegetarians and heaven knows what else besides, certainly members of every conceivable religion, not all of whom are equally prone to violence and if so, then usually for reasons other than the content of the dogma itself. From different essentialist "dogmas" different deductions for conduct will be made, just as different deductions follow from different hypotheses. I can see no general objection to "essentialism," anymore than to doctrine. Certainly it is no part of my theory or doctrine of an "open society" that people may not have irrational beliefs. Liberalism does not consist in believing in nothing. Toleration does not consist in the presumption to empty both one's own mind and everybody else's of all prejudice, but in recognizing a diversity of moral viewpoints and in limiting one's undoubted disapproval of the other viewpoints to argument, persuasion and example, rather than prohibition and coercion.[4]

But with these two caveats, I would maintain that the contrast between the ideal of an open society and the ideal of an ideological society is real and important.

[3] See the appendix, "A Footnote to Rally the Academic Professors of Politics" in my *In Defence of Politics* (2nd ed., Harmondsworth, Pelican, 1964) and "On Theory and Practice" in *Political Theory and Practice, op. cit.*

[4] On toleration see the special issue of *Government and Opposition* (Spring, 1971), especially the contributions by Maurice Cranston, Ernest Gellner, Preston King, D. D. Raphael and Alan Ryan.

SENSES OF IDEOLOGY

Never has a new and influential concept of the modern world been used and abused in so many different senses. Six main senses are distinguishable:

(i) *Impractical and visionary ideas.* Napoleon first used the word this way to mock the Old Jacobins. (ii) *Argument from some abstract formula.* The early conservatives thought that this was typical of radical and revolutionary thought; they contrasted ideology to experience. Michael Oakeshott has said that ideology is politics derived from a book. (iii) *Persuasive ideas.* Ideas advanced in a form aimed at persuasion and action rather than verification or truth: thus "instrumental" or "interested" ideas. The "ideologically correct" can even be accepted when known to be empirically false. (iv) *A comprehensive explanation of social processes.* Looking at the totality of factors involved in explaining social phenomena, an assumption that there is a social *system* analogous to natural and mechanical systems. (v) *A comprehensive explanation which prophesies or predicts systematic change.* The fourth sense of ideology can have conservative or traditionalist implications, but this fifth is revolutionary: world views can anticipate or create new worlds. The conservative says, 'things are so systematically related to each other that nothing important can be changed without risk of the breakdown of society"; but the revolutionary says, "things are so systematically related to each other that everything must be changed at once, partial or particular reforms are impossible or a delusion." (vi) *The derivation of ideas from circumstances.* Simply the academic study (as in Karl Mannheim's sociology of knowledge) of the *degree* to which ideas are products of or dependent on social structures and the interests of particular groups.

The language of political theory would be less confused if we were to use the term ideology to stand for a fusion of the second, third and fifth concepts above that is, to assert that in the modern world a distinctive and secular way of thinking has grown up which is based on highly abstract assumptions yet seeks an essentially popular and persuasive formulation in order to achieve what it believes will be a total transformation of society. This is the strong and distinctively modern sense of ideology. Following much actual usage, one could call the third or the persuasive sense, the weak sense of ideology; but there is already a perfectly good word in "doctrine," and it seems very weak to argue that ideology is simply any political idea which can have an effect, which involves action – particularly when some of us would argue that this is a general characteristic of all political ideas.[5] And to call *all* "belief-systems" "ideologies" is to add or subtract nothing, for all belief-systems have sought to be internally consistent, systematic in that sense, but only in the modern world have there been secular belief systems which have claimed to be comprehensive and of universal applicability. Certainly there is a special case to be made for the academic study of "ideology" in the sixth sense – although even then one may as well say "sociology of knowledge" and "ideas in their social setting" to avoid confusion, but only while it is assumed that ideas are to *some extent* explicable as products: once it is assumed that all ideas are necessarily and entirely products of circumstance, then it follows that one must either be a traditionalist or a revolutionary – as involved in the fifth concept above.

Let me deal with each of these senses in turn, and state the grounds for the kind of synthesis and usage I have already suggested.

(i) Ideology as the impractical and the visionary

The word ideology was a deliberate invention, to mean "the logic of ideas," by a minor French philosopher, Destutt de Tracy, in a paper read in 1795 before the semi-official Institut National des Sciences et Arts called "Une Mémoire sur la Faculté de Pensée." He wished to create a science of the true connotation of ideas based upon the crude nominalist belief that for every idea there was a unique word, and on the still more crude materialist belief that for every word-as-idea there was a unique physiological stimulus in the brain. "Every science," he wrote, "is reducible to a well made language; and to make progress in a science is nothing but improving its language, whether by changing its words or by rendering its meanings precise."

Somehow Napoleon got to hear of this and he made the word famous, taking de Tracy's modest attempt to reform language as an example of the whole class of crack-pot ideas of the old Jacobins with plans in their pockets for the reform of society based on one or two, or three or four, or ten or twenty, self-evident basic principles.

> Well, you're right, it's true that these metaphysicians are my pet aversion. I have classified all these people under the head of ideologists, which, by the way, is peculiarly and literally suited to them: idea seekers – hollow ideas, as a rule. Now the apt application of the term ideologist to that class has cast even

[5] Quoted by H. B. Acton in his "The Philosophy of Language in Revolutionary France," *Proceedings of the British Academy,* XLV (1959), pp. 199 ff.

more ridicule upon them than I dared to hope. The expression stuck – I think because it came from me. There's no harm in it. There will be less ideology around . . . those poor scholars don't understand themselves. How could I come to terms with them to govern the way they think I ought to? Yes, they have a craze for interfering with my policies. They talk, talk, talk. My aversion for this breed of ideologists goes to the point of hatred. I don't care who knows it.[6]

Certainly the idea did catch on. Many people still use the term primarily to draw a contrast between an impractical and dogmatic politics and one based on experience.

(ii) Ideology as an Abstract Formula

But Napoleon himself carried the idea further. In a speech to the *Conseil d'Etat* of the 20th December, 1812, facing impending defeat, he cried:

It is to this ideology, this shady metaphysics which would base political legislation upon subtle principles derived from First Causes instead of adapting it to our knowledge of human psychology and to historic lessons, that every misfortune experienced by our beautiful France must be attributed. These errors were bound to, and in fact did, bring about the reign of terror by the blood-stained men. Who fawned upon the people by proclaiming its sovereignty, which it was incapable of exercising? Who destroyed the awe and sanctity of the laws by making them depend, not on the sacred principles of justice, but on the Natural Order, not civil law but merely on the will of an assembly whose members were ignorant of civil, penal, administrative, political and military laws. He who has been called upon to regenerate a State must follow absolutely opposite principles. History paints the human heart. In history we must seek the advantages and disadvantages of the various systems of law.[7]

Napoleon had a point, though he exaggerated vastly.

In England, Tory pamphleteers took up the term and used it in their polemic against political reform. Burke had already attacked abstract ideas in *Reflections on the Revolution in France*, saying that in matters political it was better to trust "the farmer than the metaphysician," so the general argument was familiar to them. But they saw "ideology" as the specifically French belief, they thought, that politics could be conducted according to some rational formula. They called Jeremy Bentham an ideologist – which, in that sense, he plainly was. A contemporary Tory, Michael Oakeshott, means much the same thing by his polemic against "Rationalism." He has said in conversation that ideology is something derived from a book, just as in his *Political Education* he mocks those who think that you can even

[6] See J. Christopher Herald (ed.), *The Mind of Napoleon: A Selection From His Written and Spoken Word* (New York, Columbia University Press, 1961) pp. 68-69.

[7] *Ibid.*, p. 69.

practice cookery, let alone politics, by reading a book. (God help us, indeed, from those who practice politics, cook, drive cars and make love by reading books of instruction. But Oakeshott does not explore either how people can be led into attempting those things by a book, although they may throw it away at a very early stage; nor how an already good politician, cook, motorist or lover may improve his or her performance by reading a book).

There are people who pursue politics according to some such set of abstract formulae. Many of them today are, in fact, called liberals. But is it helpful to call them ideologists? I think not. This sense is too general. For there is a type of thinking which is not merely abstract but claims to be total and comprehensive. I prefer to call ideas about particular things "doctrines," so that most of Napoleon's ideologists become doctrinaires, and reserve the term "ideology" for those views of society as a whole in which it is asserted that society can only be seen as a whole. But before coming to that point, one other usage of ideology needs to be noted.

(iii) Ideology as Persuasive

The Catholic Church early had a special Office of the Propaganda, concerned simply with the propagation of the faith. But it was the French Revolution which gave wide currency to the idea of secular ideas popularized and used as weapons. The primary purpose of such formulations was to persuade, sometimes to frighten and intimidate, sometimes to prophesy and to create expectations of better things to come. We take this now so much for granted as part of modern politics that we forget how specifically modern it was. For a while with some of the French Jacobins and the American and English radicals, it was both revolutionary and democratic: there were no true ideas which were not comprehensible by the ordinary people, and if ordinary people understood the business of government, the consequences would be revolutionary. But almost at once ideologies, in this sense, certainly before Marxism, either compromised with the aristocratic learned traditions of the past or else took on the new elitist arguments of science and technology: there was a difficult and fully true ideology, but also a less true popular version. And sometimes the popular version was called "ideology" as distinct from science, and was what was needed, how people needed to be made to think, before the true, imminent ideology could be realized. One of St. Simon's followers, Enfantin, could

> see the time approaching when the 'art of moving the masses' will be so perfectly developed that the painter, the musician and the poet will possess the

power to please and to move with the same certainty as the mathematician solves a geometrical problem or the chemist analyzes some substance.[8]

The poet Shelley, who was a radical and a democrat by conviction, proclaimed that "poets are the legislators of mankind" (one of the first practitioners of an esoteric art to fool himself that he was reaching the people). It is worth pausing to reflect that the claim to be the unique popularizers of an esoteric reforming doctrine was made by artists about the same time, possibly slightly before, sociologists and social scientists began to make it. The horrible Wagner certainly carried forward this idea of art as didactic into our next category, that of the comprehensive or total explanation of society; indeed, he carried it right forward – such was his dark genius – into the idea of a total reformation of society. For to Wagner the future will show:

the great united art-work, that must embrace all the *genres* of art and in some degree undo (*verbrauchen*) each of them in order to use it as a means to an end, to annul it in order to attain the common aim of *all*, namely the unconditioned, immediate representation of perfected human nature – this great united art work we cannot recognise as the arbitrary need of the individual, but only as the inevitable (*notwendig denkbare*), associated work of the humanity of the future.[9]

In bad times to come there was, of course, to be a Soviet or Stalinist version of this same complicated thought, and also a Nazi version. I suspect that it was not unfamiliar in Japan when traditional thought responded to an accelerated modernization by ultra-nationalism.

And also there was a gentler version of ideology as persuasion in Protestant evangelism. As many historians have pointed out, notably Elie Halevy in his great history of English radicalism, it was Methodism, trying to bring a bureaucratized State religion back to life and back to the people, who invented many of the techniques of modern politics: the mass meeting, the meetings in the fields and in the streets preached to by travelling preachers. Some of them travelled as far as Africa and China and one may speculate that many of the popularizing techniques proved more influential in the long run in politics than in religion.

(iv) Ideology as Comprehensive Explanation of Social Processes

Hegel had, of course, prepared the roots, even though his philosophy was

[8] Quoted by F. A. Hayek, *The Counter-Revolution of Science* (Glencoe, Ill., Free Press, 1962), p. 145.

[9] Quoted by Ernest Newman, *Wagner as Man and Artist* (New York, Alfred A. Knopf, 1924), p. 187.

still, what proved to be young Marx's final breaking point with Hegelianism, inseparable from religion, not inherently secular like sociology. From Hegel came the idea of *Weltanschauung*, that each epoch was characterized by a unified world-view defined by philosophy. But the history of this term was to become inseparable from that of the French and Anglicized "ideology": both came more and more in the mid-nineteenth century to carry the connotation of not merely *being*, the rational structure of the world as it was, but of *becoming*, of making the world more rational. And this was a more commonsense view than it is often made to sound, if by "more rational" one really means less inconsistent and less contradictory (just as "more equal" is better understood as "less unequal" and "more just" as "less obviously unjust").

The idea at times seems a truism or a platitude, but there is a basic contrast between the old *political* tradition, going back in one way to Aristotle and in another to Machiavelli, which had always been concerned with particular things and with the compromising of fundamental moral viewpoints rather than their secular solution, and the newly emerging sociological world-view: that all things are interconnected. Only to pause to remind ourselves that there was a conservative version of this new sense of the totality of social relationships, in a word of "system," found in de Maistre, Burke and Hegel himself, before there was a socialist version, found in Robert Owen, Fourier, Proudhon and Marx.[10]

Marx drew an explicit distinction between the political and the social: "politics" was partial, concerned with particular things, indeed particularly bourgeois, concerned with retaining things; whereas "the social" was comprehensive, concerned with understanding the pattern of emerging new social orders.[11] But before Marx there was Proudhon:

> The social life from which the worker is *shut out* is a social life very different in kind and extent from that of the *political* sphere. The social life . . . is *life* itself, physical and cultural life, human morality, human activity, human enjoyment, real *human* existence. Human life is the *true social life* of man. As the irremediable exclusion from this life is much more complete, more unbearable, dreadful and contradictory, than the exclusion from political life, so is the ending of this exclusion . . . more fundamental, as *man* is more fundamental than the *citizen*, human life more than *political life*.[12]

[10] As brilliantly argued in Leon Bramson's *The Political Context of Sociology*, (Princeton, New Jersey, Princeton University Press, 1961).

[11] Relevant quotations of Marx's use of the term "political" are found on p. 166 of my *In Defence of Politics*, Pelican edition.

[12] Proudhon, *Oeuvres Complètes* III, p. 43, quoted by Sheldon Wolin in his *Politics and Vision; Continuity and Innovation in Western Political Thought* (Boston, Little Brown, 1960), p. 417.

Proudhon explicitly lays the blame for the troubles of his times on: "Une certaine maladie de l'opinion . . . qu'Aristote . . . a nommé 'POLITIQUE'" [13] which I would colloquially translate as "a certain sick opinion that Aristotle called 'politics.'" (May one pause to comment that both Proudhon and Marx make much better sense if they are understood as attacking contemporary politicians rather than the whole activity of politics. Certainly modern Marxism has not escaped from politics, indeed the most interesting modern Marxist writers are now trying to show that there is a place for politics in the theory: that there are choices, that all values are not predetermined, that uncertainty is not wholly a product of societies based upon the exploitation of labor).

The concept of ideology, of course, really enters into modern social thought with Marx's celebrated essay *The German Ideology,* and elsewhere it is less used and defined than many of the faithful believe. But remember what happens in *The German Ideology.* He starts off polemicizing against the official German Professors who held the State chairs. Their great philosophy, he says, is simply the ideology of political self-interest. At first he uses the term almost as Napoleon did, abusively and pejoratively of a set of ideas impossibly abstract but also, the new twist, flagrantly self-interested. But how can they be anything else, but self-interested? They are what they are as creatures of their class. And he generalizes this thought so that instead of continuing a conventional polemic, to show in grim detail what lick-spittles and hirelings they are of the Prussian State and all that it stands for, he suddenly turns the essay into a highly abstract and generalized assertion that *all* ideas are the product of the interests of social classes; the classical theory of ideology is born: that ideas are products. "It is not the consciousness of men that determines their existence, but, on the contrary, their social existence which determines their consciousness." Hegel is turned upside down indeed. The way is now clear for the emergence of revolutionary ideology.

(v) Ideology as Comprehensive Explanation which Prophesies or Predicts Systematic Change

Such that one fine day there will be no further social change. I will go quickly over familiar territory. Communist ideology is, after all, famous. Unlike so-called utopian socialism, it claims to be *scientific* (indeed the only explanation implicit in *The German Ideology* of how Marx's own ideas are *not* simply a product of his social class, which was emphatically

[13] *Ibid.,* p. 414.

not proletarian, is that his ideas are scientific, whereas other peoples' ideas are ideological: I simplify a little, but not much; all the subsequent arguments about the special role of the Party were not Marx's). But unlike social-democracy, Communism claims to be comprehensive, indeed revolutionary: there is the high theoretical argument about inevitable stages of society which is very implausible; but on a lower level, there is the implicit argument that gradualist or evolutionary means towards socialist goals simply will not work – alas, far more plausible.

But Marxism after Marx creates a subsidiary philosophy of ideology as persuasive ideas. Marxist theorists (or some of them) understand the true situation but the masses have to be persuaded or led, if necessary by half-truths, into the consciousness that somehow anticipates the next stage of historical evolution. I do not wish to consider whether the famous phrase of European Communists in the 1930s "it is ideologically correct" (which meant ask no questions about the lies and cruelties of Soviet internal politics and their self-defeating tactics in Spain) is in some sense inherent in Marxism; or whether totalitarian ideology is inherent in Marxism. All I need to do is to point to the actual existence of this kind of argument. There was Stalin's famous crude remark that "apart from the Party there is no working class consciousness" which is somewhat different from Lenin's "the party can alone formulate working class ideology." But Lenin had also said that: "To belittle socialist ideology in any way, to deviate from it in the slightest degree means strengthening bourgeois ideology." Certainly ideology had by then become remarkably removed from philosophy, or simply truth. Even then there was more than one socialism, if not the "thousand flowers" of today.

Certainly it seems hard to reconcile any belief in one body of men being sure of a comprehensive explanation of the direction of social change with any tolerance of differences either about objectives or methods. In the history of religion in the West, tolerance did not mark the end of religious belief, but originally simply a new context of restraint in which religious debate was conducted. For a long time Catholics and Protestants tolerated each other but both believed that the other would go to hell. Perhaps scepticism is more difficult if only this world counts, but since only this world counts (to my knowledge) it can also be argued that scepticism is more necessary.

One can equally well illustrate from Nazi thought the contingent tendency (I am less sure of the logical tendency) for this kind of ideology to become totalitarian. One should not underestimate the intellectual cohesion of Nazism as an ideology, nor the plausibility and influence of racial thought in general (Hannah Arendt has said, obviously using ideology in my fourth and fifth comprehensive senses, that there have been only two ideologies: that of economic causation and that of racial causation – but the question of religious ideology is a difficult one). Hitler put it clearly enough in *Mein Kampf* (Part II, Chapter 5)

A world theory is intolerant and is not content with being one party among a number of other parties; it insists on exclusive and persistent recognition of itself and on an absolutely new conception of the whole of public life in accordance with its views. Thus it cannot tolerate continuance of a force representing the former conditions . . . Political parties are always ready to compromise; world theories never are. Political parties bargain with their opponents; world theories proclaim that they themselves are infallible.

And he even dressed this up in some intellectual pretensions of comparison to Marxism and to a mythical initial period of self-criticism.

The first task of a young doctrine, containing new and great principles, must, however much individuals dislike it, be the probe of sharp criticism. Marxism possessed an objective and is aware of constructive ambition (even if this is merely creation of a despotism of world Jewish finance); but it nevertheless gave itself up to a shattering criticism for a whole seven years. Then began its so-called 'constructive work.' All this was perfectly right, natural and logical.[14]
Totalitarianism may not be logically necessary in the area of comprehensive ideology, but the danger is there at least.

(vi) Ideology as a Theory of the Derivation of Ideas from Circumstances

But always there remains the study as well as the use and misuse of ideas. (I treat this most important issue with absurd brevity, not being concerned here with different theories of the derivation or function of ideology in this sense but simply to distinguish such a sense from all others). If it is held that all ideas are products of social structure or external events, then there is probably no alternative in the practical world either to suffering or enduring things as they are, making the best of it, as the true conservative would say, "it is not such a *bad* world"; or to changing them utterly, for only by changing social structure or shaping events on a massive scale can ideas be affected at all. But if one believes, as Weber and Mannheim did, that it is sensible to study the *degree* to which ideas are the rational

[14] As translated in Hitler, *Mein Kampf*, Library Edition, (London, Hurst and Blackett, 1938), pp. 181-82, although this is a very abbreviated edition indeed. The same matter is found in Chapter 5 of Book Two in Ralph Manheim's complete translation, now in an excellent edition introduced by Donald Watt: Hitler, *Mein Kampf* (London, Hutchinson, 1969).

expression of the peculiar system of social forces of any society, and that such a study is possible, that is to say that one can particularize, then it is possible to believe that some things can change and others not; that some things should be changed and others not. As Masao Maruyama has notably argued, assumptions about types of knowledge are closely related to assumptions about types of politics. One of the worst vices of old autocracy, almost universally, was to base its system of authority on claims to some religious function removed from ordinary people. One of the worst vices of the new autocracy is the belief that the Party (whatever its doctrines) must alone determine the relevance of all important ideas, or else social order suffers. It is necessary to say with common sense that this is simply not true. Ideology, in fact, is never either politically or intellectually comprehensive. The sense in which societies are, indeed, conceivable as interrelated systems is highly abstract: there is no logical warrant for passing from either classical Marxism (as Althusier seems to recognize) or Parsonian social science to any practical judgments. Put thus more formally: the sociology of knowledge cannot ever demonstrate that all ideas are products of circumstance, that they are, in this sense, merely ideological; but it is perfectly legitimate to enquire into *the degree* to which they all are, and some are more so than others. Perhaps some ideas are purely ideological, in almost every sense I have set out; but not all ideas are purely ideological. I cannot believe, for example, that freedom, equality, authority and justice do not have residual meanings through all particular societies; certainly one could not analyze any society without such terms.

CONCLUSION

However, this has not been my main task. My main task is a simpler one. It is to suggest that we need to be more precise in our use of key terms, but not to deny for a moment that there is a political as well as an intellectual point to my argument. All I deny is that from political studies one can or should prove any particular commitment – except to tolerance and freedom in quite obvious senses: they are involved in the very study and also, as again Maruyama has argued, the study is needed for them. But the study must be relevant. We cannot be neutral, we can never be sure that we are fully objective; but we can always invoke relevant facts and

[13] See Masao Maruyama, *Thought and Behaviour in Modern Japanese Politics*, (London, Oxford University Press, 1963), especially Chapter 7, "Politics as a Science in Japan."

relevant arguments. We may be limited by ideological considerations, but we are not bound by them. Certainly those who claim to be bound by ideology, servants of history despite themselves, literally not responsible for their own actions (which is so near to a definition of lunacy that advanced spirits on the Far, Far Left in the West, at least, now claim that lunatics are the only free men in a capitalist society: Hippie, Yippy ideology) are in historical facts often astonishingly flexible within their own intellectual prison.

So I would distinguish between ideology as a scholarly study of the social setting of ideas and ideology as a special type of political doctrine. Most of the viewpoints in the first three usages of ideology which I have set out can easily enough be referred to as "doctrines." I call them "doctrines" because they may be true or false, practical or visionary, rationally based or almost wholly rhetorical, moral to me or immoral to you, but they are partial and particular: they have an object which is less than total reaction or total reform. And to the degree that doctrines are partial, there is room for other doctrines, simply by virtue of attaching more importance to other things; and there is usually a political relationship between different doctrines; that is, they recognize each other's existence and while seeking for dominance and predominance, do not believe that their success is only possible by elimination of all other doctrines. Literally, they tolerate each other: that is, they may disapprove of or dislike each other, but they limit expression of their disapproval or dislike to methods and means compatible with the other's existence.

The ideologist, on the contrary, is the person who believes that his "doctrine" cannot, on any terms, coexist with others, except perhaps as temporary tactics. An ideology, then, purports to be a total and a uniquely true explanation of the nature and direction of society such that the holder of the ideology is necessarily involved in action to lessen mercifully the period of emergence before there is a society free of conflict. For it is conflict alone that breeds, to the ideologist, what the sociologist of knowledge studies as the ideologies of different group interests.

Whether or not ideology in my "strong" sense is inherently totalitarian is a difficult question, and possibly a rather meaningless one since it largely depends on the definition of "totalitarianism." But ideology in my strong sense is certainly revolutionary, certainly both aims at and prophesies a total transformation of society.

But so, to come to the point at last after a long clearing-up operation, is the concept of "openness," even in the minimal sense that I have defined it, so much more mundane than the Bergsonian vistas opened up by Dante

Germino. If governments and individuals could withstand the speaking of all or any truths about themselves, we would be living in a very different world from the one we at present inhabit: one that I think fair enough to describe, without following that term as closely as I have tried to follow "ideology," as a revolution, a transformation of values.

The modern world is necessarily involved in the transformation of society, which gives the impetus both for totalitarianism and for planning based on freedom, freedom and knowledge. (Knowledge needs some freedom and freedom – if it is not to limit or destroy other people – needs some knowledge of them, their behavior and beliefs). In the pre-modern world systems of legitimacy or ideologies of power were basically static – concerned with the retention of power, the unchallengeability of power, rather than the effectiveness of power to transform or to guide change purposefully (which is why Wittfogel's claim that Oriental Despotism was a pre-modern form of total power is only an ambiguous half-truth).

If we see transformation as "revolution," we must insist that revolutions can be conducted by, through and for freedom. They will not, in fact, ever be total. For societies are not wholly systematic: to think that they are is basically a confusion between tendencies and laws, between relationships and necessary connections, and between abstract analytic models and empirical generalizations. (True, once again, everything does condition everything else, but mainly in trivial and in inessential ways). So revolution in the sense of total change will only be total in the sense of some abstract model (which may be useful so long as we realize that it is abstract) or "total" for some intellectually defined sector of human activity, the class structure and the governmental structure, but not for ideas as well. The content of ideas will change, but they constitute the continuity of human activity, understanding and moral judgment, so they will not change utterly. Freedom, equality, fraternity and justice are all inextricably both descriptions of social conditions and also ideals of development. To say that we can only know what they will mean after the revolution, so that the revolution cannot be judged in terms of their pre-revolutionary meaning, is either a deliberate deceit or a piece of feckless anarchism motivated either by unnecessary despair or by a complete – and sometimes deliberately cultivated – alienation. If we seek to discredit "the whole present system" utterly, we are also destroying the only possible rational basis for judgments as to what is desirable and possible in the future.

If we are no longer slaves to the past, we need neither be slaves to the future. It is brave and spectacular, theatrical indeed in a precise sense, to jump through a plate-glass window with one's eyes shut; but it is completely irrational. We cannot rationally foresee any fixed and certain pattern in the future, but we can reason about possible alternatives and choose boldly. We are unlikely to be completely right, all suffering and conflict will not vanish whatever we do, but are we unlikely to be wholly mistaken; and we can rectify many of our mistakes if we maintain freedom and strive for scientific objectivity in history and the social sciences (even though that is never completely attainable, a moving ideal, an horizon rather than ever an attained actuality). But we will be wholly wrong and will destroy all possibilities of rectification and freedom if we use, as can be used, massive violence and oppression, whether in the name of knowledge, the people or the nation, to coerce the behavior of people into some semblance of fitting our failed or incomplete prophecies. But perhaps we spend too much time arguing with unhumanistic "idiots" who happen to have an elaborate and fascinating but false logic; we need to get back to something that the social democracy had: a rational analysis based on freedom of how to transform the world from one of oppression and needless suffering, poverty, disease and inequalities, into a society based upon the ideals of freedom, equality, fraternity and justice, even if in practice we know that all we will attain is less-oppression, less-inequality, less-discrimination and less-injustice. Convictions are needed – tolerance and openness are not enough. But convictions that are tolerant. . . .

POSTSCRIPT ON SENSES OF "OPEN"

In the actual discussions, I noted seven different senses of "open" being used.

1. Open as *empathetic*, thus an open mind as distinct from a closed mind, the dogmatic or the prejudiced; but a different value-judgment could be applied to this sense by implying that a mere "open mind" is usually an empty mind or personifies liberal indecisiveness: as it were, "soft ecumenicity."

2. Open as *uninhibited* and free from repressions, the permissive society, ego-fulfillment and all that – but the psychiatrist who was supposed to be arguing this didn't show up.

3. Open as *communication* – simply, narrowly, but usefully, open to influence, the influence of words, information, research, theories and knowledge; hence an open society would simply be one with no censorship, or with minimal censorship (we never, in fact, discussed censorship and in what circumstances *it is* justified – which was remiss of us), and with the

greatest possible flow of truths about how governments work and why individuals are motivated to do as they do.

4. Open as *trial and error,* Mill's "fallacy of infallibility" and Popper's duty to attempt to falsify one's own generalizations, generally the avoidance of irreversible actions: thus Popper's account of scientific method, indeed of knowledge in general: the impossibility of proving laws, only of accepting the probability of hypotheses if not disproved, which hypotheses must be logically capable of disproof.

5. Open as *democracy* or publicly exercised liberties or free-politics, or consent plus liberty, or as – more elaborately – a society in which individuals can be effective publicly or can be left alone privately, and need for the stability of society to exercize both roles on different occasions.

6. Open as *empathy plus righteousness,* or tough ecumenicity – someone said in the discussion (I took careful notes and checked with a reliable colleague afterwards): "openness is the process of breaking down the walls which separate us needlessly and arbitrarily from ourselves, from each other, from nature, from reality, above all from 'non-existent reality,' or the ground of all existing things and of human existence itself." Opening our minds will thus let the truth flood in, if we open them very, very carefully.

7. Open as *creative (spiritual) evolution,* as in Bergson, the gradual unfolding of truth, creative evolution, degrees of openness as we spiral up towards a comprehensive vision of final human purpose, etc.

The second and fifth seem simply to be talking about something else, the one too narrow and the other too broad to be worth specifying as peculiarly "open." The first may be a necessary condition for an open society, but it far from exhausts other conditions. Three and four would together seem to provide most of those other conditions, perhaps "communication" by itself is too narrow but it corresponds, I suspect, more to what people ordinarily think of as an open society than does Popper's subtle account of scientific and intellectual methods, although he may better explain the significance and the justification of an open society as communication – which by itself is simply descriptive. Six and seven completely reverse the ordinary meaning, both are exactly what holders of the third, fourth and fifth meanings would suspect to be a "closed society"; that Bergson used the term before Popper has little significance – his is a metaphysical sleight of hand to make his anti-democratic sentiments sound generous and enlightened – and Popper's usage has had far more influence; both six and seven are forms of the positive liberty argument, so often exposed – accept my complicated value-system and you will feel free (but you won't be free any longer)! Bergson, indeed, is far closer to an ideologist, in the significant senses I have set out, than to anyone who could ordinarily or sensibly be thought of as a believer in an open society. With friends like that the Open Society would need no enemies.

THE HIGHER REACHES OF THE LOWER ORDERS: A CRITIQUE OF THE THEORIES OF B. F. SKINNER

DAVID SPITZ

There is only one serious question in political philosophy: What manner of men do we take ourselves and others to be? All other issues – not least the next fundamental question, By what right does any man or class command the services of another? – derive from the answer we give to this central question.

I wish to consider here B. F. Skinner's answers to these questions.[1] They constitute, if I understand them correctly, an argument in contempt of man, turning on a currently fashionable, though age-old, thesis: that the bulk of mankind is unable or unfit to be free; that men should accordingly be divided, on the basis of some fixed criteria, into superior and inferior orders; and that some version of the closed rather than the open society is consequently the proper (and indeed unavoidable) medium for realizing this principle. I shall argue against these notions, which I take to be morally deficient, politically pernicious, and unworkable. They are not, however, without certain elements of plausibility, a circumstance that lends poignancy to the human situation in our time. All the more so since the political authoritarianism entailed by Skinner's teaching comes bedecked in fashionable "scientific" credentials and wins the approval of some people who even think of themselves as humanists and liberals.

I

In every society – save perhaps for the "primitive" – there are pyramids of status and power, reflecting differences of wealth and birth, income and occupation, race and religion and sex, capacity and willingness to employ force and fraud, mental and moral attainments.

I mean here by a closed society one in which inherited or assigned standings in the pyramids of status and power are approved and maintain-

[1] In his book *Beyond Freedom and Dignity* (New York: Alfred A. Knopf, 1971).

ed. By an open society I mean one in which those at the base or on the lower rungs of those pyramids refuse to accept their assigned roles and struggle to rise toward the top, *and* where the beliefs and social and political arrangements make it reasonably possible for nearly all of them to engage in that struggle, if they so wish.

Merely to state so bald a polarity should rightly arouse the suspicion that these are at best ideal types. No closed society – apart, perhaps, from the extreme caste systems of fiefdoms in an earlier India or the great dynasties of an earlier Asia – has been completely closed; almost always there have been some areas in which men were at least partially free to rise. So too with open societies. There is always a considerable gap between rhetoric and practice: even those states we label democratic are disfigured by arrangements that hinder or block legitimate access to higher place and power. In the real world *all* societies have probably been mixed rather than pure types. The intriguing questions then are, How closed or open can a closed or open society be if it is to maintain and perpetuate itself? and what kinds of human beings live in and are likely to be produced by relatively closed or open societies?

In raising this last question I am returning to John Stuart Mill's insistence that the true test of a good government is not its power or wealth but the qualities – the virtue and intelligence – of its citizens. For if the state exists for man rather than man for the state, the only justification of a state is not mere survival but progress – understanding by progress a change in the quality of men's lives that will enable them to move from the sorry creatures many are to what they might and ought to be.

But what ought a man to be? What is the essence of a man as distinct from his historical or momentary existence? To this question political philosophers have given a multiplicity of answers.

Man, they have said, is a featherless biped. If so, replied the skeptic, he is a plucked chicken. Man is a rational animal. If so, how do you account for the madness with which he misgoverns himself? Man is a fragmented being, with many roles and faces, an entire *dramatis personae* within a single individual, and one therefore who will never be fully known. He is a stranger even to himself. If so, how shall we treat him, how indeed shall we know who he is? So the debate has gone.

But throughout this long debate one belief at least has seldom been challenged: that man is a sentient and (at his best) reflective creature; consequently, though he may at times act chaotically, more commonly he acts in accord with his feelings – whether we call these passions, sentiments, impulses, or desires – and what he thinks right. Disagreements concerning the nature of man have thus turned not on whether he feels and thinks but on the *character* of his thoughts and emotions, and on the relation of those thoughts and emotions to his actions: on whether "right" desires and "right" thoughts are the province of all men or only a gifted few, whether man's reason is the servant or the master of his passions (or whether reason is itself but one of the more compelling passions), and whether his behavior follows from those thoughts and emotions or is sometimes in conflict with them.

Now, however, we are told that these are mistaken grounds of disagreement. B. F. Skinner, author of one of our less genial and more authoritarian utopias,[2] and of other works denigrating man's freedom,[3] has in *Beyond Freedom and Dignity*, the Summa Scientifica of his life's work, spelled out what man really is.

Man, according to Skinner, is a behaving, not a feeling and thinking animal; as such, he must be conditioned to behave rightly, not be permitted to act wrongly; and we can so condition him only if we understand that the causes of his behavior lie beyond the individual himself, not in his attitudes or states of mind but in his cultural and social environment. As Skinner puts it:

> What is being abolished is autonomous man – the inner man, . . . the man defended by the literatures of freedom and dignity. His abolition has long been overdue. . . . A scientific analysis of behavior dispossesses autonomous man and turns the control he has been said to exert over to the environment. . . . What is needed is more control, not less. . . . The problem is to design a world which will be liked not by people as they now are but by those who live in it. . . . It is science or nothing. . . .[4]

From this perspective, the issue of closed versus open societies turns on different conceptions of what it means to be a man – not, be it emphasized, man as he is but as he might and ought to be. In Skinner's view, man is and ought to be – indeed, he *must* be, for there is no choice – a controlled being, a creature rather than a creator of his environment. In another view – and I shall here oppose to Skinner only that liberal tradition which may be said to run from John Stuart Mill through Russell, MacIver, and Morris R. Cohen to Camus and the democratic socialists of our own day – man is the one creature on earth who refuses, and ought to refuse, to be what he is. If he is to acquire the full stature of a human being, he must

[2] *Walden Two* (New York: Macmillan, 1948; paperback ed., 1962).
[3] E.g., *Science and Human Behavior* (New York: Macmillan, 1953) and "Freedom and the Control of Men," *American Scholar*, Winter 1955-56, pp. 47-65.
[4] *Beyond Freedom and Dignity,* pp. 200, 205, 177, 164, 160.

be a discontented and, more important, a self-protecting and self-dependent animal.

He must be a discontented man, according to this liberal tradition, because, as a perceiving animal, he is aware that he lives in a disharmonious and (in certain crucial respects) an unjust world. What is needed, then, are power and intelligence and above all the passion for justice that will enable the legitimately discontented man (and others like him who will always exist in our imperfect world) to alter the seemingly unalterable order of things.

This is why Mill and other liberals insist that to be a man one should exercise one's own judgment, make one's own choices. It is of course impossible to imagine a life deprived of all choices; for even the failure or refusal to choose, which is a surrender to persons or impersonal forces outside one's self, is itself an act of choice. But the crucial choice, which is the ability and right to make choices, is above all others the distinctive quality of what it means to be human. Why, it must be asked, does a man have a mind if not to exercise it? And what does it mean to exercise one's mind if not to reflect upon and choose among alternatives? And what is the point of such reflection and choice if, after that decision, he is told that it is of no account, he must abide by the decision of another? That, if left alone, he may in fact choose wrongly is a distinct possibility. But apart from the fact that fallibility also attends the choices of a superior (even if allegedly wiser) power, it is the meaning of freedom that a man take the risk of his own option. The right to be wrong, the right to be different, is (in this view) precisely what determines his manhood.

Now it is axiomatic that rights are not self-enforcing. Nor, on the historical record, are the rights of men in the lower orders likely to be held inviolate if entrusted to the higher orders. To be a self-dependent (autonomous) man requires not merely intelligence but also power to resist the will of those whose judgment runs counter to his own. He must look not to the forbearance of others but to himself. He must be able to protect himself effectively. And this means not that he be given more power than they – for what then would protect the others from his possible encroachments on *their* right to be wrong or different? – but that he be given an equal power and opportunity to use it.

This conception of equality, so necessary to the idea of liberty and of a self-dependent and self-protecting man, merits special emphasis as a distinguishing feature between closed and open societies. In closed societies, no matter how enlightened and virtuous the ruling or despotic class, inequality and degradation remain the fate of the lower orders; for the one thing even the best of despots cannot do is to produce a self-sufficient and virtuous citizenry. In open societies, despite all deficiencies in institutions, the egalitarian principle remains central. If Camus and Silone are right in saying that man is a rebel who affirms his existence by fighting against his own condition, then without equality of power and opportunity, neither reason nor passion will enable him to transcend his miserable existence.

So, too, the conception of liberty alluded to here requires special emphasis. Every society, closed or open, professes a love of liberty. Every society, closed or open, means by liberty at least the absence of alien rule. But what is characteristic of closed societies is that they also mean by liberty the right of the government officially to suppress undesirable views, most commonly on matters of morality and political right. Closed societies generally mean by liberty what has come to be called "true" or "real" freedom. This is, the freedom to do and say only the "right" things – as stipulated by God or nature or tradition or, what is decisive in practice, by those earthly powers who claim to know, and who therefore claim the exclusive power to apply, those alleged teachings. Or, if we move from normal to bizarre closed societies, that is, to those totalitarian societies based not on some alleged objective truth or binding principle but on the sheer exertion of power – as embodied, for example, in the Nazi and Fascist systems – "true" or "real" freedom becomes no more than compliance with the dictator's intuitive will.

"What is curious about this position," to cite but one of our previously mentioned liberal writers, "is the belief that if impartial investigation were permitted it would lead men to the wrong conclusion, and that ignorance is, therefore, the only safeguard against error." [5] But even if we do not, for the moment, press this objection, it remains altogether clear that the point of view embraced by proponents of the closed society cannot be acceptable to any person who conceives of man as a rational and autonomous creature and who consequently wishes our action to be guided by reason.

Open societies not only tolerate but encourage the free expression and examination of "objectionable" ideas. In the open society *all* questions are, or ought to be, open to discussion; all rulers subject to public criticism and expulsion from office; all opinions, including – indeed especially – those of the government, viewed with greater or lesser measures of doubt. What is entailed is man's freedom to articulate not only the "right" but the "wrong" ideas. Also entailed may be a predisposition, in the name of

[5] Bertrand Russell, *Why I Am Not a Christian* (New York: Simon & Schuster, 1957), pp. 182-83.

freedom, to leave men alone, to allow them to pursue their actual rather than allegedly real wills, at least in realms (such as religion) that do not require them to come into injurious conflict with one another.

So we return to the central questions: What, really, is this thing called man? What do closed and open societies make of man and do with man? No less important, what do they require man to do for himself? And what justifications attend these different understandings and practices?

II

Surely we must distrust all those who give simple answers to these questions, and Skinner gives simple answers. But what lends some verisimilitude to his answers is the undeniable fact that human or social conditioning has always been attempted and has often, in some measure, been successful.

Consider education and law. Education has always had as a primary purpose the influencing of men's minds. It seeks to control (modify) human behavior by instructing (instilling, training, indoctrinating, manipulating) children in proper codes of belief and modes of behavior. And surely it is one of the functions of law to control (modify) human behavior, in part through a system of punishments, in part through persuasion. Nor are education and law the only instruments through which men have sought to control (modify) human behavior. Force has regularly been employed to compel men to behave in ways they dislike. And more recently drugs, whether tranquilizers or stimulants, have come into widespread use for the same purpose. The techniques depicted by Koestler in *Darkness at Noon* and by Orwell in *1984*, and those utilized by the Chinese Communists in the "brainwashing" of prisoners, are testimonials to the power of this idea in the modern world.

All this is familiar enough. If a society is to function as some sort of cohesive entity, it must favor some doctrines and practices over others. It must develop or reflect a consensus on values and procedures that "define" it. Without such a consensus, however limited, a society can form neither a nation nor a state but must remain an amorphous conglomeration of beings. But in another sense, this closing of the environment may entail what Mosca has called "a real unbalancing of the spirit," an overly careful circumscribing of life. Then, unless the child is one of those rare individuals whose intellect and circumstances enable him to think for himself, he will, if raised a religious or political fanatic, become such a fanatic. To admit rays of light from other moral and intellectual worlds is to encourage doubts and desertions. In this way not only do the sane sometimes lead the mad but the mad often force the sane to keep them company.[6]

Insofar, then, as Skinner puts his faith in some form of conditioning, and stresses in this context the importance of environment, he offers not a new idea but simply a new technique to improve or more effectively implement an old idea.

It is Skinner's contention that it is misleading and unscientific to describe men in terms of "personalities, states of mind, feelings, traits of character, plan, purposes, intentions, or the other perquisites of autonomous man." Men are nothing but behaving animals, and human behavior is the automatic outcome of environmental forces. We are what our environment compels us to be. Through proper environmental manipulation or engineering – what Skinner calls "a technology of behavior" or "operant conditioning" – it should then be possible to structure the environment (design the right culture) so as to produce (control) right behavior. This involves a carefully planned (programmed, scheduled) sequence of contingencies or reinforcements, positive rather than negative (or aversive), because negative reinforcements not only lead to undesirable consequences – e.g., they reinforce the nagging parent rather than the submitting child – but are ultimately self-defeating. As Skinner says:

> All control is exerted by the environment. . . . No one directly changes a mind. By manipulating environmental contingencies, one makes changes which are said to indicate a change of mind, but if there is any effect, it is on behavior. . . . In the scientific view . . . a person's behavior is determined by a genetic endowment traceable to the evolutionary history of the species and by the environmental circumstances to which as an individual he has been exposed.[7]

But while Skinner talks of genetics and physics, what he means by environment is not the biological or physical – which one might suppose are what his theory requires – but the cultural or social. It is this cultural or social environment that "can be changed" (manipulated, repaired) to produce consequences that will modify behavior.

Now one might think that by expressing a preference for one type of culture or pattern of behavior rather than another, Skinner is introducing a moral dimension into his analysis – as indeed he is. But he insists throughout that these issues are discussed "from a scientific point of view." One might also think that if the environment can be changed, it cannot also be true that *all* control is exerted by the environment. The argument is thus

[6] Gaetano Mosca, *The Ruling Class,* trans. Kahn, ed. Livingston (New York: McGraw-Hill, 1939), pp. 184-87.

[7] *Beyond Freedom and Dignity,* pp. 82, 92, 101.

flawed from the very outset, and becomes all the more egregiously wrong as one traces out its consequences.

If the environment is a culture, and a culture is defined as "a set of contingencies of reinforcement" or "a set of practices," what does it mean to say that the environment "acts," that "it does not push or pull, it *selects*." that it "is 'responsible' for objectionable behavior" (e.g., juvenile delinquency), that it can "induce" people to change their behavior? A culture is a concept, not a person, and to reify a concept by giving it a will, with the power to judge and direct, is to move not into the science of human behavior but into a realm of verbal magic. It is also to deny what Skinner no less vehemently affirms: that "the environment can be manipulated," that "we can arrange contingencies," that "man must repair [the damage he has done to his environment] or all is lost," that while man is indeed controlled by his environment, "it is an environment largely of his own making," that "the individual controls himself by manipulating the world in which he lives." If these latter statements are to be taken at face value, then the environment, the culture, is not some abstract or even concrete thing "out there," which moves as a monolithic entity upon the individual or nation, molding it to that environment's will, whatever that might be. It is rather persons who make and mold the culture, which in turn constitutes the conditions within which and through which individuals function.

Skinner cannot have it both ways. Either he is an environmental or mechanistic determinist (which he avowedly is), in which case man is the creature but not the creator of his environment, or he holds (as he also does) that man can arrange "environments in which specific consequences are contingent upon it [*sic*]," in which case man is the creator and not the creature of his environment. If, however, man is both creature and creator, if there is some sort of reciprocal relationship or feedback – a doctrine that Skinner also affirms – then there is no determinism at all. It is hard to understand precisely which view Skinner holds, since he variously asserts all of them.

But this is not all. Skinner recognizes that environments differ considerably. "People," he says at one point, "are extraordinarily different in different places, and possibly just because of the places." And when he argues for planned diversification – of which more later – he concedes that the environment even within a nation (or culture?) is not monolithic. It follows, though Skinner does not draw this inference, that people are often different even in the same place, and may be the same even in different places. What then should the controllers do? Should they adjust (say) the rich child to the slum environment, or the slum child to the affluent environment, or maintain each child in his own or in still another environment? Does it even follow, given genetic and other differences, that the same environment will have the same effect on all persons within that environment? Clearly the controllers, if they could do through "operant conditioning" what Skinner believes it is possible for them to do, must make an ethical along with a scientific choice: they can take the world as it is and fit man into it; they can take man as he is and change the world to conform to man's nature and requirements; or they can change both man and the world so that both will be other (and presumably better) than they are. But if the controllers no less than the controlled are environmentally determined, how can they choose? And if they can choose, they are not only *not* the subject of deterministic forces, they are confronted by the need to provide justifications for their choices. All of which is to move them from "behaving" to autonomous men.

I would dwell a bit longer on this problem of the controllers. If the values implanted in the controllers' minds are determined by environmental forces – or if, to adhere to Skinner's terminology, the behavior of the controllers is determined by the culture – as are the values (or behavior) of the controlled, on what grounds can Skinner argue that the controllers should arrange the contingencies that will alter people's behavior rather than the reverse? Clearly, this cannot be defended by invoking the environmental forces themselves, for these are common to both controllers and controlled and should, precisely because they are the same, produce the same behavior (or values) in both. Indeed, given this common impact, where did the controllers come from in the first place? Since none of us, in the pre-Skinnerian world, is a controller, what in the environment selects a fortunate (and gifted?) few and transforms them from the controlled creatures they (along with the rest of us) are, into a new ruling class that will now control the environment that up to this moment has controlled us all? What, that is to say, destroys the controlling power of the environment? Further, if the behavior of the controllers is different – and it must be different, otherwise there is no point to Skinner's argument that the controllers can (and must) change the world from its present unsatisfactory state to a better one – then either there are different environmental forces at work or the same environmental forces produce different forms of behavior. On Skinner's terms, the latter possibility is self-evidently absurd. But the former possibility, if true, only returns us to the controllers' problem of choice. Skinner excludes choice, holding that men do not in fact choose, that the environment chooses for them, in which case of course it is meaningless to ask whether they ought to choose, and by what criteria. Yet it is impossible to escape the fact that the controllers must choose. Skinner concedes this in a revealing passage:

Man as we know him, for better or for worse, is what man has made of man. . . . When a person changes his physical or social environment "intentionally" – that is, in order to change human behavior, possibly including his own – he plays two roles: one as a controller, as the designer of a controlling culture, and another as the controlled, as the product of a culture. . . . The man that man has made is the product of the culture man has devised.[8]

To the extent, then, that the controllers can and do choose – and they *must* choose if man is to be made by man – then Skinner denies his own case on empirical grounds. If he says (as he also does) that the controllers *ought* to choose one set of contingencies rather than another, to select one pattern of desired behavior over another, he denies his case on normative grounds. In the latter situation, of course, he needs to provide appropriate criteria for his preferences, which leads us again into the ethical realm.

"Operant conditioning" is attended by at least two other difficulties. One is the role of accident and of the unanticipated consequences of intended actions. Chance has played an unascertainable role in human history, yet no one will deny its importance – in scientific discovery, military engagements, the resolution of economic and political conflicts, the everyday occurrences of human behavior. Even Skinner admits (though typically by overstatement) that "accidents have been responsible for almost everything men have achieved to date, and they will no doubt continue to contribute to human accomplishments." He goes on to add, however, that "there is no virtue in accident as such." This last statement is of course unexceptionable, but it does not remove the difficulty accident poses for Skinner's thesis. For if it is true that accident has played the major role Skinner concedes to it, how can he argue that it is always the environment that determines human behavior? Surely accident cannot be explained by contingencies of reinforcement. And if accident is likely to play as important a role in man's future, how can he place so much confidence in the efficacy of his behavioral engineering? Surely even carefully programmed sequences of contingencies will be afflicted again and again by unforeseen and uncontrollable events.

If Skinner seeks to design a better culture, he must know at least two things: that the culture he prefers is indeed "better" and that the contingencies he would arrange are appropriate means to achieving that end. It is more than problematical whether, qua scientist, he knows, or can know, either of these things. If he knows the former at all, he can know

[8] *Ibid.*, pp. 206-208.

it only as a moral philosopher, not as a scientist; and he cannot know it as a moral philosopher because, on his own terms, it is not merely the environment which does the selecting but it is behavior, not knowing, that defines the human animal. Man, after all – including, presumably, Skinner and his "controllers" – is not a thinking or feeling animal, only a behaving animal; he does not possess a plan or purposes or intentions, nor is he governed by a state of mind or the other perquisites of autonomous man. Hence he designs only what he is compelled by his environment to design; he can neither choose that design nor know that it is better than what presently exists. In the same way, the contingencies he would schedule cannot produce "a better world," for they will be frustrated by accident, by the unanticipated consequences of the controllers' actions. And these actions, in turn, cannot even be "intended," for the controllers can have no purposes or intentions, since they are merely behaving animals in an environmentally determined world. If, to rescue his case, Skinner would retreat from his mechanistic determinism to the voluntaristic choices of men "intentionally" seeking to remake themselves (or others), he not only repudiates his central doctrine but relies on the foolishness of choice he has consistently decried.

A second difficulty plagues the idea of "operant conditioning." It is, as I have tried to point out, truistic to say that societies attempt to condition (socialize) their children (and also, perhaps, their adults), and that in some measure they frequently succeed. But it is not always simply truistic. Consider the following possibilities:

(1) In heterogeneous and pluralistic societies, socialization or conditioning takes different forms and produces a variety of results. Differences of behavior may (probably will) make for conflict, in which case the controllers, if they are to achieve Skinner's better world, must resolve those conflicts by rearranging contingencies so as to produce a harmonious order. But which differences shall be suppressed and which contingencies chosen? Unavoidably, we are back once again to the problem of choice and its relation to environmental determinism.

(2) Where a society values (behaves so as to produce) critical and inquiring minds, that is to say, people who go about asking questions and seeking answers, it may be possible to arrange a sequence of contingencies that will bring about (or perpetuate) the very autonomous men Skinner deplores and seeks to abolish. Indeed, the very fact that Skinner seeks to abolish or dispossess autonomous men presupposes that they already exist. If so, to abolish them entails a judgment that autonomous men are evil or harmful or wrong and *ought*, therefore, to be eliminated. But how, if men

are merely (and deterministically) behaving animals, can they be termed evil or harmful or wrong? If they are so judged, we require ethical criteria by which to validate such a judgment and to vindicate their calculated transformation to "better" men. Moreover, what are "better" men? Again, this is not a scientific but a moral determination. Accordingly, let us now turn to Skinner's conception of ethics and a better (just?) society.

III

Skinner cannot really be said to have an ethical system, for in an environmentally determined world – that is, a world bereft of conscious choice – men (including of necessity Skinner himself) behave as they must, not as they think they ought to. And where men do what they must do, they have no responsibility for their behavior, so that neither praise nor censure attaches to their actions. Those actions cannot be termed good or bad; they are merely forms of behavior to be observed.

If, furthermore, all this were true, there would be no point in seeking to change the world (and human behavior) from what it is to something else. Yet Skinner does mean to change the world. He wants men to be "happy, informed, skillful, well behaved and productive." He wants them to be not heroic but "automatically good." He wants them to

> live together without quarreling, maintain themselves by producing the food, shelter, and clothing they need, enjoy themselves and contribute to the enjoyment of others in art, music, literature, and games, consume only a reasonable part of the resources of the world and add as little as possible to its pollution, bear no more children than can be raised decently, continue to explore the world around them and discover better ways of dealing with it, and come to know themselves accurately and, therefore, manage themselves effectively.[9]

Above all, he wants the culture to survive, for survival is not merely the principal value, it is "the only value according to which a culture is eventually to be judged."

This last assertion, of course, is self-evidently untrue. If the elements mentioned by Skinner in the quoted statement – peace, affluence, creativity, decency, self-knowledge, effective management – are what he esteems, then not survival per se but survival of a particular kind of culture is the crucial value. But what, apart from such impossible (for a determinist)

[9] "Freedom and the Control of Men," p. 47; see also *Beyond Freedom and Dignity,* p. 214.

expectations as self-knowledge, can be meant by the survival (or death) of a culture?

We have already been told that a culture is "the social environment," "a set of practices," "a set of contingencies of reinforcement." Can these perish or die as an individual may be said to die? Is this the sense in which Athenian culture (say) may be said to have died? If so, it can only be because culture is something that is bound in space and time, in which case no culture can be said to have survived and no culture can hope to survive. But if culture embraces entities (or practices) that permeate and transcend spatial and temporal boundaries, then Athenian culture did not die with Sparta's conquest of Athens or with the emergence of the Roman Empire. The identity 'Athens" may not have survived, at least not in the form we associate with classical Athens, but its culture survived. In this sense cultures do not die but are adapted and adopted by later cultures. Skinner himself does not seek totally to destroy our old culture, only to alter some of its practices so as to correct what he takes to be shortcomings. He values much of what it already contains. "Our culture," he tells us, "has produced the science and technology it needs to save itself." Surely, then, in designing the new culture, the needed science and technology will remain; some contingencies, some part of the environment will survive.

In point of fact, the term "culture" is not a wholly convincing unit of analysis. One cannot study American culture at any point in its development without taking account of a wider set of (conditioning) influences originating outside of America. We may grant that American culture can be made intelligible by a consideration of historic forces operating on a restricted geographic scale. But science and technology and even the idea of a national state were not sired in America. Nor can America claim exclusive paternity of its language and literature, art and music, dress, games and manners. To view the landscape of culture through Skinnerian eyes is to move into a grossly distorted world; it is also to miss the ever-continuing cross-fertilization of both American and non-American cultures.[10]

That Skinner attaches his ill-conceived notion of culture to the equally ambiguous (and long-discredited) theory of the survival of the fittest only compounds the implausibility of his doctrine. To say that what is fittest to survive, survives, is really to say no more than that we shall choose to call

[10] Cf. Morris Watnick, "Toynbee's Nine Books of History against the Pagans," *Antioch Review,* vol. 7 (1947), pp. 587-602.

fittest that which survives.[11] For it does not know what is fit to survive until after it has survived; and it can only say it was fit to survive because it survived. All of which is not merely a circular argument but is to beg the question, What in fact is the fittest? The reputable trader may be put out of business by his unscrupulous competitor, the thoughtful statesman be thrust aside by the demagogue. If these survivors are the fittest, it ill behooves Skinner to recommend their cause.

Survival of a culture, then, is not a viable but an empty and meaningless value, recommending itself only to those who feel more comfortable with concepts of stability and adjustment than with the more difficult notions of freedom, justice, and equality. Can anything more be said for Skinner's other ethical prescriptions?

Consider his idea – if a behaviorist (in Skinner's understanding of the term) can be said to have an *idea* – of "automatic goodness," Skinner wants men to be happy and well behaved. But what does it mean to be happy, and why should men behave well? How, in fact, do we distinguish behaving well from behaving badly? And is not the very drawing of a distinction between good and bad behavior (for in Skinner's lexicon to "behave well" is to "be good") an affirmation of morality rather than of science?

To a moral philosopher these might appear to be difficult (and clearly ethical) questions. But to Skinner they are scientific and readily answerable. He begins by posing the issue this way: "If a scientific analysis can tell us how to change behavior, can it tell us what changes to make?" This is not (he insists) a question of morality but

> a question about the behavior of those who do in fact propose and make changes. People act to improve the world and to progress toward a better way of life for good reasons, and among the reasons are certain consequences of their behavior, and among those consequences are the things people value and call good.... Those who observe cultures do not see ideas or values. They see how people live, how they raise their children, how they gather or cultivate food, what kinds of dwellings they live in, what they wear, what games they play, how they treat each other, how they govern themselves, and so on. These are the customs, the customary *behaviors,* of a people. To explain them we must turn to the contingencies which generate them.... The social contingencies, or the behaviors they generate, are the "ideas" of a culture; the reinforcers that appear in the contingencies are its "values."
>
> To make a value judgment by calling something good or bad is to classify it in terms of its reinforcing effects.... Good things are positive reinforcers.... The things we call bad ... are all negative reinforcers.... Things are good

[11] Skinner has repeated this tautology in a recent article, where he says: "A practice that makes a culture more likely to survive survives with the culture." In "Humanism and Behaviorism," *Humanist,* July-August 1972, p. 20.

(positively reinforcing) or bad (negatively reinforcing) presumably because of the contingencies of survival under which the species evolved.[12]

The problem, then "is to induce people not to be good but to behave well." Indeed,

We can conceive of moral training which is so adequate to the demands of the culture that men will be good practically automatically, but to that extent they will be deprived of the right to moral heroism, since we seldom admire automatic goodness. Yet if we consider the end of morals rather than certain virtuous means, is not "automatic goodness" a desirable state of affairs? [13]

Skinner, then, seeks to make it easier for men to be good (behave well). He wants to reduce what is (for autonomous men) the agonizing tension between individual inclinations and social precepts by habituating (conditioning) them to the requirements of proper ("virtuous") behavior, as this proper behavior is defined in the society. Such conformity is not to be achieved through repression, e.g., fear of punishment, but through that "operant conditioning" that will make them "automatically" desire, and consequently act in accordance with, what is socially approved. This, of course, requires a thorough understanding of human nature (behavior), a knowledge so complete that (as the skeptical Hobbes said) it would enable us to eliminate avarice and ambition and "enjoy . . . immortal peace." Skinner admits that we do not yet have such complete knowledge, that his behaviorist psychology "is not yet ready to solve all our problems"; but, he goes on to say, "it is a science in progress, and its ultimate adequacy cannot now be judged."

One might suppose that if Skinner's present knowledge is short of what is required for the implementation of his teaching, he would be loath to press his argument as vigorously as he does. But let this go for the moment. What is crucial here is his notion that if men can be conditioned to behave as society (or his controllers – and it is not clear that these are always the same, for the controllers, it must be remembered, are charged with *changing* the culture) requires them to behave, they will be automatically good; that this is the proper conception of what it means to be a man; and that such men behaving in those required ways will be happy.

Doubtless some things can be said in support of these views: that we will, in all likelihood, continue to increase our knowledge of human nature (behavior); that in consequence of this better understanding and of the further progress that will be made in behavioral engineering we will be

[12] *Beyond Freedom and Dignity,* pp. 103-105, 127-28.
[13] "Freedom and the Control of Men," pp. 60-61.

able more effectively to condition (control) children, and thus men; that such conditioning will, to the degree that it is succesful, eliminate the need for painful thought and thereby ease anxiety; that if proper behavior becomes effortless it becomes more certain, and society as a whole will benefit (in the sense that it will get what it demands); and that if "goodness" becomes automatic, and therefore less difficult, human energies can be channeled more efficiently into other needed tasks.[14]

But all too much can be said against these views, not least that the hope it holds out is of a drab and morally deficient world. For suppose Skinner is correct, that he can do all he claims, that he can make men behave well (be "good" or "virtuous") through habit, without effort and thought. What, then, is he making of men? What is he doing with and to men? Is he not converting them into automated beings or humanized robots? Is he not reducing them to untroubled innocents dwelling in a state of perpetual childhood? If a better world means better men, what shall we say of a doctrine that quite literally imprisons man, substituting for one kind of containment a more radical and dangerous restriction of the mind? It may of course be argued, in strict adherence to Skinner's behaviorist psychology, that man has no mind, in which case we are dealing not with imprisonment but only with nonviolent (and presumably benevolent) control of man's behavior. Still, it is difficult to see why such control (conditioning) is not in fact the replacement of one form of power by another. It operates as a sort of prenatal excision or molding, which is not significantly different in principle from control exercised after the act. It may, indeed, because such prenatal control is more subtle and more difficult to detect or correct, constitute a far more threatening affront to man's critical faculties than if we were dealing with open and visible dangers. No less than violence, it is a form of coercion in that it compels man to act, or refrain from acting, in accordance with another's will. And where man has no choice but to do as he is told, where indeed he is compelled to do this even without being told, he is surely no more than a puppet on a prearranged stage.

From this perspective, as George Kateb has argued, Skinner is a kind of playwright creating a world of strictly patterned activity. Men move about in expected (stipulated) ways. They substitute no words (for language, which is "verbal behavior," [15] is subject to the same Skinnerian rules) or

[14] See George Kateb, *Utopia and Its Enemies* (New York: Free Press of Glencoe, 1963), chap. 6 – though it should be noted that Kateb's careful and searching analysis, which appeared prior to the publication of Skinner's *Beyond Freedom and Dignity,* contains the most trenchant criticism of Skinner's views known to me. Kateb has commented on Skinner's last book in the *Atlantic,* October 1971, 122-25.

[15] B. F. Skinner, *Verbal Behavior* (New York: Appleton-Century-Crofts, 1957); see also the now classic review by Noam Chomsky in *Language,* vol. 35 (1959), 26-58.

gestures of their own, perform no unexpected acts, alter no scenes, introduce no improvisations. What they say and do is always controlled. They are predictable men.[16]

Now it is true that men whose actions are completely unpredictable are regarded as beyond the moral range, perhaps as lunatics. But there is a vast difference between normal (somewhat educated, somewhat socialized, perhaps somewhat conditioned) men and men totally conditioned to do what their controllers require. Such men lack all sense of, and must be relieved from, what we understand by moral responsibility; only their controllers are responsible for what they do. Such men, who are not men at all, are clearly incapable of performing Mill's self-protecting and self-dependent roles. Nor, since they are "automatically good" (behave well), can they be discontented men, or exercise – or worry about exercising – freedom of choice. That discontent, that freedom of choice, is reserved to the controllers, the new men of the higher orders, about whom, in spite of the awesome duties he assigns to them, Skinner says very little.

Here, perhaps – and we are still speaking, it must be recalled, of the moral realm – we confront the most damaging element in this indictment of Skinner's teaching. For by excluding choice from what he clearly considers the lower orders of men, he deprives them of the one quality that would still enable them to retain their humanity. To live is to think, for what but reason distinguishes man from the other animals? What but his critical and creative faculties separates the cultivated from the primitive man? And what does it mean to reason if man must then set his reason aside and forgo the right to choose? It is, I suppose, plausible to say that in primitive societies customary responses are generally sufficient to meet the problems of the day. But in complex societies, what are accounted moral problems are not choices between good and evil – such a choice is so simple (i.e., morally undemanding) as hardly to be accounted a choice at all – but choices between alternatives that are both good, or seemingly good, or sufficiently ambiguous as to require the determination of the good, or mixtures of good and bad so that in choosing to do good we may find, to our discomfiture, that it is also necessary to pay the price of doing some harm. How, in this setting, is it possible automatically, without painful reflection, without, at times, inordinate suffering, to do good (behave well)? And if to these considerations we add the further fact that no moral act makes sense that does not take into account the probable consequences of

[16] See also Andrew Hacker, "The Specter of Predictable Man," *Antioch Review*, vol. 14 (1954), pp. 195-207, and "Dostoevsky's Disciples: Man and Sheep in Political Theory," *Journal of Politics*, vol. 17 (1955), pp. 590-613.

one's actions, we can see that moral choice is the most taxing, and elevating, demand put upon the individual. It is precisely this quality that – to revert to the liberal conception of the autonomous man – constitutes the hallmark of what it means to be a man. Nowhere was Mill more eloquent than in pressing this point:

> He who lets the world, or his own portion of it, choose his plan of life for him, has no need of any other faculty than the ape-like one of imitation. He who chooses his plan for himself, employs all his faculties. He must use observation to see, reasoning and judgment to foresee, activity to gather materials for decision, discrimination to decide, and when he has decided, firmness and self-control to hold to his deliberate decision. And these qualities he requires and exercises exactly in proportion as the part of his conduct which he determines according to his own judgment and feelings is a large one. It is possible that he might be guided in some good path, and kept out of harm's way, without any of these things. But what will be his comparative worth as a human being? It really is of importance, not only what men do, but also what manner of men they are that do it.[17]

Yet precisely these are the qualities Skinner would exclude in the name of automatic goodness.

Can there, however, be such a thing as automatic goodness or conditioned virtue? To do good (behave well) without knowing what, or why, or with what consequences, and in the face of what alternatives, one is doing it, is simply to do – not to do good, or, for that matter, evil. A man who acts automatically, that is, "unconsciously," without awareness of principles and reasons, causes and consequences, is at best going through certain motions. No rational conduct is involved here, no moral choices are made, nothing good – or bad – is done, for such a man knows nothing of good or bad; indeed, he knows nothing at all. He simply does.

He does what society (or the controllers) requires him to do. Conformity, not individuality (or creativity), is what Skinner esteems. It is true, says Skinner, that "life, liberty, and the pursuit of happiness are basic rights." But he quickly adds two things: first, these are the rights of the individual and "have only a minor bearing on the survival of a culture"; and second, apart from the fact that survival of the culture is the paramount, indeed the only value, what counts is not *being* free but *feeling* free.

Now to *be* free is to be able to act undeterred by external restraints. To *feel* free may entail no more than one's recognition of this objective condition. It has also, however, been taken to mean one's voluntary and happy compliance with the dictates of authority – either because one welcomes the imposition of those external restraints or does not recognize them to be

[17] John Stuart Mill, *On Liberty* (1859; Everyman's ed., 1910), chap. 3, p. 117.

constraints at all. Conditioning, it is clear, operates at this last level. By focusing on the internal and anterior causes of human behavior, it seeks not to impose external restraints on "improper" desires but to alter man's nature (behavior) so that he will desire only what is "proper," i.e., what he *ought* to desire. Skinner confuses here the philosophical problem of determinism versus free will with the quite separate social problem of freedom and restraint. Hence, despite his repeated animadversions against such "mentalistic expressions" as the word "feeling," he can innocently – without embarrassment and indeed with approval – say that a young Chinese follower of Mao may feel freer and happier than most young Americans in doing what he is required to do, if he does them because of positive rather than negative reinforcements.[18] Such is the wisdom of our prophet.

It is also true, says Skinner, that man's "individuality is unquestioned. ... No intentional culture can destroy that uniqueness." But he qualifies this too by adding that "the individual nevertheless remains merely a stage in a process," and that it is "the culture which induces him" to act as he does. These remarks may help us to understand the cavalier way in which Skinner deals with the problem of the dissenter in contemporary America. He says:

> A serious problem ... arises when young people refuse to serve in the armed forces and desert or defect to other countries, but we shall not make an appreciable change by "inspiring greater loyalty or patriotism." What must be changed are the contingencies which induce young people to behave in given ways toward their governments.[19]

Why is *this* the correct behavior to be induced? Why not, instead, change the contingencies that will induce the government to behave in different ways – toward their young people or toward the role of the armed forces? Surely this is an ethical question of the greatest moment, but it is noteworthy that Skinner does not address himself to the issues involved, least of all to the question of what justice requires. Justice, to Skinner, is an empty word. But if behavior is to be changed, how can this determination be made without both a power of choice and a sense of justice?

It may be objected at this point that I have been unfair to Skinner's portrayal of a viable (better? just?) society, in that Skinner explicitly argues against uniformity or regimentation, which "might indeed work against

[18] See Skinner's article, "Freedom and Dignity Revisited," *New York Times*, August 11, 1972. And compare K. J. Scott, "Conditioning and Freedom," *Australasian Journal of Philosophy*, vol. 37 (1959), pp. 215-20.

[19] *Beyond Freedom and Dignity*, p. 157.

further evolution," and for "*planned* diversification, in which the importance of variety is recognized." But this does not really militate against the image of conformity I have imputed to him. For one thing, if in a given situation uniformity rather than diversity can be shown to promote the survival of a culture, and if that survival is the overriding (or only) value, then not change but uniformity is clearly to be preferred. But the more important key to Skinner's teaching here is his underscored term "*planned* diversification." His notion of variety is not that of the open society, in which men are free to become (even if within limits) what their desires, opportunities, and circumstances allow them to become, but rather of the closed society, in which variety is carefully (and officially) circumscribed. He draws a revealing analogy when he says: "The breeding of plants and animals . . . also requires planned diversity." The variety that Skinner conceives is one in which the kinds and degrees of diversity, and the manner in which they may exist, are the result not of accident or free choice by the lower orders but of deliberate design, by the contingencies of reinforcement set into operation by the controllers.

Since the issue of fairness has been raised, it may be well at this point to insert Skinner's observation that "nothing in the behavioral process guarantees fair treatment, since the amount of behavior generated by a reinforcer depends upon the contingencies in which it appears."

In the face of all this, in what sense can men be deemed to be happy in Skinner's world? "The problem," I have already quoted him as having said, "is to design a world which will be liked not by people as they now are but by those who live in it." But how, in Skinner's scheme of things, can people "like" anything? To like something is to have a feeling, or to manifest a state of mind, or to employ what Skinner calls a "mentalistic expression"; and these, he has repeatedly said, do not exist. "What is ultimately good or bad," he insists, "are things, not feelings." Yet he falls back again and again on this prescribed word. Somewhat curiously, he maintains that "a world that would be liked by contemporary people would perpetuate the status quo," as if contemporary people were a monolithic entity, all feeling content with things as they are and none of them seeking major, or even minor, changes. He believes that contemporary people like the status quo because they "have been taught to like it. A better world will be liked by those who live in it because it has been designed with an eye to what is, or can be, most reinforcing." This is in keeping with his view that "feelings about any institution depend upon the reinforcers the institution uses." If this is so, what people will like turns not on *their* preferences but on the preferences of the controller, who, Skinner affirms, will (to some extent) "necessarily design a world *he* likes." It is this world, this environment, that will shape (condition) people. They will "like" it because they will be taught (conditioned) to like it. Yet it is surely an elementary psychological truth that such a process of regression is likely to produce just the opposite result. As our rebellious youths have amply made clear, men do not and cannot really love those whose authority restricts their autonomy. If, despite this, they are happy, that happiness – if happiness it be – can only be the contentedness of men who are boring and do not even know they are bored.

IV

It is a commonplace that in politics and religion irrational beliefs and conduct are no bar to success. It is even arguable, perverse though this might seem (though not, of course, to a Dostoevsky or an Orwell), that all too many people look to a power in the universe greater than themselves; they seem to crave mystery and authority; they seek someone to whom they can entrust their conscience, someone who will remove the awful burdens of freedom, someone who will give them bread, security, and perhaps amusement, someone who will make them happy. It may well be, therefore, that Skinner's utopian vision will not founder – at least in its initial appeal – because of scientific and moral deficiencies. The fundamental question, or so he would have us believe, is not whether that vision is right or wrong (in any case meaningless terms) but, "Would it really work?" In Walden Two, he has argued, it did; and if there, why not everywhere?

Now we did not need a Marx to tell us that men have always been affected (somewhat conditioned) by impersonal forces outside themselves. Nor do we require unusual insight to understand that where there are monopolistic (or near-monopolistic) controls of the media of communication, not to speak of the deliberate use of terror, surveillance, and the concentration camp, the alternatives to which men are exposed are drastically limited; and that, if their horizons are narrowed, their thoughts and behavior are more easily channeled in desired directions. As techniques of conditioning are perfected we may expect greater and more effective socialization to take place.

Indeed, it was precisely because he recognized these things that Mill pleaded for a more autonomous man. Along with Tocqueville, he feared the increasing pressures of conformity. He understood that many (perhaps most) men were not free, did not wish to be free, and might not – in the absence of true understanding – become free. He sought, therefore, to set forth principles and institutions by which men might achieve what he believed only a very few superior intellects had thus far been able to achieve – the status of autonomous, self-reflective and self-dependent men. Such a status is not vouchsafed by history; it must be fought for and, with great difficulty, attained.

But this status, says Skinner, has not, cannot, and should not be attained. On the contrary, behavioral engineering ("operant conditioning") must prevail. There are, however, considerations that militate against his expectation.

Take, first, the problem of complexity and scale. It is one thing to control the behavior of rats in a maze or pigeons in a cage or infants in a carefully constructed box. It is more difficult (though according to Skinner quite possible) to control individuals and small groups of men. But it is surely an entirely different matter to control (as Skinner understands "control") hundreds of millions of people in a nation, or billions of people in the world. In the face of the variability and intractability of human nature, of qualitative as well as quantitative differences among men, to assume, as Skinner does, that "the behavioral processes in the world at large are the same as those in a utopian community, and practices have the same effects for the same reasons," is to gloss over the many (and I believe insuperable) difficulties that attend the vast distance between intention and achievement. For one thing, it does not follow that controls that work over many (even most) people will work over every individual; there will always be the odd person or (more likely) numbers of persons who will stray from the fold. For another, even if we think only of the generality of men, the number and quality of the controllers required to perform the close supervision of the upbringing of children, not to speak of the ongoing behavior of adults, would be simply fantastic. If Skinner really means to apply his many and diverse contingencies – in a degree of control (though not of savagery) that exceeds the practices of even the totalitarian states – to all sorts of people in varying stages of mental and moral development, in diverse social environments and levels of economic and political evolution, he requires an unimaginable number of qualified personnel in constant attendance upon them. It is instructive to note how Skinner, almost as an incidental thought, deals with this problem. He says: "Ethical control may survive in small groups, but the control of the population as a whole [which whole – the nation? the world?] must be delegated to specialists – to police, priests, owners, teachers, therapists, and so on, with their specialized reinforcers and their codified contingencies." How, and by what criteria, do owners (of what?) and police (as we know them in what country? as they might become?) emerge as equivalent to such therapists as the almightly Frazier, founder and czar of Walden Two? Clearly, Skinner's methods, if they apply at all, are applicable only to some (perhaps many, but certainly not all) individuals and small communities.

(I must note, if parenthetically, Skinner's curious failure to confront the problem of class and class consciousness with respect to his controllers. He talks throughout as if his controllers will behave [create contingencies] in a remarkably consistent and proper way so as to bring about his desired results. This presupposes not simply a community of rulers but of their interests, purposes, shared values. But Skinner offers no evidence that his rulers will constitute such a class. It is, after all, one thing to have a single person [and mind?], the scientist-king Frazier, direct a society. It is quite another to form [by labeling] police, priests, owners, teachers, therapists, and the like, into a ruling class and expect these disparate persons to behave in a unified way. Since they have no "purposes" or "interests" but only behave as the environment compels them to behave, what in that environment will make them do the same things at the same times? Why should we expect them to act *as a class* when they lack the very consciousness that is crucial to their existence as a class?)

Modern societies are complexities of large-scale organizations, involving vast and complicated systems. The rules and codes employed in those systems are numerous and by no means unambiguous. Their internal arrangements are imperfect. The messages sent (the contingencies put into operation) – and errors or accidents may of course enter even at the point of origin – are neither consistent nor constant, and so too with the course they follow. If the message employs language (verbal behavior?), this is notoriously vague and its reception, by that strange and complex animal called man, often involves a transformation of the sender's intent into a variety of misinterpretations. The whole process makes certainty of transmission a very risky business.[20] Skinner seems utterly unaware of this problem.

He seems oblivious, too, to the vast problems entailed by the modification of a complex environment. Problems are not merely many and complex in our chaotic (at least disharmonious) universe; they are interrelated, so that to deal (say) with the problems of the blacks in contemporary America, we must come simultaneously to terms with poverty, education, employment, housing, medical care, family structure, and the like – as well

[20] On this point see Martin Landau, "Redundancy, Rationality, and the Problem of Duplication and Overlap," *Public Administration Review*, vol. 29 (1969), p. 349.

as with (though Skinner will reject the phrase) the psychology of prejudice. What is the demonstrated competence of Skinner's therapists – or teachers, owners, police, and priests (and are there really to be priests in Skinner's utopian world?) – to resolve these problems? They cannot adequately solve any one of them without simultaneously solving all the others, and if, as Skinner proposes, they deal with them in piecemeal fashion instead, he must confront the further fact that a change in any one of these matters is itself likely to produce a change in another, and that this latter change (more accurately, series of changes) may be one of the unintended consequences of the controllers' actions. Thus to speak, as Skinner does, of modifying behavior and changing the environment is to ignore the complex realities hidden behind these simplistic terms.

Take, now, Skinner's idea of *planned* diversification. It has already been noted that the kinds and measure of diversity to be found in Skinner's new society will be determined by the controllers. The question now to be raised is, How shall we know in advance whether the prescribed diversities will blend together into a coherent unity or be disruptive of that unity? And further: what shall we do if the controllers make a mistake, or misuse their power? One all too obvious answer is that *we* – if members of the lower orders – will not and cannot know these things. For not only can we not "know" (we can only behave); we will have been conditioned to behave as the controllers want us to behave, which is to say, we will do as we are told. But surely, unless the controllers are gods (and even Socrates did not contend that his philosopher-kings were gods), they are likely to make *some* mistakes, they are likely to misuse some of their powers some of the time and thereby endanger the working of the system. Is there, within Skinner's arrangements, a self-correcting mechanism or principle that will deal adequately with this problem?

Here is what Skinner says:

> The misuse of a technology of behavior is a serious matter, but we can guard against it best by looking not at putative controllers but at the contingencies under which they control. It is not the benevolence of a controller but the contingencies under which he controls benevolently which must be examined. All control is reciprocal, and an interchange between control and counter-control is essential to the evolution of a culture.

And again:

> Self-government often seems to solve the problem by identifying the controller with the controlled. The principle of making the controller a member of the group he controls should apply to the designer of a culture. . . . *He* will select

goods or values which are important *to him* and arrange the kind of contingencies to which *he* can adapt.[21]

I have underscored certain words in the foregoing quotation to make it clear that what Skinner is talking about is not self-government (or counter-control) at all. Like the Persian potentate (as recounted in the *History* of Herodotus) who addresses a group of fellow conspirators, he in effect says: "Let *us* choose out from the citizens a certain number of the worthiest, and put the government into their hands." Or, in keeping with a celebrated line in the *Iliad,* he argues: "Good sir, sit still and hearken to the words of others that are thy betters." The controller is a member of the group he governs only in the way in which an absolute monarch or tyrant may be said to be a member of the group he governs. He is *in* but not *of* the group. He is certainly not chosen *by* the group. Above all, if he too is a conditioned man, if he too is subject to contingencies of reinforcement designed to control his behavior, he is conditioned not by other persons – as he conditions others – and is subject only to contingencies of his own making – whereas others are subject to the contingencies that he has made.

In what sense, then, can it be said that there is a reciprocal relationship between the controller and the controlled? Only in the sense that there may be said to be a reciprocal relationship between the jailer and his prisoner. An influence there may well be: the behavior of the prisoner may elicit pity or compassion and kind treatment, or contempt or hatred and harsh treatment, from his superior, but this does not make them equals or promote effective control of the jailer by the prisoner; for it is still the superior who determines, and alone has the power to determine, the treatment that shall be accorded the fellow-member of his "group." After all, did not Skinner say that it is the controller who will select goods or values important to him, not to them, and that he will arrange the kind of contingencies to which he, not they, can adapt?

In effect, there is no way within Skinner's system to correct the misuse of power by the controller. Skinner has divided his world into higher and lower orders, and between the two there is an unbridgeable gap. The members of the lower orders are conditioned, not conditioning, men; creatures of automatic goodness, they behave properly not because they have an awareness of problems and make intelligent choices, but because they have no awareness and make no choices but do as they are required (have been conditioned) to do. How, then, can such men, who are not men but mindless beings, question the policies of the controllers? How can such robotlike creatures correct unwise or unworkable policies? If it be said

[21] *Beyond Freedom and Dignity,* pp. 182-83, 172.

that the controllers too are conditioned men, the response must surely be that they are conditioned, if conditioned at all, in a quite different way – not by other men, other controllers, but by contingencies that they have themselves made, in other words, by themselves. And while history may be said to teach many and diverse (perhaps inconsistent) things, there is one thing it teaches that transcends all reasonable doubt: namely, that the possession of power is dangerous (even if also useful) and that to guard against its wrongful uses is the first obligation of a responsible society.

To all this we must add: the great technical difficulties in planning a harmonious and efficient social order; the extraordinary qualities required in the men responsible for such planning (and it ought not to be forgotten that Skinner's planning – both in range and intimate details – goes far beyond all hitherto known schemes for human control); and the fact that such planning must take place in ongoing, not *de novo* societies, populated by previously (and, from Skinner's standpoint, erroneously) conditioned men, passionately committed to the traditional and the familiar. We can see that the feasibility of his proposals rests on a morass of perplexities.

Take, finally, Skinner's notion of a stable (though evolving) society. He does not mean by stability a static order, for central to his teaching is a program of deliberate change. But the changes he proposes have a particular purpose, to transform the existing order and bring into being a new culture. This new culture, once achieved, will approximate if not embody utopia. Hence, though it will continue to evolve, its evolution cannot be expected to admit major alterations. Tranquillity, or the removal of tension, and peace, or the removal (or near removal) of conflict, become the hallmark of Skinner's stable – and if not static, certainly not dynamic – society.

Would such a society really work? Is it even attainable? I do not believe so, and for two reasons primarily. One is psychological, turning on the tensions and discontents that always attend differences and inequalities. The other is structural, turning on the resentments and ambitions that always attach to hierarchy. Together these make for perpetual conflict and occasional rebellion, and require, therefore, a method of resolution appropriate to a turbulent rather than a tranquil society. Let us consider these points in turn.

One striking omission in Skinner's book is his failure to treat the problem of equality. He talks, to be sure, of differences, which he prefers to uniformity. But he does not confront the problems that emerge when men impute attributes of superiority or inferiority to these differences. There is, of course, no necessary reason for such imputations, any more than there would be if we were talking of the differences between an apple and an orange. But for thousands of years men have somehow believed that differences – whether of race, sex, religion, nationality, intelligence, talent, creativity, or any number of consequential and inconsequential things – do and should entail such judgments. Indeed, the striving for preeminence is so pervasive as to warrant the suspicion that inequality in *some* form is an abiding characteristic of the human condition.

I am arguing, that is to say, that by nature *and by inclination* men are *and want to be* different, that they associate differences with imputations of superiority and inferiority, and that if they can no longer hope to better themselves they seek to improve the status of their children.

From time to time, moreover, some men and groups see themselves as outside of (alienated from, often because they believe they are regarded as inferior to) the larger group of which they are allegedly a part. Thus, when a black man today says, "I have nothing in common with whites," we may deplore his statement as a betrayal of his humanity, but we cannot fail to recognize the reality (and intensity) of his belief (feeling). And when any man, black or white, resents the superior position held by another man, generally because he believes that the other man is no more and perhaps less deserving than he, we can regret or sympathize with his judgment, but we cannot, if we seek a stable society, ignore it. Skinner may tell us that beliefs and feelings and attitudes do not exist, that only relevant behavior counts. But the fact is that the behavior of such men draws upon such feelings and beliefs and can be understood only in terms of such attitudes. For Skinner to hold, therefore, that his controllers can both assign men to fixed tasks and also (through "operant conditioning") keep them there in some sort of cooperative action, is to flout all we know of human behavior.

As long, then, as differences and inequalities of some sort exist – and they will always exist – not tranquillity but tensions and discontents will constitute essential characteristics of the social order.

These reflections are reinforced when we consider the further problem of hierarchy. In modern industrial society, specialization of function and the division of labor are not matters of choice but technical necessities. Workers cannot be freely interchangeable. Differences of function entail inequalities of skill and (generally) productivity, and consequently inequalities of reward. Now if the ideal of equality of opportunity had been, or could be, fully realized – if all men had been, or could be, given the same opportunities to reach higher positions – men at various levels in the pyramid of hierarchical power and reward might feel no sense of injustice. But the reality, of course, is that this ideal has never been realized, and if we are to take seriously the Socratic teaching that equality of opportunity requires, among other things, that all children be taken from their parents immediately after birth and raised in common – and I see no other way to achieve complete equality of opportunity – it is unlikely that the ideal can ever be fulfilled. Even if, with Edward Bellamy, we look also to equality of income or reward, the problem of differentiated power and the touchy question of incentives (which has bedeviled even the "socialist" countries of our time) remain.

It follows, then, in the face of the heterogeneity in power, fame, reward, and the like, produced by hierarchical structures, that men at the lower levels will (as they do) resent their positions and strive in various ways to rise above them. They object, too, to the arbitrary rules (or what they take to be arbitrary rules) and the irresponsibility (lack of democratic accountability) of men at the higher levels of those pyramids. Whatever the merits of their complaints, certain facts are clear: that hierarchy makes for a variety of differences, that these differences entail a variety of inequalities, and these inequalities produce not merely a variety of tensions but also a striving for betterment that cannot (Skinner notwithstanding) be programmed out of existence.

What is true of hierarchies in the industrial sphere is true of hierarchies in other areas of society, e.g., the political, the religious, the educational. The difficulties – the resentments, tensions, conflicts, strivings – are thus all-pervasive. How implausible, then, is the extraordinary remark by Skinner's alter ego, the psychologist Frazier in *Walden Two*: "We simply arrange a world in which serious conflicts occur as seldom as possible or, with a little luck, not at all." Conflicts will be absent only in a world where men have ceased to be human, where they have been converted into robots and are consequently "automatically good"; or in an entirely just world populated by entirely just men, which is to say, Heaven. But as Lucifer demonstrated, not even the most perfect ruler can order the continuance of perfection.

Skinner's recipe – conditioned virtue – is both ineffectual and destructive. Ineffectual, because it cannot eliminate the conflicts that endanger the stability of a state. Destructive because, in seeking only to eliminate those conflicts, it provides no mechanism by which to contain them when they erupt. Thus Skinner's theory not merely invites the rebellions of the lower orders; it ensures that those rebellions, when they occur, will be unmanageable.

V

Two considerations more than any others seem to underlie the idea of a closed society: that the truth is known and that it can and should govern human societies. Both are demonstrably false.

The truth is not known, at least not the whole truth. Always we know only a fraction of what there is to be known; always the things we do not know vastly exceed the things we know; hence we cannot be sure that we know even what we think we know. We act, of course, on the basis of what we think we know, and we must do so. But action dictated by faith or circumstance or limited (because partial) understanding is a far cry from absolute knowledge.

Since *the* truth is not known, it follows (as Mill argued) that men must be free to inquire into the validity of conflicting claims to truth. The alternative is the imposition of an alleged truth on the ground that power is rightfully employed in a true cause. But whether that cause is a true cause is precisely what is at issue. Hence domination not merely evades the issue of truth, it corrupts the process by which it might be ascertained.

What is distressing about Skinner, who is presumably committed to scientific method, is that he not only claims to know the truth, or enough of it to warrant the conviction that in time he will embrace it all, but wants the power to preclude the possibility of anyone ever again challenging that truth, or the men who implement it.

From this point of view, it is less important to argue that Skinner is wrong in his conception of what human nature (or behavior) is, than it is to argue that uncertainty is the first condition of rational thought, and that whatever one's conviction about his own or another person's ideas, it is never legitimate to hold that those ideas are beyond criticism. For the moment Skinner is content to meet this requirement, as is evidenced by his participation in public discussions of his work. But the logic of his position is such that should he obtain the power to put his ideas into practice, those ideas and that power could not be reversed. If he can do what he claims to be able to do, and if he has the power to do it, then men conditioned by his methods will no longer be capable – as they are now – to make the free choice to reject his system. This irreversibility converts Skinner and his controllers into authoritarian, oligarchical men.

This authoritarianism, inherent in Skinner's thought, should come as no surprise to a reader of *Walden Two*. There Skinner has Frazier say:

> The government of Walden Two has the virtues of democracy, but none of the defects.... We have no election campaigns to falsify issues or obscure them with emotional appeals, but a careful study of the satisfaction of the membership is made. Every member has a direct channel through which he may protest to the Managers or even the Planners. And these protests are taken as seriously as the pilot of an airplane takes a sputtering engine. We don't need laws and a police force to compel a pilot to pay attention to a defective engine. Nor do we need laws to compel our Dairy Manager to pay attention to an epidemic among his cows.
>
> Let's not stop with democracy. It isn't, and can't be, the best form of government, because it's based on a scientifically invalid conception of man. It fails to take account of the fact that in the long run *man is determined by the state*.[22]

And if one should wonder what is entailed by channels of protest and studies of satisfaction of the membership, Frazier explains that Walden Two has effectively controlled the *inclination* to behave; that through a wise choice of techniques what has been increased is the *feeling* of freedom; and that in any case a social structure has been built "which will satisfy the needs of everyone and in which everyone will want to observe the supporting code."

Skinner underscores these points in *Beyond Freedom and Dignity* when, to avert possible misunderstanding, he says: "People who get along together well under the mild contingencies of approval and disapproval are controlled as effectively as (and in many ways more effectively than) the citizens of a police state."

Thus Skinner moves, not simply "beyond" (by which he means "short of") freedom and dignity, but "beyond" ("short of") science and rationality. He moves "beyond" science in that he removes his system and the men who operate it from the self-corrective controls of experience. One of the great merits of democracy is that it can provide an effective mechanism through which those who live under a system are able to inform the rulers of their experiences under that system. But this information is worthless if it has been prearranged. Nor is it consequential if it enters only as a petition or prayer, dependent for its reception on the arbitrary will of the ruler. But in Skinner's system, apart from an individual's presumed capacity to reveal his suffering as a cow reveals its affliction or an engine its defect, there is no way for a citizen to express his discomfort or to compel a change in its cause.

Skinner moves "beyond" rationality in that he does not understand the limits of reason in politics. It is a truism that in politics *the* truth, in whatever measure known, does not wholly govern men. There is a certain

[22] *Walden Two* (paperback ed.), pp. 269, 273. Italics in the original.

recalcitrance in human nature, a grim resistance to the surrender of one's habits and prejudices, a love for what is, a commitment to people and places and possessions. What *can* be done is vastly different from what a scientist-king believes *ought* to be done. This is why Aristotle carefully distinguished theorethical wisdom (knowledge of the truly good) from practical wisdom (knowledge of what is possible in a given situation). Totalitarian rulers, not knowing or indifferent to this distinction, resorted to terror in the abortive attempt to achieve their unattainable ends. Similarly, Skinner, who would use the carrot rather than the whip, requires manipulation (a form of coercion in that it violates man's autonomy) to pursue his stated objectives, and would put that manipulation outside the reaches of popular control. All of which becomes particularly irrational when we understand that many problems are not capable of permanent solution at all.

I mean here no more than that, where diversity and thus conflict are permanent features of the human condition, it is necessary to provide not "a" solution but a method that will admit of continuing (and at best partial) resolutions. This is why Mill and other writers in the liberal tradition have stressed the crucial importance of democracy and the open society, from which there emerges a certain conception of dignity, embodied in the rights of man.

Among these rights three are of such importance that they merit special emphasis: the right to be wrong; the right to be Left; and the right to be left alone.

It is often said that while every man has a right to speak as he may please, it should please him to speak only what is right and good; for no man should wish to utter false or wicked things. He has a right to be right, but not to be wrong. This is pernicious doctrine. He who claims to know what is right and true and good really asserts no more than that he thinks he knows. Even if he does know, he knows not by authority – for as Hobbes remarked, when a man says that God spoke to him in a dream he is really saying he dreamed God spoke to him – but by observation and reasoning. As these were open to him, so they must be open to other men.

It is also often said that men should not disturb accepted traditions and practices, especially since (as would be the case if Skinner's policies prevailed) they are the "right" practices. What is most objectionable here is the notion that conformity and tranquillity are the noblest of virtues. One need not insist that all traditions and practices are wrong in order to insist on the right to question them. The right to be Left is the right to point out derangements and propose remedies. The right to be Left denies that tranquillity is the highest achievement of the human race.

Finally, the right to be left alone. It is often said that what liberalism lacks is a sense of and respect for community, that it sets men apart in isolation from each other and thereby deprives them of their brotherhood. This is surely a tawdry caricature, both of Mill and other liberals (Russell, MacIver, Dewey, Cohen, etc.). Man does not and cannot exist apart from community. Community forms him, gives him his substance and identity. What liberals contend is that community is a necessary and ennobling reality, but not the only or complete reality. Individuality is a reality, and a value, too. Men must be given room for their own differentiation. To realize oneself as a unique person, a man must in some measure be left alone.

Nor does this mean that he will be the straw man Skinner attacks – a fully autonomous creature. There is no such thing as a completely free and autonomous man. What autonomy means in the real world is not freedom from all restraints, not the denial of socialization (some "conditioning"), but the insistence that where an individual's practices do not militate against the interests of others, his mode of life has a privileged claim to respect. Where his actions do not directly violate the welfare and interests of others, he should be left undisturbed.

We live, in some respects, in a deranged world. Through accident and design, men have been divided into higher and lower orders. But it is not written in the stars that those at the bottom are forever destined to reside there, or were properly put there initially. The right system, the only just system, must have as its prerequisite a mechanism that will enable the lower orders not merely to reach out for their legitimate higher claims but actually to attain them. Equality in all things is an impossible goal. But equality in crucial things is a reasonable goal. What those crucial things are is properly a matter of dispute. Hence men must be free to discuss and resolve that dispute. In this at least they must be equal. Such freedom and such equality are the core of what we mean by dignity. The "right" human objective, then, is not to move beyond freedom and dignity but to secure them.

VI

Despite all that has been said here, some sensitive and idealistic persons have found in Skinner's theory a plausible answer to their concerns. Why is this so?

(1) Clearly, they do not see in that theory and its explanatory account

anything markedly different from what they conceive American practices already to be. In their view, America is not a liberal or democratic state but a society ruled by hidden elites. These elites condition us now – through controlled "information" from the government and mass media, through authoritative indoctrination from the churches and schools, through programmed advertising from the controllers of Madison Avenue. This conditioning works. It has produced a conformist culture made up of one-dimensional men.

The choice before us, therefore, is not between programming and the absence of programming but between two kinds of programming – that of Skinner and that of hidden elites. It is not a choice between two ideal types – authoritarian rule and democracy; but between two realities – the benevolent authoritarianism of Skinner's scientist-kings and the inchoate (and wicked) authoritarianism of the political-military-industrial complex. Indeed, they do not even take Skinner's controllers to be scientist-kings or authoritarians at all; rather, the controllers (as Skinner has repeatedly emphasized) are themselves controlled men, they are like us, of us. Hence their programming is more likely to be "right."

(2) They are attracted as much by Skinner's methods as by his promised results. Some see him as he sees himself, as a humanist, "one of those who, because of the environment to which he has been exposed, is concerned for the future of mankind." [23] Others (rejecting his world outlook) are attracted by his techniques, which they see as improved shortcuts of technological manipulation that may be used to achieve their own ideological ends.

It is a grim fact, they note, that good ends are not always attainable by good means. If economic development is to take place in the "backward" nations, for example, despotic rather than democratic rule may be required. If children are to be taught mathematics, language, and "right" principles, authoritarian rather than democratic methods may be the more effective. And if good men are to realize their right causes in a world where persuasion, addressed to previously conditioned (and therefore unreceptive) men, can never be effective, Skinnerian techniques may be the only device to break the bonds of conformity.

(3) They are bemused, then, by the quest for certainty. Like Hobbes, they want peace and tranquillity and a commodious life, and they believe that Skinner will help to provide these. Here many correctly sense what Skinner himself does not see: that Skinner is essentially a mystic, not a

[23] Skinner, "Humanism and Behaviorism," p. 20. This queer definition may help to explain the incredible designation of Skinner as "Humanist of the Year" for 1972!

scientist or behaviorist at all. What drives Skinner, and what attracts them to Skinner, is his faith – not in reason, or science, or scientists, or even that limited breed of scientists known as behaviorist psychologists, but in a sort of Invisible Hand that will transcend environmental determinism to control the environment that controls us, and in that way lead us to utopia. And Skinner's utopia, like all utopias, cannot be said to be harmful or wrong, for how can one criticize what does not exist and never has? There are no imperfections, no meannesses, no inequities, in Skinner's world. We cannot disprove empirically what is not yet real. His hypothetical utopia, like all mystical systems, is invulnerable to criticism.[24]

This fascination with utopia must not be minimized. For well over two millennia men have been gripped by the Socratic portrayal of an ideal Republic ruled by philosopher-kings. Bacon's *New Atlantis* anticipated much present-day disillusionment with philosophy by putting scientists at the helm instead. What Skinner does is to plumb the hearts of those who want freedom but do not want to make choices, who want to *feel* free but not to *be* free, by giving them what they want (or will want after proper conditioning) while absolving them of all the burdens – the fears, uncertainties, and responsibilities – of decision-making. He offers them a royal road to salvation – led and controlled by behaviorist scientist-kings.

Similarly, we must not mistake the profound appeal of the doctrine of environmental determinism. Listen again to Skinner:

> Do I mean to say that Plato never discovered the mind? Or that Aquinas, Descartes, Locke, and Kant were preoccupied with incidental, often irrelevant by-products of human behavior? Or that the mental laws of physiological psychologists like Wundt, or the stream of consciousness of William James, or the mental apparatus of Sigmund Freud have no useful place in the understanding of human behavior? Yes, I do. And I put the matter strongly because, if we are to solve the problems that face us in the world today, this concern for mental life must no longer divert our attention from the environmental conditions of which human behavior is a function.[25]

Here, at one stroke, Skinner imputes responsibility for our many problems not merely to all the thinkers who have preceded him but to the fact that they exercised "thought" at all. Skinner thus presents himself as a humble, not an arrogant man. It is not *his* "mind" that is superior to theirs. It is rather the environment that is above us all. The "evil," the weakness, the fallibility in man – these are not the products of man's will, or of his "nature," but of an uncontrolled environment that makes us what we are.

[24] Cf. Neil Postman, "My Ivan Illich Problem," *Social Policy,* January-February 1972, p. 35.

[25] "Humanism and Behaviorism," p. 19.

Control the environment and you control the conditions of life; control the conditions of life and you control man.

(4) It follows, paradoxically, that Skinner appeals precisely to those who would argue men should not be governed by forces outside their own control. That, he contends, is how they are governed now – with catastrophic results. Consequently, with the help of science, men who wish to be ("feel") free must seize control of those external forces (the environment) which determine their behavior in order that they may themselves determine that behavior "correctly." Not to control the environment is in fact to surrender to the forces that now control them.

Doubtless there are further reasons for Skinner's widespread appeal, but these may be sufficient to suggest why that appeal is widespread, and why the grounds that sustain it appear so plausible.

It is pointless to repeat here the considerations I have already advanced to show that *all* of these interpretations of Skinner are either erroneous, in that they mistake Skinner's teaching, or warrant condemnation, in that they lead to harmful results. A few additional remarks, however, may be in order.

(1) Skinner's system *is* markedly different from current American practices in at least two major respects: it substitutes for the present conditioning from a variety of uncoordinated sources a carefully coordinated and univocal pattern of conditioning; and it substitutes for the present reality of imperfect democracy an ideal or perfect, because total, system of authoritarian rule.

It may or may not be true that America is governed rather than merely (or widely) permeated by "hidden elites." But to the extent that it is true those elites are not merely many, they are often discordant and opposed. They are also specific rather than general, in the sense that while an elite may dominate a realm of activity at a particular time, it does not dominate all sectors of the society always. It is contested by other elites, and it depends for its success on its ability to win the support of the masses. And where elites compete for mass support, that support is forthcoming only where the masses can exact a price in return. To this extent at least, the masses do choose. A particular elite does not always ascend to power, as business elites have learned to their discomfiture in the age of the welfare state, and as labor elites learned in the age of capitalism and are still learning in the age of the mixed economy. In Skinner's system, however, the masses never choose; a particular elite always governs.

The very fact that Skinner is free to prescribe wholesale remedies for change; even more, the fact that he believes those remedies not only should but can be implemented – these testify to the relative openness of existing arrangements, both in ideas and political practices. It is all too clear that under his system there can be no opposing ideas, indeed no "ideas" at all, and no political instruments for change counter to the will of his new ruling class.

(2) Skinner is not a humanist, for he dehumanizes man. No less important, in scorning process for results, he deprecates humanistic values in the procedures he advocates.

I know it is fashionable, today as always, for men convinced of the rightness of their cause to become impatient with and ultimately to reject the tedious delays and inevitable compromises that emerge from formal rules of consultation, bargaining, and popular acquiescence. They want not "right" procedures but "right" results; hence they are prepared to jettison those procedures when they do not get what they want.

This is the principle of oligarchy, a principle that respects "superior" minds and is contemptuous of the "inferior." But it is not a principle consistent with humanism. In the humanist conception, all men require opportunities for education and growth, all men count. To neglect their judgments, to impose the judgment of an allegedly superior will, is to diminish their humanity. And if it is the business of a people to correct the errors of government, procedures that enable them to criticize, to participate, and effectively to remove rulers are vital.

The bad-means/good-ends relationship accepted by Skinner's devotees is equally dangerous. This is of course the ancient problem of "dirty hands," the notion that good men may have to do unjust things in order to achieve just goals. But this is a false and pernicious statement of the problem. If a particular means is *necessary* to the achievement of a "good" end, such means – even though it may entail painful acts, such as the surgical removal of a leg to save a man's life, or the resort to war to save a people from Nazi barbarism – cannot be condemned. Means and ends are never to be judged in disjunction. They must always be taken together and assessed in terms of the total situation.

From this perspective, despotism for the advancement of "backward" peoples and authoritarian techniques for the improvement of children have little or no relevance for what Mill called mature and enlightened peoples. It is even questionable whether despotism will "advance" a "backward" people rather than more effectively bind it in subjection, or whether authoritarian controls will "educate" children rather than turn them into mechanical beings. Certainly, the ineffectiveness of Chinese "brainwashing" lends little support to the notion that modern techniques of conditioning can effectively re-educate men.[26] It requires more than a little faith to believe that Skinner's conditioning of rats, pigeons, infants, and retardates proves his ability to condition mature adults.

(3) Skinner is indeed a mystic, and his utopia is much to be feared. Utopia, to be sure, has always appealed to men conscious of the injustices of an existing order and attracted to an ideal commonwealth where disharmony and inequity no longer prevail. But this is not the lot of men. Utopias of whatever kind are always rooted in a right authoritarian mold. This is because the new system, being perfect (or nearly perfect), cannot admit of change lest it lose its perfection. Utopias are thus static societies, and men within them, frozen into higher and lower orders, are soon frustrated and bored. The impulse to change cannot be eliminated, for while men have limited needs they have unlimited wants; but if suppressed, that impulse will assume unorthodox and revolutionary forms. Hence the inevitable dilemma of utopia: to assure the maintenance of its perfect arrangements, it must preclude orderly processes of change; by precluding those processes, it only facilitates the emergence of other, disorderly, and (probably) violent social movements. The reality of utopia becomes the death of utopia.

Like Plato, whom he oddly dismisses, Skinner believes that knowledge – *his* knowledge – is virtue that *his* understanding of human behavior will lead always to the "right" controls, the "right" results. He should hearken instead to the words of sanity uttered by a madman:

> Knowledge and pain go together. The more we know, the greater our despair. The more we advance, the more we clash with the immensity of evil. . . . Not all your scientists put together could guarantee the serenity of a single human being.[27]

Skinner looks to external (environmental) forces as determining the nature (behavior) of men. But the curious fact (I must repeat) is that if his notion of environmental determinism is correct, Skinner *cannot* bring about the changes he prescribes. If we are what we are because of deterministic forces outside our control, we *cannot* become other than what we are or are destined to become. To be other than we are, to become other than what we are already destined to become, we would have to control the environment that controls us. But if *it* controls us, we cannot control *it*. Hence Skinner's proposal is self-defeating.

[26] Cf. Robert Jay Lifton, *Thought Reform and the Psychology of Totalism* (New York: W. W. Norton, 1963); see also Edgar H. Schein, *Coercive Persuasion* (New York: W. W. Norton, 1961).

[27] From Elie Wiesel, *A Beggar in Jerusalem*, trans. L. Edelman and E. Wiesel (New York: Random House, 1970; Avon paperback, 1971), p. 52.

To put this another way: If Skinner's goal is survival of the culture, and if survival requires that his controllers gain power, then his doctrine of environmental determinism precludes their getting that power and hence of providing for that survival. To get that power they would have to break the chains of environmental determinism. The logic of Skinner's theory makes it impossible for them to do this, though Skinner curiously believes that they can and should do this. If they can do it, despite his theory, then his theory is wrong: the environment does not deterministically control men. And if they can do it, we are back of course to the ethical question: survival for what? Why is X culture – *our* culture – worthy of survival? Why is it more worthy of survival than Y or Z (*their*) cultures? Indeed, given a deterministic doctrine, in what sense can it be said that we choose survival at all? It is really no answer to say, as Skinner said in a television broadcast (October 17, 1971): "We do not choose survival as a value. It chooses us." For if it chooses us, we need neither Skinner nor his concerns; all will be done despite him or ourselves.

(4) To avoid being governed by forces outside their own control, Skinner would have men seize control of their environment. But which men? If Skinner's controllers, the new men of the higher orders, in what sense can men of the lower orders be said to control? Clearly, whether the environment controls men, or Skinner's controllers control the environment that controls men, the bulk of mankind remains subjects, not citizens. A citizen is one who rules and is ruled; a subject is only ruled. In Skinner's world there are rulers and subjects. There is, in this relationship, no significant difference between the current world as Skinner depicts it and the world he would create. The future world is not better or worse than the present world; it is fundamentally the same. But to the extent that the actual world is different from the world he depicts, what he envisions is decidedly worse; for to turn citizens into subjects is effectively to bind them to governments and forces he would set permanently outside their own control.

VII

A final word: No credit or blame should attach to Skinner for the achievements or failures of *Beyond Freedom and Dignity,* or of his life's work. Clearly, these are the products of external circumstance, the environment, over which as a determinist he can have had little or no control. For the same reason, no credit or blame should attach to this writer for what is said here, or to the reader for his reactions. As Skinner would be the first to insist, both writer and reader are also behaving only as they must. If, then, none of us is an autonomous man, if none of us is responsible for what we do and say, what is the point of writing, reading, reflecting upon, or talking about this book?

PSYCHIATRIC RESPONSIBILITY IN THE OPEN SOCIETY

ANTHONY STORR

For the purpose of this paper, there is no need to define the term 'open society' too closely. As Karl Popper delineates it, the open society is an ideal towards which men should strive, rather than an actuality. But, however imperfectly realized, the open society is one in which personal freedom is highly valued, in which individuals are, to use Popper's phrase, "confronted with personal decisions" and in which decisions, both personal and collective, are based upon reason rather than upon authority or tradition. What part has the psychiatrist to play in such a society; and has he anything special to contribute to it?

A hundred years ago, the role of the psychiatrist in society was both limited and clearly defined. His job was to look after the insane; an occupation which was largely custodial, since the insane were mostly untreatable, or at any rate incurable. As cities grew in size, both in Great Britain and the U.S.A., large institutions had to be constructed to accommodate the mentally ill from these urban populations. These institutions, at first called lunatic asylums, and only recently named mental hospitals, were, at any rate in Britain, often placed at considerable distance from the community whose needs they were designed to serve, in order that the distasteful phenomena of insanity should impinge upon the ordinary citizen as little as possible. Psychiatry was a backwater speciality in which those out of mind were as far as possible put out of sight, whilst those who cared for them were similarly circumstanced.

Psychiatrists, therefore, tended to be men of little professional distinction. There were honourable exceptions: men like Tuke and Connolly in England or Pinel in France, who were responsible for replacing brutality with enlightened regimes for lunatics; but psychiatrists in the nineteenth century

* Part of this paper has already been published in "The Ciba Foundation Symposium" No. 16 "Medical Care of Prisoners and Detainees." Amsterdam (Associated Scientific Publishers) 1973.

were all too often indolent failures content to carry out a perfunctory 'round' of their charges once a day and to spend the rest of their time playing cricket. The idea that such men had a special role to play in society other than that of seeing that their patients were safely confined and treated with reasonable humanity would not have occurred to anyone.

The custodial role of the psychiatrist is still important. In Great Britain, at the end of 1969, there were 66,000 women and 50,000 men resident in mental institutions. One man in 14, one woman in 9 can expect to be admitted to a mental hospital at least once during their lifetime. In the U.S.A the figures are comparable. One out of every twelve Americans will enter hospital for mental illness at some time during his life. There are over one million patients on the books of the mental institutions, occupying more than half of all hospital beds. These figures are often not appreciated by the general public. During the last twenty years, advances in the discovery of tranquillizing drugs and other physical methods of treatment have made it possible for a number of patients to live outside mental hospitals who would formerly have had to remain as in-patients. The news media have publicized this and given the public the false impression that the mental hospitals are rapidly emptying. The figures belie this hopeful supposition.

Although there is certainly a more rapid turnover of patients than there was, many of those discharged are re-admitted and there remains a chronic core of patients who are unable to take their place in the ordinary community. How far this chronicity is the consequence of living in hospital is as yet undetermined. On both sides of the Atlantic a great deal still requires to be done to transform mental hospitals from places of confinement into truly therapeutic institutions; to integrate these hospitals into the community; and to prevent the deterioration which inevitably occurs in persons deprived of liberty who are confined for any long period in any institution.

It is worth noting that, in England, four fifths of those admitted to mental hospitals are 'voluntary patients'; whereas, in America, four fifths of admissions are involuntary. American psychiatrists working in public mental hospitals are, therefore, compelled to assume the distasteful role of gaolers to an even greater extent than are their British counterparts.

That there is bound to be some conflict between the roles of therapist and gaoler is obvious. What is not so generally appreciated is that society's greater appreciation of the possibilities of psychiatric treatment has resulted in an increased threat to personal liberty. We shall return to this topic at a later point.

Around the beginning of this century, society's attitude to psychiatrists began to change; very largely because of the rise of psychoanalysis. Psychiatrists started to emerge from their remote seclusion in mental hospitals to become, increasingly, the guides and mentors, not of the insane but of those troubled people we call neurotic. The popular image of the psychiatrist changed from that of gaoler to that of crank or eccentric; a label which has, with some justification, been attached to him ever since. However, as with other eccentrics in other societies psychiatrists tended to become invested with special, almost magical powers, supposedly gained from dredging in psychic depths to which no ordinary person would care to descend. It was even assumed that their new knowledge of human nature could somehow come to embrace the whole range of human affairs and be used to transform society. Gradually these eccentrics began to be consulted by persons from the upper strata of society; partly because no one else could afford their fees, and partly because psychoanalysis and its offshoots had an intellectual appeal to which the less educated were unable to respond. This tendency was further underlined by the fact that the psychoses, to which psychoanalysis has but a limited application, occur more commonly in the underprivileged; whilst neurosis, though no respecter of class, is more often found amongst the sophisticated and complex. In Europe, and later in America, psychoanalysts began to be consulted by intellectuals; a social phenomenon to which, perhaps, too little attention has been paid. On the face of it, it is surprising that the highly educated and socially secure should have apparently demeaned themselves so far as to seek analytical help at a period when self-esteem, far more than today, depended upon position in society. It is, I think, no coincidence that this phenomenon should have been contemporaneous with the decline of belief in conventional Christianity and with the dissolution of a class structure based upon land and family in favour of a less secure hierarchy based more upon the acquisition of wealth. Nowadays, we take it for granted that psychoanalysts will be consulted by distinguished figures, from politicians to philosophers; but in the 1900s it must have seemed an odd thing to do to those who were brought up to think that they were the elite and that no one else was likely to know more than themselves about human nature and the conduct of human relationships and human affairs in general.

Moreover, the idea of progress, of a general tendency towards the improvement of society and the world in general as a result of increasing civilization, so dear to the Victorians, was still operative. Disillusion with Western civilization had not yet overtaken its protagonists, nor had anthropology revealed that so-called 'savages' might be better adapted to their environment than we to ours. Psychoanalysis, as it gradually gained recognition, was regarded as a scientific discovery on a par with the discovery of radium or the like; a way of ameliorating man's lot by abolishing neurosis. Freud himself was no Utopian. Indeed he became increasingly pessimistic about psychoanalysis as a therapeutic method, though remaining convinced of its scientific status. Many of his followers, however, both in the early days and even today, believed that psychoanalysis was far more than a therapy designed to relieve a few neurotic sufferers. Melanie Klein, for example, writes in one passage of her hope that child analysis will one day become universal. Admittedly, she refers to this hope as 'Utopian'; but even to imagine that "child-analysis will become as much a part of every person's upbringing as school education is now" is an extraordinary flight of fancy.

This tendency towards Utopianism has persisted to some extent amongst psychoanalysts, although it is probably rather less than it was. It is reinforced by the fact that many analysts lead isolated, dedicated lives, seeing few people other than patients and colleagues, and playing less part than most other professional men in public affairs. It is easier to sustain the belief that one has the answer to the universe if one has no idea how the universe works. Psychoanalysis is primarily an interpretative discipline; a method of making sense out of the previously incomprehensible, and a way of helping individuals to understand themselves better. Although Freud did apply psychoanalytic interpretation to social phenomena to some extent and, for example, conducted correspondence on the subject of war, he was never unrealistic enough to suppose that a method of individual treatment of neurosis could readily be transferred to solve all the problems of society.

That psychoanalysis has not proved to be a universal panacea, nor even the therapeutic success for which enthusiasts hoped, does not mean that psychiatrists and psychoanalysts have nothing to contribute to the study of society. It is a truism to say that society is composed of individuals and that political institutions are, or in an open society, should be designed to promote the well-being of society's members. What constitutes individual well-being and what best contributes to this end are both arguable matters. Whether the health and happiness of individuals is best achieved by material prosperity, by sexual fulfillment, through faith or through agnosticism, by being reared in a kibbutz or in a small family, by being encouraged to be, or discouraged from being, competitive; all these and many similar topics are themes to which the psychiatrist may legitimately address himself and upon which he is entitled to something of a special hearing because of his intimate knowledge of the emotional problems of individuals.

It does not, however, follow that he should therefore be regarded as an expert upon education, the control of crime, the resolution of colour prejudice or the abolition of war. To all these subjects, the psychiatrist has something to contribute but it is a limited contribution, derived from his experience with comparatively few individuals.

The analytical treatment of neurotics takes a very long time; which is one reason why psychoanalysis has so far been available, with very few exceptions, only to the privileged rich. This state of affairs is bound to create the hope, however Utopian, that if only greater resources of time, money and trained personnel were provided, many of the misfits in society could be better fitted to take their place in it. Moreover, this hope contains the unspoken assumption that psychoanalysis, or some such psychotherapeutic method, is likely to be as effective a treatment for social deviants as it is for neurotics; and that, if only all criminals, drug addicts, sexual perverts and the like were treated as patients rather than offenders, their problems and the problems they create would be solved. Hence, there is a strong tendency to exaggerate what psychiatric treatment can accomplish and to suggest that more facilities for treatment exist than is in fact the case. Readers of Popper's "The Open Society" will be familiar with his thesis that Utopianism inevitably leads to tyranny. The present tendency in society to idealize the therapeutic approach to misfits is a good example. I do not mean to suggest that, were greater resources available, nothing further could be done for the mentally ill. There is an enormous amount which could and should be done but, as things are at present, the resources do not exist, and psychiatrists are being asked to undertake more than they can possibly accomplish and to direct their therapeutic efforts towards a clientèle who are less likely to respond to their efforts than are neurotics who seek help voluntarily. This has led to a number of abuses, of which unnecessary deprivation of liberty is the most obvious. It has been demonstrated that, as one might expect, the majority of psychiatrists and psychoanalysts are mildly left-wing, liberal and anti-authoritarian. It is perhaps paradoxical that the therapeutic approach to persons who would, in previous generations, have been considered wicked or feckless, has resulted in a decline in liberty, but such is the case. In what follows I am heavily indebted to "The Right to be Different" by Nicholas N. Kittrie (The Johns Hopkins Press, 1971). It is significant that a professor of criminal law should be moved to write such a powerful indictment of what he calls the 'therapeutic state.'

In his book, Professor Kittrie demonstrates, with a wealth of examples, that misplaced therapeutic enthusiasm has led to many persons being confined for indefinite periods with few of the safeguards against wrongful confinement which are available to criminals being effectively operative. Thus, thirty-three states of the U.S.A. have laws allowing the indefinite commitment of drug addicts to therapeutic institutions from which they can only be released if 'cured.' Since, even after extensive exposure to the best treatment programmes, only about three per cent of addicts remain abstinent after release, it is obvious that many persons are being confined indefinitely upon false premises.

It is surely the duty of the psychiatrist to society to point out that he has, as yet, no effective method of treating the personality disorder which, it is generally agreed, underlies the phenomenon of addiction to narcotics; and, whilst pursuing research which may lead to effective treatments, it is his duty to refuse to act as gaoler for those he cannot as yet help. He might add that, in the recent exacerbation of anxiety about the taking of drugs, it is often forgotten that the legal control of narcotics is of very recent origin, as is the supposition that crime and addiction are necessarily linked. Before 1914, there were no laws in the U.S.A. regulating the traffic in narcotics and there is little doubt that, in the U.S.A., the association of drug addiction with crime is the result of punitive legislation.

In Great Britain, the poet Crabbe took opium for over forty years; yet it did not interfere with his literary output and he died at the age of seventy-eight. Wilkie Collins took increasing doses of laudanum (tincture of opium) from 1862 to his death at the age of sixty-five in 1889. His novels may have deteriorated but he did not cease production. Addiction to even heroin and morphine does not cause as much physical damage as does addiction to alcohol; and it is often preferable, as the law allows in Britain, for addicts to be allowed to obtain a regular dose of narcotic upon prescription than to try and fail to forcibly wean them from it.

Similarly, in the mistaken belief that psychiatrists can cure large numbers of alcoholics of their addiction *against their will,* 26 states of the U.S.A. have laws which allow the commitment of alcoholics to institutions from which release is conditional upon cure. Since the treatment facilities available fall far short of what is required, the effect of this compulsion, intended as a liberal, therapeutic device, is simply to extend the period during which an alcoholic offender is confined, without in fact improving his condition. This is, of course, not to argue that no alcoholics can be cured. Some can and are helped by psychiatric treatment to achieve and sustain total abstinence: but, in my limited experience, this is entirely dependent upon the *voluntary* co-operation of the alcoholic.

More dubious still are the laws determining the confinement of so-called 'psychopaths'; a category of mental abnormality so hard to define that "a 1950 New Jersey report cited twenty-nine different definitions of the condition by twenty-nine medical authorities." (Kittrie, p. 193). At least twenty states of the U.S.A. have made use of statutes relating to psychopaths, with the result that mental institutions are overloaded with people for whom they have no effective treatment. Kittrie gives examples of offenders who have often committed only trivial offences: for example, indecent exposure, who have been committed to institutions for indefinite periods. I will add one example from Great Britain. The Mental Health Act of 1959 unfortunately included provision for the forcible confinement of psychopaths. In the words of the Act, psychopathic disorder is defined as "a persistent disorder or disability of mind (whether or not including subnormality of intelligence) which results in abnormally aggressive or seriously irresponsible conduct on the part of the patient and requires or is susceptible to medical treatment."

In 1968, Eric Edward Wills, aged 21, who had been charged with larceny and with obtaining money under false pretences, was sent to a mental hospital for a report. He was there diagnosed as a psychopath. The medical report submitted to the magistrate revealed that he was a compulsive gambler and recommended that the operation of prefrontal lobotomy be performed upon him. The magistrate promptly ordered that this operation be carried out. Fortunately, the Press heard of the case, realised the implications and the decision was rescinded.

Deprivation of liberty on the grounds of insanity, whether or not accompanied by the intention of enforced therapy, is also open to abuse. In the USSR, confinement in a mental hospital may be instituted if the 'patient' is regarded as being a 'public danger.' More particularly, Soviet law allows for forcible commitment if an individual is said to suffer from a "hypochondriacal delusional condition, causing an irregular, aggressive attitude in the patient towards individuals, organizations or institutions." Even more sinisterly, the law recognises that "externally correct behaviour and dissimulation" may mask what is supposed to be the individual's true intention.

It is well-known and amply documented that mental hospitals are used in the USSR to confine persons who are thought to be hostile to the regime; and that psychiatrists have co-operated in this misuse of their medical function. Perhaps some psychiatrists are such dedicated Communists that they do in fact believe that anyone who does not share their faith must be insane. Others may well be threatened with dismissal and loss of livelihood if they do not agree to treat as patients those whom the

Government wishes to remove from society. As readers of "A Question of Madness" by Zhores and Roy Medvedev will known, whatever the reasons may be, it is clearly not difficult for the Soviet Government to find psychiatrists who will co-operate.

In the West, it is less likely that individuals are wrongly committed to mental hospitals on purely political grounds, although the cases of Earl Long, the Governor of Louisiana and, more especially, the case of May Kimbrough Jones, both quoted by Kittrie, must give rise to doubt. But it is very easy indeed for individuals to be judged insane upon dubious criteria; to be committed indefinitely to mental institutions where they will receive no treatment; and to be deprived of liberty, perhaps for life, in spite of the fact that they may be causing no harm to themselves or to anyone else.

In the U.S.A. Thomas Szasz, a psychoanalyst, has propounded the thesis that the inmates of mental hospitals are the scapegoats of society, fulfilling the same function for society as did witches in the Middle Ages. He believes that any form of coercion applied to the so-called 'mentally ill' is unjustifiable and that the psychiatrist's function should be confined to elucidating the 'problems in living' of those who voluntarily seek his help. This, to my mind, is oversimplifying the issue. There are a number of persons in any society who are, and should be, regarded as mentally ill and who may, unfortunately, require confinement against their will, at any rate temporarily. In his essay on Liberty, John Stuart Mill wrote: "The only purpose for which power can rightfully be exercised over any member of a civilised community against his will is to prevent harm to others. His own good, either physical or moral, is not a sufficient warrant." Although Mill admits of some modification of this principle in the case of juveniles, he does not really consider the case of the mentally ill, in spite of the fact that, in a footnote to a later passage of the essay, he has sharp observations to make about the inadequacy of the evidence as to insanity which is often accepted by jurors. According to Mill, it would obviously be right to certify and confine an individual who was suffering from paranoid schizophrenia and threatening to murder his imagined persecutors.

[In this connection it is of interest to note that acute paranoid episodes, in which individuals go berserk and do in fact kill others, is one of the few forms of mental illness common to all cultures and one universally recognised as calling for the forcible restraint of the sufferer.]

But how about the sufferer from melancholia, who announces his intention of committing suicide? Although it is true that suicide does usually harm those nearest to the suicide, I doubt if Mill would have thought this kind of harm sufficient to come within the category he defines. Suicide is primarily a matter of the individual harming himself; and this, Mill considers, he should be left free to do. Yet every psychiatrist will have had many patients who have been actively suicidal and who may have made more than one attempt to kill themselves yet who, on recovery from their disorder, have been extremely glad that they were restrained from doing so and grateful for any treatment which led to their recovery. Moreover, there are patients in a state of mania or hypomania who may undertake all kinds of ill-judged commitments, financial and otherwise, which result in harm to themselves and from which, upon recovery, they have been grateful for being restrained. Should one deny treatment to those suffering from these types of mental disorder on the grounds that it is an unwarrantable interference with their personal liberty to do so?

In Great Britain it has been the practice to certify and confine against their will not only those who are obviously likely to harm others but also those who are likely to harm themselves, either by suicide or else by overreaching themselves whilst in that state of high excitement and overconfidence we designate as hypomania. I think it right that this should be so and I can see no way in which psychiatrists can in conscience entirely avoid the distasteful role of acting as temporary gaolers and exercising coercion over some patients which conflicts with their function as therapists.

But I also think that psychiatrists have a special duty, in the open society, to see that this coercion is kept to an absolute minimum. So far as I can see, this involves two principles. First, no psychiatrist should be misled by his own therapeutic enthusiasm or by the well-meaning therapeutic hopes of others into promising treatment for social deviants which he cannot carry out. Thus, because he believes that a criminal, or an alcoholic, or a psychopath or a psychotic might be helped by a full-scale analysis of fifty minutes five days a week, he should not agree to his confinement in a mental institution where he will get, if he is lucky, a ten minute interview once a week. It is not disputed that some patients in these categories can be helped by analysis; or indeed by psychotherapies less drastic, although it must be admitted that the patients who benefit most from such treatment are generally those who are too inhibited to be social deviants, rather than the reverse. But there is no point in depriving people of liberty if one has no treatment to offer them. As Norval Morris of Chicago University has put it: "The rehabilitative ideal is seen to impart unfettered discretion. Whereas the treaters seem convinced of the benevolence of their treatment methods, those being treated take a different view, and we, the observers share their doubts. The jailer in a white coat and with a doctorate remains a jailer – but with larger power over his fellows." So much is this the case that Professor Morris advises that no criminal should plead not guilty upon grounds of insanity.

Second, no psychiatrist should co-operate in coercion unless he is convinced that the person concerned is a danger to others or to himself. If we exclude the mentally defective, the intoxicated, the physically ill and the senile, who raise problems beyond the scope of this paper, this will in practice involve only those individuals who are murderous, suicidal or obviously manic. A few paranoid individuals may remain murderous throughout life, but they are very few. Manic depressives, whether manic or depressed, almost invariably recover from any given attack of their disorder. Therefore, by far the majority of those who are forcibly confined will need to be so for only short periods.

Twenty-five years ago, when I was a newly-fledged psychiatrist, I should have been in favour of casting the coercive net far wider. It seemed obvious, for instance, that the schizophrenic with delusions and hallucinations and other clear-cut manifestations of mental illness should be in a mental hospital where, if he could not be cured, he would at least be treated with tolerance and understanding. If he had not the insight to see this, then reluctantly, he should be certified insane. Now I realise that our criteria of mental illness are sadly inadequate; that many harmless people have 'delusional systems' by which they live; and I am against depriving anybody of liberty, however 'mad' he may appear, unless he is a danger to others or to himself.

In the open society, the psychiatrist has a second duty which is equally important. That is, he must do his best to ensure that techniques of psychiatric investigation and treatment are not misused for other purposes by Governments or other agencies such as the police or military. I have already drawn attention to the misuse of mental hospitals as places of confinement for those whom society or Government find inconvenient. There are many other possibilities of abuse. Prefrontal lobotomy is an obvious example. The misuse of drugs which alter mood or which release inhibitions so that information can be obtained is another. The techniques of conditioning used in 'behaviour therapy' could easily be used for the convenience of society, rather than to promote the well-being of the individual. So could the new electronic techniques of modifying brain function by the implantation of electrodes into the brain substance. Such dangers, thanks to the publicity given to them by books and newspapers, are beginning to be widely appreciated. However, there is still a pressing need for vigilance. I shall end this paper by giving an example of the misuse of psychiatrict research by Government in which I was personally involved in protest.

The history goes back a long way. In 1960, the late Professor Kennedy, then Professor of Psychiatry in the University of Edinburgh, was rash enough to reveal that he had been employed, during the last war, at an interrogation centre in Cairo, in giving advice as to how methods of psychological pressure could be brought to bear upon prisoners from whom information was wanted. This disclosure created a certain amount of unease; more, I think, amongst the general public than amongst the medical profession. What, they asked, was a doctor doing in this context? Surely a doctor's job was to heal the sick, not to instruct governments in how to break down prisoners, mentally in such a way that they would yield up information. I took this point of view myself, although I knew that not all my psychiatric colleagues shared it. At the time, there was considerable interest in 'brainwashing' techniques, as practised by the Russians and the Chinese. The Korean War, with its revelations as to how nearly a third of the Americans captured had been persuaded to 'collaborate' was still fresh in people's minds. There was still a lingering feeling that the British Army did not behave like that, although, of course, no one expected that they would invariably behave to prisoners with saintly forbearance. The best I could do at the time was to write an article, which was published in the 'New Statesman' entitled 'Torture without Violence.' In it, I deplored the fact that doctors should lend themselves to use by Government in the way which Professor Kennedy had indicated, and suggested that this conduct was contrary to the Hippocratic oath, as indeed it was. He made no riposte to the article; perhaps because of ill-health; since in fact he died within a few months of its publication. There were various repercussions to this article. One lawyer wrote from Cyprus to say that he had knowledge of British methods of interrogation, and that these included what he called 'drug-induced hypnosis.' It emerged that there was a special training centre for interrogators – it still exists – at Maresfield in Sussex: though what went on there proved difficult to find out. Eventually, we got so far as to persuade Mr. Francis Noel-Baker to ask a question in the House of Commons of the Prime Minister, then Mr. Harold Macmillan. He evaded the issue, saying that it was not in the public interest to reveal what methods of interrogation were taught to British interrogators since such information might be of use to potential enemies. He did, however, write "... I can give an unequivocal assurance that in the training of British interrogators the use of 'brain washing,' drugs or physical violence is expressly and emphatically forbidden."

I gave up enquiry at this point. It seemed difficult to carry matters beyond the Prime Minister. From time to time various rather disturbing allegations of brutal conduct on the part of the British Forces emerged from Cyprus, Aden and other trouble spots. Then came the revelations about Northern Ireland. We learned that men were being starved, deprived of sleep, made to assume uncomfortable postures standing spread eagled against a wall for hours at a time; and, more sinisterly, that they were being hooded and exposed to continuous noise at the same time. These revelations shocked a great number of people, and, eventually, an enquiry was instituted under the chairmanship of the former Ombudsman, Sir Edmund Compton. This resulted in a report which, though deploring the use of 'brutality,' alleged that the methods of interrogation employed in Northern Ireland were not in fact brutal. The hooding, the posture on the wall, and the continuous noise were, so Compton alleged, designed primarily to stop internees communicating with each other. A secondary effect, the report went on, might be to render the men so treated more susceptible to interrogation. "It can also, in the case of some detainees, increase their sense of isolation and so be helpful to the interrogator thereafter."

I think that any uninformed person reading the Compton report would have concluded that, although what was done to internees was not pleasant, there was little evidence of severe *physical* pressure being employed. Some men had complained of being knocked about, or being forced to do unaccustomed physical exercises, or of being forced to stand up against the wall again when they had collapsed from fatigue and the effects of being given only one slice of bread and some water every six hours or so. But the tenor of the report was that although more supervision of interrogators was desirable – and it must be remembered that the interrogations were carried out primarily by the Royal Ulster Constabulary and not by British Armed Forces personnel – not much harm was being done, and possibly some unpleasant procedures were temporarily necessary if the IRA was to be stopped from pursuing its policy of terrorism.

It is at this point, I think, that specialised psychiatric knowledge became relevant. Anyone who had read the literature on sensory deprivation and its effects must have concluded that a variant of sensory deprivation was being used as a method of breaking down internees. The hooding and the continuous noise were designed, not to isolate men from each other, as the Compton report alleged, but as a deliberate method of producing mental confusion and disorientation. I was no expert in the field of sensory deprivation: but I knew that the effects were so disturbing that, even amongst healthy volunteers who were acting as experimental guinea-pigs and being paid for it, a high proportion pressed the 'panic button' long before the experimental period was up. In mild sensory deprivation conditions, male volunteers endured only an average of 29 hours; and in more rigorous conditions, only one man in ten endured more than ten hours. If no limit in time has been set to the termination of the experiment, fears of insanity and confusion may come on within as little as two hours. I knew that many people lost all sense of time; that others became hallucinated; that the experience could, at any rate for some people, be compared with a bad 'trip' as a result of taking LSD. I knew, moreover, that an interesting fact had emerged from the Princeton experiments. If the experimenters used Princeton students, a number became paranoid, thought the experimenter had abandoned them and so on. But when the experimenters had run short of their own students, and had to seek volunteers from further afield, the proportion who became paranoid was much higher. If the very mild degree of distrust which one might feel at entrusting oneself to the care of university professors not of one's own university became so quickly magnified under sensory deprivation, what, one wondered, would be the effect of sensory deprivation upon men who knew themselves to be in the hands of actual enemies?

At the time of publication of the Compton Report I was asked if I would write an article on the psychiatric aspects of the Compton Report for the 'Sunday Times' and did so on the following day. In the article, I tried to make it clear that physical brutality was not the only kind of brutality which mattered; that sensory deprivation techniques could be used to produce what was equivalent to a temporary episode of insanity; that no one could possibly know what the long-term after-effects of such procedures would be upon the men to whom they had been applied; and that the Home Secretary had no business to say that these methods had no serious sequelae, as he had been rash enough to do in the House of Commons. I thought it important to do this because I surmised that the general public would have no idea that any method of psychological pressure without actual physical torture could be expected to have serious effects. Psychiatrists who spend most of their time only in interchanges with other psychiatrists take for granted a number of things which it is actually rash to assume that non-psychiatrists have any idea of.

After various further protests in the House of Commons and elsewhere, a group of three Privy Councillors, Lord Parker, Lord Gardiner and Mr.

Boyd-Carpenter, were appointed to investigate the whole question of interrogation further, and I found myself giving evidence before them. I repeated to these distinguished men what I had said in the 'Sunday Times' article, further reinforced by a study of the literature on sensory deprivation. I discovered that some of this literature is still not available, as it comes under the heading of 'classified' information. It seems that Government departments are quick off the mark in spotting what psychological and physiological techniques might be of use to them in war. A great deal of this research had, of course, been undertaken at the request of Governments interested in the effect of isolation, weightlessness and the like upon potential astronauts. What the Parker committee were primarily interested in was whether the techniques of sensory deprivation employed in Northern Ireland could, as it were, be used in moderation without much risk of serious after-effects. They told me that it was undoubtedly true that much useful information had been obtained from internees by the use of these methods, and no doubt many lives had been saved as a result. I was, of course, unable to answer this question, since there was no literature available to me which could tell me whether sensory deprivation employed as an interrogation technique upon enemies had the dire effects which any psychiatrist must guess it would be likely to have. All I could say was that so-called 'traumatic' neuroses had been known to result from traumas which were less severe; that producing psychotic symptoms in 'normal' people by other methods like the use of LSD, for instance, was fraught with risk; and that one could only tell what the effects would actually be after a long-term follow-up of the people concerned. In the event, the Parker Committee produced a report in which Lord Parker and Mr. Boyd-Carpenter thought that the methods employed in Ulster could continue to be used if subject to more stringent safeguards; whilst Lord Gardiner produced a minority report saying that these methods were wholly detestable, their results unpredictable, and that they were unworthy of British traditions in the treatment of prisoners. The Prime Minister, after the publication of the report, said in the House that these methods would henceforth be forbidden.

The moral of this story is not so much that it is possible for psychiatrists, on occasion, to participate effectively in protest, important though this is. It is to underline the fact that psychiatric techniques and research, designed originally to be helpful to disturbed individuals, can, in many instances, be extracted from their therapeutic setting and used for exactly the opposite purpose. It is the duty of the psychiatrist, in the open society, to be aware of this possibility, and to prevent it when he can. In my view, it is also his duty to refrain from giving professional advice or in any way participating in such abuse. "The condition upon which God hath given liberty to man is eternal vigilance: which condition if he break, servitude is at once the consequence of his crime and the punishment of his guilt."

NEITHER STICKS NOR STONES*

HENRY S. KARIEL

> "Any trumpets in it?"
> "No."
> "Any drums?"
> "No."
> "Call it *Neither Trumpets nor Drums.*"
> – François Truffaut,
> "Bed and Board"

Whoever is now composing that epitaph for a monument to a successful revolution is surely too old to enter the new world himself. He remains the victim of old languages, responsibilities, and deadlines. Still, he must have gotten the message. The past is transcended: all caverns of the body are touched and familiar, the mind has expanded, and there is no one who has not risen to fly with Yeats's falcon without falconer, "turning and turning in the widening gyre," gently whirling, easily switching from role to role, celebrating amateurism, openness, and love. We are in permanent revolution, bringing the world into museums, life into plays and plays into courtrooms. At last, a world stage, a divine festival. The arts – all of them, politics included – provide fluid prototypes that are almost redundant: artist-designed earthscapes, radar-directed bombings, diplomatic receptions, lunar flagraisings, press conferences. Angela Davis, Daniel Ellsberg, Howard Hughes, Clifford Irving, Benjamin Spock, Bernardine Dohrn, Hugh Hefner, William Calley, Ralph Ginzburg, Muhammed Ali, Jerry Rubin, the Berrigan brothers – deserters, misfits, outcasts, imposters, drop-outs, dissenters are cast as models of heroic innocence, violating the law but no one's canons of justice. Well-plotted lives have become unreal, not to be mourned when finished, no longer suitable for films or novels. "Straight lines are monsters," we would chant with Delacroix if we cared to remember him saying it. Plots, sequences, endings, frames, instruments are broken and scattered to make room for individuals as unmoved movers, protean in their encounter with an ever-yielding reality, able to escape the confinements of the past and the future. No end is fated. We can deliver ourselves to chance – Luke Rhinehart has recently invented a useful mechanism in *The Diceman* – and become willing victims with nothing to lose but our guilt. For self-sustaining therapy, Rhinehart's diceman,

* This paper originally appeared in *Politics and Society* (Winter, 1973), pp. 179-199.

named Luke Rhinehart, keeps throwing his die so that it will give him six feasible future options whenever his last commitment winds down. His basic vision is clear:

> We want people to greet each other on the street and not know who is who and *not care*. We want freedom from individual identity. Freedom from security and stability and coherence. We want a community of creators, a monastery for joy-filled manmen. . . . I'm talking about converting QSH into a Center in which patients will be systematically taught to play games with life, to act out all of their fantasies, to be dishonest and enjoy it, to lie and pretend and feel hate and rage and love and compassion as determined by the whim of the dice. I'm talking about creating an institution where the doctors periodically pretend to be patients, for days, for weeks, where the patients pretend to be doctors and give therapy sessions, where the attendants and nurses play the roles of patients and visitors and doctors and TV repairmen, where the whole fucking institution is one great stage upon which all walk free.[1]

In this fantasy – our reality – we joyfully obliterate monuments and records, birth certificates and academic grades, wanting no past to serve as index to our future, determined to make it easy to get into and out of schools, careers, neighborhoods, and – who knows? – cemeteries. We are impatient with the patina and characters of De Sica's "Garden of the Finzi-Continis": why don't Micòl and Giorgio *do* something? Aren't men and women free to make history? The frontier has beckoned and we have crossed over. Who among the late romantics – Rousseau, Schiller, Blake, Delacroix, Baudelaire, Nietzsche, Proudhon, Sorel, Wilde – would not believe that the future has happened?

Who (to double back) among the living really believes it? The year 2000 is but the present, only more so. The avant-garde mythology of the frontier confirms the betrayal of romanticism: all the new Westerns give the lie to the promise of the holy land. We have known the truth ever since Gary Cooper revealed in "High Noon" that the peace of his Quaker wife had to be violated for one more job and that the community of frontiersmen was impotent without him and his gun. Butch Cassidy as well as the Sundance Kid finally search for the frontier in Bolivia and the Wild Bunch moves down and out to Mexico. "Five Easy Pieces" starts at the last frontier, easing Jack Nicholson out of L.A.'s freeways into the most northwestern corner of the land, broke (but alive) at the end. "True Grit" – like a score of movies putting Frederick Jackson Turner's frontier thesis into jeopardy – reveals the sag and sourness of the cowboy come of age. (Three years later, in "The Cowboys," John Wayne unwittingly mocks all that's left – a herd of cows and a bunch of boys.) McCabe and Mrs. Miller

[1] Luke Rhinehart, *The Diceman* (New York: Morrow, 1971), pp. 140-141.

are both done in by corporate power, one dying in the snow, the other returning to opium. What is told and retold in cinematographic myth – "How the West Was Won" ends with the sun going *down*, way out in the Pacific where Norman Mailer placed his great American Western, *The Naked and the Dead* – is no longer unhinged from ordinary experience. Somehow we are being had – being schooled, due processed, confined, starved, and emasculated, being developed and executed in stages, taught to perceive ourselves as ready-mades framed for hanging. Inchoate, unnamed forces inexorably shape our lives and diminish us, making it easy to speak of ennui and alienation, of growing up absurd and meeting death at an early age. We are doomed by the Environmental Crisis, that autonomous ungovernable force out there about which we are calmly lectured by sensitive and powerless scientists, belatedly experts in futuristics. We hear the lectures helplessly, guilty and disarmed, believing that Nature – not a mindless elite – is at last taking its toll. And within areas that Nature still permits us to reduce to our own designs, we are no less condemned, and know it. Our inventions have ceased to be liberating: nation-states, highway intersections, metropolitan governments, communication grids, hotel chains, school systems, hospital complexes, television networks, defense departments, double-entry bookkeeping are not the value-neutral institutions they once seemed to be. Adding little to our pleasures, they are hard to appreciate as innocuous instruments. Can weapons systems which include napalm *ever* be used to reduce our miseries? We remain fundamentally and deeply committed to a technology which divides and consumes and drives us, arresting the development not only of subordinates but also of superiors, making everyone a functionary. Our governors, it turns out, are not actors after all but typecast naturals – stereotyped men and women who have thoroughly learned how to function in but one role. And our dissenters are as fixed in the hierarchies of power as their guardians. Patients and doctors, students and teachers, prisoners and guards confront one another like natural forces convinced that this is what they truly are, that their roles are no mere roles, no put-ons, no acts. It is the real thing, the way to live, the way to go. There is no mass liberation, no greening, no jump into freedom. Bentham's world. Skinner's. IBM's. The landscape is flat and gray, and only the computer gives the appearance of playing. Walden III (2) 1.

The half-truths expressed by these two caricatures may help to undercut my obsession with the specific texture of nothingness, for they point to polarities of experience that must somehow occupy the most empty and open society if it is to reveal with concrete exactness how empty and open it is. They may make it easier to realize that we can enter the promised land only through acts of controlled idiocy, only by working our way *through* the present, not getting lost en route, determined to come out (travel kits intact) on the other side. Salvation through perdition, in the old romantic formula that gave credence to order and discipline, leading us to *encompass* traversed territory, to map and recollect it, to give a coherent account of the voyage, ourselves included. Clearly, we should welcome the trip and whatever temptations it offers to stop somewhere, to become captivated by some finality, some nonpolitical private passion which might enslave us fully. Failing to act *as if* taken in by finalities, we will be as innocent as we were when we departed. The new-won silence will have no resonance.

I am of course insisting on the difference between not doing anything and knowing precisely what one is not doing. "Rendering oneself unarmed," in Nietzsche's words, "when one had been the best-armed, out of a height of feeling – that is the means to authentic peace. . . ." [2] The new state is not one of simple vacuity but rather one in which specific things are *known* to be absent because previously confronted and overcome, one in which healed wounds explicitly testify to the absence of heroic deeds, final solutions, impregnable armor, total victories – some whole thing. "You keep throwing in your hand because you haven't got the whole thing," Alex's mother says in Penelope Gilliatt's "Sunday Bloody Sunday." Reflecting on what gives the illusion of being a meaningless marriage, she adds, "You think it's nothing, but it's not nothing."

Because there are no unmistakable clues to something which is *not* nothing, it is easy to misread the promises of nothingness, to mistake the intonations of writers such as Roland Barthes, Norman Brown, or Charles Castaneda, to disguise the absurdities of the *I Ching,* the pelvic posture, *The Aquarian Gospel of Christ*, astrological charts, and the signs of witches. These seem to offer but a formless existence, inviting us to assume we can keep performing without interdiction, discipline, protocol, and grammar. Yet their very style makes the point that we cannot save ourselves, save the various selves implicitly present in our being, by letting go and falling free. True, we may aim to purge myth, ideology, and authority, write at degree zero, paint pure white on pure white, compose resounding silences, celebrate the nonrepressive society, blueprint empty analytical frameworks, play games without rules. We may feel drawn toward the spaces beyond the door held open by R. D. Laing, toward the agraphia of

[2] "Human, All Too Human," in Walter Kaufmann, ed. and tr., *The Portable Nietzsche* (New York: Viking, 1954), sec. 284.

Rimbaud, or toward the desperate negations of Nietzsche. But to save a self that *knows* the pleasures of being observed in action, to give significance to our appearances by referring them to structures of possibilities shared by others, we require order, continuity, convention, redundancy – beads to pray with and count on, to get our bearings, to give us bearing and composure. Nothing, to say it sententiously, can be salvaged without form: no ecstasy without stasis.

Yet what form among the infinite possible ones is likely to serve our interests? We recurrently assume that we have made some sensible choice when of course we have merely slipped or responded to pressure. Seeking to discriminate and act, we see ourselves in motion – know that we are merely busy reacting and responding, perhaps vaguely sensing that others call the shots or that some singular abstraction designed by men long dead determines the rhythm and direction of our lives. Nature, Tradition, Manifest Destiny, Historical Necessity, Technological Momentum, Organizational Inertia are in charge of us. We perceive and embrace a "logic of the situation" – a rationality – which we finally believe to be our very own.

To return to our own senses, to reactivate ourselves, what is to be done? How can we open existing societies and yet accept the constraints we need to take our measure, to find pleasure in ourselves and one another? It would be useful, I think, to single out and capitalize three modes of action – the *indicative*, the *transactional*, and the *anticipatory* – and note how these might function to open society not so as to transcend it and reach some final state but so as to *keep* our social selves in a state of openness, in a condition of permanent conflict, tension, and excitement.

When we express ourselves in the indicative mode, we remain calmly in the midst of the stream of human events, accepting what appears within our range of vision, what is said and done and believed, moving ourselves as close to the phenomena under study as we can without losing our perceptual apparatus, our epistemology, our composure. We embrace the prevailing definitions of "event," "problem," "fact," "cause," and "decision," ignoring the possibility that boundaries might be drawn differently by men who are less equipped, secure, and calm, more involved and bloodied than we are. For us (and our patrons), the existing solutions are *not* seen as problems. Education is never miseducation, use never waste, progress never regression, official coercion never violence, pacification never terror. Acting in the indicative mode we are servants of reality, control ourselves, and let things be what they are known to be. We take account of them – literally recording, transcribing, documenting. We conform to the great dogmas of scientific empiricism, literary naturalism, and early positivism, tell it virtually as it is, or at least as it is widely said to be. At best, we so arrange and enliven the facts that they appear to speak for themselves. We imply that not men but 'natural forces" make history, that no one decides on beginnings and endings, causes and effects. Our chronicles begin as if the story somehow told itself ("It so happened that . . ."). And they end on the note experimentally parodied by Henry Adams's nine volumes on the Jefferson and Madison administrations, by Sartre's interminable studies of Genet and Flaubert, by Vonnegut's resigned "so it goes." [3] Adhering to the indicative mode of action, we insinuate that our work will fully attend to the structures inherent in nature. We assume that by not intervening in the way things appear the world becomes luminous.

The plausibility of such work is assured by the way it appears to conform to contemporary experience. It *is* illuminating. Is it arbitrary, after all, to be offered pictures of men being no more than they appear to be, precisely what meets the eye? Are men not dependent on some psychological or economic substructures of forces immune to their control? Isn't it evident – haven't the critics of the mass society from Tocqueville to Mumford made it evident – that things have ceased to be different than they seem to be? It has become all right for films to treat background as foreground, to assimilate action to street motion and street noises, to subordinate actors to the furnishings of living rooms, the shiny hardware of hospitals, the exciting litter of grubby hallways. The background becomes equal, if not autonomous: walls acquire a life of their own. The camera is not clearly wrong in showing characters to be no more than the credit cards they carry or the drugs they take. Nor are the on-location accounts of social science which exhibit men as functions a form of naive scientism. "The trouble with modern theories of behaviorism," Hannah Arendt has said, "is not that they are wrong but . . . that they actually are the best possible conceptualization of certain obvious trends in modern society." [4] If the works of literary realism and behavioral social science are compelling, this is because for us – and our authors – the surface facts of life have emerged as the whole of life.

Of course, no "realistic" works exist in their purity: a representation of reality is merely that, a part of a larger whole. Even the most passive effort

[3] The subversiveness of Adams's commitment to positivism deserves attention; see his "Letter to American Teachers of History" in *The Degradation of the Democratic Dogma* (New York: Macmillan, 1920), pp. 137-263. I have touched on it in "The Limits of Social Science: Henry Adams's Quest for Order," *American Political Science Review,* 50 (December 1956), 1074-1092.

[4] Hannah Arendt, *The Human Condition* (Chicago: University of Chicago Press, 1958), p. 322.

to indicate that something is only natural assumes a larger nature to which it belongs. To point to man's determined behavior – the ways he is driven and eliminated – is still to place it in some larger context. The facts of life, not life as such, are always human constructions. Whoever relates them discloses not only the way men fail to see and help themselves but also their missed chances, their derailed plans. He will reveal the ironies of life, showing how the assertion (for example) of a seemingly charitable impulse is "really" something more – perhaps a form of displacement, defiance, status envy, or glandular imbalance. He will unavoidably magnify the implied tendencies of manifest behavior. Seeing more fully and deeply than his subject matter, he will expose backgrounds, motives, and dispositons. He will say more than they care to say (or are able to say without jeopardizing what they have become) and will thereby disclose the presence of unexpressed phenomena. This is as true of the accounts of social science (Gans's *The Levittowners*) as it is of novels (O'Hara's and Cheever's short stories), sculptures (Segal's "Motel Room"), films (Bagdanovich's "The Last Picture Show"), plays and skits (those of Elaine May, Mort Sahl, Ken Kesey, and Lenny Bruce), reportage, profiles, and observations (Tom Wolfe's, Calvin Trillin's, E. J. Kahn's).

Nevertheless, distinctions are useful. There are head-on, dead-pan, sharp-focus products which seem to be nothing but prosaic manifestations of the indicative mode. They leave the surface virtually undisturbed, consecrating things as they are, their flat prose a match for the flatness of the social landscape. To be sure, outside the offered case histories, their authors may lead lives which show them to reach further – as when Truman Capote actually committed himself to reflect on the *merits* of capital punishment. Within the confines of their art, however, they remain composed in accordance with established expectations. Capote's *In Cold Blood* does permit us to learn that the two thugs who committed murder had repressed their altruistic sentiments. But beyond this, there is nothing about how the underlying structure of society deflected such human aspects, nothing about the punitive institutions of the state of Kansas, the self-imposed frugality of its legislature, the hierarchical social order that made it impossible for Capote's killers to dream up and stage a performance that might have given more life to *all* prospective players – to themselves, their guards, their victims, their witnesses, their biographer. Capote's observations skim the accredited surface, scarcely carrying him beyond the ideology of the day. Insofar as his work is in the indicative mode, it reveals the narrowness of his imagination, his alienation from the political dimension of life, his tacit acceptance of things as he found them.

The effects of being preoccupied with the apolitical surface become even more evident in projects whose authors strain to cut deeper. Where exactly are we after Walker Evans's photography? No doubt, photographs and prose can be so intensively precise that they will succeed in violating the immediate present: Agee's and Evans's *Let Us Now Praise Famous Men* surely broke up some of its readers, changing their conventional view of the subjects on which the book focused. So did Frederick Weiseman's "Titicut Follies" or Bruce Davidson's photographic essay, *East 100 Street.* Similarly, "On the Waterfront" revealed the complex underside of its hero – but remained stuck precisely there, contented with a one-dimensional portrait (hardly remembered by anyone who has seen the film) of the villainous financier whose actions, whose repressed generosity, turned dock workers into brutes.

The project which has engaged Robert Coles since 1967 is a no less striking illustration of the sway of the indicative mode, for he, too, has tried to go beyond it, to *move* people, to produce whatever changes might reduce the miseries he describes. In the second volume of his *Children of Crisis,* Coles allows that "it is the duty of people like me, who would claim some knowledge of how certain people feel way down in the lowest possible 'layers' of their subconscious minds, to witness at first hand the effort made by mountaineers or tenant farmers or migrants to achieve a kinder, more decent world, and to witness also the defeats they suffer. . . ." [5] What Coles perceives is lodged below the familiar exterior; it is what he calls (with his own stress on the word) the *lives* of people – sensibilities alive below the misshapen, intimidated, frustrated, ruined appearances, buried beneath the wreckage and wastage of America. But Coles, having travelled, comes to rest, declining to witness more in either himself or others. He does not approach and embrace the concealed aspects of those secure in positions of power. There are no accounts of the suppressed compassion and affection of financiers and managers, only of those whom established America has categorized as The Poor – migrants, miners, mountaineers, sharecroppers. Coles betrays no feeling for the poverty of the affluent, for those who seem so graceful and fluent, authorities who only *seem* not to require spokesmen as open and articulate as Coles. Nothing is said about the defeated passions of the powerful, Coles's included. He locates no one to whom he might give credit for those impulses within him that he is unable to display and use. His work generates no awareness of the underlying structure of our lives – the sensibilities of a technologically advanced country, of its rigid sense of space and time, of the complex ways it man-

[5] (Boston: Atlantic, Little Brown, 1972.)

ages men and women, detaching them from their needs. Coles's work is unobtrusive and clean; it offers no intimations of the existence of a political realm. A book of the month, it leaves its readers a touch more guilty, but precisely where they are.

Possessed by what Lionel Trilling has aptly called the liberal imagination, our most marketable authors (Coles, Capote, Hershey, Mitchner) write as partisans: they are loyal to the nonpolitical, psychological segments of individual lives, unable to make politics their subject even when they use the word. Writing in the indicative mode, at home in the territory immaculately managed by *The New Yorker*, they and their readers remain detached from their most central need – the need to transcend their meagre private preoccupations and emerge as persons capable of acting. Plays, histories, films, photo albums, scholarly studies are designed to keep us stunned. They are priced for the powerful, those with the education and leisure to scrutinize the powerless, to examine how people officially categorized as outsiders carry on when placed against a background the outsiders themselves cannot discern because they are alienated from it, unfamiliar with part of themselves, and unable to change because not conscious of their condition.

I have already suggested that, given half a chance, no artist or social scientist will in fact perform purely in the indicative mode. Plainly, men are inclined to imagine alternative futures and to make some of them real. We are impatient, anxious to interfere with the present organization of life, determined to *force* ourselves on others to make sure that some larger promise will be kept. Even our most one-dimensional acts contain ambiguities that direct us to depart from the obvious. We frame our works so that we can abandon them and go on to new things, continuously upsetting ourselves and others. We violate what is alleged to be real, placing in jeopardy not only "the poor" but our very notion of poverty, not only familiar "groups" but the very notion of membership. We enlarge consciousness – gain knowledge – in action, through continuous involvement with our subject matter. Such involvements – exercises of the will in an unbounded field which is, as Nietzsche proclaimed, but "a monster of energy," nothing but "a play of forces" – transform all at once the person in quest of knowledge, the world he seeks to know, and the existing body of knowledge. Such involvements keep renewing the field; they transform actors and the records of their action. They constitute a simultaneous change of mind and reality, an unending transaction.[6]

[6] A transactional persuasion is explicated in Paul Kress, *Social Science and the Idea of Process: The Ambiguous Legacy of Arthur F. Bentley* (Urbana: University of Illinois Press, 1970). This study, however, does not stress how the so-called observer is activated by the epistemological assumption that knowledge of phenomena is

I have no reason – no life-enhancing words – for assuming that there is any real purpose above or beyond such transactions, though it may be useful to pretend otherwise. It is sufficient to assume that we seek to control experience – that is, to enlarge the sphere of known life, of life lived deliberately. When we have opportunities for becoming aware of the incomplete (hence intolerable) nature of presently controlled experience, we proceed to act. We regard every known structure of power as offensive for no other reason, in the final analysis, than its sheer being. Its mere existence annoys. Imperviously present – a natural force like a mountain – it begs to be assailed, to be measured and scaled and mastered because it is said to be indubitably there. It should not *be* – for the sole reason that, for us, nothing whatever should finally be. What disconcerts us is precisely its alleged imperturbability, its sense-dulling, obtuse presence. To quicken our own sensibilities, we have no choice but to test what are said to be its powers of resistance, to act upon putative reality, to expose those who claim to know the true boundary between the realm of necessity and that of freedom.

Our ability to keep renewing reality depends on our capacity for fusing imagination with power, for obliterating the distinction (as Dewey persistently argued) between imagined ends and the practical means for attaining them. That so-called means are indistinguishable from so-called ends becomes evident, I think, when one considers the *immediate* rewards of acts by which we free ourselves from the present, from what is *made* present, from all that which those in power treat as logical, inevitable, rational, factual, real, timely, normal, or successful. Such acts carry their own reward. Engaging in them allows us to be continuously gratified as we confront and manage larger contexts of our lives. Given form by us as we play the role of the artist, we deprive the world of its current success, making evident that it only appears to be successful. At best, we will not only lead ourselves up to some situation in order to be stunned but will also induce ourselves to recover and proceed. Our discipline will make us realize both that there is always more than has met our eye and that whatever we have presented has been presented not by Nature or by History but by us.

Because it is hard to see the relevance of this discipline for activating us outside the domain of "art," I might repeat what is readily acknowledged to be true of works of art, namely that to give us a new vision and a new life they must leave gaps, open up hard surfaces through ambiguities, give

gained only by acting on them, by violating what they seem to be, by interrogations which activate the interrogator's subject matter – stimulating and arousing it, inducing it to identify its own character and voice – as well as the interrogator himself, changing both.

villains and heroes their moments of doubt and humanity, embody ironic constructions, undercut by making light of grave things and by treating light things with mock seriousness. And to enable us to realize that reality is not "given," the artist must leave traces of his own presence, revealing his props and scaffolding, leaving his imprint, his smudges, his own distinctive voice. Disclosing that it is *his* work, he implies it is *merely* his and that we might work differently and establish different realities by *our* work. When he leaves the frame vague and the center ambiguous, he implies that his expressions do not settle the boundaries and the meaning of a situation, that others might draw new boundaries and create new meanings. By devices which detach us from his work, he moves us to encompass and appropriate more reality, to enlarge the contexts of known experience, our own cramped lives. His work serves first to attract us by indicating (in documentary fashion) that something is "out there" and then to activate us by refusing to place things out there so definitively that we let them have the last word.

I am restating this conventional aesthetic so as to call attention to the way it applies to our political culture as well. Art, narrowly defined, is characterized by a discipline – a disciplined commitment to the use of dialogical techniques – which may be seen as the essence of law making processes which demand recognizing interests other than the lawmaker's own, of methods of inquiry which demand confronting of counter-arguments, or of educational programs which demand enrolling in courses other than vocational ones. *All* are artistic works which demand placing some private interest in an unfamiliar setting that subjects it to continual testing. Although these processes are ostensibly concerned with outcomes – a law, a scientific proposition, an educated individual, a work of art, in any case, always an end result designed to amplify our lives – the results actually do not come at the end of the process: they occur every instant, and they give the pleasures which inhere in politics, in action, in play. They suspend the distinction between means and ends while disabusing us of the notion that gratification comes only at the end, that everything preceding the end is but burdensome preparation from which the majority of men must be spared. An artist's work, accordingly, should be seen not as some end-product but rather as the ground on which men keep from ending.

In the transactional mode, the artist will confront the present state of things – himself included – but not accept it as it appears to be, as complete, as having ended. He will ask his subjects (and himself) questions not likely to have been previously asked. How would men behave under changed conditions? How would they perform on different stages? If he added something not now on the stage – money, love, disaster – how would they respond? What potentialities would be realized? What new dimensions would come into play?

In such interrogations, he treats the present as ambiguous and proceeds to contradict it. The order of symbols he creates will inevitably violate what is so clearly the case. He puts what he knows to the test and thereby exhibits unknown possibilities, inarticulate forms, hidden capacities for action. Works of art – whether novels or communities of living men – are thus experiments: they put existing worlds into crucibles and transform them under controlled pressure. Students are placed into a curriculum. A character is placed on a ship, made to travel, left to his fate. Kafka's Joseph K. is placed on trial, Mann's Castorp in an Alpine sanitarium, Malamud's Levin in the English Department of Cascadia College. All are transported. All are pressured – and released in the end, orphans anew.

In the social sciences, the case for merely literary experiments has been argued especially by Herbert Blumer and Harold Garfinkel, while Erik Erikson and Erving Goffman have demonstrated its rewards. But at its most powerful – in the forms advocated by Marx, Dewey, and Sartre – overt action concretely expresses alternatives, constituting visible displays of previously unacknowledged options, public demonstrations of the practical feasibility of continuous social development – the kind exemplified not by the books but by the field work of Mailer, Malraux, Duvignaud, Russell, Mishima.[7] Each of these authors have included themselves in their field of operation, communicating (like the best of actors) not only what they did but also what transpired in their minds. They have shown themselves opening up, taking things in, changing in the process of observing. In each instance, as they have been exhibiting themselves, they became spokesmen of the smothered elements in the lives of others, representing suppressed realms of being. Just as their acts have threatened to become unbearable because of their impending end – just the moment before we shudder and break out in embarrassed laughter or tears – they have enabled us to *see*. They have made more of life bearable by inducing us to acknowledge that the world, viewed comprehensibly, must be ours, that is assuredly is both the best and the worst of all possible ones. Their transactions have vindicated not only the refractory givenness of our existence, the dense, authoritative inevitability of the way we happen to be, but also our being orphaned, free like Ishmael to put all remaining authority to the test.

[7] See especially Jean Duvignaud, *Change at Shebika: Report on a North African Village* (New York: Pantheon, 1970).

To be sure, reality testing frequently turns out to be disastrous: it leaves those engaged in it damaged and dispirited. When this is the probable result of experimental action, we have no choice but to stay where we are. We might then withdraw our support from existing structures of power, at least not *add* our weight to them, at least not contribute to the harm being done. Jeopardizing masculinity, we can *wait* for things to happen. One ground for not despairing should be our conviction (daily confirmed) that the future is open and empty, that, though we *know* the present to be a horror, we have no evidence that the future (and the *un*known past) must unavoidably be the same. Assuming a feminine posture, we can seek to share our concern for the silences and spaces before us, letting others watch until they, too, feel as we do. Listening and waiting for life, remaining in a state of tense, alert anticipation, we can acknowledge that expectancy is not the least honorable mode of action.

As part of our holding operation, we can also give public recognition to others whose irritating, defiant transactions have impressed us as memorable and telling, as exemplary ways of relating new human possibilities. We become accrediting agents as we reiterate and confirm the specific scenarios of political actors such as Thoreau or Malcolm X and make explicit how their work extends an established balance of interests, how it draws in and implicates men who subsist on the margin, outcasts arrested in their development. We thereby legitimate projects which have transformed not only their authors but also some subject matter – whether the economy of Walden Pond or life in Harlem. We explicate work whose authors are exposed and vulnerable, who have violated convention and risked appearing foolishly off balance. We acclaim records of experience which include author and subject and which, in turn, have the power to *move* others, making all of us accomplices in crime.

The conditions which free us to move, which cause us as well as society to open up, are secret only to the mass of men. For the rich, the able, and the well-born (in Hamilton's inclusive phrase) the discussion of the conditions of growth – the so-called requisites for development – was inaugurated in the Western world by Plato's dialogues on education, or more precisely, by his demonstration of the uses of the inconclusive dramatic form.[8] But what has become known about learning and creativity, about the variables facilitating personal and social growth gets scant circulation. Certainly the social sciences have been neither communicative

[8] See R. C. Lodge, *Plato's Theory of Education* (New York: Harcourt, Brace, 1947).

nor disruptive.[9] Public tranquility has not been threatened by the news that the available insights and lessons might be applicable to developing *all* sectors of our lives: divine providence or scarce resources can always be credited with forbidding the development of underdeveloped mass of men (the underdeveloped parts of ourselves). The conditions for growth, it is widely asserted, exist – or should exist – only for the few in select arenas. If the masses (repressed aspects of ourselves) are to augment themselves at all, it must be during their spare time; they may indulge in spectator sports and hobbies, all extracurricular activities, all frivolous except insofar as they help keep men fixed in their roles. Thus we speak of the extrinsic functions of play, not its intrinsically self-fulfilling nature. We do not publicize the delights and rewards of imprecision in language, contradiction in terms, fusion of opposites, duplication of effort, proliferation of incompatible theories.[10] We find it embarrassing to engage in pointless play, in games in which nothing – not status, not money, not pride – is at stake.[11] Instead, we expect models of society to be unambiguously bounded, to accept conflict because the forces of law and order have reserves enough to keep the populace under control. What Marcuse has called repressive tolerance – the appreciation of dissent as long as dissent gives vitality to the status quo – is the tacit order of the day.

The ideological predispositions of advanced industrial societies make it hard to universalize and democratize what is known about ways for giving men a progressively larger sense of self and of others. Asked to incorporate an ever greater range of experience within themselves, men feel threatened: they may lose a fixed center, their integrity, their very nature. Play and politics are seen as costly means for greater goods, not as the ultimate ground of personal development. It is widely believed (certainly widely taught) that the treatment of politics as play and play as self-sufficient end is unsupportable both economically and morally: the costs are exorbitant and even if we escaped bankruptcy we would be driven to nihilism and despair. The economic issue, to be sure, is no longer seen

[9] Compare Rousseau's *Émile* with Max Bruck, "A Review of Social and Psychological Factors Associated with Creativity and Innovation," in Charles Press and Alan Arian, eds., *Empathy and Ideology* (Chicago: Rand McNally, 1966). Ch. 1.

[10] Consider P. K. Feyerabend's advocacy of proliferation: "Invent and elaborate theories which are inconsistent with the accepted point of view, even if the latter should happen to be highly confirmed and generally accepted." ("Reply to Criticism," in Robert S. Cohen and Marx W. Wartofsky, eds., *Boston Studies in the Philosophy of Science* [New York: Humanities Press, 1965]. Vol. II, 223-224; see also "Against Method: Outline of an Anarchistic Theory of Knowledge," in Michael Radner and Stephen Winokur, eds., *Minnesota Studies in the Philosophy of Science* [Minneapolis: University of Minnesota Press, 1970].)

[11] See Clifford Geertz, "The Balinese Cockfight," *Daedalus,* 101 (Winter, 1972), pp. 1-37.

in absolutist terms; to enlarge the arenas for play, there is a good deal of testing what is alleged to be economic necessity. But the moral issue remains alive. If there are no limits to play, if we cannot finally justify the use of any specific stakes for which we might play, what will keep us from opting for hell on earth and winning? Won't we move (in Irving Howe's nightmare) toward "a frolic of emptiness," a horrible future of "publicity and sensation, the kind of savage parody which may indeed be the only fate worse than death"? [12]

The response to these rhetorical questions has been available for some time. The prophets of emptiness, Nietzsche the most probing, have not only pronounced the death of the ultimate ends for which men have murdered one another – weighty qualities such as Honor, Country, Integrity, Truth, Women, Workers, Whites, Justice, God – but have also dramatized their perceptions and thereby remained alive well this side of inhumanity. Oriented by existentialism, pragmatism, and analytic philosophy, we have been encouraged to grope for a *natural* basis for defining violence, exploitation, cruelty, and ugliness, recognizing that it is unnatural to tolerate policies that keep men where they are – listless, submissive, inert.[13] Despite the myth that leaving things indeterminate makes brutes of us all, we have begun to feel uneasy as we *see* men reach their end. We are no longer unnerved when we discover that the belief in some center is dispensable, that the highest state has no final qualities, no point, that it manifests only that pure Nothing which Hegel identified with Being.

It is precisely this image which can now be affirmed as ideal ground for being – this along with whatever practices will actually sustain our continuous journey, with whatever variable but determinate institutions and ideals (illusory finalities) will actually keep us moving and make a "frolic of emptiness" a going concern. Thus while we may be unable to escape the dead-ends of privacy, we can nevertheless regard openness – unfilled space and time, purely political space and time, the empty essence of mere play – as the touchstone for specific policies, acts, institutions, and values. Whether specific finalities are indispensable becomes thereby just as much a practical, testable question as the economic question about the

[12] Irving Howe, *Literary Modernism* (New York: Fawcett, 1967), p. 40.

[13] Men are literally sickened by violence, cruelty, exploitation, and ugliness. Conversely they are restored by their opposites. The question to which I have no answer is to what extent the conditions which induce sickness and restore health are universally human or characteristics of specific cultures. Do certain kinds of situations deaden (or conversely, enliven) everyone? Or does our culture-conditioned capacity for extending contexts determine how specific phenomena are experienced? May artists (and politicians) be seen as successful insofar as they extend contexts and thereby deprive phenomena of their flatness, simplicity, dullness, and familiarity – their alleged ugliness?

availability of resources for play. Experimental action alone will disclose how scarce action-sustaining resources are. And the answers will necessarily be tentative ones, to be taken lightly, pragmatically, skeptically.

The appropriate form of consciousness for such action has been described by Hegel as embracing

> the aimless fickleness and instability of going to and fro, hither and thither, from one extreme of the self-same consciousness, to the other contingent, confused and confusing consciousness. It does not itself bring these two thoughts of itself together. It finds its freedom, at one time, in the form of elevation above all the whirling complexity and all the contingency of mere existence, and again, at another time, likewise confesses to falling back upon what is unessential, and to being taken up with that. It lets the unessential content in its thought vanish; but in that very act it is the consciousness of something unessential. It announces absolute disappearance but the announcement *is*, and this consciousness is the evanescence expressly announced. It announces the nullity of seeing, hearing, and so on, yet *itself* sees and hears. . . . Its deeds and words belie each other continually. . . .[14]

Henry James embodied this form of consciousness in one of his characters, Lord Mellifont:

> He directed the conversation by gestures as irresistible as they were vague; one felt as if without him it wouldn't have had anything to call a tone. This was essentially what he contributed to any occasion – what he contributed above all to English public life. He pervaded it, he coloured it, he embellished it, and without him it would have lacked, comparatively speaking, a vocabulary. Certainly it wouldn't have had a style, for a style was what it had in having Lord Mellifont. He *was* a style.[15]

How hard it is to overcome one's ambivalence toward the case for pure style (James himself added that, in whatever place Mellifont had been, "the place was utterly empty . . . he had ceased to be") is shown by Robert Jay Lifton's mixed feelings about what he has described as an emerging style, that of protean man who conducts "an interminable series of experiments and explorations, some shallow, some profound, each of which can readily be abandoned in favor of still new psychological quests."[16] Lifton's own studies make clear how desperately one wants to reintroduce some nucleus, some secure human nature. If James expressed no such hankering, perhaps this is because he created the very network that holds

[14] Georg W. F. Hegel, *Phenomenology of Mind* (London: Allen & Unwin, 1949), pp. 249-250.

[15] "The Private Life," in *Works* (New York: Scribners, 1909), Vol. XVII, 227. I am indebted for this quotation and the questions it raises to John Helmer, "The Face of the Man without Qualities," *Social Research,* 37 (Winter, 1970), 547-574.

[16] *Boundaries* (New York: Random House, 1970), p. 44.

However promising their speculations, they nonetheless persist in making their case for executives who do not execute and organizations which stay loose on the ground that such openness will *really* contribute to productivity and reduce the costs of the end-product. Pay-offs all around, the cyberneticists proclaim. Yet the new models still have firm attributes: the newly celebrated informal flow behind the hard organizational façades turns out to be not formless but merely formed differently.

The currently approved diffusion of managerial authority also makes it more difficult to identify and establish a dialectical opposite. Perhaps we have no alternative to first *envisaging* the prevailing structures of power – the institutions now at the top and center of our lives and our consciousness – as firmer than they seem so that we can then envisage what they are not and bring what is absent (or barely present) into being. We would have to elicit and expand whatever within current institutions seems ineffective and wasteful, fragile and vulnerable, easy to miss and ready to dissolve. In an anticipatory posture, we should expect the new antithetical politics to be playful, experimental, flirtatious, elusive, and equivocal, continuously subverting fixations and reifications, standing for nothing secure and dependable.

To uphold it, to treat it sympathetically, is to assent to the transactional mode. It is to define no theoretical model, merely an image of a society which confirms the human disposition to keep one's balance while in circulation, to combine stasis with ecstasis, pain and pleasure, reason and feeling, Thanatos and Eros – all those states of being which become hardened when not seen in terms of their opposites. It is an image which includes both of the caricatures with which I began – but treats both as disguises, as evidence of man's willful determination to express himself in as many guises as he can bear.

To give recognition to this image of the expressive society is to perceive repressed, still disreputable parts of ourselves and to bring them into the balance of our interests. It is to make it respectable to remain discursive, playful, inconclusive, and open-ended, certainly less well punctuated than my remarks, but just as questionable.

Change," in Herman D. Stein, ed., *Social Theory and Social Invention,* (Cleveland: Case Western Reserve University Press, 1968), pp. 93-141. Literature in the Marxist tradition is no less relevant: see A. Hegedüs, "The Division of Labor and the Social Structure of Socialism," in Peter Berger, ed., *Marxism and Sociology: Views from Eastern Europe* (New York: Appleton-Century-Crofts, 1969).

THE ECOLOGY OF OPENNESS[1]

JOHN RODMAN

Discourses on 'the Open Society,' especially since Popper's World War II book,[2] have tended to share four characteristics. They have assumed the distinction between Open and Closed Societies to be a clear and meaningful distinction corresponding to something in reality. They have assumed that an Open Society was good and a Closed Society was bad. They have assumed that 'we' (moderns, Westerners, Anglo-Americans, etc.) live in a more-or-less Open Society, which, however, is threatened by forces of closure (fascism, communism, barbarism, etc.). Above all, they have tacitly selected certain elements of the overall system of social control for attention, ignoring others. To the extent that these assumptions have gone unexamined, talk of 'the Open Society' has been more the defensive ideology of a Liberalism-turned-conservative in the face of threats, than it has been political or social philosophy. My thesis is that the challenge posed by the contemporary 'ecological crisis' forces us to become more philosophical, to make explicit, reconsider, and radically redefine the formerly tacit dimension of the Open Society paradigm.

I. PARADIGMS

A major component of ideological thinking is the hypostatized adjective. For example, we are told that some idea or institution is inappropriate today because it originated in an Age of Scarcity whereas we live in an Age of Abundance. Scarcity and abundance of what? Our attention has been directed to one category of 'goods,' the desirable fruits of technology and mass production, and away from other classes of 'goods,' such as those

[1] An earlier version of this paper was presented at The Open Society Conference, Villa Serbelloni, Bellagio, Italy, June 28-July 4, 1972, under the title "The Open Society and the Final Frontier." The paper was heavily revised in July, 1973.

[2] Karl Popper, *The Open Society and Its Enemies* (London, Routledge and Kegan Paul, 1945).

sometimes called 'natural resources.' In actuality, the latter have become scarce while the former have become abundant. Thus, one class of goods is treated as if it were the only significant class, or as if it were the whole. Such tacit selection is the normal basis for theories of social "progress."

The situation is no different in discussions of Open and Closed Societies, since the nouns are so general (as with Affluent Society) that they give no significant information. To what, we may well ask, is a society open, and to what is it closed? May we say that medieval society was less open to individual entrepreneurial activity, while modern society is less open to ritual experience? That primitive societies were less open to freedom of conscience, while modern societies are less open to the experience of nature? Or shall we act as apologists for modernity and simply ignore the avenues it has tended to close off?

Within any particular society, precisely what is open to which classes of people, and what is closed to whom? How open did slaves find even the Athenian polis, or women the empire of Napoleon ('careers open to talent')? A society that tolerates philosophers may persecute homosexuals, or vice versa.

Even societies that congratulate themselves on their openness have their points of closure, as deviants as diverse as Socrates and Ralph Ginzburg have discovered, and it may be that some societies seem more open than others simply because we do not consider them as wholes. Certainly we select our data in accordance with tacit criteria, and there has been a rough consensus among intellectual defenders of the Open Society over the last several decades as to the most important items: freedom of expression (speech, publication, worship) and the social-economic-political mobility of 'the individual.' An Open Society is defined, in effect, by contrast with both 'traditional' and 'totalitarian' societies: an Open Society is one in which the life of 'the individual' (this kind of abstraction from status is essential to the model) is 'free,' i.e., not determined by a hereditary caste system or unbreakable custom, by a church-state or party-state, or by a monolithic public ideology. In other words, an Open Society is marked by a high degree of 'disestablishment,' by a 'separation' of spheres that once were fused: public and private, church and state, government and economy, political office and social status, etc.

But, as Mill and Marx pointed out over a century ago, the absence of governmental control in any sphere of life does not necessarily amount to an absence of social control, which may be exercised by religion, the family, the economic system, public opinion, 'morality,' or (Freud added) social taboos internalized as superego, or (contemporary writers add) the system of technology and the mass media.[3] Thus the Sherman Antitrust Act was premised on the notion that the concentration of economic power had reached dangerous proportions in the United States and needed to be broken up by governmental intervention. Consider also Tocqueville's remark that the United States of the 1830's could afford weak government because American families transmitted such a strong sense of religious morality;[4] from which it might seem to follow (as indeed it has) that a weakening of the family or of religious belief, as well as any shift away from a moral style of religiosity, might be compensated by an increase in governmental control.

Following out the implications of this line of thought, we can postulate an alternative to the Open/Closed Society paradigm. Could it be that in all societies, at all times and in all places, the overall amount of social control is roughly constant, and that the major variable is the *mode* of social control – i.e., the number of sources and channels of control, the extent to which these sources/channels are complementary and mutually reinforcing rather than conflicting, and the type of control that is predominant (custom, conscience, law, the market, etc.)?

We might then be tempted to suppose that an Open Society would be a society in which there was a plurality of sources and channels of social control which were not mutually reinforcing, so that 'the individual' had a choice between family loyalty and the edict of Creon, between the will of God and the law of Caesar, between wealth and virtue, etc. But situations of conflict among authorities have not normally been experienced by their heroes/victims – from Antigone to the Berrigan brothers – as situations of openness, but rather as situations of tragedy in which the moment of freedom has been contained within a larger structure of coercion that impinges as a fate. When the sources of social control are greatly out of joint with one another, are in a state of 'contradiction' (Marx), we normally have dissolution or revolution (e.g., the Europe of Bruno and Galileo, the England of Cromwell, or the France of Robespierre), when the presence of violent coercion is so marked that we know this cannot be what is meant by those who defend the Open Society.

Perhaps the Open Society paradigm can be assimilated to the Social Control paradigm in this way: an Open Society is a society that is divided

[3] J. S. Mill, *On Liberty* and *On the Subjection of Women;* Karl Marx, "On the Jewish Question" and "Economic and Philosophic Manuscripts"; Sigmund Freud, *A General Introduction to Psychoanalysis* (1924); David Riesman et al., *The Lonely Crowd* (New Haven, Yale University Press, 1950) and Herbert Marcuse, *One Dimensional Man* (Barton, Beacon Press, 1964).

[4] Alexis De Tocqueville, *Democracy in America,* Vol. I, Ch. XVII.

into spheres of influence (government, economy, religion, family, etc.), and in which government plays a relatively limited role, while 'law' is nevertheless regarded as the major control mechanism, so that a large proportion of the actual control is exercised by politically 'invisible' agencies (e.g., the market, the system of technology, an internalized puritan ethic, and 'public opinion.' [5]

The distinction between Open and Closed Societies is, then, a perfectly tenable one if we keep in mind that the phrase 'Open Society' refers to a particular mode of social control, and that the superiority of this mode to that of a more Closed Society is not immediately self-evident. That is to say, the advocate of the Open Society must give persuasive reasons why a relatively invisible (non-political) mode of social control is preferable to a relatively visible (political) one. In the process he must confront the logic of social contract theory, which provided the major intellectual foundation for modern Liberal society and which seems to point in the opposite direction.

2. SOCIAL CONTRACT

The minimal thesis of social contract theory is that rational-legal constraint is less 'inconvenient' than other forms of constraint. Specifically, a reasonable person will prefer the rule of law to being at the mercy of arbitrary individual whims and unpredictable social forces (the 'state of war'). A settled system of publicly known rules at least limits the area of coercion, provides a kind of security that is associated with freedom from fear of the unpredictable, replaces chaos with a kind of Newtonian social universe that a rational man can consent to as being in accordance with nature (including his own). The maximal thesis of social contract theory is that consent based on a recognition of a rational order transforms constraint into freedom, so that the laws liberate rather than restrain us, as if civil

[5] Robin Williams' remark is pertinent here: "A major implicit cultural premise in the dominant valuation of freedom [in American society] has been *the equating of 'freedom' with control by diffuse cultural structure rather than by a definite social organization.* Thus, it has seemed to make a great difference whether the individual receives a certain income or has a certain type of occupation as a result of an apparently impersonal, anonymous, diffuse competitive process, as against 'being forced' to accept that employment or remuneration by law or by the command of a visible social authority. A foreclosed mortgage has been culturally defined in a radically different way from governmental confiscation of the same property. To be tied to a given locality by diffuse cultural pressure and lack of economic opportunity is regarded as a quite different kind of constraint from such controls as a police order or a governmental regulation." (emphasis in the original) Robin M. Williams, Jr., *American Society: A Sociological Interpretation,* (New York, Knopf, 1951), p. 419.

government brought only benefits and no costs, no loss of freedom (spontaneity).

Whenever a new social issue of great magnitude has arisen (e.g., the 19th century 'urban crisis' stemming from the impact of the Industrial Revolution,' the Great Depression of 1929 and after; the contemporary 'ecological crisis') modern societies have had to confront the prospect of a new (or at least an additional) social contract. That is, the question periodically has arisen: would we be better off to suffer the continuation of disorder and non-governmental coercion or to extend the role of government in an attempt to end or ameliorate the oppressive social condition? At each stage, champions of governmental action have been opposed by those whose notion of freedom has become fixated at some previous balance of public-private coercion, who have fallen into the perennial 'politicist fallacy' of assuming government to be the only source of coercion,[6] or who cling to a stubborn faith that the play of 'natural forces' (meaning the social forces that caused the crisis) will, if not interfered with, resolve the crisis. And at each stage, the prophesy of 'the road to serfdom' has been countered by the paradoxical claim that 'true freedom' resides in an extension of governmental authority.[7]

Will the creation and enforcement of a 'national policy for the environment' involve a kind of socialist dictatorship run by ecologist-kings? Or will it bring us freedom from the oppressive forces of technological-industrial society that are waging deadly war upon Nature and, ultimately, upon Man? To some extent, the debate over the ecological crisis repeats old issues. The opponents of governmental action seem to think that the status quo is a state of freedom, despite their prudent decision not to play tennis during the smog season. Advocates of governmental action, concerned to expose the coercive character of environmental pollution and to lay bare its social roots, seem to believe, despite the sad history of incremental reform in other fields, that the passage of new and better laws will restore our lost freedoms. Yet the kind of perspective that arises to diagnose the current disorder as 'ecological' has the potential for shifting the parameters of political discussion. Put briefly: it is now more difficult (than, say, in Marx's time) to depict the crisis as a 'problem' that can be 'solved'

[6] The specifically American version of the politicist fallacy is that only the *federal* government is a source of coercion.

[7] Although the phrase 'the road to serfdom' is borrowed from Friedrich Hayek's book of that title (University of Chicago Press, 1944), the basic structure of the confrontation goes back to T. H. Green's 1881 "Lecture on Liberal Legislation and the Freedom of Contract." See John R. Rodman (ed.), *The Political Theory of T. H. Green* (New York, Appleton-Century-Crofts, 1964) esp. pp. 51ff, and Herbert Spencer's *The Man Versus the State* (1884).

by an adjustment of the accepted paradigm.[8] If the ecological crisis has taught us anything, it is that 'tack-on devices' do not work, because they affect only specific elements of a complex system. The modern Newtonian state now staggers awkwardly under the weight of several centuries' accretion of laws, regulations, semi-governmental bodies, and other 'adjustments,' which appear increasingly like smog-control devices added to the internal combustion engine.

3. THE ECOLOGICAL OUTLOOK

The ecological outlook is at bottom a disposition of mind that, like philosophy, looks to wholes rather than parts. The propositions in which it can be (incompletely) expressed are in one sense applications of basic principles of biology, physics, and economics;[9] in another sense, they are generalizations drawn from the frustrations of recent practical experience.[10] Thus the last decade's experience has taught us that many forms of pollution (air, water, solid waste) are interchangeable (hence the need for a coordinated policy of pollution control); that pollution control is closely linked to the older issue of resource use (e.g., stricter emission standards may necessitate a change in the type of fuel); and that both are closely connected with such general social factors as population level and density, the rate and type of economic growth, and the prevailing forms of technology.[11] Recent experience has also shown that the logic of competition (among corporations, individuals, and political jurisdictions) makes reliance upon self-sacrifice and self-control futile, that a necessary (though not sufficient) condition of altering behavior is the formulation of general

[8] For another, and somewhat different, treatment of the ecological crisis in relation to a received paradigm, see John Rodman, "What Is Living and What Is Dead in the Political Philosophy of T. H. Green," *Western Political Quarterly*, XXVI, No. 3 (September, 1973).

[9] Thus Commoner formulates four "laws" of ecology: "everything is connected to everything else," "everything must go somewhere," "there is no such thing as a free lunch," and, most controversial and ambiguous of them all, "nature knows best." Barry Commoner, *The Closing Circle* (New York, Knopf, 1971), Ch. 2. To this list might be added "every action has unanticipated consequences" and (perhaps a corollary to the "no free lunch" law) "there are no technical solutions to an ecological dilemma." In section 5, below, I restate Commoner's "first law" in a more radical form.

[10] For a more detailed interpretation of 'recent experience' (primarily American) set in a longer-run historical context, see John Rodman, "Ecopolis: Prolegomena to the Development of a National Environmental Policy" *IDOC Seminar*, No. 47 (New York, IDOC – North-America, October 1972).

[11] For analyses of these relationships, see Commoner (note 9, above), Paul R. and Anne H. Ehrlich, *Population, Resources, Environment*, (revised edition, San Francisco, Freeman, 1972); and Donella Meadows et al, *The Limits to Growth* (New York, Universe, 1972).

rules by government, and that the working-out of this logic moves the major locus of regulatory authority from the local community to the most comprehensive level of government that has effective power (presently the national state).[12] The symbolic climax of these two trends was marked in the United States by the National Environmental Policy Act of 1969, when the Congress declared "a national policy for the environment" and forced upon a reluctant President an advisory Council on Environmental Quality. I call the climax 'symbolic' because there was no substantive policy involved, only a formal requirement that the 'environmental impact' of federal projects be considered as one factor among others, and because the ensuing policy recommendations of the Administration advised by the Council have amounted to a hodgepodge of heterogeneous proposals that presuppose the 'normal' (i.e., government-abetted) patterns of population growth and economic growth and are premised on the faith that the same technological genius that helped create the ecological crisis can and will resolve it.[13]

To this contradiction between systemic diagnosis and piecemeal policy – and on top of the old economic paradox of simultaneous wealth and poverty – is now added the technological paradox represented by the coexistence of an incredibly inventive space technology and a hopelessly incompetent technology of automotive emission control. What happens in technology seems to depend greatly on the extent to which government manages to mobilize social resources to focus on specific targets (e.g., the development of an atomic bomb or a space program), which is to say that the direction and pace of technological development is, to a large extent, a matter of political economy. Yet political priorities seem to be strongly determined by military considerations and by the influence of corporations with a vested interest in existing technology (e.g., petroleum), within the general framework of a political culture that seems as committed to 'growth' and to 'technical' (non-political) solutions as its leaders.

[12] The *logical* upshot, of course, is an environmental policy at the level of effective *world* government. The UN Conference on The Human Environment (Stockholm, 1972) reflected both the logic (pollution can be 'exported' across national boundaries; the resources of the ocean bottom are an international 'commons'; etc.) and the difficulties of the matter (an Environmental Secretariat is not a world government). For theoretical formulations of (aspects of) the general 'logic' involved, see John Locke, *Second Treatise of Government,* § 13 et *passim;* Garret Hardin, "The Tragedy of the Commons" *Science* (13 Dec. 1968); and Rodman (note 10, above).

[13] See the Council's annual reports, beginning in 1970, each published under the title *Environmental Quality* (Washington, D.C., U.S. Government Printing Office), as well as "Environmental Awakening: President Nixon's Third Annual Environmental Message to Congress," 9 Feb. 1972. Some of the same presuppositions are evident in the "Declaration on the Human Environment" adopted at the Stockholm conference.

But there may be no 'technical' solutions. Experience suggests that every attempt at a technical solution creates new problems. That is the story of chemical pesticides, artificial fertilizers, auto emission controls, nuclear power generation . . . the list is endless. If there is no technical solution, it is because there is no 'environmental problem' but rather a systemic ecological crisis brought about by the very forces of 'progress' that have brought us 'affluence.'

The systemic character of the crisis is suggested by the fact that action at individual, corporate, and governmental levels tends to find itself involved in 'double binds' and 'vicious circles,' since elements of the 'problem' are built into the instruments of 'solution.' A person tries to protect himself from air pollution by bying an air conditioner; in the process he adds to air pollution and resource depletion by increasing the demand for electric power production. Another person moves to the suburbs or the country to escape smog; he commutes to work by automobile, adding to the smog he seeks to escape. Environmental activists in Southern California drive their cars to anti-smog strategy meetings, polluting as they go; how else get there, the way Southern California has been laid out? Successive national Administrations try to cope with 'the water pollution problem' by funding the construction of more sewage treatment plants, all of which require additional power generation. Southwestern power companies, blocked by environmental activists from constructing new nuclear plants and from expanding fossil fuel-burning plants in metropolitan areas, construct coal-burning plants in the distant 'unpopulated' desert, stringing the countryside with utility lines, and bringing air pollution and strip-mining to hitherto 'undeveloped' areas. Nuclear power plants replace the conventional problems of air pollution and oil/gas depletion with subtler, longer run hazards, especially atmospheric radiation and the dilemma of radioactive waste 'disposal' (storage).

Meanwhile, the existence of an Environmental Protection Agency testifies to the national government's recent concern to 'protect' the public from pollution, but the continued existence of the Corps of Engineers and the Bureau of Reclamation testifies to the longer-standing commitment of the same government to the promotion of economic development and environmental disruption. The government agency charged with protecting the public from radiation hazard by setting safety standards for nuclear power plants and the government agency charged with promoting the commercial use of nuclear energy turn out to be one and the same agency (AEC). The National Forest Service allows clearcutting and the overcutting of timber quotas on the public lands in at least partial fulfillment of the spirit of the founder of American Conservation, Gifford Pinchot, who made it clear that the purpose of conserving forests was not to preserve wilderness but to assure a steady supply of timber "for the making of prosperous homes." [14]

Should a person think to escape this tangle of knots by 'returning to nature,' he may discover that access to 'Wilderness Areas' has begun to be rationed because of overcrowding. Nor are things much better abroad, or not for long, since the same basic conditions foster the same effects in Communist as well as capitalist countries, and developing societies are making great strides to match them. The ecological crisis is perhaps the greatest evidence of 'convergence' in the contemporary world.[15] To the extent that its clutches are inescapable and efforts to escape it or 'solve' it become enmeshed in vicious circles, the ecological crisis approaches the dimensions of an increasingly totalitarian system of constraint that is rapidly eliminating some of the options that individuals, economic enterprises, and political systems have traditionally enjoyed.

Meanwhile the policy of governmental tinkering under the guise of 'environmental policy' gives the public a temporary, symbolic reassurance that things are under control, protects regulated industries against the possibility of ecological guerrilla warfare that might, but for regulation, seem legitimate, and perhaps slows the rate of deterioration sufficiently for the public to 'adapt' gradually to worsening levels of pollution.[16] This process is punctuated by periodic micro-disasters, disturbing revelations (e.g., that radioactive nuclear waste storage facilities are leaking), and shortages that raise the cry for additional governmental intervention (e.g., for gasoline rationing to ensure that farmers get their share) – the net effect of which is to obtain more governmental responses along the same lines, so that a pattern of legislation and administration grows up that is both elaborate and ineffective. This has been the trend under both Democratic and Republican Administrations.

In this context it is pointless for intellectuals who affirm the ecological outlook in principle to devote their time to internecine quarrels about which single causal factor – population, affluence, or technology – is the

[14] For the Pinchot quotation, see Samuel P. Hayes, *Conservation and the Gospel of Efficiency: The Progressive Conservation Movement, 1890-1920* (New York, Atheneum, 1969), pp. 41f. See also Pinchot's autobiography, *Breaking New Ground* (New York, Harcourt, Brace, 1947).

[15] See Marshall Goldman, "The Convergence of Environmental Disruption" *Science* (2 Oct. 1970).

[16] The analysis of the largely 'symbolic' role of regulatory agencies developed by Murray Edelman *The Symbolic Uses of Politics* (Ann Arbor, University of Michigan Press, 1964) fits the case of pollution control excellently, with some obvious modifications.

most important and should be given top priority in policy-making.[17] Population growth, economic growth, and technological change are three facets of a single process, the social revolution of modernity. Surely the upshot of ecological diagnosis is to bring the continuation of that basic process itself into question.

4. THE FRONTIER OPENS...AND CLOSES

Although the distinction between Open and Closed Societies is in one sense perennial, appearing in different historical periods and applied so as to distinguish different societies of the same historical type (e.g., one polis, one nation-state, one tribe from another),[18] there is another, more world-historical version that draws the distinction between the social-political forms that characterize different periods, as when Hegel or Fustel de Coulanges contrasted 'the ancient city' with the freedom of the modern state.[19] In this section I shall discuss the uniqueness of modernity, the special type of 'openness' (and 'closedness') that characterizes 'modern' as distinct from pre-modern and still-traditional societies.

For all its dynamism, commerce, warfare, and regional hegemony, a polis like Athens was bounded, like most ancient and medieval cities, by a human boundary, a city wall, beyond which lay the natural world, partly farmed and partly wild. The pattern of the natural world was defined by the diurnal and annual cycles, and the 'history' of human societies was construed on this cyclical model, save for the exceptional deed of the hero

[17] I have in mind the exchange between Paul Ehrlich and John Holdren, on the one hand, and Barry Commoner, on the other. (See texts in *Environment* magazine for April 1972; also *Science and Public Affairs (Bulletin of the Atomic Scientists)* for May 1972). While affirming a multi-factor analysis in principle, each depicts the other as committed to a single-factor analysis, and each strives mightily to prove that either population (Ehrlich/Holdren) or technology (Commoner) is the most important factor. In fact, neither position can be proven by the methods utilized by the contestants (who attempt to assign numerical weights to each factor and compute mathematical relationships), since there is no natural unit of measurement for technology (cf. population), and since 'technology' and 'affluence' are overlapping categories. The charge that each makes about the other – that preoccupation with distinguishing factors and emphasizing one of them is a way of avoiding the basic issue of radical (systemic) change – seems correct in both cases.

[18] See, for example, the contrast between Athens and Sparta in Pericles' Funeral Oration (Thucydides, *History of the Peloponnesian War*); also Mary Douglas, "Lele Economy Compared with the Bushong: A Study of Economic Backwardness" in Paul Bohannan and George Dalton (eds.) *Markets in Africa* (Evanston, Northwestern University Press, 1962). The terms 'open society' and 'closed society' were added to Douglas' analysis by Harold K. Schneider in a letter published in *Science* (19 March 1971), p. 1095.

[19] G. W. F. Hegel, *The Philosophy of Right: Lectures on the Philosophy of History*. N. D. Fustel de Coulanges, *The Ancient City* (Garden City, N.Y., Doubleday, Anchor Books, 1956).

who gained, through the grace of historians, a kind of immortality.[20] In the religious ritual of tragedy, *nemesis* regularly followed *hubris,* reaffirming the warning, 'nothing in excess.' The ancient philosophers saw the polis as properly limited in size and as internally ordered by justice and temperance; and Aristotle considered excellence a mean. Even in the Roman age of geographic empire, the philosophers (e.g., Cicero) assimilated the political order to a cyclical, nonlinear model of the natural universe. And the medieval world, for all its theoretical eschatology, was essentially static in its acceptance of temporal boundaries for the city of man.

If modern man, looking back, tends to construe 'the classical ideal' in terms of balance, moderation, harmony, and limits, neglecting the dynamic forces of expansion that dialectically provoked and eventually undermined, the insistence on measure, it is largely because his own world's values are so different. Between modern man and classical man lies a revolution that has dethroned Nature and enthroned History in its place, radically reordering the type of experience to which human societies are open. The modern revolution began with a breakthrough in spatial consciousness that was quickly expanded into a transformation of temporal consciousness. The Age of Discovery opened new vistas and the prospect of a new beginning in a 'new world' (even of a new beginning in the old world in emulation of the new).[21] The revolution gathered momentum during the commercial and industrial revolutions and the accompanying upsurge of population growth, and found articulation first in the 18th century idea of 'progress' generalized from the march of science and technology, then in the 19th century historicization of nature (historical geology and the theory of evolution). It flourishes today in 'the space race' and in 'future studies,' finding perhaps its best expression in science fiction in which the notion of a radical breakthrough in space is fused with the notion of a radical breakthrough in time. The modern age has thus been an age of the exploration and conquest of the earth's territory (and beyond); an age of continually receding and continually redefined frontiers; an age of navigators, missionaries, conquistadors, emigrants and immigrants, pioneers, settlers, explorers, entrepreneurs, reformers, inventors, the Corps of Engineers, the Peace Corps, jet pilots, astronauts, psychoanalysts, and revolutionaries seeking vindication from posterity.

What geographical expansion and temporal progress had in common was a restless refusal to accept any qualitative limit as 'natural.' Boundaries

[20] Cf. Hannah Arendt, "The Concept of History: Ancient and Modern," *Between Past and Future* (Cleveland and New York, Meridian Books, 1963).

[21] The spatial aspect of modern expansionism has been treated by Walter Prescott Webb, *The Great Frontier* (Boston, Houghton Mifflin, 1962).

were replaced by frontiers: what lay beyond the frontier was wilderness to be explored, conquered, civilized (subjected to the patterns of the city), preserved in bits as a tame curiosity in zoos and reservations, transmuted from irrationality to rationality by science ("Where id was, there ego shall be." – Freud). The 'infinite perfectibility' of man meant exactly that no limit could be foreseen for 'the progress of the human mind.' Man's virtual liberation from the constraint of natural biological cycles – mind's liberation from the body – was the upshot of the dream of Descartes and Condorcet that, through medical science, man could push back the frontier between life and death indefinitely, perhaps even abolish it.[22] Ritual activity, which imitated biological cycles, was driven underground by the modern ethic of individual 'achievement' and social 'growth,' the consummation of which lay always just outside the grasp. In the 'closed' version of the society open only to 'development,' social 'growth' was centrally planned and directed. In the 'open' version, social 'growth' was seen as the aggregative consequence of individual achievements (governmental promotion of 'growth' was important but discreet). Both versions of modern society rejected the idea of *stasis,* rejected traditional authority, and committed themselves to 'possibilities' and 'movement.' Modern societies, like modern individuals, have sought to achieve goals but have found little satisfaction therein and have continually had to project new goals into the future.[23]

Modern man has cherished in his innermost heart a faith that the world was not a closed system, that there would always be an 'outside' dimension to help him solve his problems. This 'outside' has been variously envisioned as Divine Providence or 'the cunning of Reason' (Hegel), as 'vacant spaces' to populate, colonies to exploit, natural sinks into which to dump wastes, mineral resources yet to be discovered, and new technologies yet to be devised. Social conflicts and dilemmas could thus be regarded as 'problems'

[22] Descartes, *Discourse on Method,* Sixth Discourse; Condorcet, *Sketch for a Historical Picture of the Progress of the Human Mind* (1795), tr. June Barraclough (London, Weidenfeld and Nicolson, 1955), pp. 199f. For a somewhat critical view of this type of vision, see René Dubos, *Mirage of Heath: Utopias, Progress, and Biological Change* (Garden City, N.Y., Doubleday, Anchor Books, 1959).

[23] The fragility of the goal-oriented mentality of modernity is thrown into stark relief by J. S. Mill's experience: "It occurred to me to put the question directly to myself, 'Suppose that all your objects in life were realized; that all the changes in institutions and opinions which you are looking forward to, could be completely effected at this very instant: would this be a great joy and happiness to you?' And an irrepressible self-consciousness distinctly answered, 'No!' At this my heart sank within me: the whole foundation on which my life was constructed fell down. All my happiness was to have been found in the continual pursuit of this end. The end had ceased to charm, and how could there ever again be any interest in the means? I seemed to have nothing left to live for." J. S. Mill, *Autobiography,* ed. Jack Stillinger (Boston, Houghton-Mifflin, 1969), p. 81.

that had 'solutions,' because there was always 'a way out' – new lands to open up, new places to dump, or at least a continually increasing pie to divide. That is why the prospect of 'the closing of the frontier,' of encountering 'the limits to growth,' has always aroused such anxiety and denial, why 'new frontiers' have been continually sought to substitute for old. If there were no frontier, we might have to face the internal conflicts and dilemmas of modern society.[24]

There is a sense in which the main theme of modern European and American history has been the attempt to escape the confines of time and space, the threat of a closing world, and to establish (either in a new place or by breaking with the past, or both) a 'new world' untarnished by the evils of the old. The United States is the *reductio ad absurdum* of that tendency: founded by people who fled the old world rather than confront its problems, it has been continued by people who continually moved west in quest of the dream; its youth now re-enact the tradition in a variety of ways ranging from Peace Corps missionary work to internal emigration ('dropping-out' – but where is 'out'?).

The 'vacant spaces' have been filling up, and faith in 'progress' has been compromised both by the 'betrayal' of one utopian revolution after another and by prophecies (now computerized) of incremental exponential ecological disaster. We still look for a way 'out,' but our gaze is forced back upon ourselves, and we wonder fearfully what we must confront if indeed we have reached the final frontier of modernity, when all the social costs of 'progress' must at last be internalized.

Just as the Open Society of antiquity shared with the Closed Society of antiquity a reliance on slave labor, so modern Open Societies have shared with Closed ones a deep tendency towards imperialism, towards the conquest and exploitation of what has lain beyond the 'frontier.' But if there is a frontier, it always lies within us as well as beyond us: the conquest of 'the other' is always a conquest of the self. The ultimate discovery of explorers is that life is metaphoric, that 'the heart of darkness' lies within. The revolt of external colonies against the overt imperial rule of the Western powers is largely over, but resentment at an economic system whereby the 'developed' countries consume a percentage of world resources many times their percentage of the world's population has only begun to fester. Domestically, revolts of various 'minorities' (Blacks, Chicanos, women, Indians, etc.) against deprivations of status and power are under-

[24] For a psychoanalytic interpretation of the basis of this denial, see Harold F. Searles, "Unconscious Processes in Relation to the Environmental Crisis," *The Psychoanalytic Review,* 59, No. 3 (1972).

way. An erosion of 'the Protestant ethic' – self-coercion, postponement of gratification – and its partial replacement by an ethos of 'awareness in the here-and-now' – is shared by society's youthful 'drop-outs' and by earnest middle-class adults paying the fee for weekend group therapy. Concurrent with this is a renewed revolt of 'the body' and of 'feelings' against the domination of 'reason' and superego. And behind all these trends looms the revolt of Nature against exploitation by man.

On the 'practical' level, these revolts or movements of liberation are perceived as diverse and even competing; partisans present us with rhetorical choices between Black Liberation and Women's Liberation, between 'people' and 'trees.' Yet each is a metaphor for the other: the body is Nature-in-us; the 'liberation of women' is also the liberation of the 'feminine' element in men; oppressed minorities are 'internal colonies'; and 'have-nots' are everywhere. Seen from a larger perspective, all five revolts are facets of a general revolt against the oppressive regime established by the successful revolution of modernity, a regime sometimes represented as an Open Society.[25]

Reference to colonial independence movements, to minority liberation movements, and to guerrilla warfare against the Protestant/industrial conception of time (the tyranny of the future over the present) will probably not strike anyone as intrinsically mysterious. Nor will 'the revolt of the body' puzzle anyone who is aware of the (frequently) psychosomatic character of his own backaches, headaches, ulcers, or heart attacks. But 'the revolt of Nature' may seem to require some complicated explanation, since we are not in the habit of speaking of Nature as an intentional actor analogous to individuals or groups. Modern man has not only drawn an over-sharp dichotomy between (intentional) human action and the (allegedly 'mechanical') behavior of 'natural phenomena,'[26] but he has also lost the sense of Nature as an overall balance or equilibrium in which he is embedded, a system in which certain types of actions tend to incur natural

[25] I do not wish to play down the immediate and very practical tensions that do exist among the various liberation movements. One of the best statements of the Third World's relationship with the ecological crisis was made by the Prime Minister of India, Indira Gandhi, to the Stockholm Conference in 1972. (For the text, see "What Happened at Stockholm," *Science and Public Affairs: Bulletin of the Atomic Scientists,* Special Issue, (1972), pp. 20ff.) Another, less-noticed tension lies between the here-and-now emphasis of the revolt against the Protestant/industrial sense of time and the ecological outlook's concern to take into account the long-term effects of actions.

[26] For a detailed treatment of the Cartesian version of this as a political act, see "The Politics of Nature, or The Transcendence of Humanity, being The Dolphin Papers, Part One," ed. John Rodman (presented to the Western Political Science Association annual meeting, April 6, 1973), excerpts from which will appear in *North American Review* (Winter Issue, 1973-74).

sanctions. Until the ecological outlook has re-established among us on the authority of 'science' something of the wisdom of ancient and 'primitive' peoples, we must make do with analogy: let us speak of Nature as we might speak of our bodies if we said, apropos of fatigue or indigestion, 'I think my body is trying to tell me something.'

The present situation is so anomalous in terms of our established ways of thinking that we can speak at one moment of Nature's revolt against mistreatment and warn ourselves that 'Nature bats last,' while at another moment we can despair at the impending 'death of Nature' (from resource depletion, pollution, oversettlement, 'public works,' the proliferation of a plastic environment, and the basic approach of modern, technologically-oriented science, which conceptualizes nature as a system of coercion (efficient causation) and proceeds to study natural processes coercively – e.g., by splitting the atom). What is reasonably clear is that we approach a world-historical moment when the linear march of modern history (economic growth, technological 'progress,' population increase, 'expansion' in all senses) threatens to collide with the limits imposed by biological cycles.[27]

The intense anxiety inspired by the growing environmental crisis seems inexplicable simply in terms of the calculable cost of air pollution, water pollution, etc., even when the 'negative externalities' concealed by the free-market paradigm are counted. Neither is man's 'survival' really the ultimate issue – though man's anxiety in the face of his mortality remains a powerful force – since most of us can imagine worlds so impoverished that we should not care to survive. What we witness daily is the slow 'death of Nature,' a kind of passive-aggressive rebellion against man's dominion, signalled in 'vanishing air,' diminishing wilderness, and endangered species, all of which fill us with a kind of biological-aesthetic anxiety about the future. To explain or justify our anxiety in terms of the long-term impact on *man's* survival is, I suspect, at least partly an attempt to rationalize our mood in terms of the modern utilitarian philosophy of enlightened self-love, lest we appear 'sentimental.'

What could underlie this deep anxiety, this sense of impending loss? It could be our suspicion of how much of modern society we would have to

[27] The basic structure of this confrontation was outlined by Malthus, who published his *Essay on Population* (1798) in rebuttal to the Condorcet/Godwin theory of the 'perfectibility' (i.e., capacity for unlimited progress) of the human species. Malthus' view that there were cyclical 'laws of nature' that linear progress could not ultimately escape confronting is simply developed in a more multi-faceted and quantitative way by contemporary analyses such as Jay Forrester's *World Dynamics* (Cambridge, Mass., Wright-Allen, 1971) and *The Limits to Growth* by Donella Meadows *et. al.* (New York, Universe Books, 1972).

give up to save Nature. But what would losing Nature mean? At this point we can only speculate.[28]

(1) To lose Nature would be to lose Mother, our roots, our sense of continuity with 'the great chain of being' from which we came. In this respect, trees may be of particular symbolic importance, since we are evidently descended from arboreal ancestors and still find 'the woods' the most comfortable form of wilderness.[29]

(2) To lose Nature would be to lose our bodies, at least our bodily health, for the body, with its natural functions and natural cycles is Nature-in-us. The conquest of Nature by technology is paralleled by the subjugation of the body's rhythms by the linear schedule of technological society; and the revolt of Nature is paralleled by the body's revolt in the form of heart disease, hypertension, 'mental illness,' etc., as well as in the form of movements in contemporary therapy that emphasize the mind-body continuum, awareness of the body, acceptance of the body, etc.[30]

(3) Finally, to lose Nature is to lose the metaphoric embodiment of an important regulative idea – the idea of an objective, given, eternal, recurrent order that outlasts human life, transcends the affairs of the city, and allows us to catch glimpses of ourselves 'in the perspective of eternity.' Modern industrial-technological-mass society functions, on the one hand, to close off the experience of transcendence into Nature, both by redirecting attention to more 'profitable' achievement activities, and by systematically destroying or transforming nearly all traces of the natural environment. It also functions, on the other hand, to intensify the need and demand for the same experience it is busy closing off.

If we were to depict on one chart a set of curves representing population growth, increase in per capita GNP, the production/consumption of certain new forms of technology (e.g., synthetic fibers, plastics, etc.), and per

[28] I know of no systematic attention to this issue, but for hints see Paul Shepard, *Man in the Landscape: An Historical View of the Esthetics of Nature* (New York, Ballantine, 1972) and *The Tender Carnivore and the Sacred Game* (New York, Scribner, 1973); Harold F. Searles, *The Nonhuman Environment in Normal Development and in Schizophrenia* (New York, International Universities Press, 1960) and "Unconscious Processes in Relation to the Environmental Crisis," *The Psychoanalytic Review,* 59, No. 3, (1972); Mary McCarthy, *Birds of America* (New York, New American Library, 1972).

[29] Hence the appropriateness of the action of those citizens of Stockholm who, in the course of defending a stand of old trees against being razed for a parking lot, literally 'took to the trees' at night to await the possibility of surprise attack. See also John S. Collis, *The Triumph of the Tree* (London, Jonathan Cape, 1950).

[30] See, for example, Frederick S. Perls, *Gestalt Therapy Verbatim* (Lafayette, Calif., Real People Press, 1969); Wilhelm Reich, *The Function of the Orgasm,* trans., T. P. Wolfe (New York, World, 1971); Elsworth Baker, *Man in the Trap* (New York, Macmillan, 1967); Alexander Lowen, *The Betrayal of the Body* (New York, Macmillan, 1967); and many others.

capita usage of National Parks and National Forests for the United States since World War II, we should not only see certain parallels but would also discover that the most sharply rising curve was the one for per capita usage of the Nature reservations.[31] Furthermore, it is predictable from studies of those who use National Parks and Forests that any long-run upgrading of the occupational and/or educational level of the population will further increase usage as well as commitment to 'wilderness values.'[32] In short, modern society dialectically fosters an increasingly large demand for a realm of reality that transcends the plastic society – the same realm that it is systematically destroying. This is perhaps the most basic, if also the most subtle, contradiction of modern society.

5. TRANSCENDING THE FRONTIER MENTALITY

The awareness of the closing of the American land frontier towards the end of the 19th century produced an anxiety that manifested itself in three forms: (1) the emergence of the Progressive Conservation movement, devoted to 'solving the resources problem' by applying more scientific techniques of management to achieve a 'sustained yield' so that economic development could continue;[33] (2) the establishment of a few organizations such as National Audubon and the Sierra Club, which, out of a variety of motives, some of them difficult to fit into the general ethos of modernity, devoted themselves to the preservation of wilderness and endangered species;[34] and (3) a dedication to discovering or inventing *ersatz* frontiers.

Frederick Jackson Turner, who celebrated the central importance of the frontier in American history just as it was passing, sought substitute frontiers to preserve the "pioneer ideals" ("conquest," discovery, individualism, egalitarianism) that he considered to lie at the heart of American "de-

[31] Comparisons of trends in population, affluence, and technology are argued by Commoner and Ehrlich/Holdren (see note 17). For figures on usage of National Parks and National Forests, see *Public Use of the National Parks: A Statistical Report, 1960-1970* (Washington, D.C., National Park Service, 1971) and *Outdoor Recreation in the National Forests* (Washington, D.C., Forest Service, 1965).

[32] See William R. Catton, Jr., "Motivations of Wilderness Users," in *Woodlands Section, Pulp & Paper Magazine of Canada* Dec. 19, 1969, pp. 121ff. It can be argued that the desire for nature is already there, and an affluent, technological society gives more people the means to 'go to nature' (e.g., leisure, automobiles, etc.). Or it can be argued that the urban-industrial-technological society creates, or at least intensifies, the felt need for nature. It is suggestive that people with wilderness preservation and appreciation attitudes tend to be urban in background. (See Catton, note 31.)

[33] See Hays (note 14).

[34] See Frank Graham, *Man's Dominion: The Story of Conservation in America* (Evans, New York, 1971).

mocracy." He found them in such unlikely enterprises as education (especially the public land-grant university), "the new frontiers of unwon fields of science, fruitful for the needs of the race," and the "frontiers of better social domains yet unexplored." [35] The possibility that social reform was the new frontier was echoed by Henry Wallace in the depths of the Great Depression,[36] while President Franklin Delano Roosevelt struck a broader, more eclectic note:

> Today we can no longer escape into virgin territories: we must master our environment.... The old frontier is occupied, but ... science and inventions and economic revolution have opened up a new frontier ... [based] on the resourcefulness of men and women applied to the old frontier.[37]

Vannevar Bush, drawing the moral of World War II, extolled "science, the endless frontier" in his report to the President.[38] President Kennedy directed the nation's attention to the exploration of outer space, to the modernization of developing societies, and to what later became known as 'the war on poverty.' A contemporary political scientist has propounded the comprehensive thesis that "the continuing frontier experience of the American people ... remains the central experience in American life," and that this experience – "a constant effort to extend man's domination over his environment" – has gone through three great phases, "the rural-land frontier," "the urban-industrial frontier," and "the metropolitan-technological frontier of science, suburbia, synthetics, and cybernetics." [39] Conceding that "the very process of conquering each frontier has in every case generated a host of problems" that require a governmental response, our author nevertheless presents a summary "case study" of "the impact of the automobile" that mentions only desirable impacts.[40] "Somewhere on the horizon," he concludes, "is yet a fourth frontier stage. ... The resolution

[35] Frederick Jackson Turner, *The Frontier in American History* (New York, Holt, Rinehart, and Winston, 1967): "The Significance of the Frontier in American History" (1893), "Pioneer Ideals and the State University" (1910), and "The West and American Ideals" (1914). Turner, of course, thought the frontier experience to be the key to what was uniquely American, though he was apt to illustrate the frontier spirit by quoting Kipling's poetic evocation of "The Voortrekker" (pp. 270ff.). My view is that the frontier ethos of modernity reached its most uninhibited and self-conscious expression in the United States.

[36] Henry A. Wallace, *New Frontiers* (New York, Reynal & Hitchcock, 1934).

[37] Franklin Delano Roosevelt, *Public Papers and Addresses,* New York, 1938-1949, Vol. V, p. 239 (July 3, 1936).

[38] Vannevar Bush, *Science, The Endless Frontier: A Report to the President on a Program for Postwar Scientific Research* (Washington, D.C., 1945).

[39] Daniel J. Elazar, "The Metropolitan Frontier: A Perspective on Change in American Society" (Morristown, N.J., General Learning Press, 1973).

[40] *Inter alia,* "The automotive frontier ... broadened both the opportunities and horizons of *a people previously restricted in every way ...*" (p. 13, my emphasis).

of America's present problems may be formed only in the opening of that frontier." [41]

The rhetoric of the new frontiersmen from Turner to the present is such that it is hard to tell the politicians from the historians and political scientists, the scholars from the myth-makers and myth-perpetuators. The major message that comes through is an incitement to bring to science, economic development, and even social reform the same spirit of exploration and domination (hence the 'war' on poverty and the 'conquest' of space) that is thought to have characterized the physical frontier experience. In a sense, the exhortation is redundant; in another, pathetic, since what was most interesting about the original American frontier experience – the personal confrontation with wild Nature – is difficult to re-enact in the laboratories of Dupont, the headquarters of the AEC, or even the regional offices of the Peace Corps. The new frontiersmen never discuss what may be lost in this translation.

Will the impact of the contemporary ecological crisis fall into this same pattern: absorption into the framework of modernity, with a few groups of eccentric dissenters tolerated anomalously like semi-wild animals in a zoo? The central metaphor to emerge so far – 'spaceship earth' – is ambiguous in portent. As used by writers such as Kenneth Boulding and Garret Hardin, the image suggests a planetary ecosphere, a closed system of biological cycles (even the urine of the astronauts must be recycled), the end of 'the cowboy economy.' [42] As used by Buckminster Fuller, the image carries similar implications of an intricate, closed system, but one that is a creative feat of human engineering.[43] Similar ambiguity surrounds that great symbolic moment when earth's astronauts first looked back from outer space and saw the earth as a finite sphere: the earth was revealed as a fragile, limited system at the very moment that man broke out of that system. Who can tell which aspect of that experience will prevail – the chastened sense of limits or the sense of man's godlike powers to create worlds, the image of our world as organism or as mechanism? Along with talk of restoring disrupted ecosystems go bold visions of the endless exploration and conquest of space, along with more pedestrian visions of solving the earth's problems by sending our surplus population and garbage to the moon. In the fantasy of the human race's 'starting over again' on another

[41] Elazar, p. 19.

[42] Kenneth Boulding, "The Economics of the Coming Spaceship Earth" in Henry Jarett (ed.), *Environmental Quality in a Growing Economy* (Baltimore, Johns Hopkins University Press, 1966). Garrett Hardin, *Exploring New Ethics for Survival: The Voyage of the Spaceship Beagle* (Baltimore, Penguin Books, 1973).

[43] R. Buckminster Fuller, *Operating Manual for Spaceship Earth* (Carbondale, Ill., Southern Illinois University Press, 1969).

planet, after life on this world is destroyed in an ecological version of the Deluge, are combined the extremes of optimism and pessimism that have always characterized the frontier mentality.

Is it conceivable that, instead of proliferating plastic frontiers, we could bring ourselves to decide that the frontiers of modernity were truly closed; that the frontier style has been a style of escapism and avoidance, of projection, domination, and self-domination; that there will henceforth be no spatial-temporal 'outside' to conquer, escape to, or draw help from; and that it is time to make peace with ourselves and rediscover that ultimate boundary that was once called 'the nature of things'? It may be that modern man has opened himself to History as far as is prudent, that through History he has rediscovered Nature, and that the time is now ripe for a reopening of ourselves and our society to the world of Nature. What is, from one point of view, a closing off is, from another point of view, an opening up. Frontiers make for conquest, and conquest never satisfies because the object of conquest always remains alien, always distant; otherness is subjugated but not penetrated. Boundaries, on the other hand, allow transcendence, which is a qualitatively different experience, involving an awesome discovery and acceptance of the self in the other and of the other in the self.[44] Underlying Commoner's "first law of ecology" ("everything is connected to everything else") is a more ultimate "law" that can be validated only experientially, that no relations are merely external, that "I am in everything, and everything is in me."

I have depicted the modern Open Society as having been, in substantial measure, a system of invisible coercion. We have been ruled by a myriad of social controls less visible than overt legal controls. Among these controls has been the internalized paradigm of modernity that has committed us to an endless conquest of the untamed nature lying beyond the 'frontier.' That untamed nature to be subjugated has lain within ourselves as well (the 'beast,' the 'wildness' in us). The hidden dimension of the modern Open Society has thus been a state of war that has cast man as a scientific/technological/economic frontiersman waging war upon Nature and the Nature-in-himself. The ultimate law of ecology has an important corollary: as man conceptualizes and treats Nature, so he will eventually conceptualize and treat himself and his fellow men, e.g., as a self-determining subject

[44] Examples of transcendence via encounters with Nature can be found in Thoreau's *Walden*. See also Laurens van der Post, *The Lost World of the Kalahari* (New York, Morrow, 1958); John S. Collis, *The Triumph of the Tree* (London, Jonathan Cape, 1950). The attitude of sympathetic openness in the encounter with Nature is exhibited in different ways in Jane van Lawick-Goodall, *In the Shadow of Man* (New York, Dell, 1972) and John Cunningham Lilly, *The Mind of the Dolphin* (New York, Avon, 1967).

to be respected and cooperated with, or as an object or thing, as material without intrinsic value, to be subjugated and exploited. Thus the logic of Descartes' 'animal machine' is fulfilled in B. F. Skinner's view of man.[45]

Can the circle of domination in which we are enmeshed be broken? Even if we can transcend the compulsions of the frontier mentality, is not the vision of an ultimate 'liberation' incompatible with the Social Control paradigm, which sees the 'amount' of social control as ever constant? The question is legitimate and important, and I cannot fully answer it. At this point I can only suggest several considerations.

We need a fuller exploration – going beyond the Newtonian world of social contract theory – of the conditions under which certain forms of control are preferable to others. This would include a critical examination of the modern assumption that dependence upon technology is always preferable to dependence upon natural systems. The ecological outlook suggests that in a healthy ecosystem there are internal checks and balances that tend to return it to an equilibrium condition. The artificial simplification of ecosystem diversity by man (e.g., the deliberate introduction of monoculture) upsets the natural balance, divides inhabitants into 'friend' and 'foe,' and produces the felt necessity for large-scale external coercion (e.g., the 'massive retaliation' of chemical pesticides that destroy indiscriminately). The analogies are striking. The production of 'mass society' by the economic-technological-population revolution of modernity has been accompanied by the development and use of devastating weapons of political control. The ecological outlook suggests that monoculture is a mistake, and that diverse ecosystems are, other things being equal, superior in respect to stability, vitality, and resistance to disease, disaster, and death. In that respect, the ecological analogy provides an additional justification for the traditional Liberal principle of 'toleration,' but it goes further in three ways. (a) The ecological analogy suggests that social forces tending to destroy diversity and create uniformity should be discouraged. (b) The ecological analogy suggests that communities are composed of many species all of which have 'rights' to the commons. A society revolutionized by the ecological outlook would therefore go beyond a merely humanistic frame of reference, concede intrinsic value to nonhuman forms of life, and manage its survival without engaging in an unnecessary 'war' upon nature. It might even extend Liberalism by incorporating into its legal system protection for the rights of nonhumans.[46] (c) The ecological analogy sug-

[45] On the Descartes-to-Skinner logic, see Rodman (note 26).

[46] See Christopher Stone, "Should Trees Have Standing?": Towards Legal Rights for Natural Objects," *Southern California Law Review* (Spring 1972) and Justice Douglas' dissenting opinion in Sierra Club v. Morton, April 1972. The ethical and

gests further that an acceptance of diversity as desirable may diminish the felt need for external control. In a sense this lesson is already implicit in Locke, who argued that it was not (religious) diversity that produced subversion and persecution, but intolerance and persecution that produced subversion.[47] Analogically, it can be argued that it is the individual who has a narrow (intolerant, oversimplified) idea of who he is (should be) who must engage in a high degree of 'self-control' (coercion, persecution, repression) in order to make that idea true in practice.

Now, to say, as I just have, that certain social trends should be "discouraged" is still to speak of social (including political) control. Operationalizing the ecological vision of society might involve a paradox similar to that of operationalizing the laissez-faire vision of Adam Smith and Jeremy Bentham. Government action is initially required to remove previously-established interferences with what Smith called "the natural system of liberty." Implementation of laissez-faire was sometimes thought of as if it were a one-time act: after government intervened to abolish tariffs, usury laws, and other legal restraints on economic activity, government could retire from the field. But, as with all aspects of the Open Society paradigm, there was actually an ongoing role for government that was assumed; it consisted of restraining those types of human conduct that obstructed the operation of the market (e.g., theft, fraud, the breaking of contracts, etc.). So the principle of a governmental role in protecting the 'natural system' from the interference of human activities that would disrupt it is already well established, if not much emphasized, in modern Liberal regimes.

The main difference between the ecological outlook and economic laissez-faire is that ecology does not mistake the particular historical stage of development of a human social arrangement ('the free market') for a 'natural system.' This mistaken view of 'nature' from Adam Smith through Herbert Spencer licensed economic and technological forces to operate without the legal, social, and moral restraints that ancient and medieval societies had imposed, with the eventual consequence of serious disruption with the real 'natural system' of biological cycles. The intent of new controls asserted in the interests of ecological balance, therefore, is to remove

political theory for the rights of animals has been tentatively developed by Joel Feinberg, "The Rights of Animals and Future Generations" in William Blackstone (ed.), *Philosophy and Environmental Crisis,* (Athens Ga., University of Georgia Press, 1974) and John Rodman, "Liberalism and the Ecological Crisis" (a paper presented at the annual meeting of the Western Political Science Association, April 1970) and "The Ecological Perspective and Political Theory" (a paper presented at the annual meeting of the American Political Science Association, September 1970).

[47] Locke, *Letter Concerning Toleration.*

a kind of oppression, to remove interferences with the true 'system of nature' of which we are a part. Since modern governments are in fact already heavily involved in promoting and guiding economic and technological 'growth' (and even population growth, via pro-natalist tax policies, etc.) – so much so that there is some suspicion that we might lapse into a 'steady-state' economy if government did not keep up pressure for 'growth' – the change needs to be only that governments should influence in the right direction social trends that they are already influencing. It is doubtful, then, that the ecological outlook demands any significant increase in the quantity of social controls, even of legal controls, even in the implementation period. In the longer run, there is reason to hope that a society imbued with the ecological outlook might require a good deal less of what we think of as social controls. The law of the conservation of energy says that energy is transformed but not destroyed; control is only a form or use of energy, and a generally uncreative one at that.

We need also to understand better the psychological roots of the modern fantasy of man's omnipotence and the identification of this with technology and 'wealth.' My suspicion is that an attempt to deny human mortality – in an age when mythological and theological answers to this dilemma have lost their hold – is basic to this neurosis, and that a shift in man's identification from technology to nature, involving an acceptance of death as an integral part of the cycle of life, could go far towards diminishing the compulsion to dominate.

We also need to know more about alternative forms of society, especially pre-modern 'steady-state' societies that apparently lived happily without the kind or degree of social domination, war, economic growth, and devastation of nature that modernity has often assumed to be either 'natural' to man or evidence of modern man's superiority to 'primitive' society. The 18th century theory of 'progress' to which we are heir now appears to have been based upon a radical misunderstanding (involving a great deal of projection) of hunting-and-gathering societies in particular.[48]

As for the Social Control paradigm, it has the heuristic value of enabling us to become more fully aware of the tacit structures of domination within and underlying an ostensibly Open Society. The Social Control paradigm may be a dialectically necessary moment in the transition from the myopia of the Open Society to a fuller liberation. Surely if liberation is possible, the path to it lies through this kind of awareness, just as personal liberation

[48] Compare Turgot, "Plan of the First Discourse," *On Universal History,* and Condorcet, "The First Stage," *Sketch for a Historical Picture of the Progress of the Human Mind,* with Paul Shepard, *The Tender Carnivore and the Sacred Game* (New York, Scribner's, 1973).

is possible only through a process of recognizing and 'owning' one's own projections and repressions.

But self-awareness involves not only an acceptance of one's complicity in a pervasive system of domination, but also an exploration of the alternative societies that are implicit in our own experience. The ecological crisis and the possibility of recovery exist within us as well as 'out there' in the larger 'environment.' Dostoevsky suggests somewhere that memories of childhood happiness are a necessary, though not a sufficient, condition of being saved. I have asked numerous people over the last several years to recall some moment of childhood happiness, and from their responses I have concluded that there dwells in most of us an underground man who is pre- and post-modern in his allegiance and profoundly subversive to the civilization of modernity.[49]

The contemporary underground man recalls being happy when he was in physical contact with Nature, and he frequently exhibits a striking ability to evoke concretely the landscape of his happiness (the warm sun, the cool wind, the beating of the waves, the grassy meadow full of wildflowers, the rough bark of the elm trees). His experiences of, and in, Nature were most often social in character. The underground man was not usually alone but with a friend or two (never a crowd or 'gang'), a beloved dog or cat, or one or more members of his family at a time when relations were affectionate. The mood of harmony permeated his relationships with Nature and his fellow human beings. Very seldom did the underground man recall happiness as connected with achievement or succes. More often he was at play, engaged in a ritual activity, or just being there in a certain place. More often invoked than achievement was grace – receiving a present or being taken somewhere. If memories of childhood happiness are any prototype of adult happiness (if happiness is a recovery or recognition), this combination of harmony-with-Nature, sociability, and non-achievement seems profoundly subversive to the traditional modern ethos of achievement and conquest.

Perhaps there is an opening towards Nature (and to the related experiences of play, community, ritual, and grace) buried in the childhood of each of us, repressed by the civilization of modernity. Periodically, this

[49] This 'experiment' has normally been performed with groups of students or adults, who were asked to close their eyes, relax, let their minds drift back to childhood, recall a moment when they were happy, dwell upon it for a few moments, then briefly describe that moment in writing. The object is not to decide which moment was happiest, but to accept the first memory of happiness that floats into consciousness. The major variation discovered is that graduate students have a slightly greater tendency (than undergraduates and miscellaneous adults) to associate happiness with achievement.

'other self' surfaces in the form of nostalgia for a less-estranged condition when we were at one with Nature, our fellow men, and our bodies, and felt more fully present in our activities. It can also manifest itself in resentment and rebellion against the dominant culture. Perhaps above all, it appears as anxiety at the prospect of an imminent 'death of Nature' that would leave us wholly at the mercy of a technological society lacking any sense of limits.

The underground man is not a revolutionary. Perhaps we should call him a secret Dissenter. But if he should ever come to connect the ecological crisis of modern society with his own internal resentment and nostalgia, and to identify himself with Nature's rebellion against the forces of intolerable oppression, then out of that experience of a limit might come the kind of re-opening of human sensibility that would signal the beginning of the transcendence of the frontier society of the modern world.